Fact File 2009

Statistics brought alive!

Copiable book with online access & CD

Digital Fact File

This year's book includes online access (single user) as well as a cd with all the Fact File pages as pdfs and the spreadsheet data to make your own charts. Email us for your username and password. info@carelpress.com

CAREL PRESS
http://www.carelpress.com

Welcome to Fact File 2009

What's new

This year's book includes online access (single user) as well as a cd with all the Fact File pages as searchable pdfs. In addition you receive the spreadsheet data to create your own charts plus the Fact File archive from 2001. Email us for your username and password. info@carelpress.com

A site licence is available for a small extra charge allowing you not only to network Fact File but to also permit home use.

Once again Fact File has been closely linked with its companion resource, Essential Articles. Statistics from Fact File will relate to pieces of writing in that publication and vice versa. For example Essential Articles 11 has both debate on the subject of an opting out system of organ donation and personal accounts of the agony of waiting for a transplant and Fact File gives the numbers of transplants and organ donations. A free guide to both publications is available on our website. This means that anyone using the two publications can put together facts and opinions to support an argument or provoke discussion.

Revised sections

The content of the sections has been decided in response to both key issues and the demands of the curriculum.

Britain & its citizens looks at population and attitudes in our society.

The section on **Family & relationships** emphasises the changing nature of the family but also how much it is still at the heart of our daily lives.

The section on **Financial issues** looks particularly at debt amongst young people and also touches on some of the most worrying aspects of money management.

As with all the sections, the statistics in **Health** will give you and your students facts about issues that are in the news: obesity, alcohol, drugs suicide, and NHS dentistry. You can be confident of having the key statistics to support an argument.

Much of the information in Fact File deals specifically with matters that affect young people. The statistics are interesting in themselves, but reflecting on them can help young people make judgements both about their own lives in comparison to others and about the nature of statistical information.

The majority of the information in Fact File deals with the countries of the UK. There is also a strong representation of EU information. Charts in **Wider world** focus on international issues.

Live links

Once again we have included links, live in the digital version, to sources and associated websites.

Finding information easily

The structure of Fact File encourages browsing and exploration but we have also tried to meet the needs of those who are seeking specific information. When the information in a chart could be categorised in several different ways the index will help you find it. A good example of this is the *Sanitation solution* page which is taken from the Unicef report *Progress for children*. Because it deals with international comparisons it is in the Wider world section but it is also indexed under: environmental issues, health and developing world, because it involves all of those issues. Anyone searching for this information has an easy route to it.

Up-to-date statistics

As always, all the charts have been newly created or thoroughly updated. There is, of course, always a gap, sometimes lengthy, between the collection and the publication of statistics and this is particularly the case with international statistics. The link on the page will lead you to the latest updates.

The nations of the UK collect their own statistics on some topics. These may be compiled at slightly different times making it difficult to find and compare across the whole country.

Supporting the whole curriculum

Fact File has been designed to support the whole secondary and further education curriculum and is an essential library resource. Those teaching citizenship and PSHE will find Fact File invaluable in providing current data related to these subjects. Teachers of business, English, general studies, geography, economics, politics and sociology will also find relevant statistics, attractively presented, to enhance their teaching.

Publication Information

4 Hewson St, Carlisle
Tel 01228 538928
Fax 591816
info@carelpress.com
www.carelpress.com

British Library Cataloguing in Publication Data
Fact File 2009
1. Great Britain – Statistics 314.1
ISBN: 978-1-905600-15-1

Research, design and editorial team:
Anne Louise Kershaw, Debbie Maxwell, Sandra Percival, Christine A Shepherd, Faye Sisson, Chas White

Subscriptions:
Ann Batey (manager), Brenda Hughes, Anne Maclagan

Printing:
Finemark, Poland

Book cover:
Carel Press

FACT FILE 2009 CONTENTS

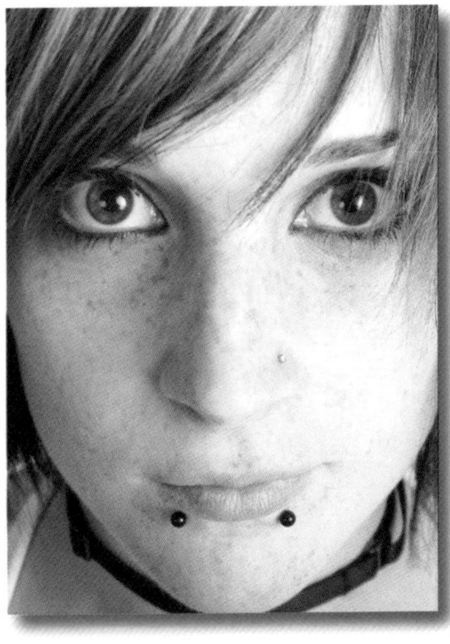

FAMILY & RELATIONSHIPS

FINANCIAL ISSUES

FOOD & DRINK

HEALTH

INTERNET & MEDIA

LAW & ORDER

SPORT & LEISURE

TRAVEL & TRANSPORT

BRITAIN

WAR & CONFLICT

WIDER WORLD

WORK

SIMONIS
Duvel

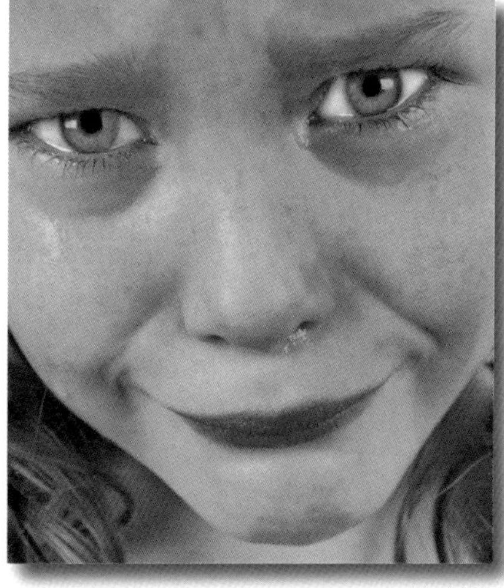

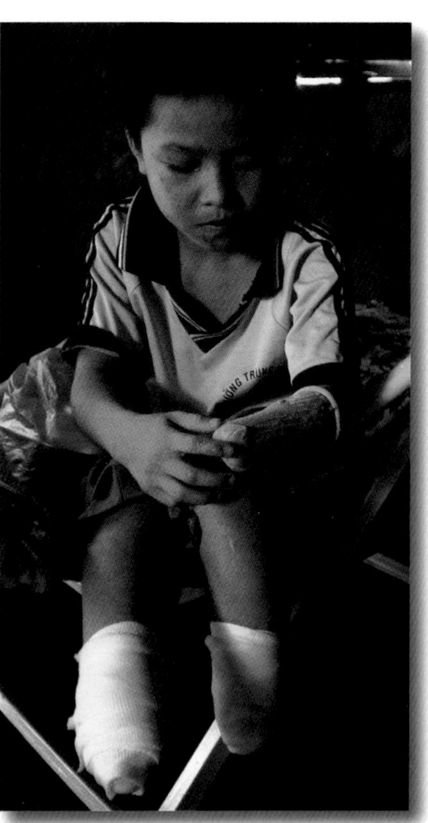

Animals

Primates in peril

Mankind's closest relatives are disappearing from the face of the Earth

50% of the world's 634 kinds of primates are in danger of becoming extinct with some being literally eaten to extinction.

Habitat destruction, through the burning and clearing of tropical forests is a major threat to primates. Other threats include the hunting of primates for food and an illegal wildlife trade.

In Asia, more than 70% of primates are classified on the IUCN Red List as Vulnerable, Endangered or Critically Endangered – meaning they could disappear forever in the near future.

In both Vietnam and Cambodia, approximately 90% of primate species are considered at risk of extinction. Populations of gibbons, leaf monkeys, langurs and other species have dwindled due to rampant habitat loss made worse by hunting for food and supplying the wildlife trade in traditional Chinese medicine and pets.

Vietnam

Grey-shanked douc langur

Critically Endangered

Photo: © Tilo Nadler

In Africa, 11 of the 13 kinds of red colobus monkeys assessed were listed as Critically Endangered or Endangered – two may already be extinct.

Madagascar

Diademed Sifaka

Endangered

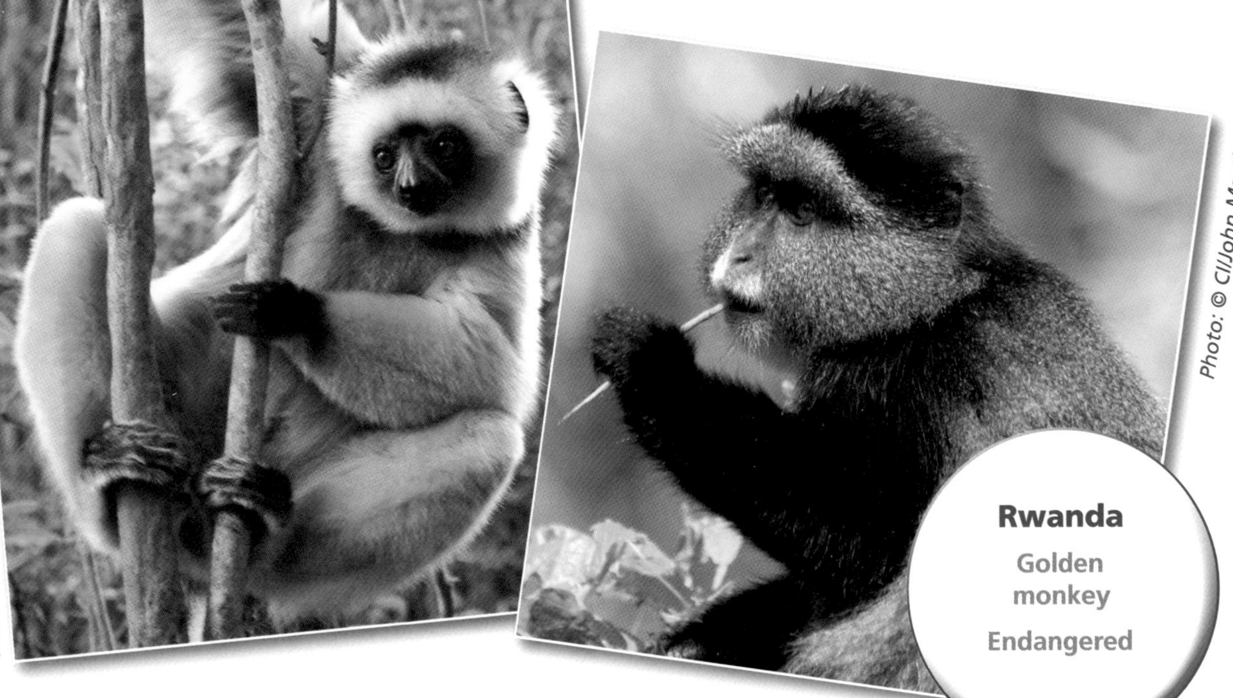

Photo: © CI/Sterling Zumbrunn

Photo: © CI/John Martin

Rwanda

Golden monkey

Endangered

Countries with the highest percentage of threatened species

(only countries with more than two species present)

	% threatened
Cambodia	90.0
Vietnam	86.4
Indonesia	84.1
Lao People's Democratic Republic	83.3
China	77.8
Brunei Darussalam	77.8
Malaysia	70.0
Guatemala	66.7
Mexico	66.7
Myanmar (Burma)	62.5
Bangladesh	62.5
Thailand	61.1
Sri Lanka	60.0
India	54.5
Costa Rica	50.0
Panama	42.9
Colombia	42.4
Nigeria	42.3
Liberia	41.7
Madagascar	40.2

Photo: © Proyecto Tití

Colombia

Cotton-Top Tamarin

Critically Endangered

Primates are important to the health of their surrounding ecosystems. Through the dispersal of seeds and other interactions with their environments, primates help support a wide range of plant and animal life in the world's tropical forests. Healthy forests provide vital resources for local human populations, and also absorb and store carbon dioxide that causes climate change.

Number of species and sub-species listed as Vulnerable, Endangered or Critically Endangered – breakdown by geographic region:

Africa:

63 species – 37% of all African primates

Asia:

120 species – 71% of all Asian primates

Madagascar:

41 species – 43% of all Malagasy primates

Mexico and Central & South America:

79 species – 40% of all Neotropical primates

Glimmer of hope?

As a result of 30 years of conservation efforts in Brazil, populations of both black lion tamarin and golden lion tamarin are now well-protected but remain very small, causing an urgent need for reforestation to provide new habitat for their long-term survival. They were downlisted to Endangered from Critically Endangered in 2003.

Researchers are also considering reclassifying the mountain gorilla to Endangered from Critically Endangered due to increasing populations in their only habitat – the protected mountain jungles of Rwanda, Uganda and Democratic Republic of Congo. However, the slaying of eight mountain gorillas in 2007 and political unrest has delayed this.

Source: IUCN Red List, Conservation International
http://www.iucnredlist.org

Sold into extinction

Humans are responsible for the decline of the tiger

Tiger numbers are very hard to assess – but all estimates point to a catastrophic decline

Tigers remaining in the wild
Worldwide, estimated numbers

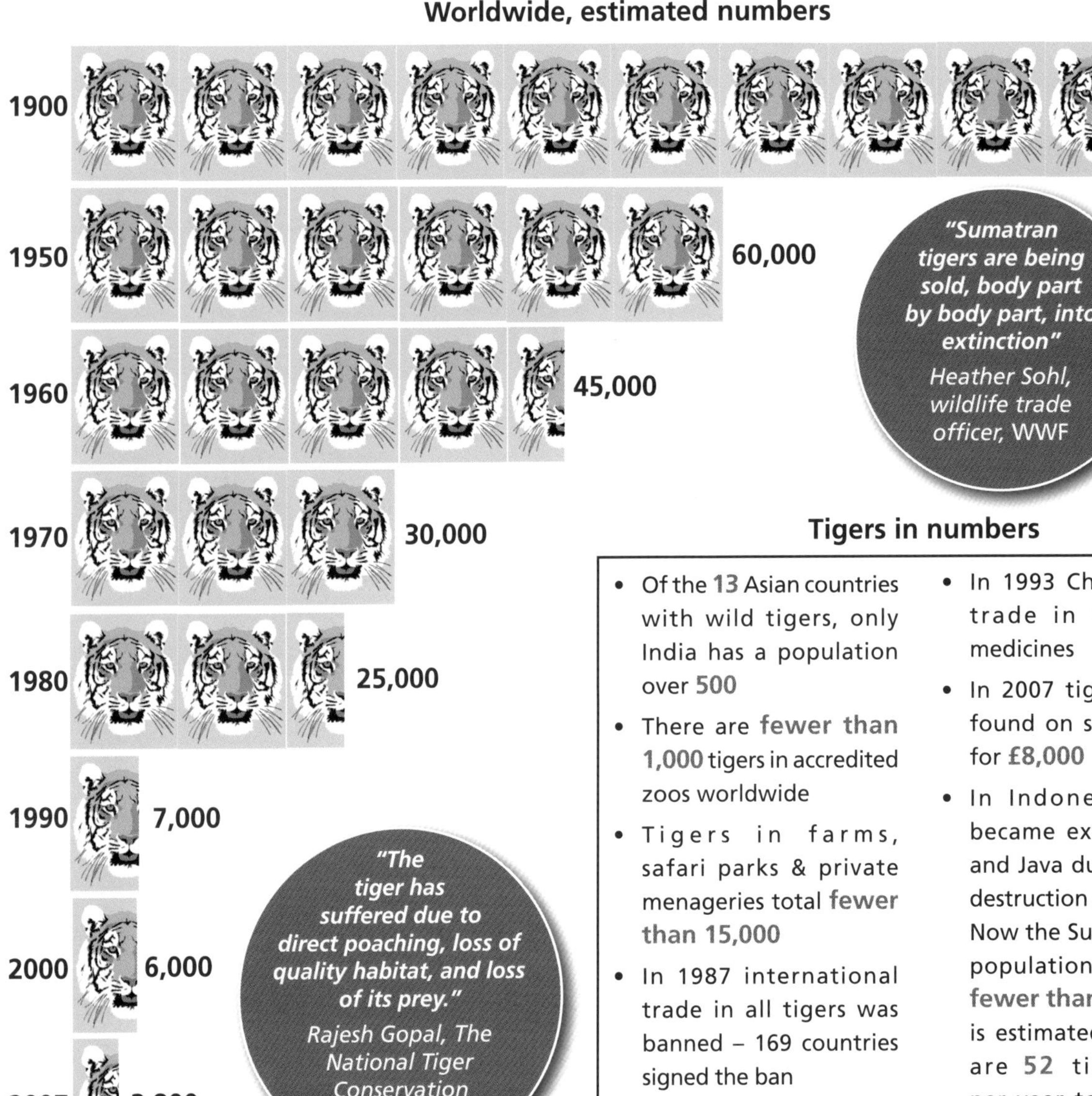
1900
100,000
1950
60,000
1960
45,000
1970
30,000
1980
25,000
1990
7,000
2000
6,000
2007
3,800
2025
Extinct in the wild

"The tiger has suffered due to direct poaching, loss of quality habitat, and loss of its prey."
Rajesh Gopal, The National Tiger Conservation Authority

"Sumatran tigers are being sold, body part by body part, into extinction"
Heather Sohl, wildlife trade officer, WWF

Tigers in numbers

- Of the **13** Asian countries with wild tigers, only India has a population over **500**
- There are **fewer than 1,000** tigers in accredited zoos worldwide
- Tigers in farms, safari parks & private menageries total **fewer than 15,000**
- In 1987 international trade in all tigers was banned – 169 countries signed the ban
- In 1993 China banned trade in tiger-bone medicines
- In 2007 tiger skin was found on sale in China for **£8,000**
- In Indonesia, tigers became extinct in Bali and Java due to habitat destruction and hunting. Now the Sumatran tiger population is down to **fewer than 400-500**. It is estimated that there are **52** tigers killed per year to supply the wildlife trade.

In India:

There were **3,642** tigers recorded in 2002

In 2007 improved measuring methods recorded just **1,411**

The Indian tiger will not survive unless humans intervene. It will require breeding areas free from any human presence. These areas will need to be linked by 'corridors' where the human population has an incentive to conserve rather than hunt or destroy the habitat

http://www.savethetigerfund.org
http://www.wii.gov.in
http://www.traffic.org

Sources: Traffic; Wildlife Institute of India: Save the Tiger Fund

Preyed on

Attacks on birds of prey are up by 40%

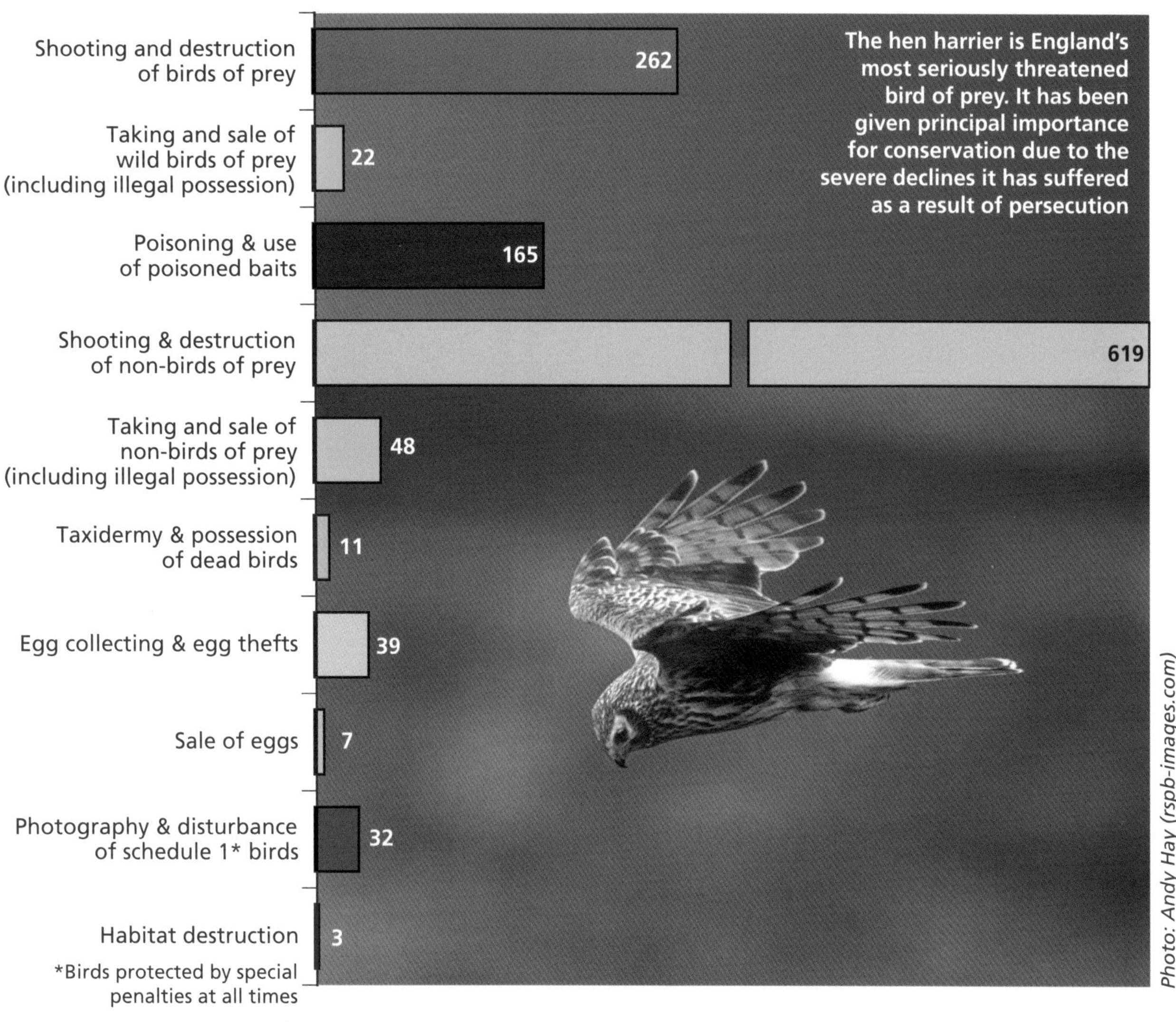

Reported offences against wild bird legislation in the UK, 2007
Shooting and destruction of birds of prey 262
Taking and sale of wild birds of prey (including illegal possession) 22
Poisoning & use of poisoned baits 165
Shooting & destruction of non-birds of prey 619
Taking and sale of non-birds of prey (including illegal possession) 48
Taxidermy & possession of dead birds 11
Egg collecting & egg thefts 39
Sale of eggs 7
Photography & disturbance of schedule 1* birds 32
Habitat destruction 3
*Birds protected by special penalties at all times
The hen harrier is England's most seriously threatened bird of prey. It has been given principal importance for conservation due to the severe declines it has suffered as a result of persecution
Photo: Andy Hay (rspb-images.com)

Killing birds of prey was made illegal 50 years ago but reports of criminal acts against all wild birds were at record levels in 2007 with 1,208 separate incidents reported to the RSPB.

The RSPB believes the true figure is much higher, with many crimes taking place in remote areas where they remain undetected and unreported.

Of the 49 reports of birds of prey being poisoned 17 were red kites – the highest number recorded in a single year.

UK breakdown:

England: 810 offences

Scotland: 229

Wales: 128

Northern Ireland: 33

Not specified: 8

There were 33 prosecutions involving 127 charges

70% resulted in a guilty outcome

Total fines for the year £19,450

Two people received custodial sentences

Source: Bird Crime 2007, RSPB

www.rspb.org.uk/birdsofprey
http://www.rspb.org.uk/youth/learn/birdsofprey.asp

Lab rats

Animals are being created just to be used in experiments

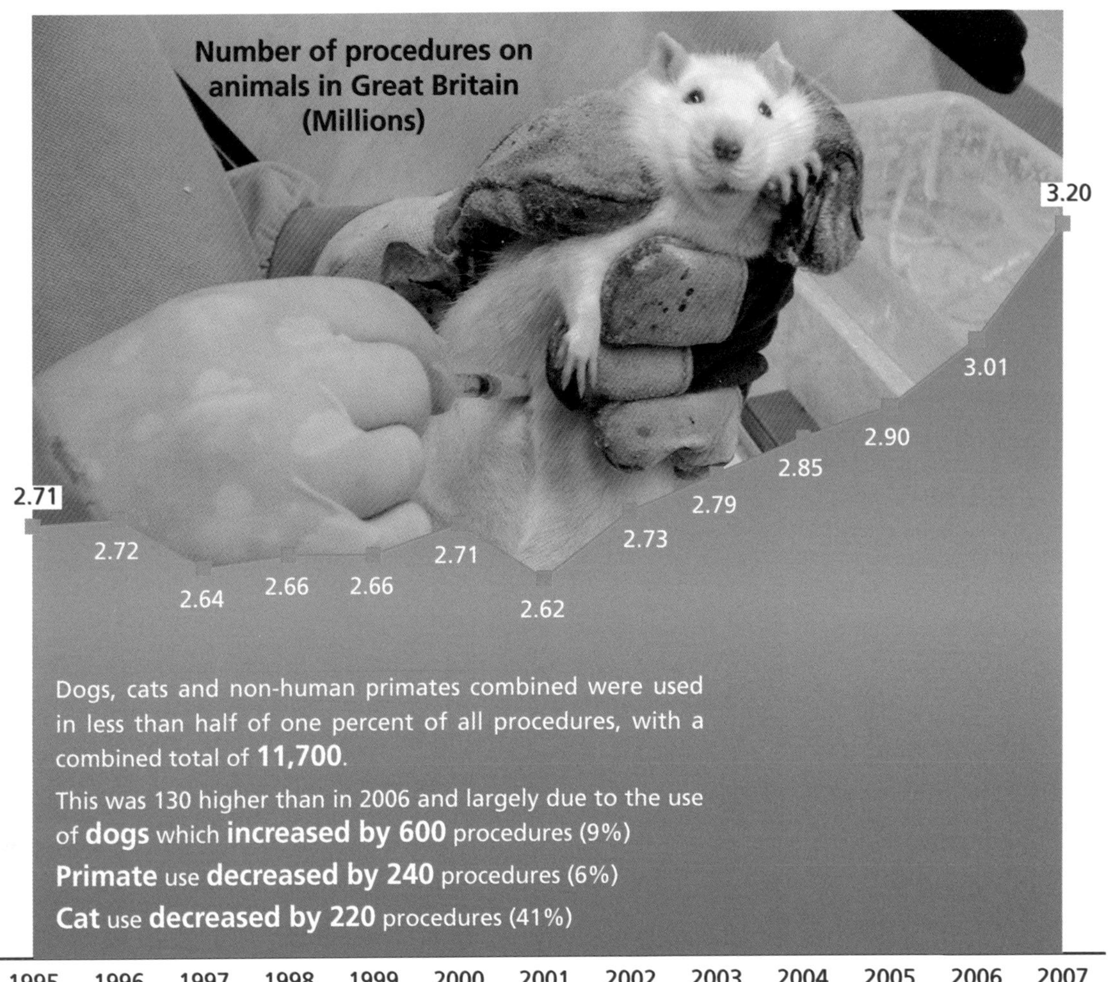

Number of procedures on animals in Great Britain (Millions)
2.71
2.72
2.64
2.66
2.66
2.71
2.62
2.73
2.79
2.85
2.90
3.01
3.20
Dogs, cats and non-human primates combined were used in less than half of one percent of all procedures, with a combined total of **11,700**.
This was 130 higher than in 2006 and largely due to the use of **dogs** which **increased by 600** procedures (9%)
Primate use **decreased by 240** procedures (6%)
Cat use **decreased by 220** procedures (41%)
1995
1996
1997
1998
1999
2000
2001
2002
2003
2004
2005
2006
2007

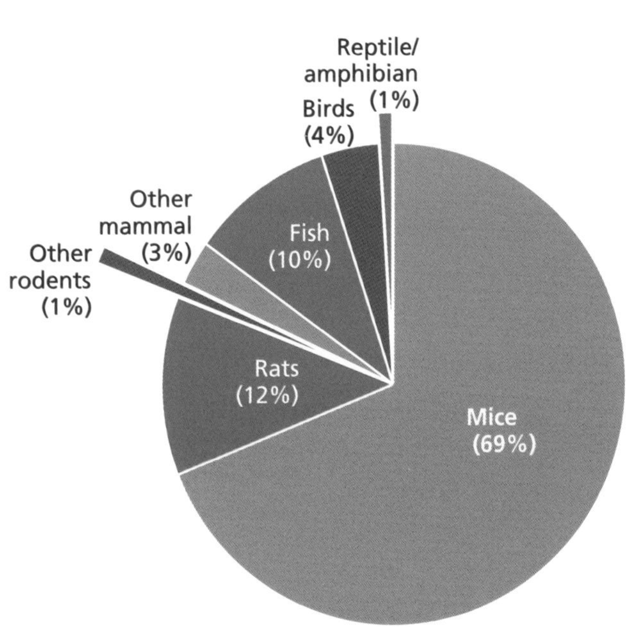

Proportion of procedures using different types of animals
Reptile/ amphibian (1%)
Birds (4%)
Other mammal (3%)
Other rodents (1%)
Fish (10%)
Rats (12%)
Mice (69%)

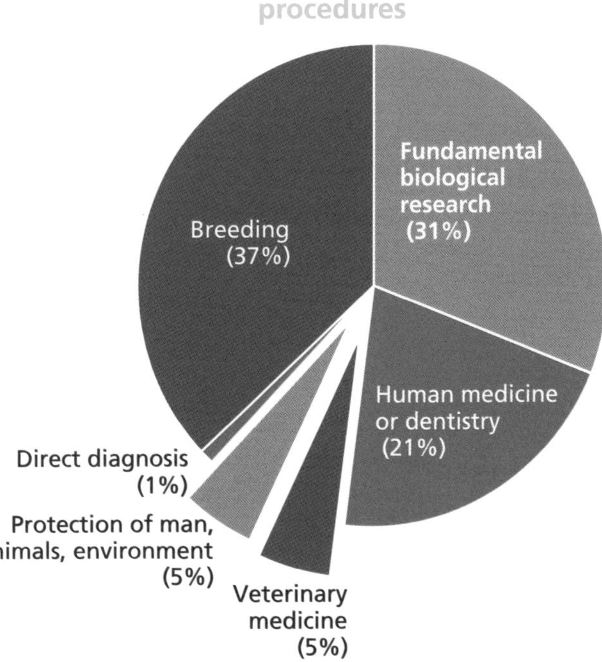

Primary purpose of procedures
Breeding (37%)
Fundamental biological research (31%)
Human medicine or dentistry (21%)
Direct diagnosis (1%)
Protection of man, animals, environment (5%)
Veterinary medicine (5%)

Other purposes amounting to less than 1% of the total include education, training and forensic enquiries

Genetically modified (GM) animals

The RSPCA is concerned about ethical and welfare issues associated with the creation of GM animals for use in experiments.

The charity feels that this is increasing at an alarming rate and it is now reversing the downward trend in laboratory animal use.

It is also concerned that the process of creating GM animals can be painful as well as wasteful. It argues that the experiments are presented as beneficial without the public being given the information to weigh the benefits against the harm.

Proportion of procedures using animals of different genetic status

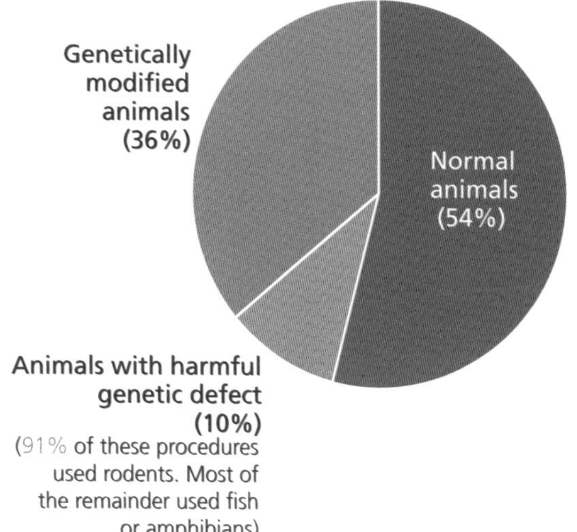

Genetically modified animals (36%)
Normal animals (54%)
Animals with harmful genetic defect (10%)

(91% of these procedures used rodents. Most of the remainder used fish or amphibians)

Number of procedures using GM animals (thousands)

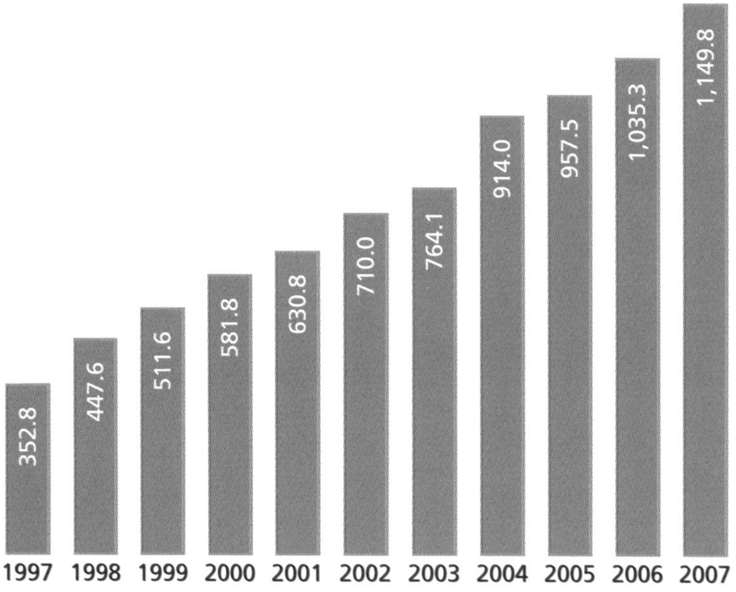

352.8
447.6
511.6
581.8
630.8
710.0
764.1
914.0
957.5
1,035.3
1,149.8
1997 1998 1999 2000 2001 2002 2003 2004 2005 2006 2007

Around 39% of all procedures used some form of anaesthesia. For many of the remaining, the use of any drugs could increase the adverse effects of the procedure or interfere with results.

Toxicological (safety) purposes accounted for 13% of all procedures started in 2007. This testing can include pesticides, medication, food additives and artificial sweeteners. 78% of these procedures were for testing pharmaceutical (medical/health) products.

'Superfoods'

Superfoods may be responsible for part of the rise in animal experiments according to some animal welfare groups.

The British Union for the Abolition of Vivisection identified experiments to test probiotic drinks and herbal supplements which required animals to be subjected to pain and distress.

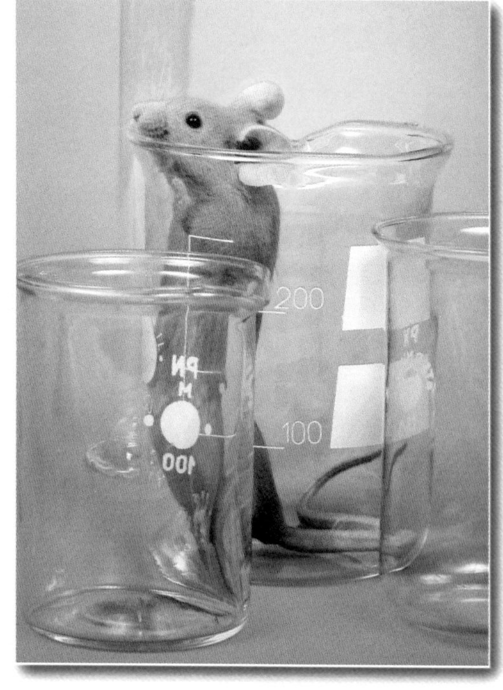

Source: Home Office © Crown copyright 2008
RSPCA, British Union for the Abolition of Vivisection

http://www.homeoffice.gov.uk
http://www.rspca.org.uk
http://www.buav.org/

Acting for animals

A new law should make it easier to help animals

The new Animal Welfare Act has made it possible to take action sooner than ever before in situations where there are animal welfare concerns.

"Without the new Act, this year's cruelty figures could have been even more horrific."
Tim Wass RSPCA

The RSPCA investigated 137,245 complaints of cruelty (up 12%) on the previous year

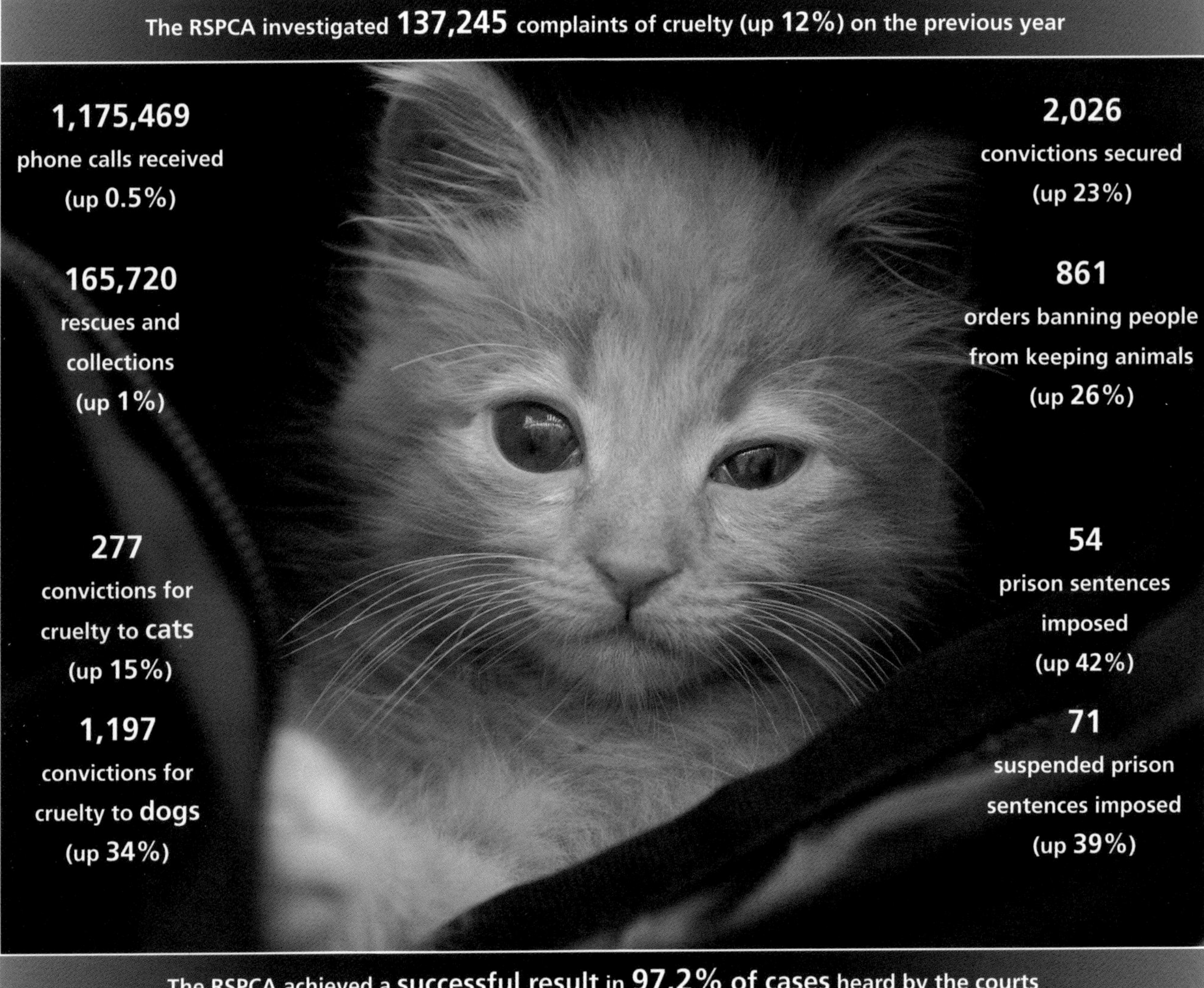
1,175,469
phone calls received
(up 0.5%)
165,720
rescues and
collections
(up 1%)
277
convictions for
cruelty to cats
(up 15%)
1,197
convictions for
cruelty to dogs
(up 34%)
2,026
convictions secured
(up 23%)
861
orders banning people
from keeping animals
(up 26%)
54
prison sentences
imposed
(up 42%)
71
suspended prison
sentences imposed
(up 39%)

The RSPCA achieved a successful result in 97.2% of cases heard by the courts

The **Animal Welfare Act** has raised the **age limit** at which a child can **buy a pet**, or **win one** as a prize, to **16 years old**.

The owner of a pet will need to provide five **essential requirements** under the **Act** –

- a **suitable environment** (where it lives)
- a **suitable diet**
- to be able to **behave normally**
- to be **housed with or apart from other animals**, (whatever is best for that particular animal)
- to be **protected from pain, suffering, injury and disease**

Offenders can be **banned** from owning animals; **fined** up to £20,000; and/or sent to **prison** for a maximum of 51 weeks.

It remains an **offence** to cause **unnecessary suffering** to an animal, or to organise an **animal fight**, but the law relating to these offences has been revised so that it is geared to tackle the types of crimes that occur in the 21st century.

The **Animal Welfare Act** obliges courts to explain their reasons if they don't impose a ban and this may have contributed to the increase.

Source: RSPCA, Defra
http://www.rspca.co.uk
http://www.defra.gov.uk

Dangerous dogs

Violent dog attacks have risen to nearly 3,800 a year

Under the Dangerous Dogs Act, it is an offence to own or keep a Pit Bull Terrier, Japanese Tosa, Dogo Argentino and Fila Braziliero

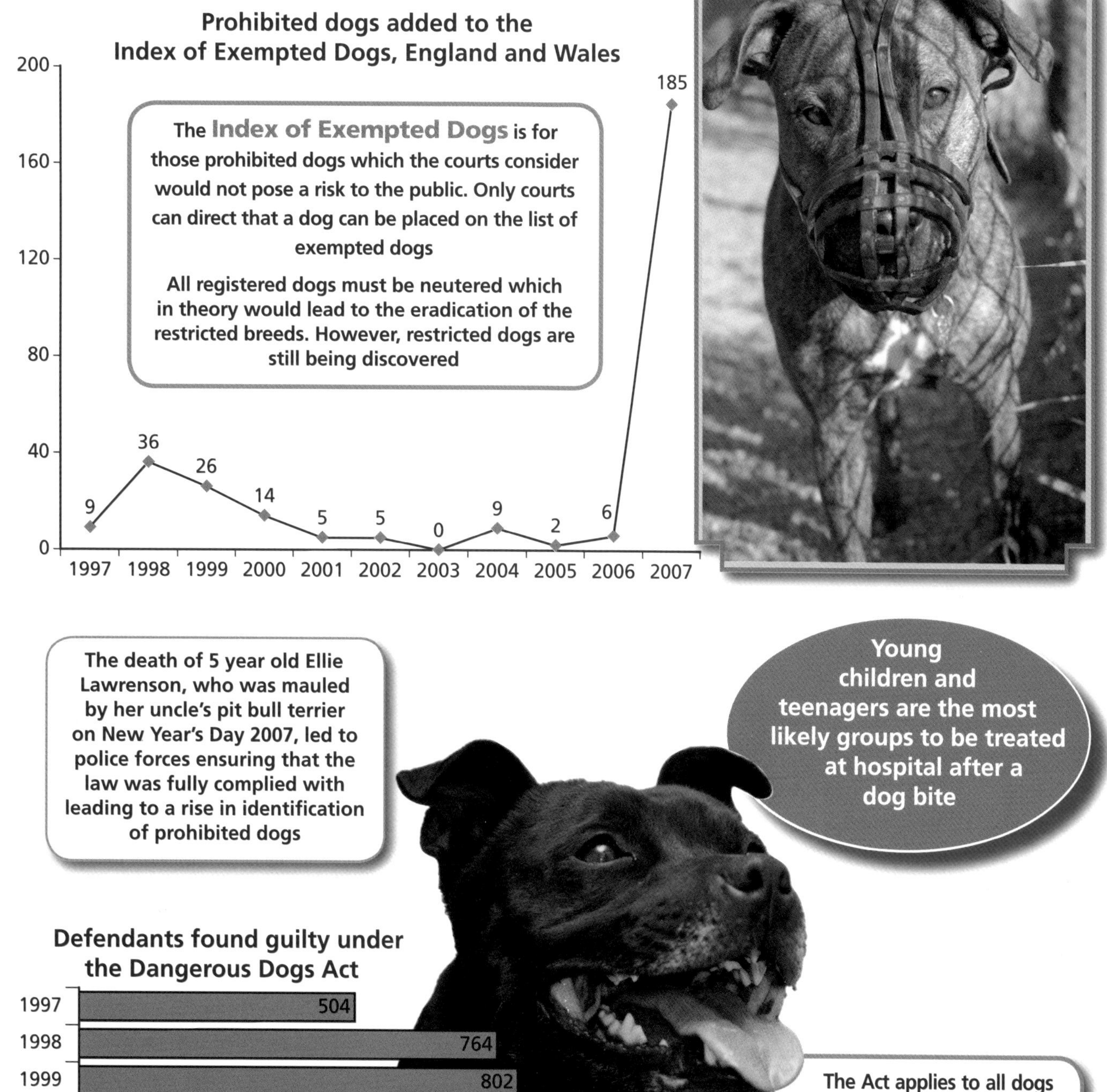

Prohibited dogs added to the Index of Exempted Dogs, England and Wales
200
160
120
80
40
0
1997 1998 1999 2000 2001 2002 2003 2004 2005 2006 2007
9 36 26 14 5 5 0 9 2 6 185

The **Index of Exempted Dogs** is for those prohibited dogs which the courts consider would not pose a risk to the public. Only courts can direct that a dog can be placed on the list of exempted dogs

All registered dogs must be neutered which in theory would lead to the eradication of the restricted breeds. However, restricted dogs are still being discovered

The death of 5 year old Ellie Lawrenson, who was mauled by her uncle's pit bull terrier on New Year's Day 2007, led to police forces ensuring that the law was fully complied with leading to a rise in identification of prohibited dogs

Young children and teenagers are the most likely groups to be treated at hospital after a dog bite

Defendants found guilty under the Dangerous Dogs Act

Year	Defendants
1997	504
1998	764
1999	802
2000	836
2001	886
2002	922
2003	988
2004	990
2005	1,025
2006	1,077

The Act applies to all dogs that are dangerously out of control in a public place (it does not apply to dogs in their own gardens who jump up at visitors).

If a dog acts in a way so that someone fears they will be attacked, then an offence is committed

Source: Defra © Crown copyright 2008
http://www.defra.gov.uk

Sniffing it out

A dog's sense of smell can make a vital difference

HM Revenue & Customs (HMRC) Detection dogs were first introduced in 1978. Dogs can distinguish smells so well because they have around 200 million receptors compared to just 5 million in a human nose.

People

Eddie is an enhanced victim recovery dog and is specially trained to detect the scent of human remains. He is able to smell through solid materials, like concrete, because of scientific training techniques.

The seven-year-old dog located parts of a child's body even though they were buried under several inches of concrete at a former Children's Home in Jersey.

Bombs

The British Army's specialists believe they, along with the Israelis, lead the world in the use of dogs to find explosives: weapons caches, booby-trap bombs and unexploded devices.

Bomb sniffer dogs often move at the front of patrols as British forces move through hazardous areas. They are trained to sit and stare at the source of a scent but not to touch it.

Insurgent fighters have tried to disrupt specialist explosive sniffer dogs from operating – by leaving dog toys and treats around hidden devices.

DVDs

Lucky and Flo, two black Labradors, can sniff out DVDs in an attempt to stop pirate imports.

Drugs

The first dogs were used to find cannabis, but they are now also trained to find Heroin, Cocaine, Ecstasy and Amphetamines, plus cash, products of animal origin (eg dairy, meat and fish) and tobacco.

In 2006/07 HMRC's detection dogs seized a total of:

£10,724,945 in cash (in various currencies)

40.6 tonnes of products of animal origin (dairy, meat & fish)

9,390,136 cigarettes

3,568 kg of hand rolling tobacco

1,434 kg of class A drugs

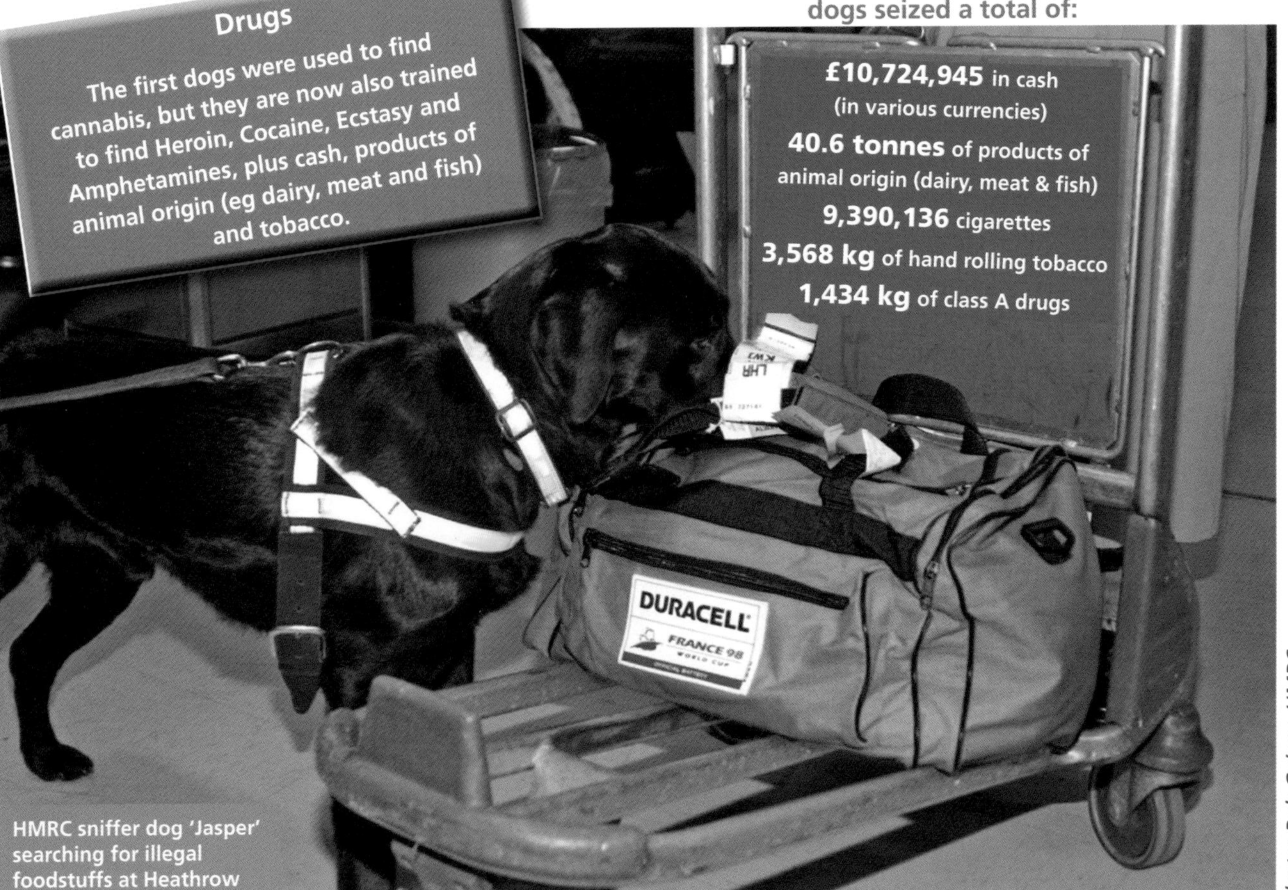
DURACELL
FRANCE 98

HMRC sniffer dog 'Jasper' searching for illegal foodstuffs at Heathrow

Photo: Bob Gaiger, HMRC

Source: HM Revenue & Customs

http://www.hmrc.gov.uk

Britain & its citizens

Accessorize
AMUSEMENTS
AMIR
AMOUD
AMOUD

Escalating nations

The UK population will rise to 71m by 2031

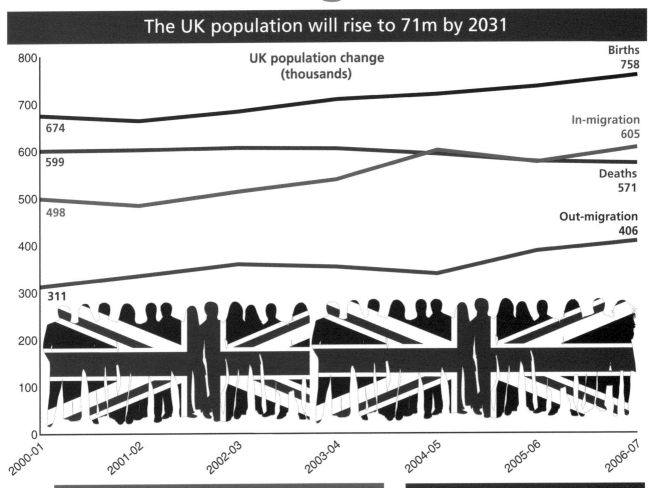

UK population change (thousands)

800
700
600
500
400
300
200
100
0

Births 758
674
In-migration 605
599
Deaths 571
498
Out-migration 406
311

2000-01
2001-02
2002-03
2003-04
2004-05
2005-06
2006-07

The population of the UK was 60,975,000 in mid-2007, up by 388,000 (0.6%) on the previous year and nearly two million more than in mid-2001.

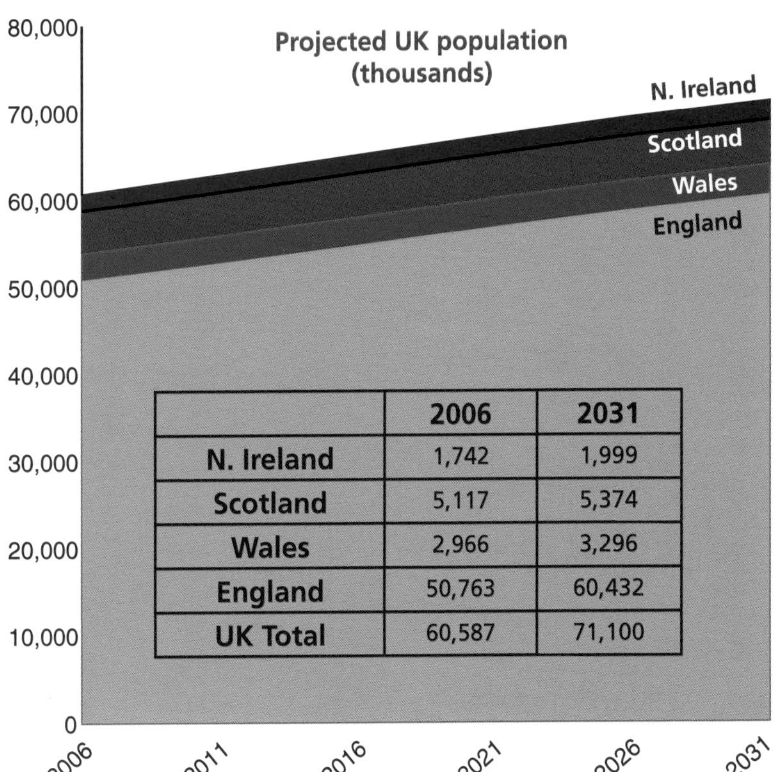

Projected UK population (thousands)
80,000
70,000
60,000
50,000
40,000
30,000
20,000
10,000
0
N. Ireland
Scotland
Wales
England
2006
2011
2016
2021
2026
2031

	2006	2031
N. Ireland	1,742	1,999
Scotland	5,117	5,374
Wales	2,966	3,296
England	50,763	60,432
UK Total	60,587	71,100

Net migration

Net international migration (the difference between long term migration into and out of the UK) was +198,000 in the year to mid-2007. This was 9,000 more than in the previous year and 11,000 more than in the year to mid-2001 (+187,000). This accounted for 52% - of all population growth during the 12 months to mid-2007, compared with 55% in 2006 and 72% in 2001.

Natural change

Natural change (the difference between births and deaths) contributed 48% to population growth in the year to mid-2007 compared with 45% in mid-2006 and 28% in mid-2001.

There were 758,000 births in the 12 months to mid-2007, 84,000 more than in the 12 months to mid-2001 (674,000). Deaths decreased by 28,000 over this period (from 599,000 in 2001 to 571,000 in 2007).

Source: Office for National Statistics
http://www.statistics.gov.uk

Death by numbers

In the early 1900s over half of all deaths occurred before the age of 45, now it is only 4%

Death registrations, aged 45 and over, UK, 2007

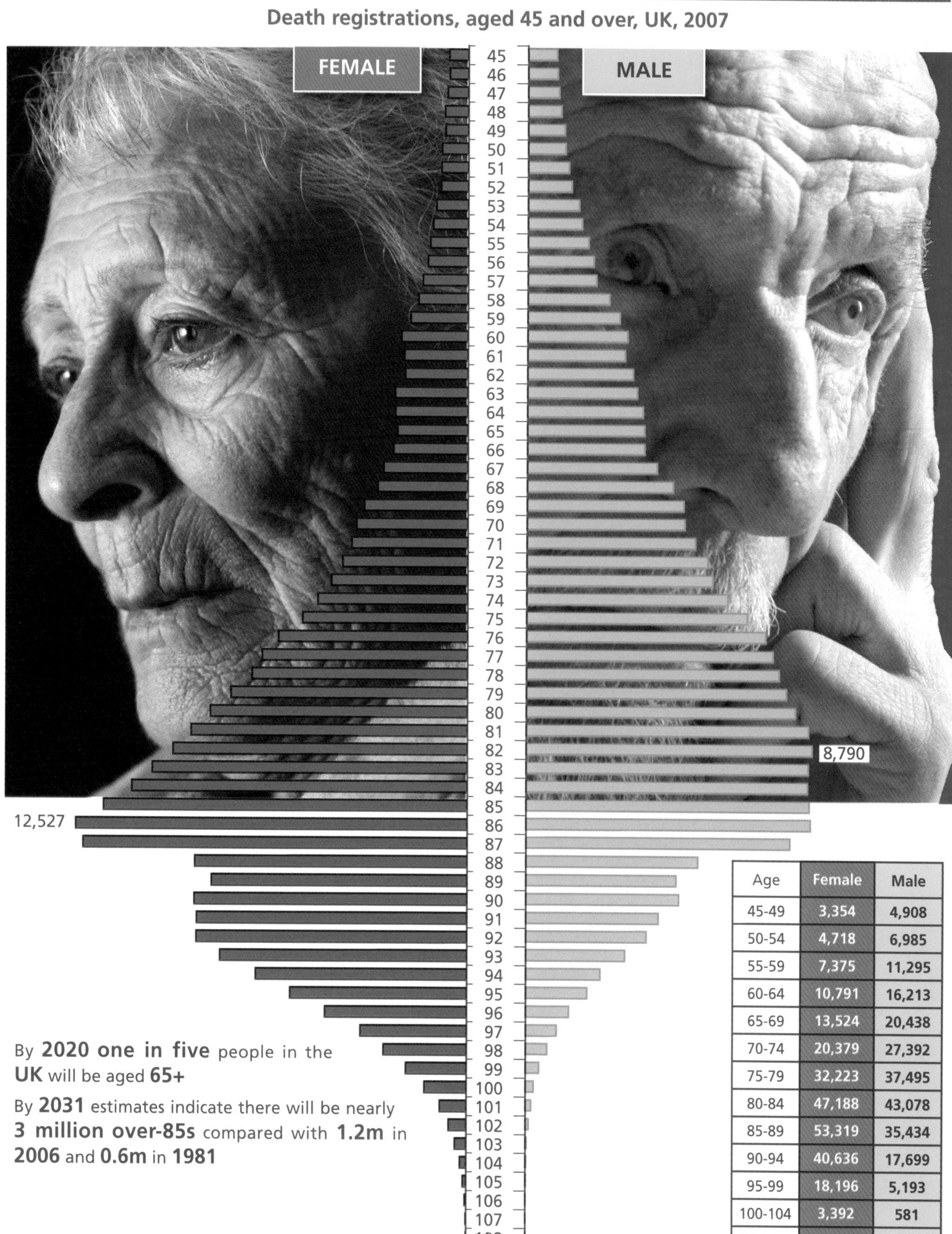
FEMALE
MALE
45
46
47
48
49
50
51
52
53
54
55
56
57
58
59
60
61
62
63
64
65
66
67
68
69
70
71
72
73
74
75
76
77
78
79
80
81
82
83
84
85
86
87
88
89
90
91
92
93
94
95
96
97
98
99
100
101
102
103
104
105
106
107
108
109
110 +
12,527
8,790

Age	Female	Male
45-49	3,354	4,908
50-54	4,718	6,985
55-59	7,375	11,295
60-64	10,791	16,213
65-69	13,524	20,438
70-74	20,379	27,392
75-79	32,223	37,495
80-84	47,188	43,078
85-89	53,319	35,434
90-94	40,636	17,699
95-99	18,196	5,193
100-104	3,392	581
105-109	205	22
110 +	4	1

By **2020 one in five** people in the **UK** will be aged **65+**

By **2031** estimates indicate there will be nearly **3 million over-85s** compared with **1.2m** in **2006** and **0.6m** in **1981**

Source: Office for National Statistics © Crown copyright 2008, Institute for Public Policy Research © ippr 2008

http://www.statistics.gov.uk
http://www.ippr.org.uk

Different class

Have attitudes towards social class really changed?

43% feel that the class system has become less rigid in the past 10 years yet we still make judgements about 'class' from the way people speak and act.

In 2008, 52% of people defined themselves as working class, 44% as middle class while 3% didn't know and 1% refused to answer.

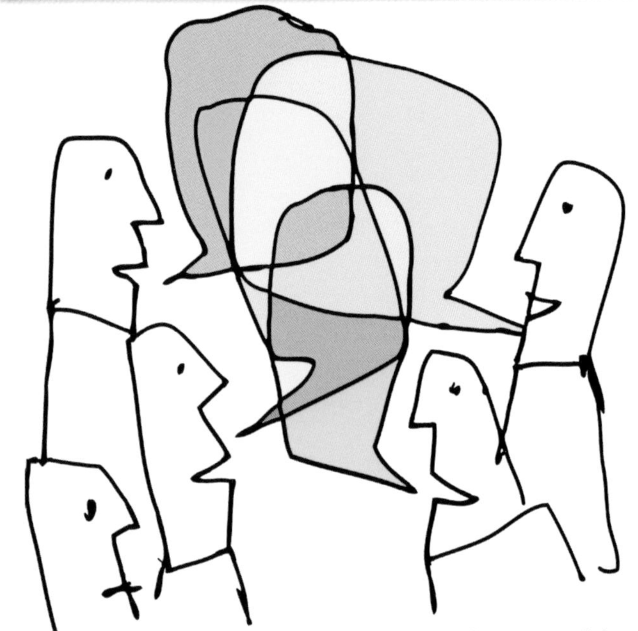

Q. How often, if at all, do you think that other people can tell which class you are by the way you speak?

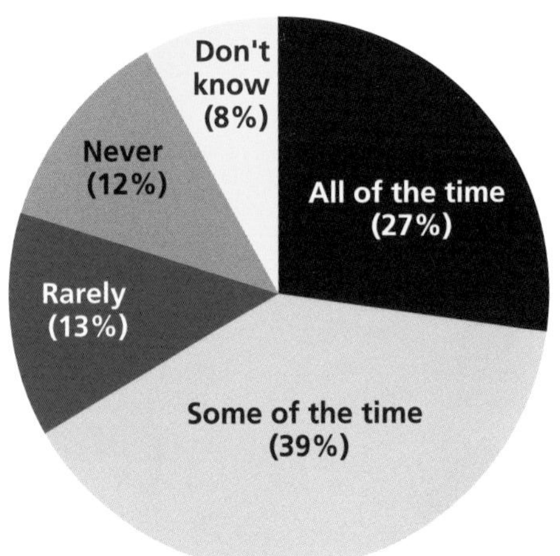

All of the time (27%)
Some of the time (39%)
Rarely (13%)
Never (12%)
Don't know (8%)

Q. Which of the following do you think would most likely be done by a working class person, a middle class person, or an upper class person?

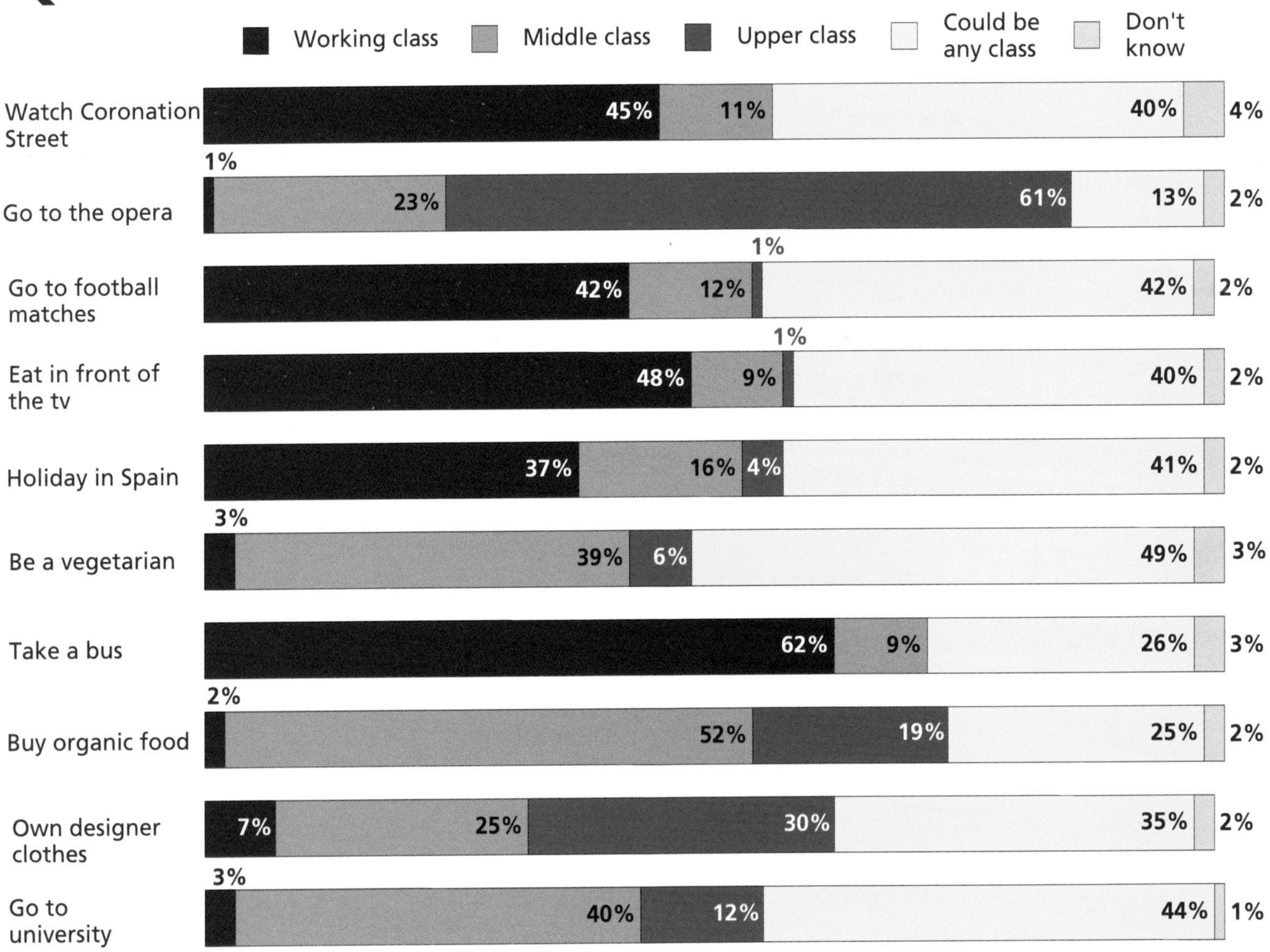

	Working class	Middle class	Upper class	Could be any class	Don't know
Watch Coronation Street	45%	11%		40%	4%
Go to the opera	1%	23%	61%	13%	2%
Go to football matches	42%	12%	1%	42%	2%
Eat in front of the tv	48%	9%	1%	40%	2%
Holiday in Spain	37%	16%	4%	41%	2%
Be a vegetarian	3%	39%	6%	49%	3%
Take a bus	62%	9%		26%	3%
Buy organic food	2%	52%	19%	25%	2%
Own designer clothes	7%	25%	30%	35%	2%
Go to university	3%	40%	12%	44%	1%

NB Figures may not add up to 100% due to computer rounding or multiple answers

Source: Mori survey on class
http://www.ipsos-mori.com

Mr & Mrs Average

The 'typical' British family

Nearest and dearest?

Mr and Mrs Average live 47 minutes drive from the nearest close member of their family

Living nearest to close family, by region (in minutes)

North East	34
Yorkshire	36
North West	37

Living furthest from their close family, by region (in minutes)

Wales	64
London	64
South West	61

Mr and Mrs Average...

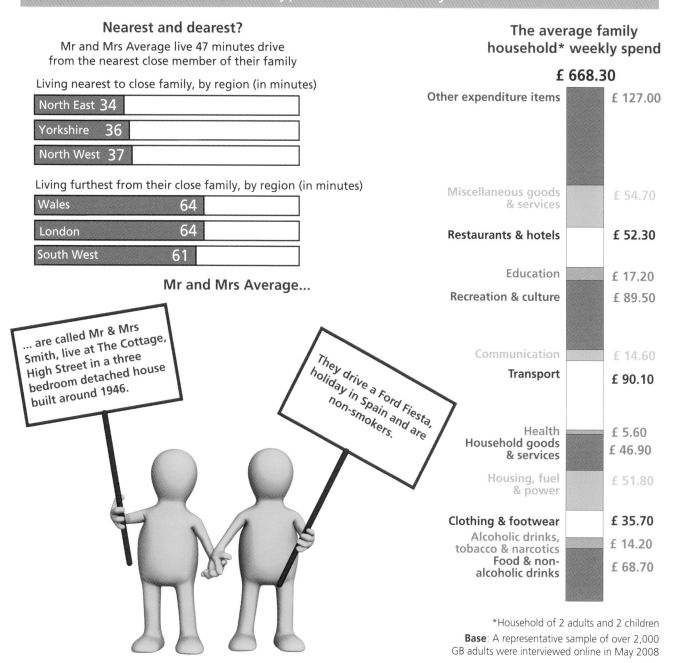

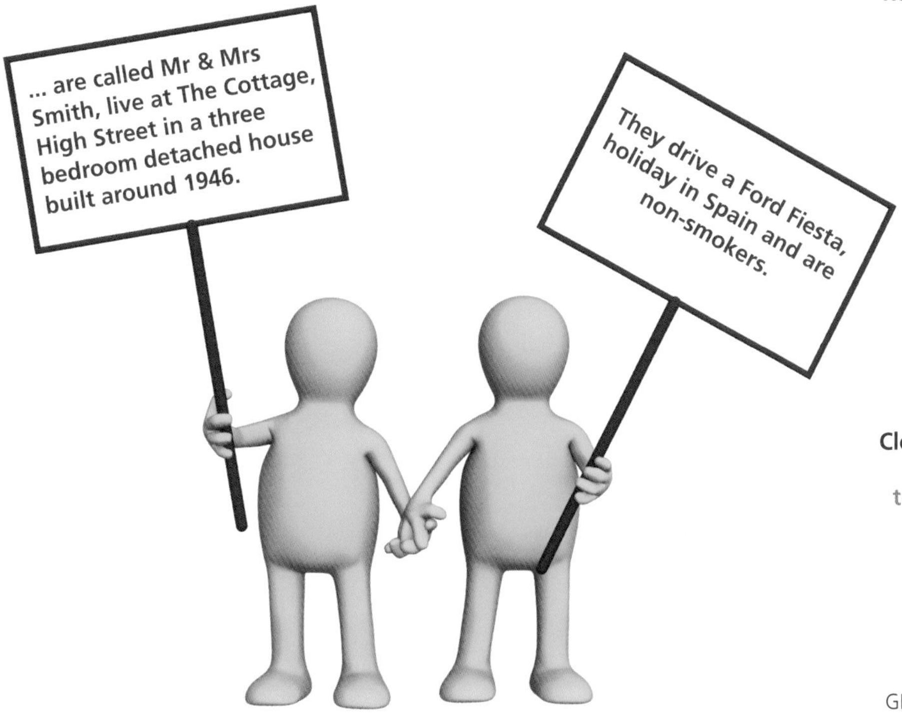

... are called Mr & Mrs Smith, live at The Cottage, High Street in a three bedroom detached house built around 1946.

They drive a Ford Fiesta, holiday in Spain and are non-smokers.

The average family household* weekly spend

£ 668.30

Other expenditure items	£ 127.00
Miscellaneous goods & services	£ 54.70
Restaurants & hotels	£ 52.30
Education	£ 17.20
Recreation & culture	£ 89.50
Communication	£ 14.60
Transport	£ 90.10
Health	£ 5.60
Household goods & services	£ 46.90
Housing, fuel & power	£ 51.80
Clothing & footwear	£ 35.70
Alcoholic drinks, tobacco & narcotics	£ 14.20
Food & non-alcoholic drinks	£ 68.70

*Household of 2 adults and 2 children

Base: A representative sample of over 2,000 GB adults were interviewed online in May 2008

Prized possessions

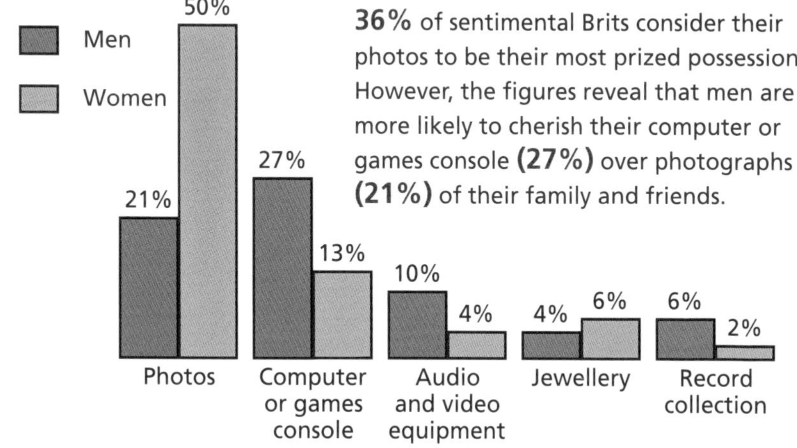

Men
Women
21%
50%
27%
13%
10%
4%
4%
6%
6%
2%
Photos
Computer or games console
Audio and video equipment
Jewellery
Record collection

36% of sentimental Brits consider their photos to be their most prized possessions. However, the figures reveal that men are more likely to cherish their computer or games console **(27%)** over photographs **(21%)** of their family and friends.

Top five British surnames
Smith
Jones
Williams
Brown
Taylor

Source: Norwich Union, Office for National Statistics © Crown copyright 2008

http://www.aviva.com

http;//www.statistics.gov.uk

It's not me...

People believe that *they* are not prejudiced, but their colleagues *are*

Q. In your workplace, do you think there is prejudice against employees who are...

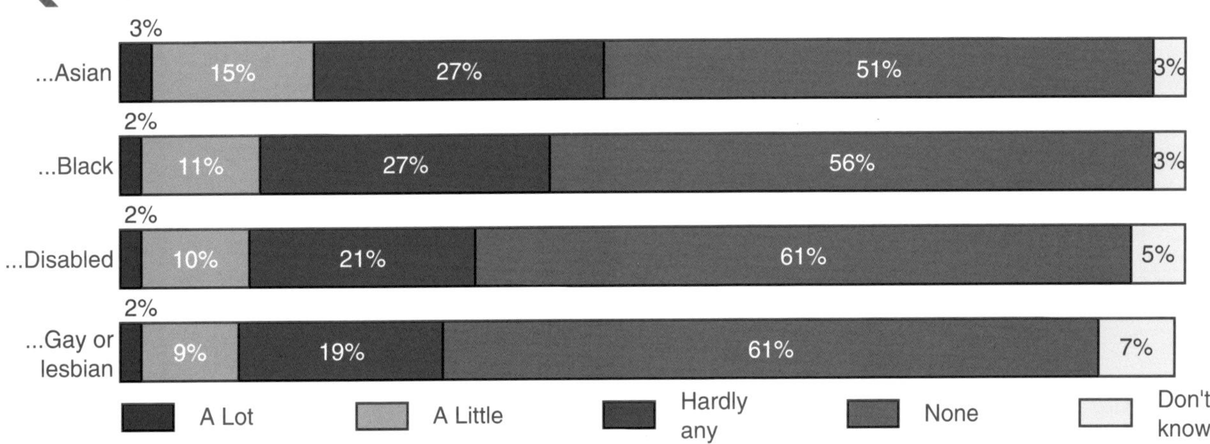

...Asian
3%
15%
27%
51%
3%
...Black
2%
11%
27%
56%
3%
...Disabled
2%
10%
21%
61%
5%
...Gay or lesbian
2%
9%
19%
61%
7%
A Lot
A Little
Hardly any
None
Don't know

Figures do not add up to 100% due to rounding

Q. If the person was suitably qualified, do you think you or your colleagues would mind having them as a boss if they were...

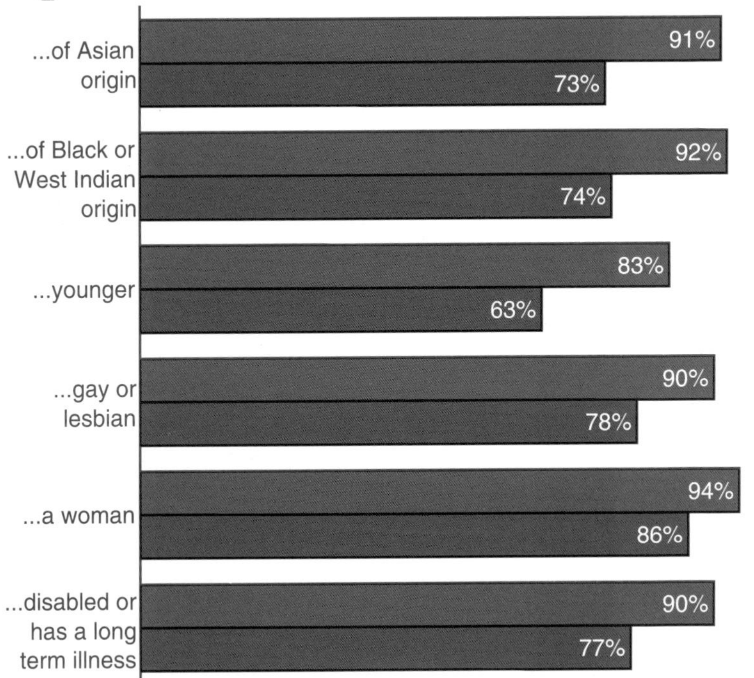

...of Asian origin
91%
73%
...of Black or West Indian origin
92%
74%
...younger
83%
63%
...gay or lesbian
90%
78%
...a woman
94%
86%
...disabled or has a long term illness
90%
77%

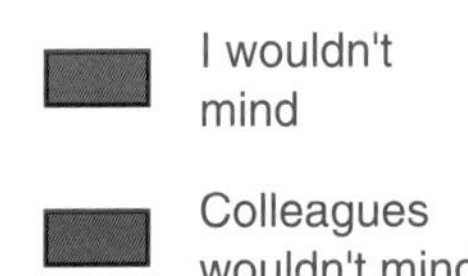

I wouldn't mind
Colleagues wouldn't mind

Even '*hardly any*' prejudice, involves some prejudice. And while, for example, most people wouldn't mind if a person of Asian origin were their boss, **8%** definitely would.

When asked whether equal opportunities in the workplace had gone too far, **36%** of people thought they had gone too far for Black and Asian people, **11%** for women, **6%** for disabled people and **18%** for gay and lesbian people.

It is interesting that there is a difference between how people see their own level of prejudice and how prejudiced they think other people are.

Source: British Social Attitudes 2007/08
http://www.natcen.ac.uk

How racist is Britain?

Views on prejudice have become gloomier

The Citizenship Survey covers a representative sample of adults in England and Wales plus a minority ethnic boost to ensure that the views of these groups are robustly represented.

In 2007 over 7,000 face-to-face interviews were conducted.

People who feel there is more racial prejudice in Britain today than 5 years ago

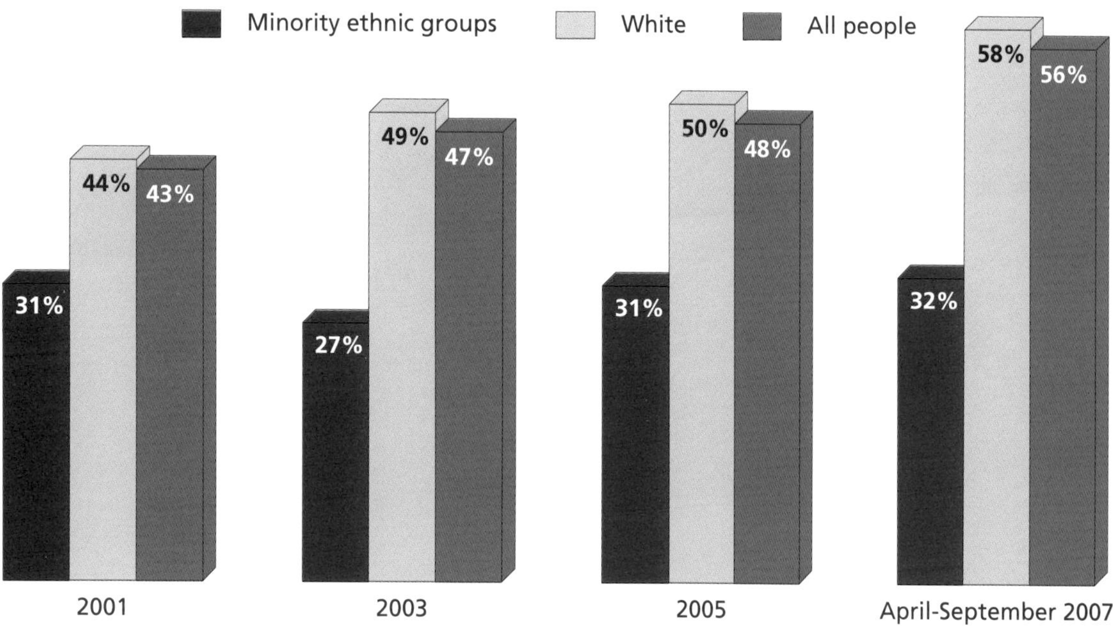

Minority ethnic groups
White
All people
31%
44%
43%
27%
49%
47%
31%
50%
48%
32%
58%
56%
2001
2003
2005
April-September 2007

Amongst minority ethnic groups: who thought prejudice had got worse?

46% of Pakistanis

39% of Mixed Race

33% of Indians

31% of Black Caribbeans

26% of Bangladeshis

26% of Chinese or other minority ethnic backgrounds

22% of Black Africans

Young people have more positive views regarding racial prejudice than older people – 43% of people aged 16-24 saying prejudice had increased compared with 65% of 65-74 year olds

Source: Department for Communities and Local Government © Crown Copyright 2008 http://www.communities.gov.uk

Bovvered!

Younger people are opting out of politics

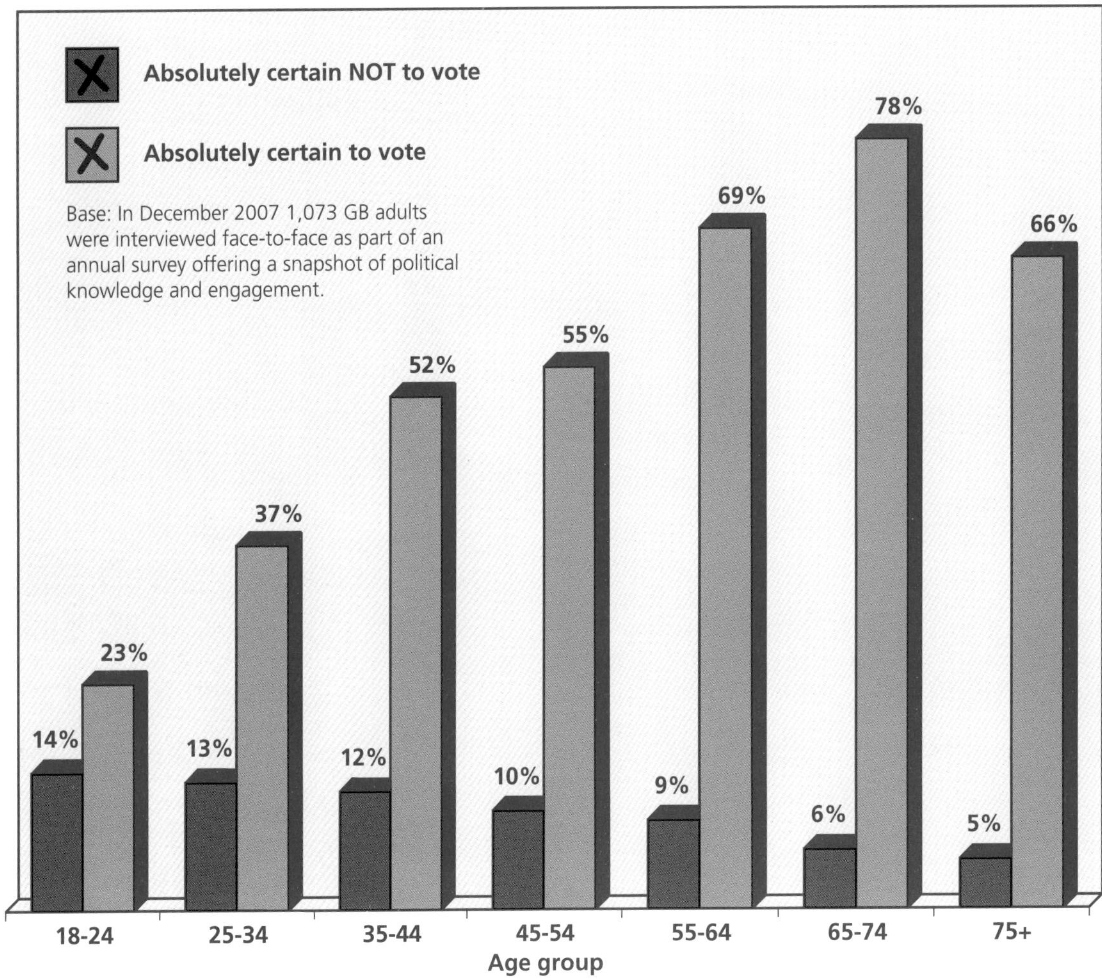

Those absolutely certain about whether they would vote in an immediate general election
Absolutely certain NOT to vote
Absolutely certain to vote
Base: In December 2007 1,073 GB adults were interviewed face-to-face as part of an annual survey offering a snapshot of political knowledge and engagement.
14%
23%
13%
37%
12%
52%
10%
55%
9%
69%
6%
78%
5%
66%
18-24
25-34
35-44
45-54
55-64
65-74
75+
Age group

- Turnout at the 2005 general election was **61.4%**, **up 2%** on the previous election in 2001
- The overall turnout figure masks variations in participation rates
- Young people were half as likely to vote as older age groups and their participation actually dropped from **39%** in 2001 to **37%** in 2005
- Younger age groups are much less likely to see voting as a civic duty than older age groups
- Research suggests that some young people have never acquired the habit of voting and that this effect will be carried forward as they age

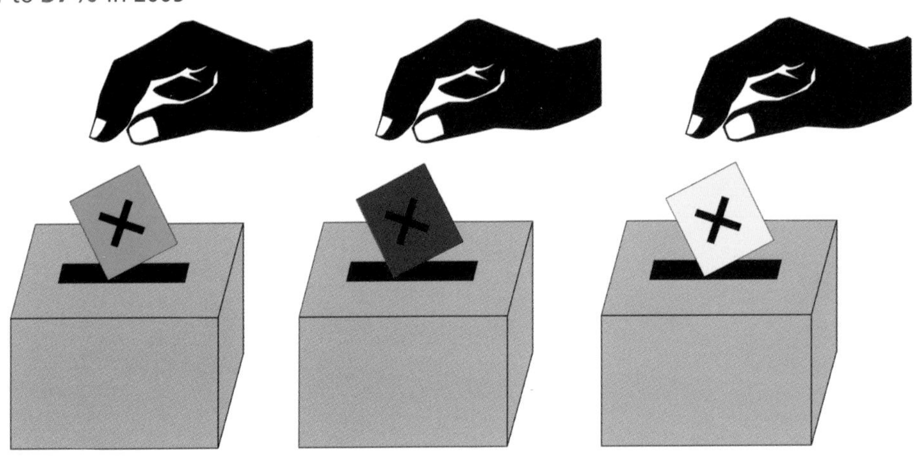

How interested would you say you are in politics?

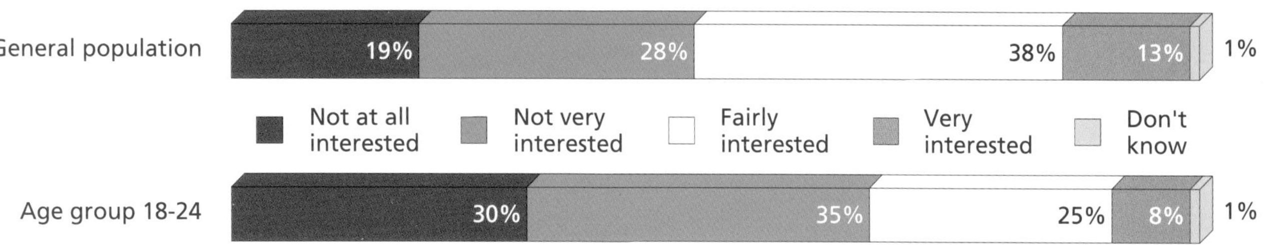

General population
19%
28%
38%
13%
1%
Not at all interested
Not very interested
Fairly interested
Very interested
Don't know
Age group 18-24
30%
35%
25%
8%
1%

Totals may not add up to 100% due to rounding

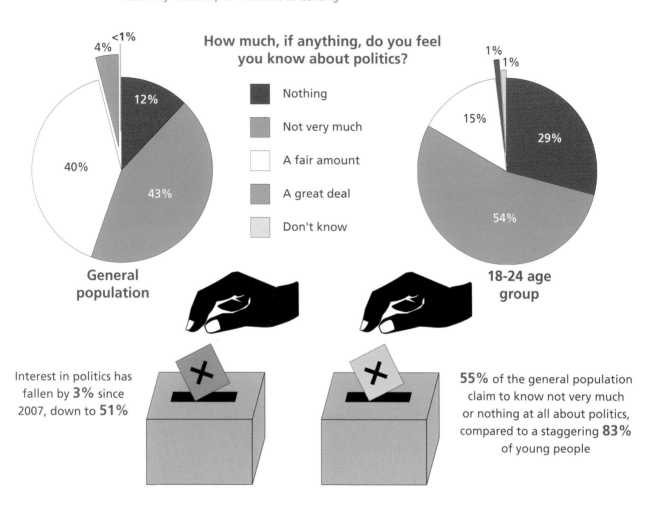

How much, if anything, do you feel you know about politics?

Nothing
Not very much
A fair amount
A great deal
Don't know

General population: Nothing 12%, Not very much 43%, A fair amount 40%, A great deal 4%, Don't know <1%

18-24 age group: Nothing 29%, Not very much 54%, A fair amount 15%, A great deal 1%, Don't know 1%

Interest in politics has fallen by **3%** since 2007, down to **51%**

55% of the general population claim to know not very much or nothing at all about politics, compared to a staggering **83%** of young people

Which, if any, of the things on the list have you done in the last 2 or 3 years?

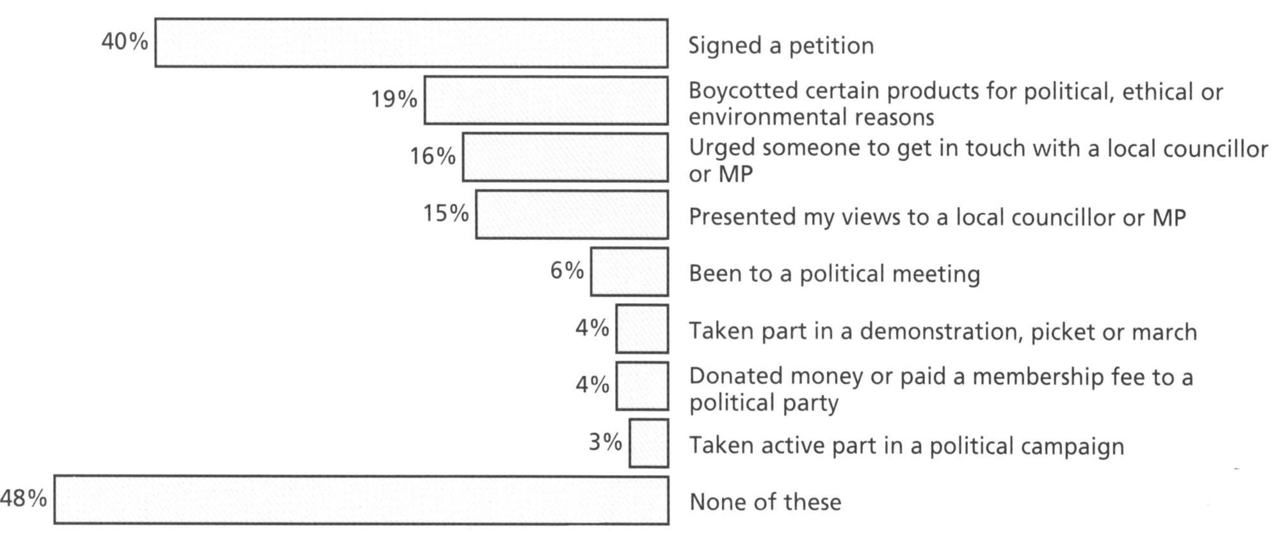

40% Signed a petition
19% Boycotted certain products for political, ethical or environmental reasons
16% Urged someone to get in touch with a local councillor or MP
15% Presented my views to a local councillor or MP
6% Been to a political meeting
4% Taken part in a demonstration, picket or march
4% Donated money or paid a membership fee to a political party
3% Taken active part in a political campaign
48% None of these

Source: Audit of Political Engagement 5 © Hansard Society 2008

http://www.hansardsociety.org.uk

Taking liberties

Is Big Brother watching you?

Britain has more closed circuit TV cameras (CCTVs) than any other country, monitoring streets, stations, shopping centres, offices etc.

Do you think this is...

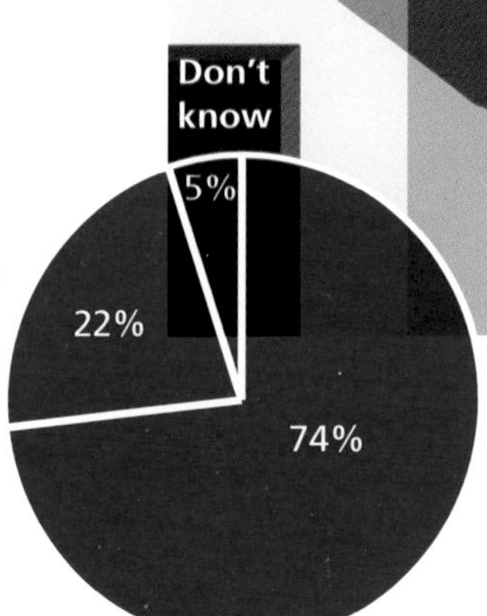
Don't know
5%
22%
74%

...broadly a bad thing, because these cameras allow the state to 'snoop' on people and invade their privacy

...broadly a good thing, as CCTV cameras help to deter criminal behaviour and catch offenders

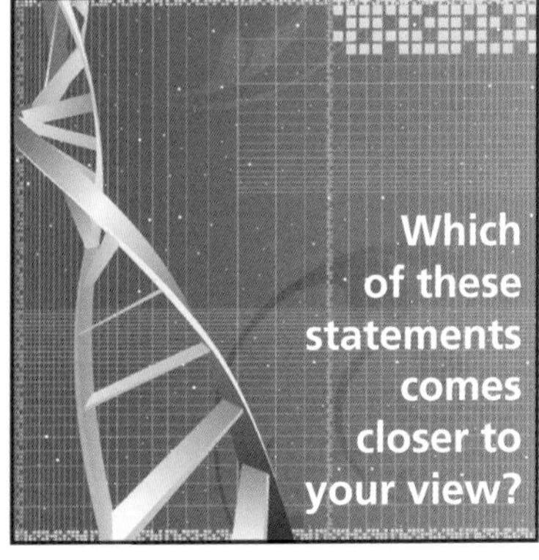
Which of these statements comes closer to your view?

Police are relying ever more heavily on DNA to solve crimes. Britain now has the largest DNA database in the world. It includes data on people who have not been convicted of any crime

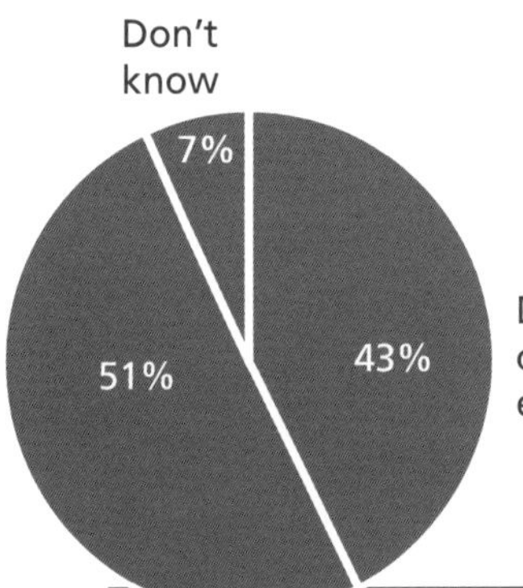
Don't know
7%
51%
43%

To be able to catch more criminals, the police should be able to build up their DNA database, so that eventually they hold DNA data on every citizen

DNA data should be held only for convicted criminals. Data on everyone else's DNA should be destroyed

Britons have not, until now, been required to carry proof of identity in peacetime. The Government proposes introducing an ID card, and backing it up with a comprehensive database including biometric information about everyone

Which of these statements comes closer to your view?

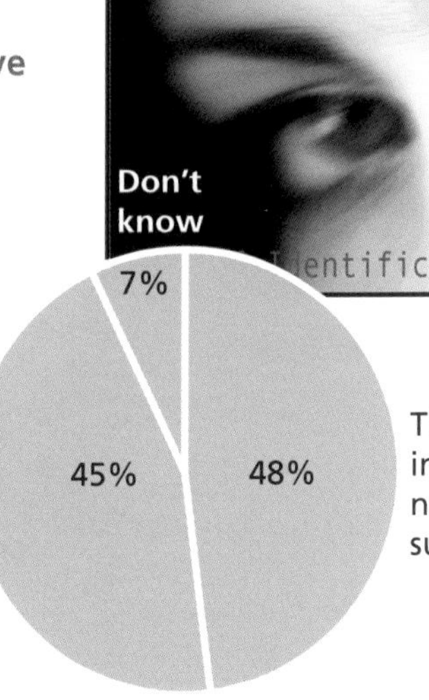
Don't know
7%
45%
48%

ID cards and biometric information are a good idea: they will make identity theft harder and keeping track of terrorists and illegal immigrants easier

The benefits of the ID card and biometric information system are few and possibly non-existent; they certainly do not justify such an invasion of our privacy

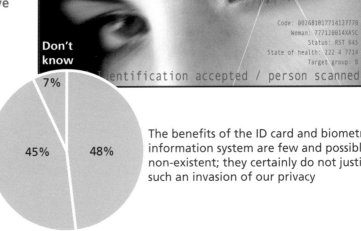

Figures may not add up to 100% due to rounding

Over 2,000 UK adults were interviewed in 2008

Source: YouGov/ The Economist
http://www.yougov.com

Royal rewards

Are the Royals an asset or a liability?

*'The money provided by the taxpayer to enable The Queen to fulfil her role as Head of State, is equivalent to **66p per person** in the country. This is the **annual** cost, not the daily, weekly or monthly cost and is **3.1% lower** in real terms than it was in 2001'*

Sir Alan Reid, Keeper of the Privy Purse

'Republic objects to the monarchy because it is undemocratic and unaccountable, and entirely unsuited to a modern democratic constitution. However, it is vital that we directly challenge the palace's assertion that the monarchy is 'value for money'.'

Republic, the Campaign for an elected Head of State

Royal public finances to year end 31 March 2008 (£millions)

What is included:

The Queen's Civil List
provided by Parliament on a 10 yearly cycle for staff costs and running expenses of HM official household

Parliamentary annuities
for Duke of Edinburgh's official expenses

Grants-in-aid
Property maintenance, utilities, telephones etc – **£15.3m**, communications and information services – **£0.5m** and royal travel **£6.2m**

Expenditure met directly by Government Departments and the Crown Estate
Administration of honours – **£0.7m**, ceremonial occasions – **£0.2m**, equerries and orderlies seconded from the Armed Services – **£1.4m**, State Visits **£0.7m**, maintenance of Holyrood House **£1.1m**, maintenance of Home Park at Windsor Castle **£0.6m**, Other **£0.2m**

Total	40.0
The Queen's Civil List	12.7
Parliamentary annuities	0.4
Grants-in-aid	22.0
Expenditure met directly by Government Departments and the Crown Estate	4.9

What is NOT included:

Money from the Duchy of Lancaster, declared at **£12,645,000** in 2008. This is the Queen's private income.

Income from the Duchy of Cornwall. This funds the official duties of the Prince of Wales. The income was declared as **£16,273,000** in 2008, with a further **£1,951,000** coming from Grants-in-Aid and **£503,000** coming from government departments. The Duchy showed a cash surplus of **£194,000** in 2008.

Cost of security – not known but estimated at **£100m** annually (in 2004).

The Republic campaign group states that amongst the hidden costs are unpaid taxes of perhaps **£5.5m** and costs to local councils of Royal visits of close to **£10m** – bringing the yearly total to above **£150m**.

Republic argues that European heads of state are much cheaper:

Ireland	**£1.5m**	**Austria**	**£3.5m**
Finland	**£7.9m**	**Germany**	**£9.9m**

The arguments **AGAINST** a monarchy – financial and otherwise can be explored at:

http://www.republic.org.uk

and **FOR** it at

http://www.monarchy.net

Source: Royal Public Finances
http://www.royal.gov.uk

Clearing the air

Most people are in favour of a smoking ban in public places – even smokers

The ban on smoking in public places came into force in England in July 2007, following similar bans in Scotland, Wales and Northern Ireland.

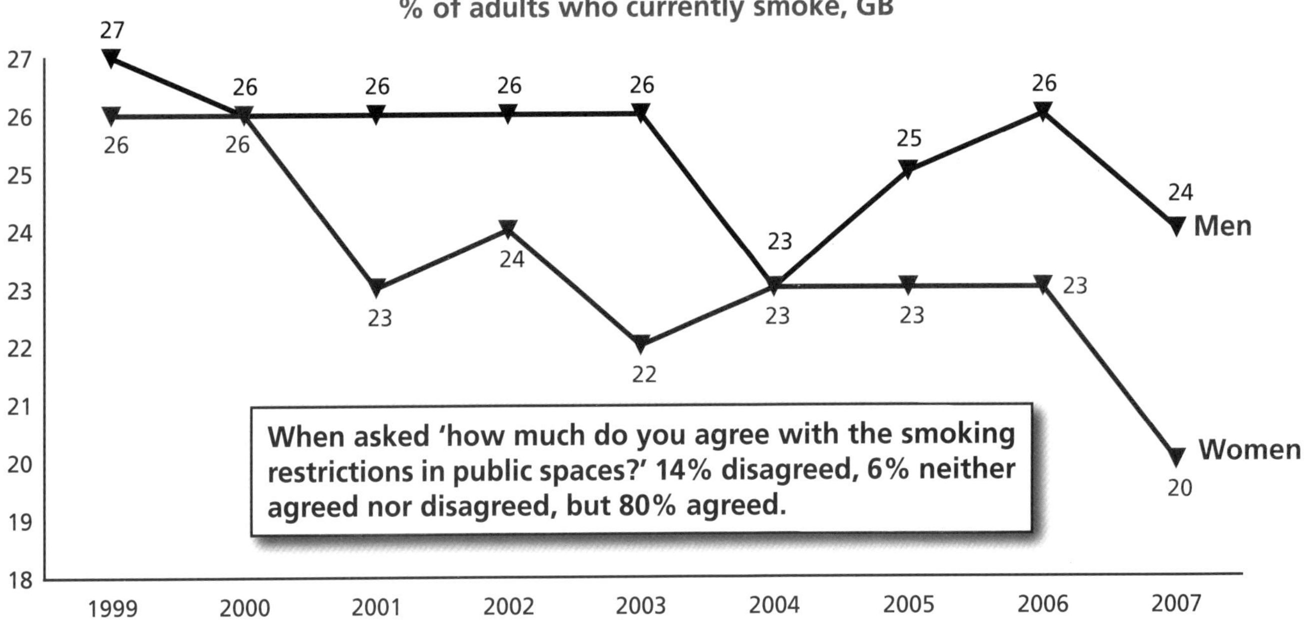

% of adults who currently smoke, GB
27
26
25
24
23
22
21
20
19
18
1999
2000
2001
2002
2003
2004
2005
2006
2007
Men
Women
27 26 26 26 26 23 25 26 24
26 26 23 24 22 23 23 23 20

When asked 'how much do you agree with the smoking restrictions in public spaces?' 14% disagreed, 6% neither agreed nor disagreed, but 80% agreed.

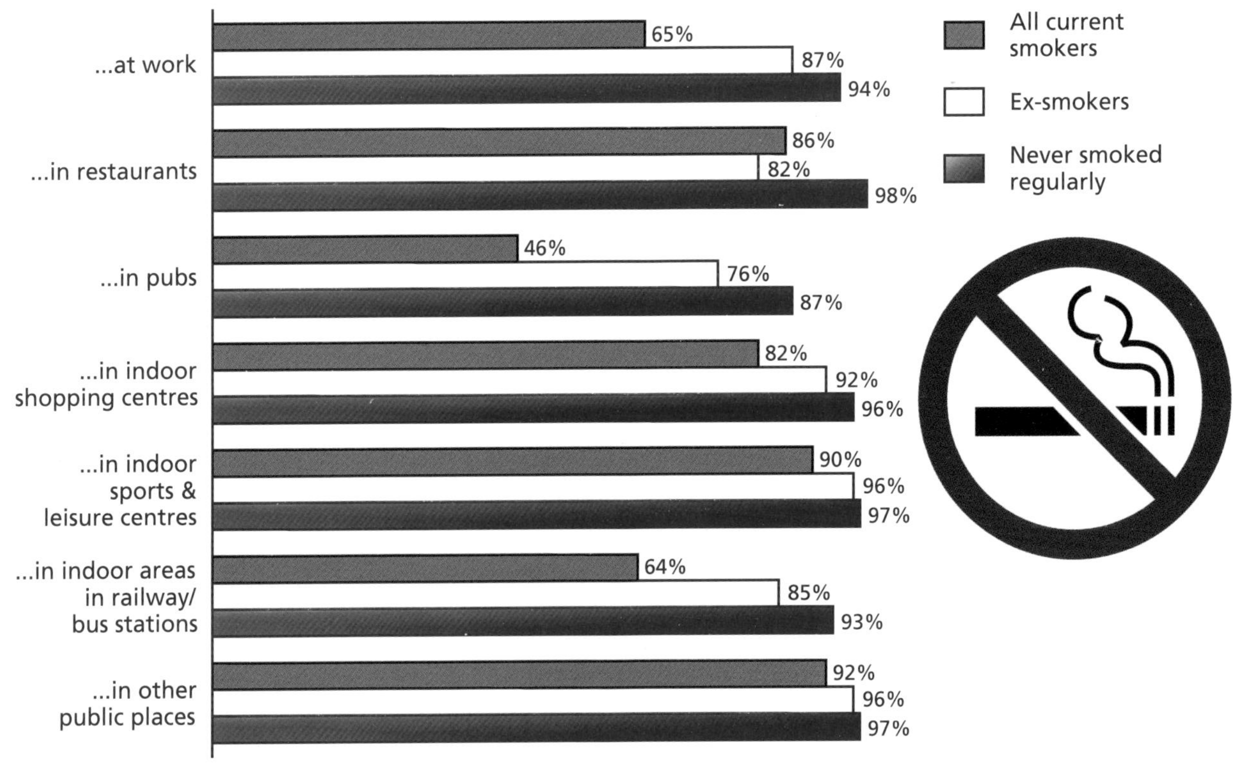

Agreement with smoking restrictions in certain places, % of all respondents agreeing with smoking ban...
...at work
65%
87%
94%
...in restaurants
86%
82%
98%
...in pubs
46%
76%
87%
...in indoor shopping centres
82%
92%
96%
...in indoor sports & leisure centres
90%
96%
97%
...in indoor areas in railway/ bus stations
64%
85%
93%
...in other public places
92%
96%
97%
All current smokers
Ex-smokers
Never smoked regularly

Base: As part of the Office for National Statistics Omnibus survey, a representative sample of the population was asked about smoking-related behaviour and attitudes.

Source: Office for National Statistics
http://www.statistics.gov.uk

Fancy a drink?

Nearly half of young people aged 11 have never touched alcohol, by 21 most are regular drinkers

Q Which describes you best?

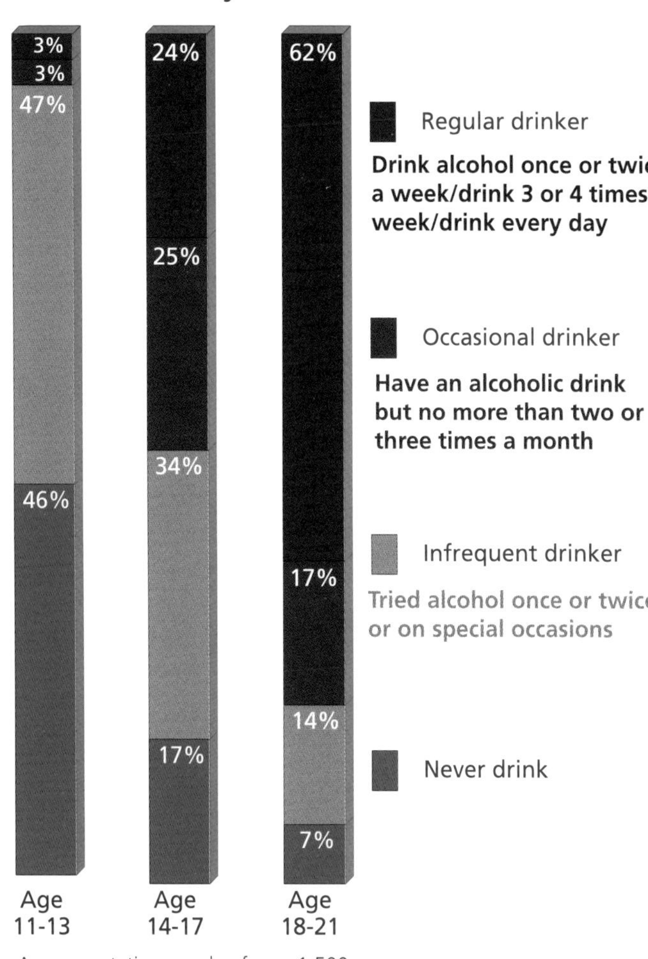

3%
3%
47%
46%
24%
25%
34%
17%
62%
17%
14%
7%
Regular drinker
Drink alcohol once or twice a week/drink 3 or 4 times a week/drink every day
Occasional drinker
Have an alcoholic drink but no more than two or three times a month
Infrequent drinker
Tried alcohol once or twice or on special occasions
Never drink
Age 11-13
Age 14-17
Age 18-21

A representative sample of over 1,500 UK young people aged 11-21 were interviewed about their drinking habits

"Alcohol is great. You just feel yourself floating and nothing can touch it."
Female, 17, Manchester 2007

"We drink wherever we can really. Could be anywhere. Just get some cans or a bottle and sit in the park with some mates."
Male, 15, Scotland, 2007

Q Have you drunk alcohol in any of these situations in the last six months?

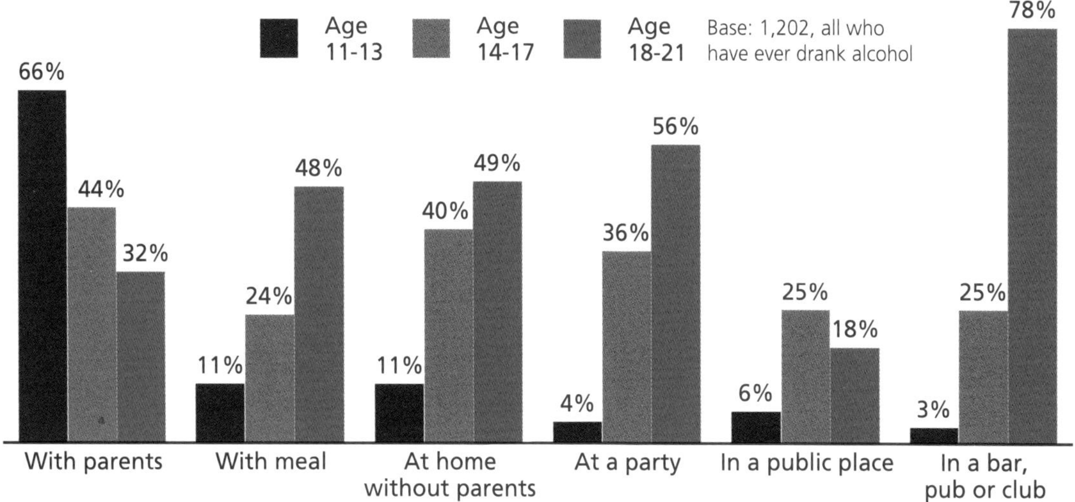

Age 11-13
Age 14-17
Age 18-21
Base: 1,202, all who have ever drank alcohol
With parents: 66% 44% 32%
With meal: 11% 24% 48%
At home without parents: 11% 40% 49%
At a party: 4% 36% 56%
In a public place: 6% 25% 18%
In a bar, pub or club: 3% 25% 78%

Source: Ofcom, Young People and Alcohol Advertising

http://www.ofcom.org.uk

Touch wood

77% of the British public deny that they are superstitious but...

Which of the following do you believe in?

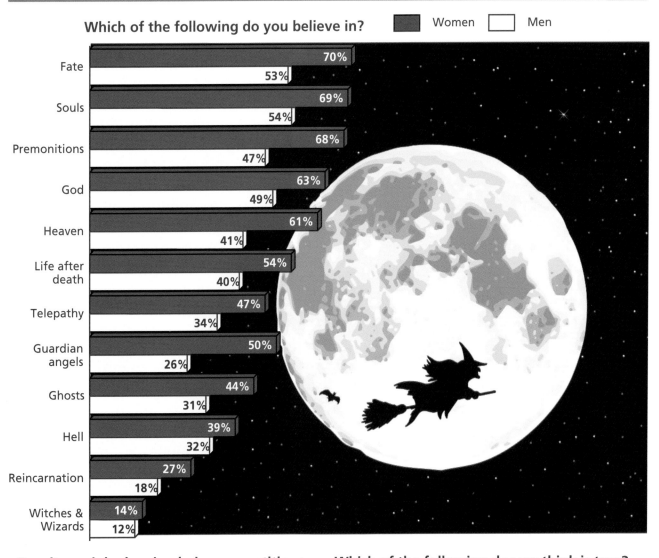

	Women	Men
Fate	70%	53%
Souls	69%	54%
Premonitions	68%	47%
God	63%	49%
Heaven	61%	41%
Life after death	54%	40%
Telepathy	47%	34%
Guardian angels	50%	26%
Ghosts	44%	31%
Hell	39%	32%
Reincarnation	27%	18%
Witches & Wizards	14%	12%

Despite mainly denying being superstitious:

51% touch wood to avoid bad luck

39% cross their fingers for good luck (in fact 30% of those who claim NOT to be superstitious cross their fingers for good luck)

16% have a lucky charm

15% consider the number 13 to be unlucky

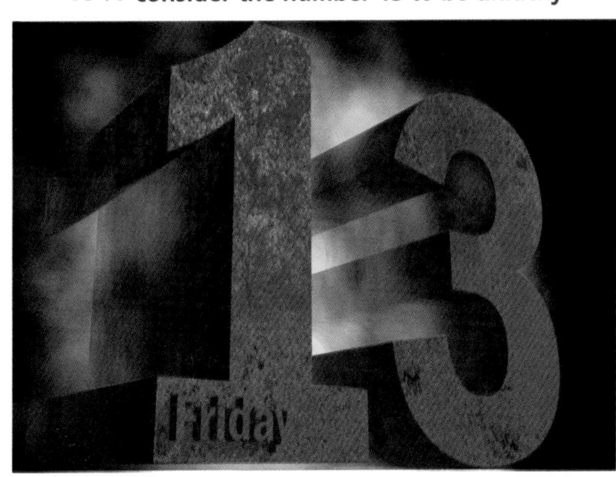
Friday
13

Which of the following do you think is true?

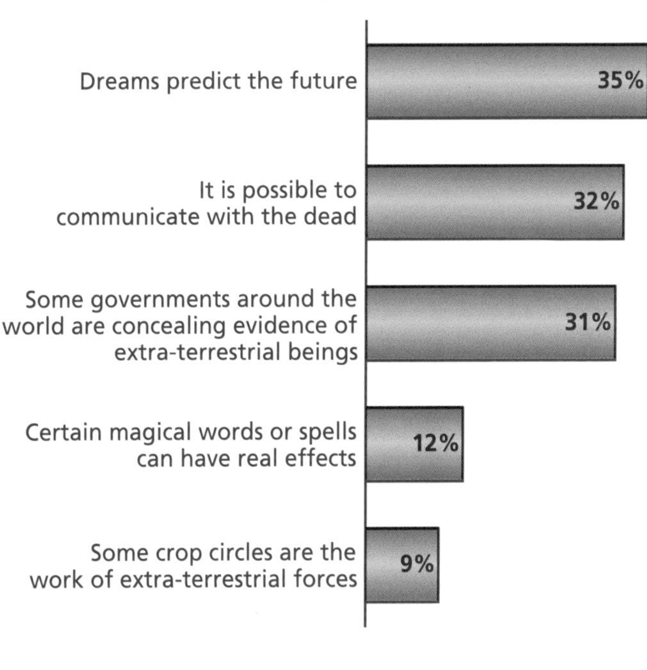
Dreams predict the future 35%
It is possible to communicate with the dead 32%
Some governments around the world are concealing evidence of extra-terrestrial beings 31%
Certain magical words or spells can have real effects 12%
Some crop circles are the work of extra-terrestrial forces 9%

Source: Ipsos MORI
http://www.ipsos-mori.com

Education

School snapshot

Pupils are mainly positive about school

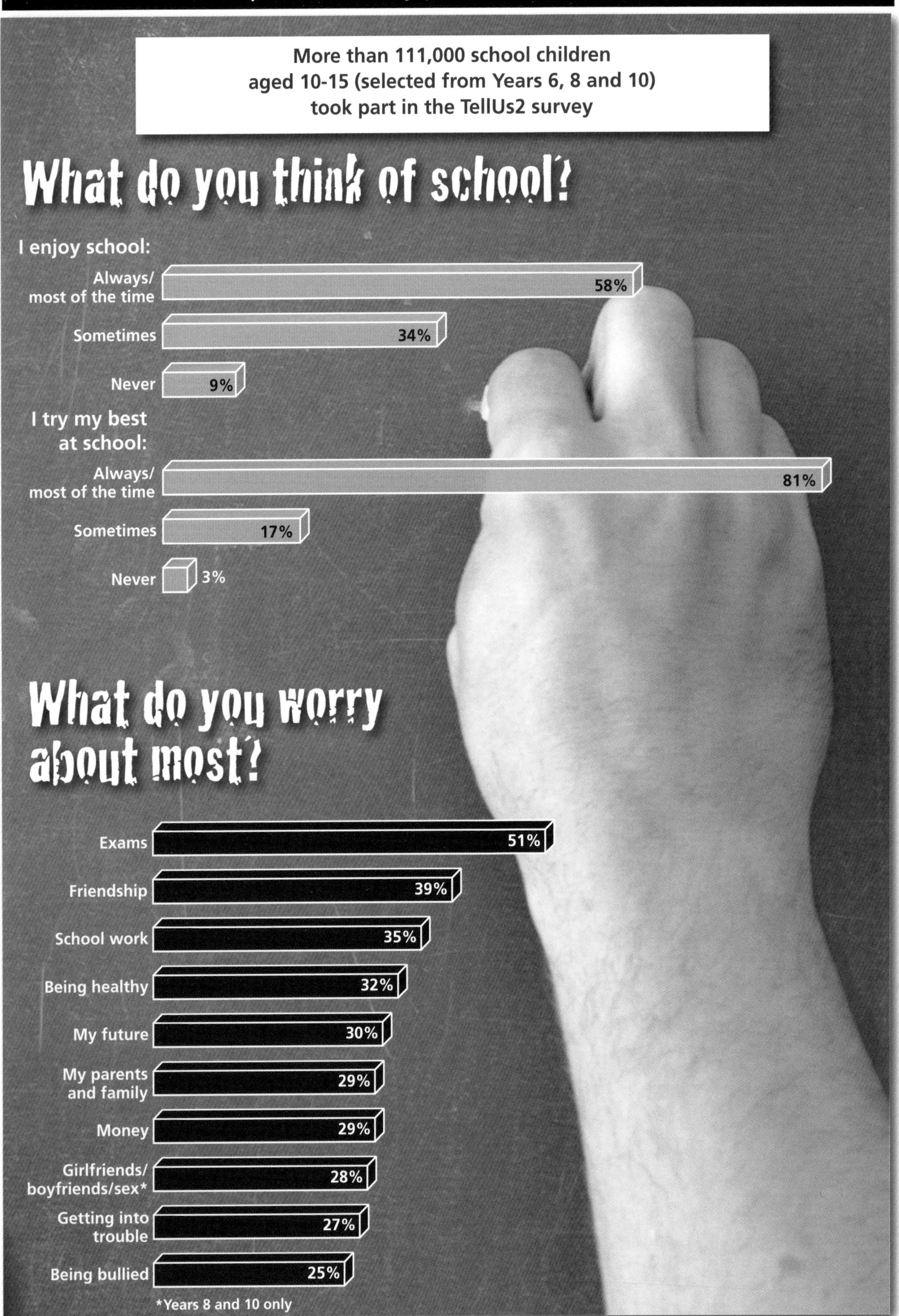

More than 111,000 school children
aged 10-15 (selected from Years 6, 8 and 10)
took part in the TellUs2 survey
What do you think of school?
I enjoy school:
Always/ most of the time 58%
Sometimes 34%
Never 9%
I try my best at school:
Always/ most of the time 81%
Sometimes 17%
Never 3%
What do you worry about most?
Exams 51%
Friendship 39%
School work 35%
Being healthy 32%
My future 30%
My parents and family 29%
Money 29%
Girlfriends/ boyfriends/sex* 28%
Getting into trouble 27%
Being bullied 25%
*Years 8 and 10 only

How often, if at all, have you been bullied in the last four weeks?

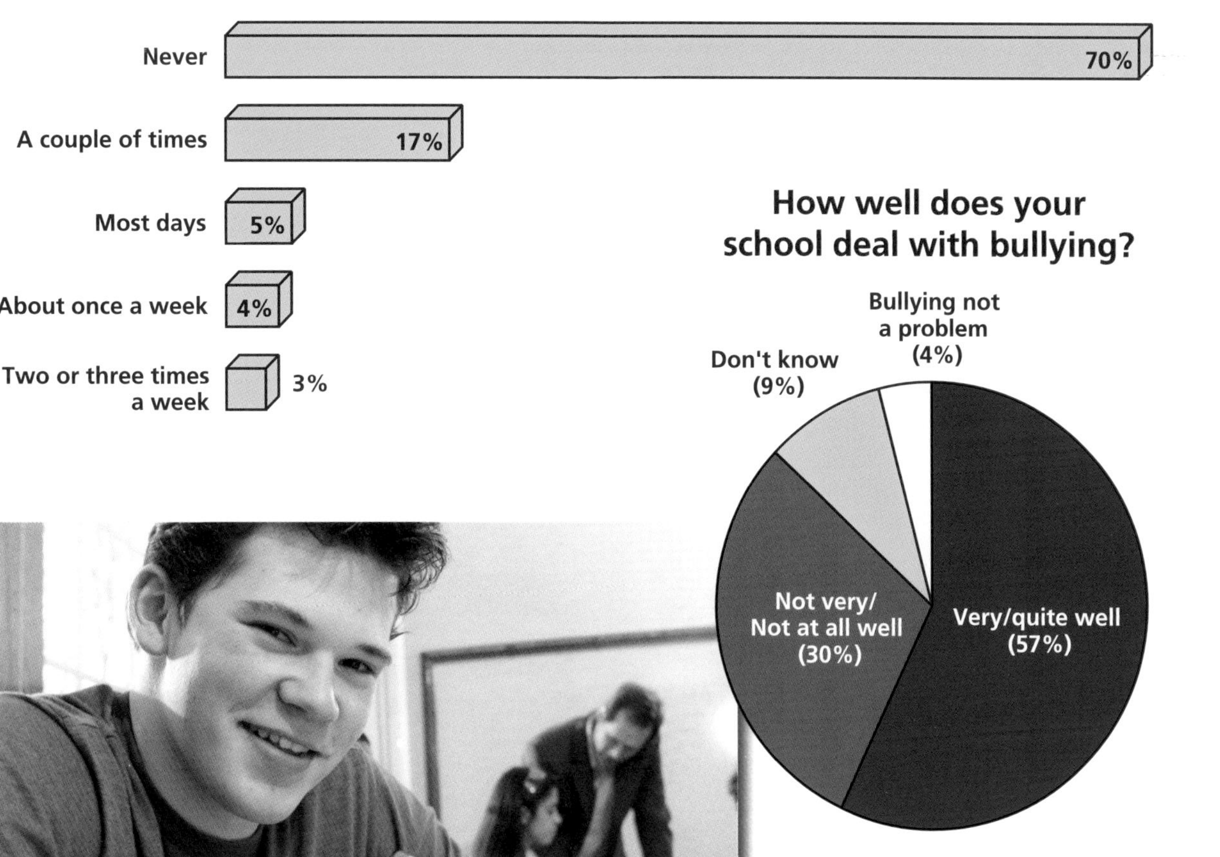
Never 70%
A couple of times 17%
Most days 5%
About once a week 4%
Two or three times a week 3%
How well does your school deal with bullying?
Bullying not a problem (4%)
Don't know (9%)
Not very/ Not at all well (30%)
Very/quite well (57%)

While teenagers generally feel safe in and around school (85%), 13% feel unsafe going to and from school and 14% feel unsafe in school.

What might help you do better in school?

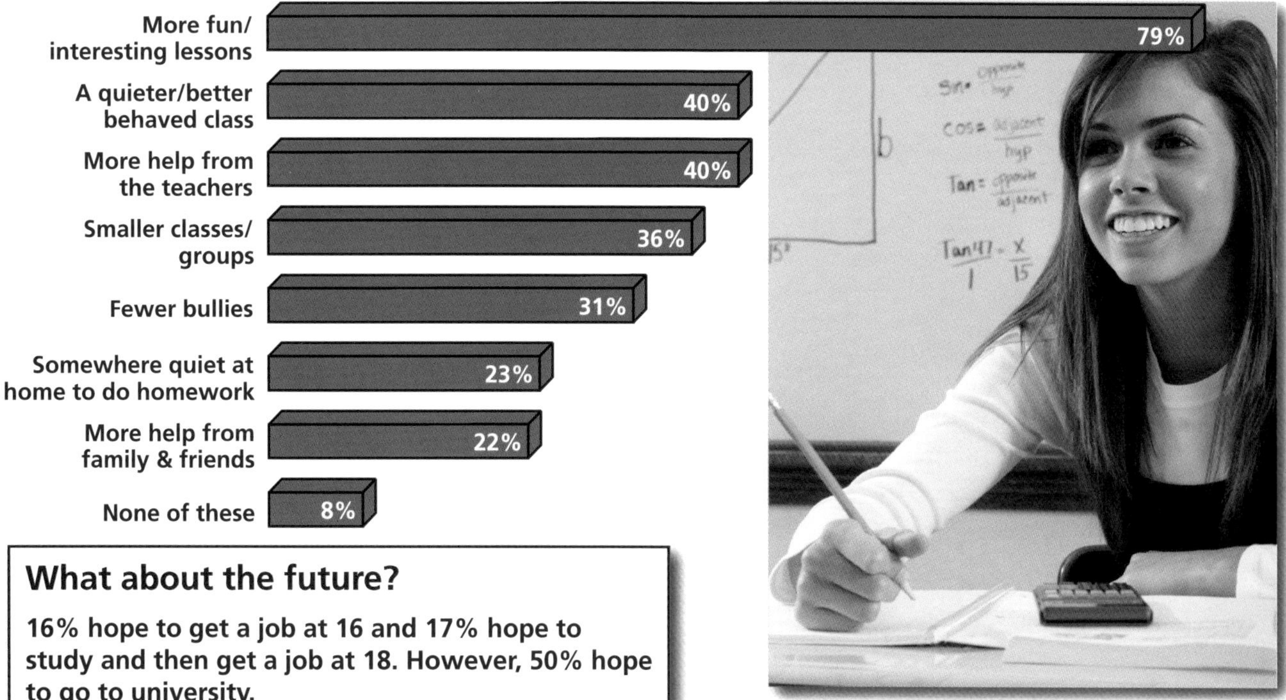
More fun/ interesting lessons 79%
A quieter/better behaved class 40%
More help from the teachers 40%
Smaller classes/ groups 36%
Fewer bullies 31%
Somewhere quiet at home to do homework 23%
More help from family & friends 22%
None of these 8%

What about the future?

16% hope to get a job at 16 and 17% hope to study and then get a job at 18. However, 50% hope to go to university.

Source: TellUs2, Ofsted © Crown copyright
http://ofsted.gov.uk

NB Figures may not add up to 100% due to rounding

Persistent part-timers

63,000 pupils truant every day in England

A pupil is defined as a persistent absentee (PA) when he or she is absent for more than **20%** of the time. This is equal to **at least 25 days** in a year

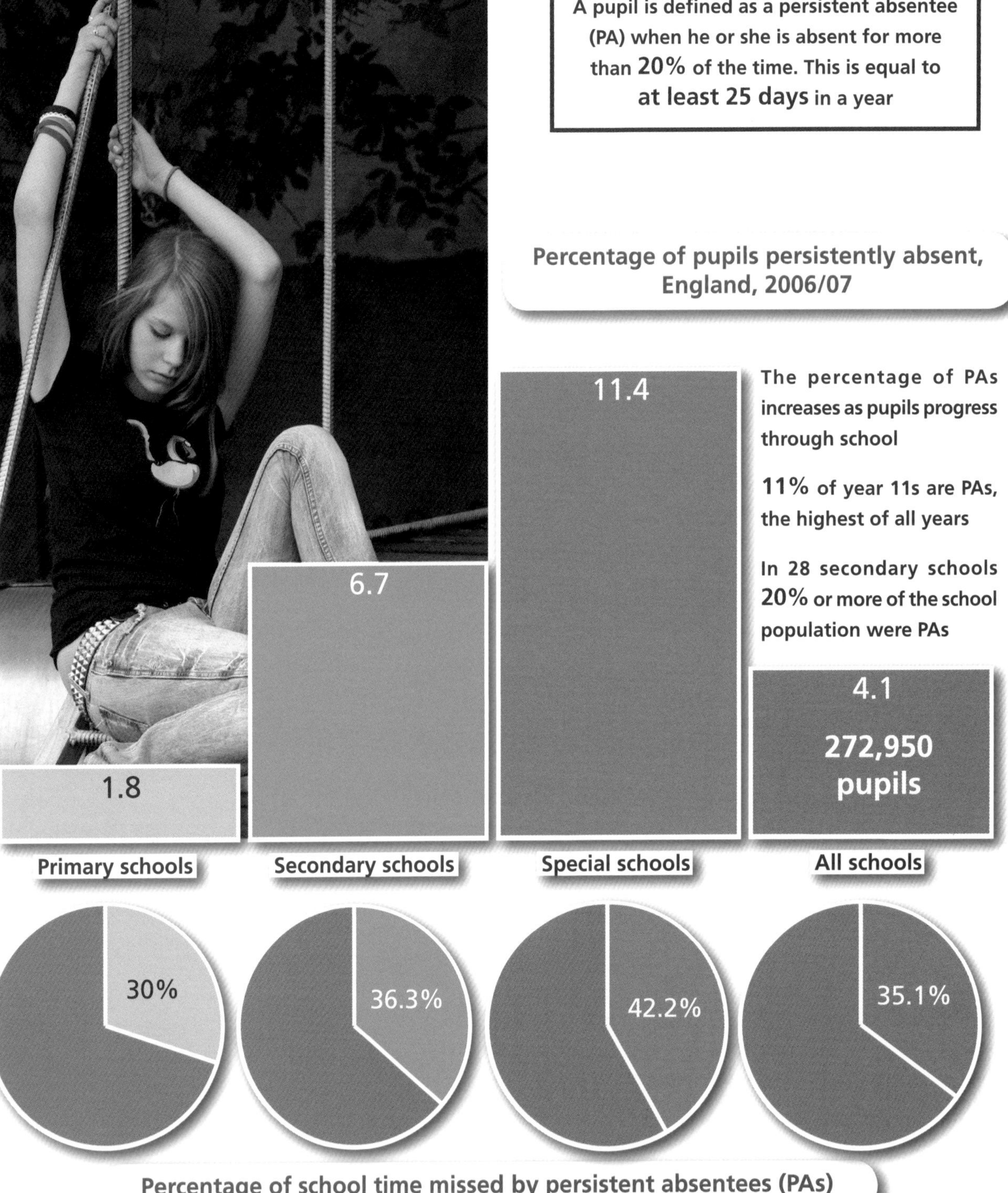

Percentage of pupils persistently absent, England, 2006/07
1.8
6.7
11.4
4.1
272,950 pupils
Primary schools
Secondary schools
Special schools
All schools
30%
36.3%
42.2%
35.1%
Percentage of school time missed by persistent absentees (PAs)

The percentage of PAs increases as pupils progress through school

11% of year 11s are PAs, the highest of all years

In 28 secondary schools **20%** or more of the school population were PAs

9% of pupils eligible for free school meals were PAs, compared with around **3%** for the rest of the school population

Every day in Scotland **5,600** pupils are truanting

Source: Pupil absence in schools in England, 2006/07

http://www.dcsf.gov.uk

Musical youth

Why don't girls choose the drums?

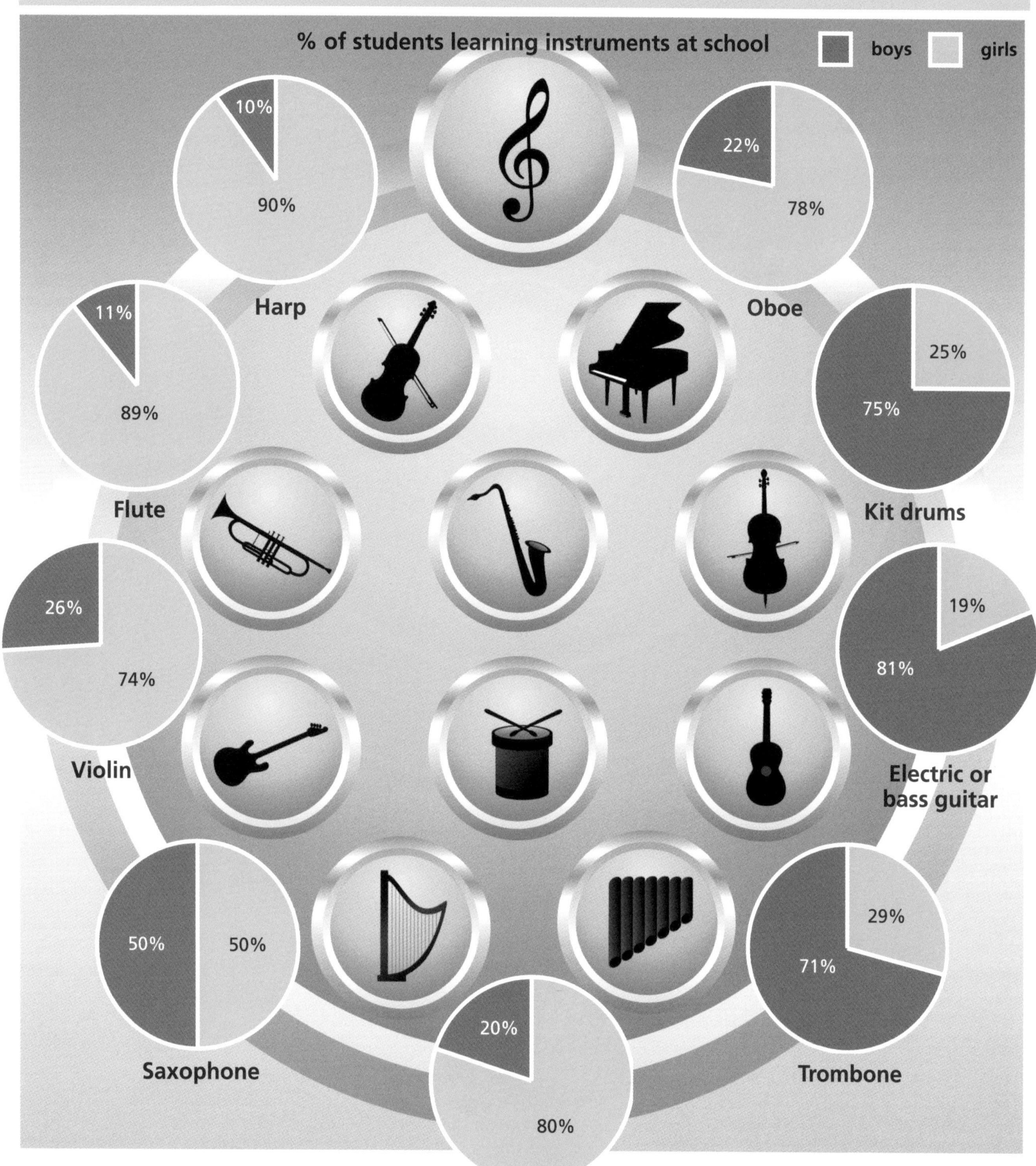

% of students learning instruments at school
boys
girls
10%
90%
Harp
22%
78%
Oboe
11%
89%
Flute
25%
75%
Kit drums
26%
74%
Violin
19%
81%
Electric or bass guitar
50%
50%
Saxophone
29%
71%
Trombone
20%
80%
Singing

Boys, although reluctant to learn any instrument, tend towards electric guitars, drum kits and music technology classes. Girls are more inclined towards smaller higher-pitched instruments.

A study by the University of London Institute of Education says: "The way that physical interaction with the instrument occurs may be important. Boys may prefer instruments that are struck or require high levels of physical exertion. The technical difficulty of the instrument and level of persistence required to play it may also play a part, as evidence indicates that boys tend to do less practice than girls."

Another factor may be that brass instruments and drums have long been used in military bands and therefore are associated with war.

Source: International Journal of Music Education
http://www.isme.org/

Levelling off

Over a quarter of A levels are awarded at the top grade

Each year the A level results are greeted with delight by most students while the newspapers are full of criticism that exams are getting easier. This is accompanied by the suspicion that some subjects are more difficult than others.

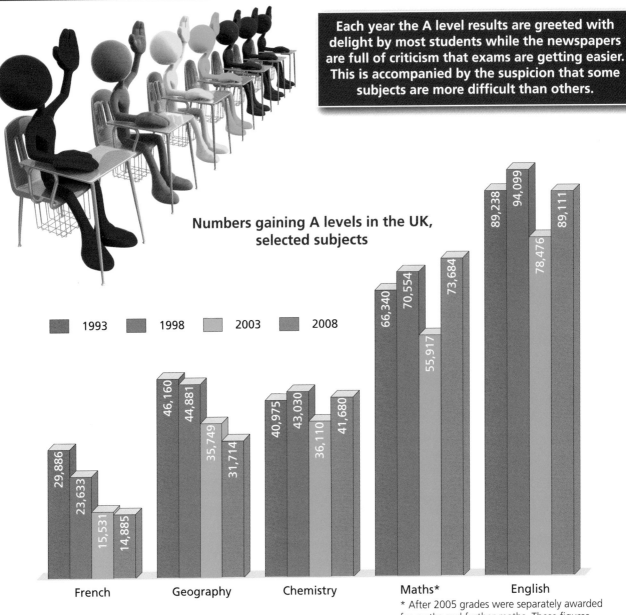

Numbers gaining A levels in the UK, selected subjects

	1993	1998	2003	2008
French	29,886	23,633	15,531	14,885
Geography	46,160	44,881	35,749	31,714
Chemistry	40,975	43,030	36,110	41,680
Maths*	66,340	70,554	55,917	73,684
English	89,238	94,099	78,476	89,111

* After 2005 grades were separately awarded for maths and further maths. These figures include candidates for both exams.

Overall A level results, by grade, 2008

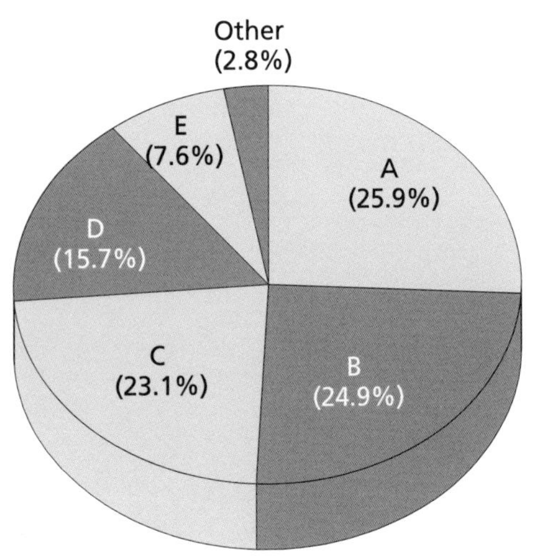

Other (2.8%)
E (7.6%)
A (25.9%)
D (15.7%)
C (23.1%)
B (24.9%)

The results from 2007/08 show that most entrants achieved good grades, with fewer than 30% of candidates scoring below C.

The pass rate (grades A-E) was more than 97% in all subjects.

Source: Joint Council for General Qualifications http://www.jcq.org.uk

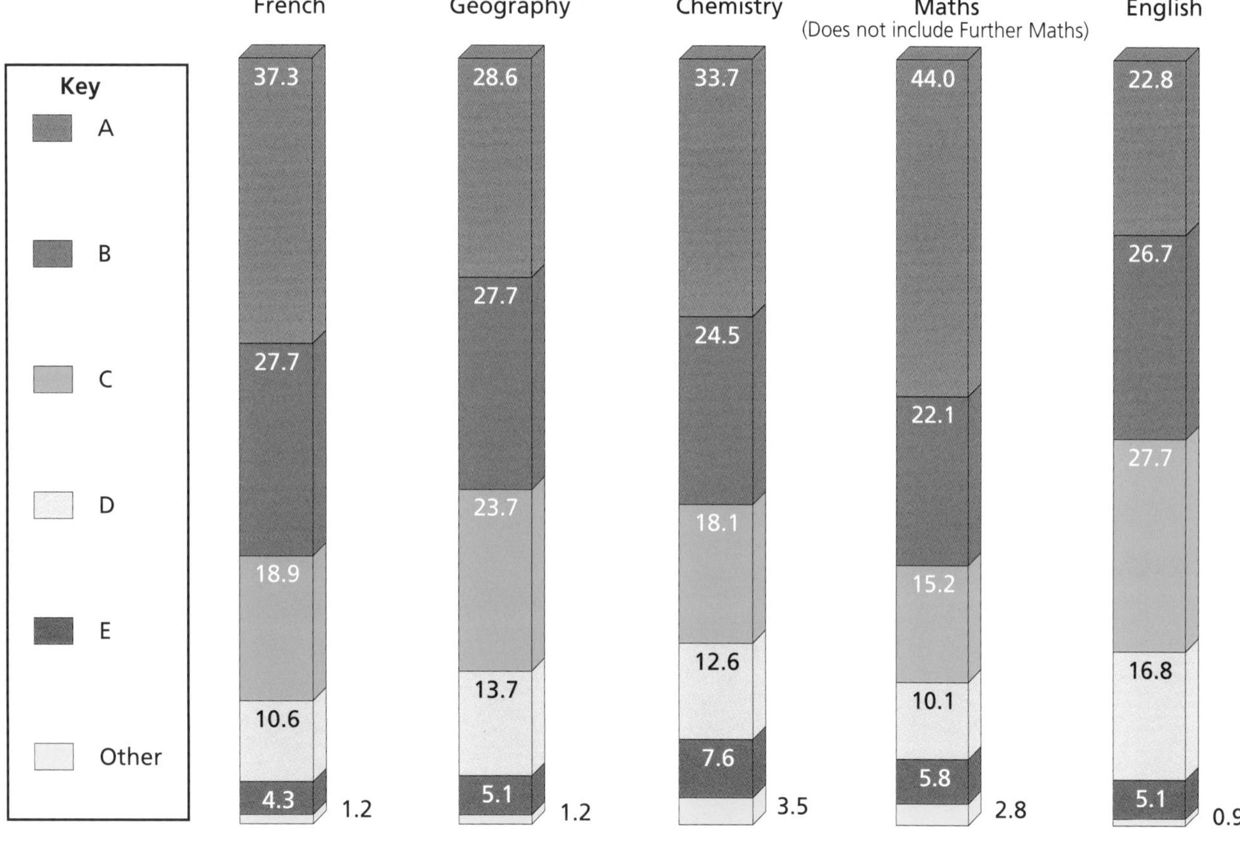
A level results for selected subjects,
by grade, England, 2008
(percentages)
Key
A
B
C
D
E
Other
French
37.3
27.7
18.9
10.6
4.3
1.2
Geography
28.6
27.7
23.7
13.7
5.1
1.2
Chemistry
33.7
24.5
18.1
12.6
7.6
3.5
Maths
(Does not include Further Maths)
44.0
22.1
15.2
10.1
5.8
2.8
English
22.8
26.7
27.7
16.8
5.1
0.9

NB Other includes ungraded, no award (absent/declined) and pending
Due to rounding the totals may not add up to 100%

The most common grade in English is C, while in French, Geography, Chemistry and Maths, the highest percentage of entrants achieve grade A – the percentage achieving A in Maths being nearly twice that in English. In Further Maths, 57.5% of candidates achieved Grade A

Top universities have drawn up lists of subjects they consider not to be a good preparation for degree studies. Cambridge University says its applicants must do at least two "traditional" subjects to have a chance of a place and has published lists of A levels which provide "less effective" preparation for a degree:

- accounting
- art & design
- business studies
- communication studies
- dance
- design and technology
- drama/theatre studies
- film studies
- health and social care
- home economics
- information & communication technology
- leisure studies
- media studies
- music technology
- performance studies
- performing arts
- photography
- physical education
- sports studies
- travel & tourism

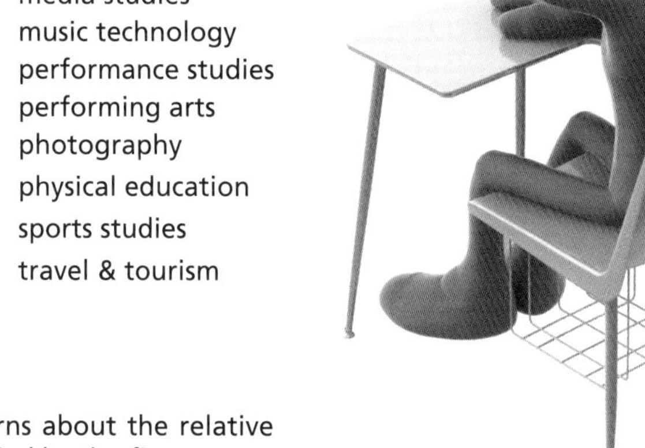

In contrast the QCA argues that concerns about the relative value of different subjects are not justified by the figures.

Source: Joint Council for Qualifications, National Provisional GCE A Level Results, June 2008

http://www.dcsf.gov.uk
http:www.qca.org.uk

Degree of difference

How does our student life compare with Europe?

The Eurostudent project aims to deliver fundamental information on the social and economic conditions of student life in Europe

How long does it take to get a degree? Selected European countries (in years)

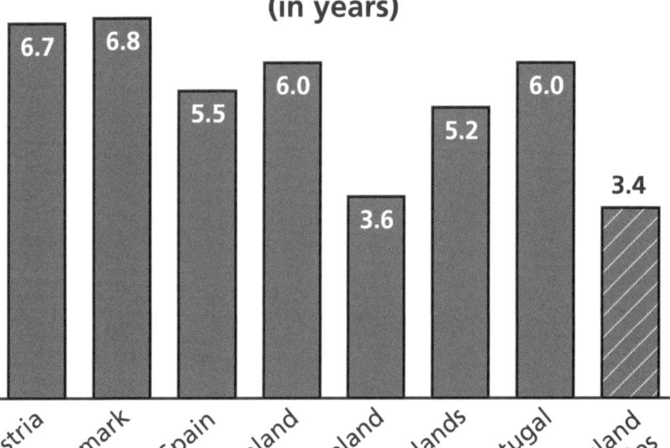

Austria 6.7
Denmark 6.8
Spain 5.5
Finland 6.0
Ireland 3.6
Netherlands 5.2
Portugal 6.0
England & Wales 3.4

How much time spent studying? selected European countries (hours per week)

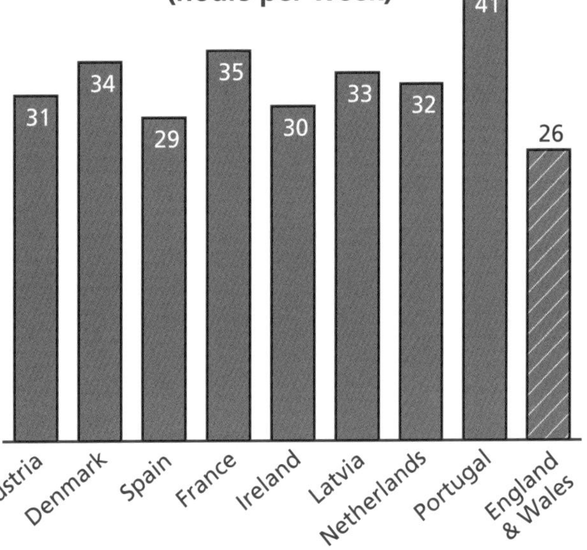

Austria 31
Denmark 34
Spain 29
France 35
Ireland 30
Latvia 33
Netherlands 32
Portugal 41
England & Wales 26

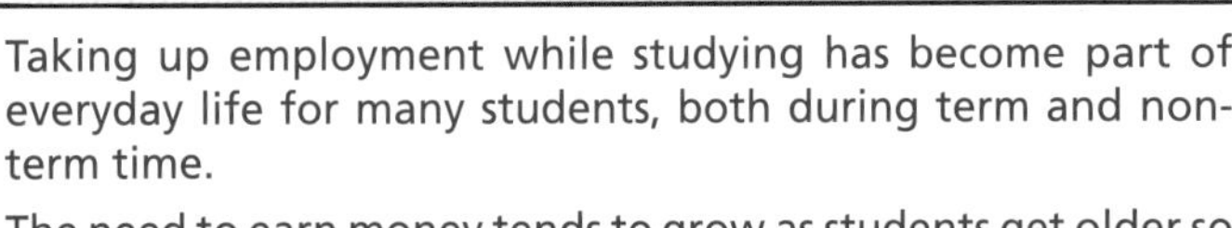

Taking up employment while studying has become part of everyday life for many students, both during term and non-term time.

The need to earn money tends to grow as students get older so some of the differences between countries might be explained by different age levels of the student population.

Student employment rate during term time

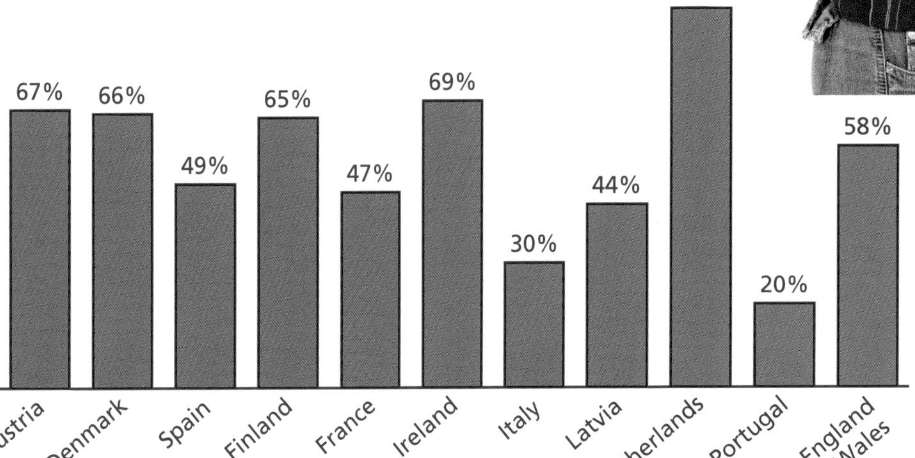

Austria 67%
Denmark 66%
Spain 49%
Finland 65%
France 47%
Ireland 69%
Italy 30%
Latvia 44%
Netherlands 91%
Portugal 20%
England & Wales 58%

Source: Eurostudent
http://www.bmbf.de/pub/eurostudent_report_2005.pdf

Facing the drop

The Government wants 50% of 18-year-olds to go university...

... but do they stay?

The major part of the government drive is to reach young people who have no tradition of university entry.

Despite the government spending £800m tackling the problem, the drop-out rate has hardly moved in five years.

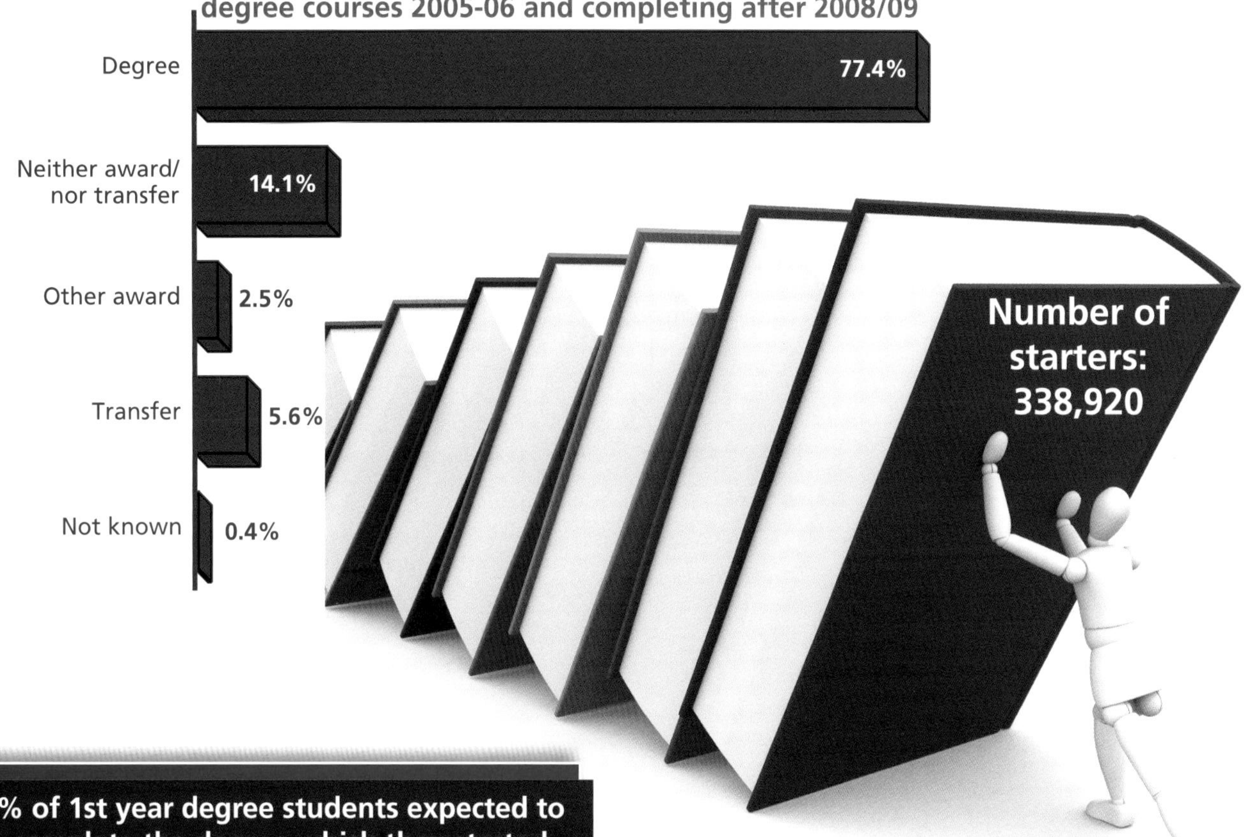

Projected outcome of full-time students starting degree courses 2005-06 and completing after 2008/09
Degree 77.4%
Neither award/ nor transfer 14.1%
Other award 2.5%
Transfer 5.6%
Not known 0.4%
Number of starters: 338,920

% of 1st year degree students expected to complete the degree which they started
Top five universities

The University of Oxford	95.3%
Courtauld Institute of Art	93.2%
The University of Warwick	93.2%
Stranmillis University College, Belfast	93.1%
The University of Cambridge	92.6%

% of 1st year degree students expected to complete the degree which they started
Bottom five universities

The University of Bolton	50.5%
Anglia Ruskin University	51.2%
London Metropolitan University	55.6%
Middlesex University	56.2%
Thames Valley University	56.5%

The projected percentage of students who drop out is less than 25% for the majority of institutions in the UK.

Source: Higher Education Statistics Agency www.hesa.ac.uk

National achievement

Around 1 in 8 adults in the UK has no qualifications at all

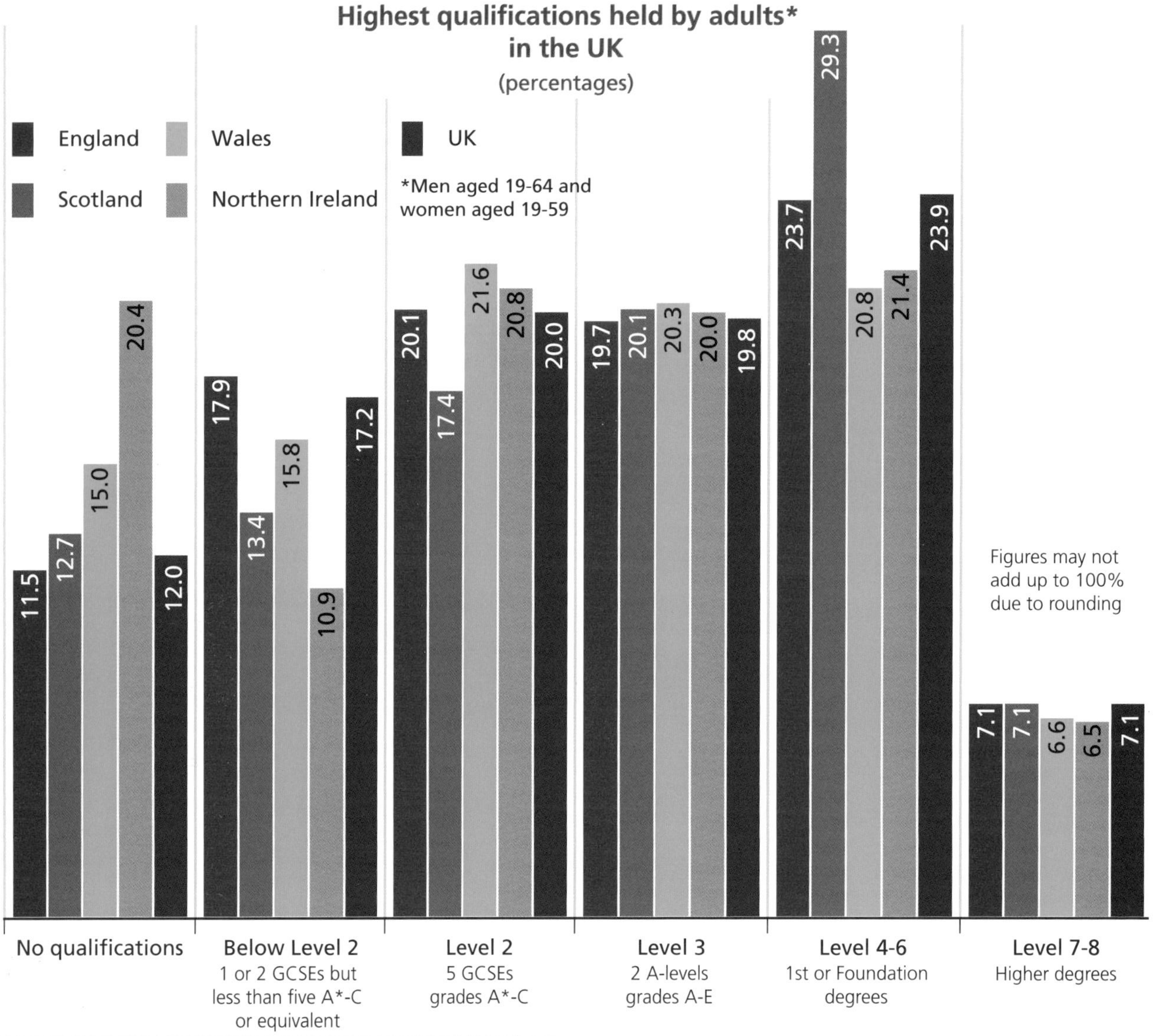

Highest qualifications held by adults* in the UK

(percentages)

Qualification	England	Scotland	Wales	Northern Ireland	UK
No qualifications	11.5	12.7	15.0	20.4	12.0
Below Level 2 (1 or 2 GCSEs but less than five A*-C or equivalent)	17.9	13.4	15.8	10.9	17.2
Level 2 (5 GCSEs grades A*-C)	20.1	17.4	21.6	20.8	20.0
Level 3 (2 A-levels grades A-E)	19.7	20.1	20.3	20.0	19.8
Level 4-6 (1st or Foundation degrees)	23.7	29.3	20.8	21.4	23.9
Level 7-8 (Higher degrees)	7.1	7.1	6.6	6.5	7.1

*Men aged 19-64 and women aged 19-59

Figures may not add up to 100% due to rounding

The 11.5% of adults in England who have no qualifications make up 3.3m people

The proportion of people with no qualifications tends to increase with age. Less than **8%** of those aged 19-30 have no qualifications compared with **20.1%** of those aged 55-64

Women are slightly more likely than men to have no educational qualifications (**11.9%** versus **11.1%**)

The unemployed are more than twice as likely as employees to have no qualifications (**16.7%** versus **7.1%**), and those who are economically inactive are even more so (**26.5%**)

Disabled adults are more likely to have no qualifications than the non-disabled (**23.3%** versus **8.7%**). The difference is even greater for those whose disability is most acute – **30.2%** have no qualifications

Source: Department for Innovation, Universities & Skills © Crown copyright 2008

http://www.dcsf.gov.uk

Environmental issues

Energy issues

Energy supplies are decreasing – global demand is increasing

The energy issue

Energy is one of the most challenging issues currently facing the world. As energy needs are growing in developing countries, and use is also increasing in developed nations, consumption will continue to rise.

Fossil fuels

Our continued increase in the use of fossil fuels such as coal, gas and oil which are not renewable, means that global carbon dioxide emissions are still rising and our energy stocks are decreasing.

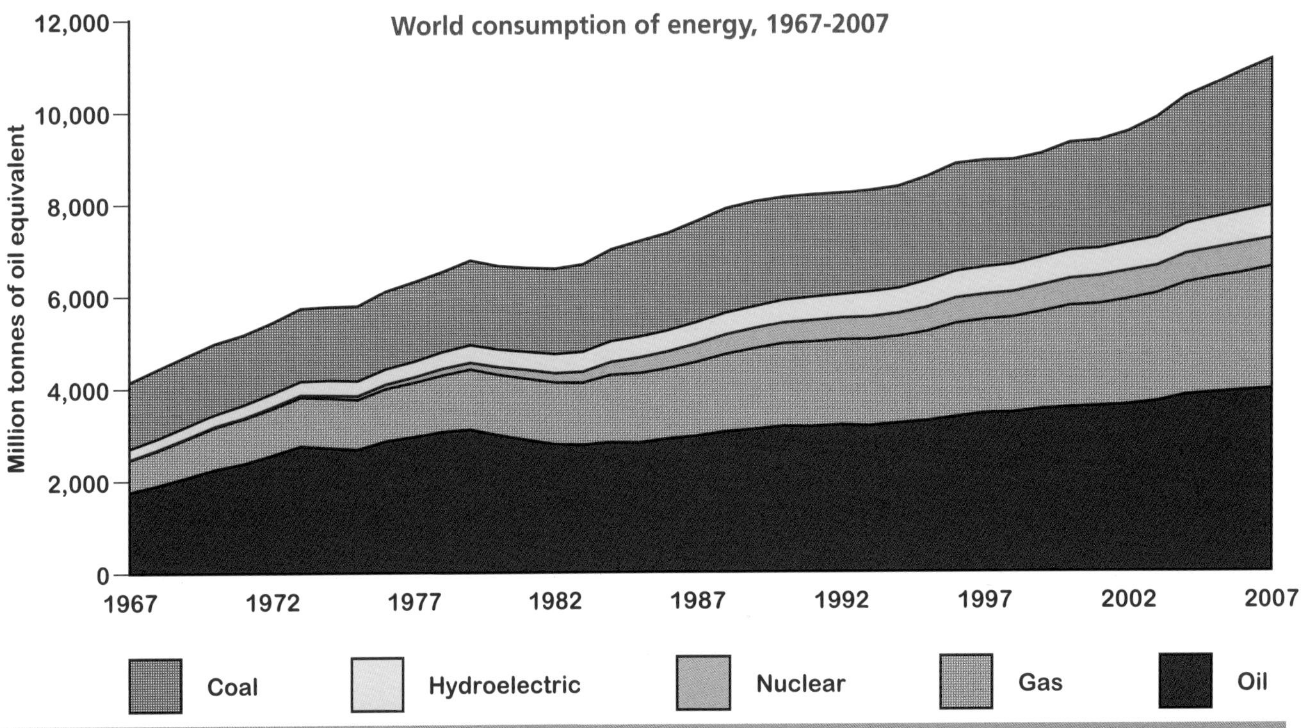

World consumption of energy, 1967-2007
Million tonnes of oil equivalent
12,000
10,000
8,000
6,000
4,000
2,000
0
1967
1972
1977
1982
1987
1992
1997
2002
2007
Coal
Hydroelectric
Nuclear
Gas
Oil

Demand

- World primary energy consumption increased by 2.4% from 2006 to 2007
- Asia-Pacific accounted for two-thirds of this growth most of which was in China, which alone accounted for over half of this increase.

Consumption

- Natural gas consumption grew by an above average 3.1%.
- Coal continued to be the fastest growing fuel in the world for the fifth year running.
- Oil consumption grew by 1.1% or 1 million barrels per day.

Alternatives

- As stocks continue to decrease and pollution continues to increase, what are the alternatives? One suggestion is increased use of nuclear power, though output fell by 2%. However, more than 90% of this decline was accounted for by Germany and by Japan, which saw the world's largest nuclear power plant closed following an earthquake. Although nuclear is an alternative, it raises many environmental issues regarding the safe disposal of radioactive waste.
- Renewable energy such as wind, solar and tidal energy, which many people seem to hope is an answer to the energy crisis, provides a very small share of global energy use.

Source: BP Statistical Review of World Energy 2008
http://www.bp.com
http://greenpeace.org.uk

Nuclear future

Is nuclear power a solution to our energy needs?

Solution or set-back?

Increased concerns over climate change and decreasing global stocks of fossil fuels are leading many countries to turn to nuclear power to solve their energy problems.

It is generally accepted that **nuclear power stations do not emit CO2** and so offer a 'clean' alternative to the use of fossil fuels.

However, **nuclear waste** will **remain hazardous for thousands of years.**

There is still no demonstrated method for isolating nuclear waste from the environment for an adequate period of time to avoid problems.

World consumption of nuclear energy, 1967-2007

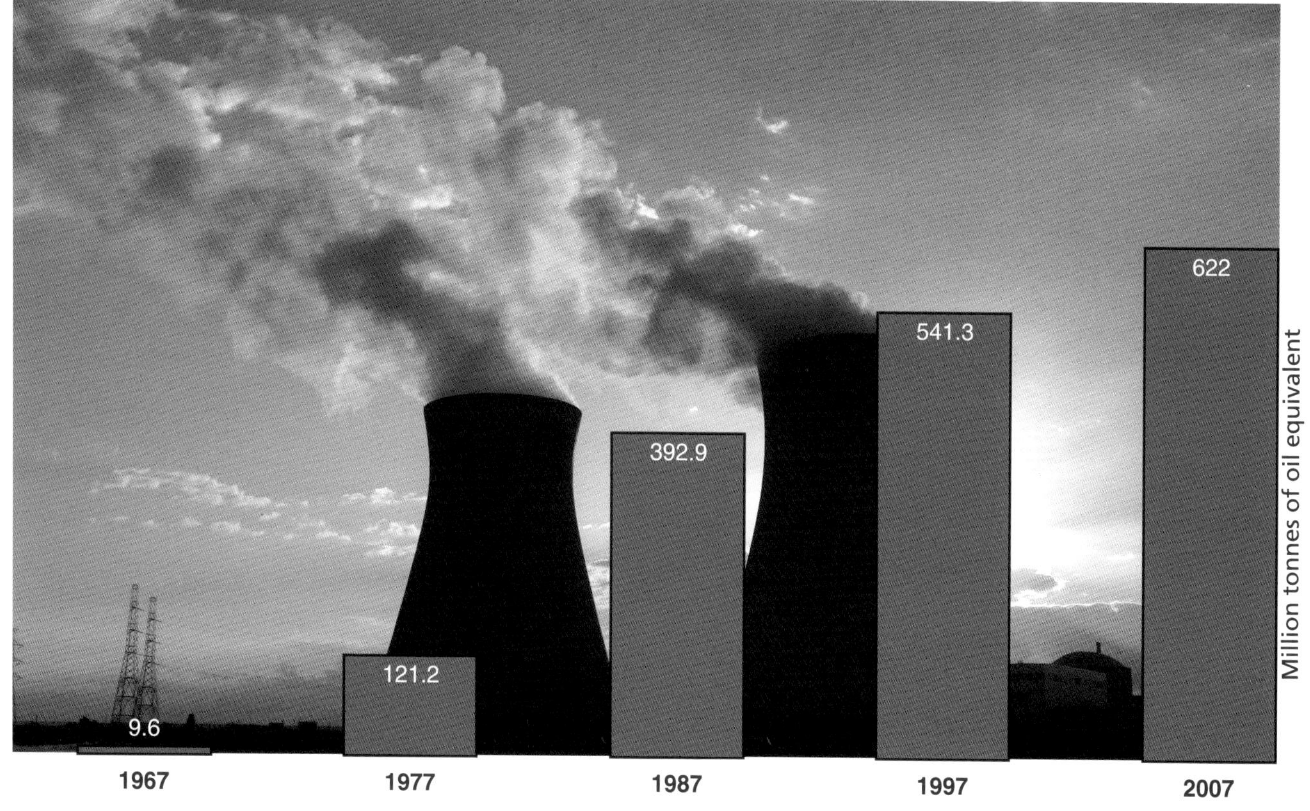

9.6
121.2
392.9
541.3
622
Million tonnes of oil equivalent
1967
1977
1987
1997
2007

A recent survey among EU citizens reveals concern over the issue of radioactive waste from nuclear energy production.

Public opinion regarding nuclear energy production appears to be strongly divided in the EU. Nearly identical shares of respondents express support **for** nuclear energy – **44%** and **opposition** to it – **45%**.

However when it comes to attitudes regarding radioactive disposal, opinion is less divided.

Do you agree with the following?
(% who agree, EU, 2008)

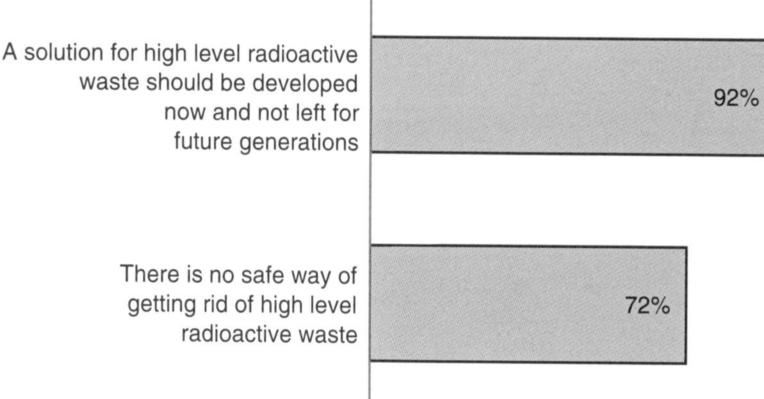

A solution for high level radioactive waste should be developed now and not left for future generations
92%
There is no safe way of getting rid of high level radioactive waste
72%

Source: BP Statistical Review of World Energy 2008; Attitudes Towards Radioactive Waste, Eurobarometer, 2008

http://www.bp.com
http://www.greenpeace.org.uk
http://www.ec.europa.eu

Fair share

Some of the countries tackling CO_2 are still the worst polluters

The CCPI (Climate change performance index), compares the climate protection efforts of 56 industrialised countries which together account for **90%** of the world's carbon emissions. It takes into account each country's emission levels, trends in emissions and climate policy.

The results clearly show that even those making the most effort have a long way to go to reach the target of 100 and halt climate change.

CO2

CCPI TOP 10

Rank	Country	Score
1	Sweden	65.6
2	Germany	64.5
3	Iceland	62.6
4	Mexico	62.5
5	India	62.4
6	Hungary	61.0
7	UK	59.2
8	Brazil	59.0
9	Switzerland	59.0
10	Argentina	58.5

CCPI BOTTOM 10

Rank	Country	Score
47	Ukraine	44.7
48	Kazakhstan	44.6
49	Malaysia	44.2
50	Russia	43.9
51	Korea, Rep.	41.3
52	Luxembourg	39.2
53	Canada	37.6
54	Australia	35.5
55	USA	33.4
56	Saudi Arabia	30.0

Top 10 CO_2 polluters – share of pollution and population (CCPI Ranking in brackets)

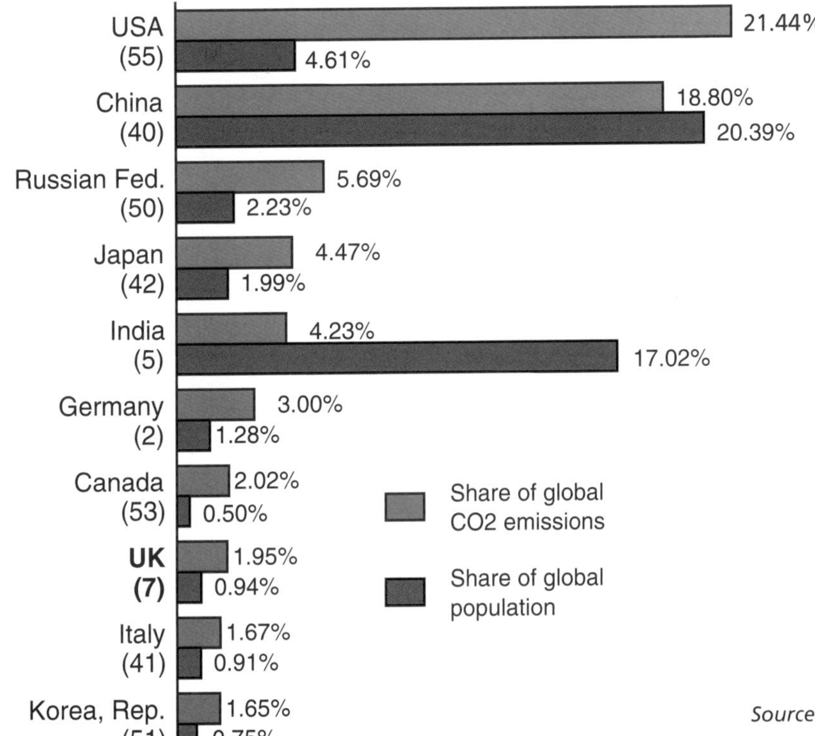

USA (55)
21.44%
4.61%
China (40)
18.80%
20.39%
Russian Fed. (50)
5.69%
2.23%
Japan (42)
4.47%
1.99%
India (5)
4.23%
17.02%
Germany (2)
3.00%
1.28%
Canada (53)
2.02%
0.50%
UK (7)
1.95%
0.94%
Italy (41)
1.67%
0.91%
Korea, Rep. (51)
1.65%
0.75%
Share of global CO2 emissions
Share of global population

10 countries alone are responsible for **64.9%** of global CO_2 emissions. In some cases, like China, their share of emissions is similar to their share of world population.

While India is the 5th largest producer of CO_2, its efforts to tackle the issue, make it 5th in the CCPI index also. Its share of population well outstrips its share of pollution. The USA, however, is responsible for over one fifth of the world's CO_2 pollution, but has only **4.61%** of the global population. Its CCPI rank of 55, suggests that little is being done to tackle the issue.

Source: The Climate Change Performance Index, 2008
http://www.germanwatch.org/ccpi.htm

Global footprint

Some countries are using more than their share of the world's resources

In order to live, we consume what the earth can offer. There are currently **1.8 hectares** of resources per person available to use.

Most people use **2.2 hectares** worth of resources – meaning we consume nearly **23% more** than the planet can sustain. This is without taking into account any other species that consumes the same resources as humans.

If everyone consumed the same amount of resources as the average African we would only use up **0.6** of a planet.

On the other hand, if everyone had the lifestyle of most North Americans we would need to have the resources of **5.3** earths to survive.

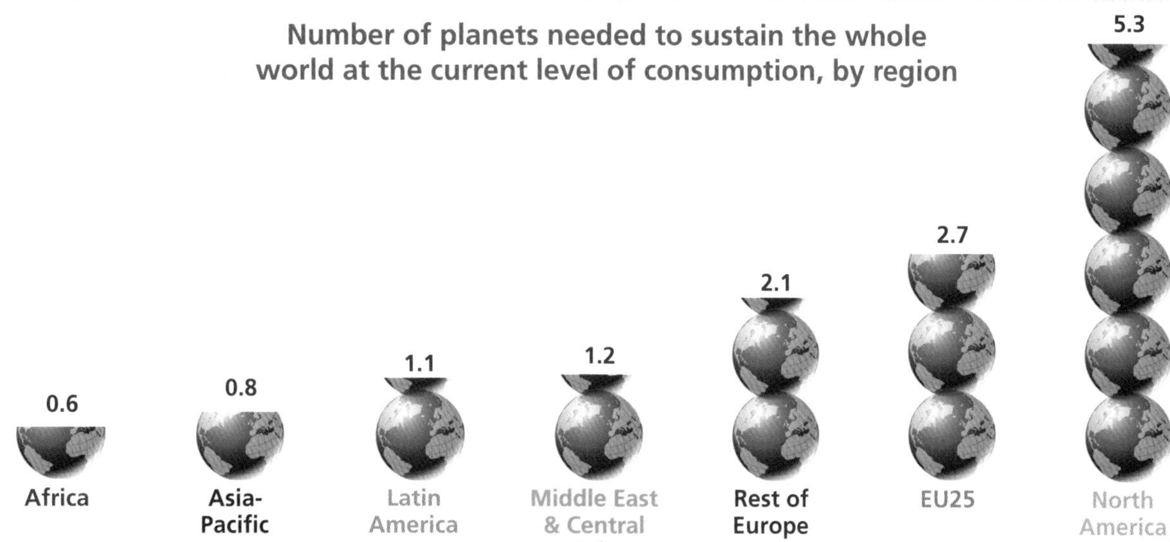

Number of planets needed to sustain the whole world at the current level of consumption, by region
0.6
Africa
0.8
Asia-Pacific
1.1
Latin America
1.2
Middle East & Central Asia
2.1
Rest of Europe
2.7
EU25
5.3
North America

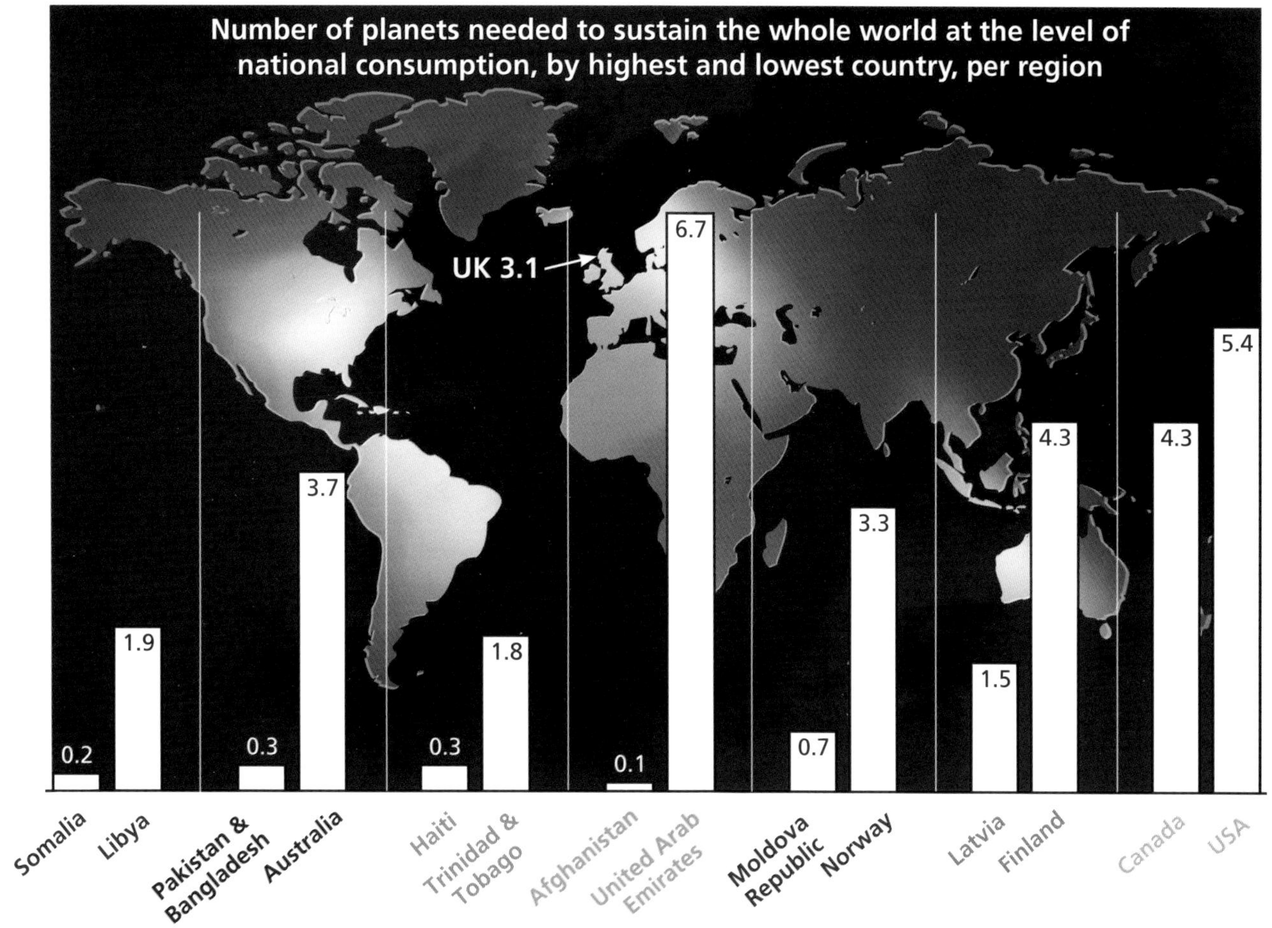

Number of planets needed to sustain the whole world at the level of national consumption, by highest and lowest country, per region

Somalia	0.2
Libya	1.9
Pakistan & Bangladesh	0.3
Australia	3.7
Haiti	0.3
Trinidad & Tobago	1.8
Afghanistan	0.1
United Arab Emirates	6.7
Moldova Republic	0.7
Norway	3.3
Latvia	1.5
Finland	4.3
Canada	4.3
USA	5.4

UK 3.1

Source: Global Footprint Network 2006. National Footprint Accounts, 2006 Edition

http://www.footprintnetwork.org

Climate of change?

Attitudes to climate change – concerned but not convinced

New research shows that while people are concerned about climate change, they have doubts about the science behind it and the government's green agenda.

How concerned are you about climate change?

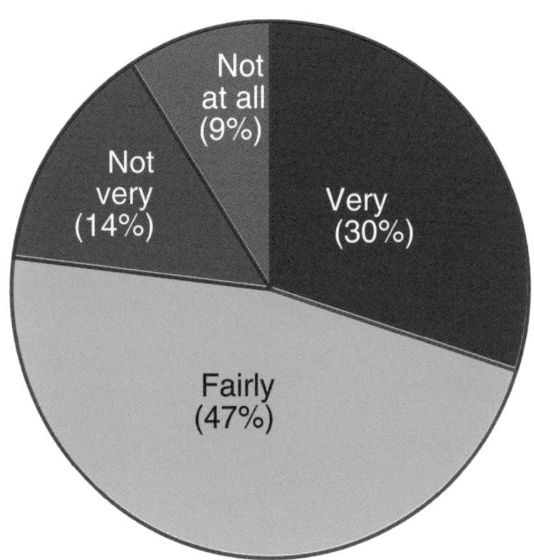

Not at all (9%)
Not very (14%)
Very (30%)
Fairly (47%)

Scientists!
Government!
Trust?

Science
There seems to remain an uncertainty about both the science and the potential impact of climate change.

To what extent do you agree or disagree?

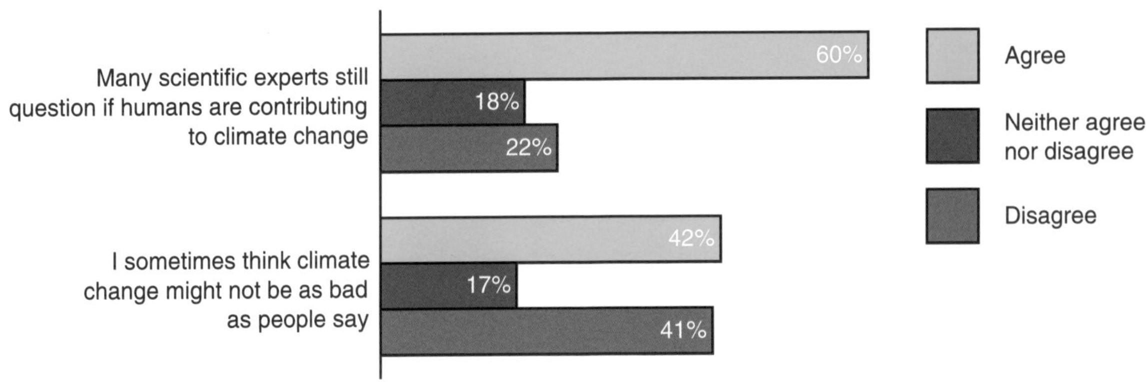

Many scientific experts still question if humans are contributing to climate change
60%
18%
22%
I sometimes think climate change might not be as bad as people say
42%
17%
41%
Agree
Neither agree nor disagree
Disagree

The government

Turning to attitudes about the role of the government, only 38% are confident the government will take the steps necessary to tackle climate change, compared to 57% who are not.

There is even less confidence in international leaders taking action (36% confident vs 61% not confident).

But only 27% of people agree that it's too late to tackle climate change.

FRAGILE
HANDLE WITH EXTREME CARE
FRAGILE
HANDLE WITH EXTREME CARE
FRAGILE
HANDLE WITH EXTREME CARE

It seems the government faces a series of challenges regarding its climate change credentials. On the one hand there's support for it to do more yet people seem cynical about its motives.

To what extent do you agree or disagree that...?

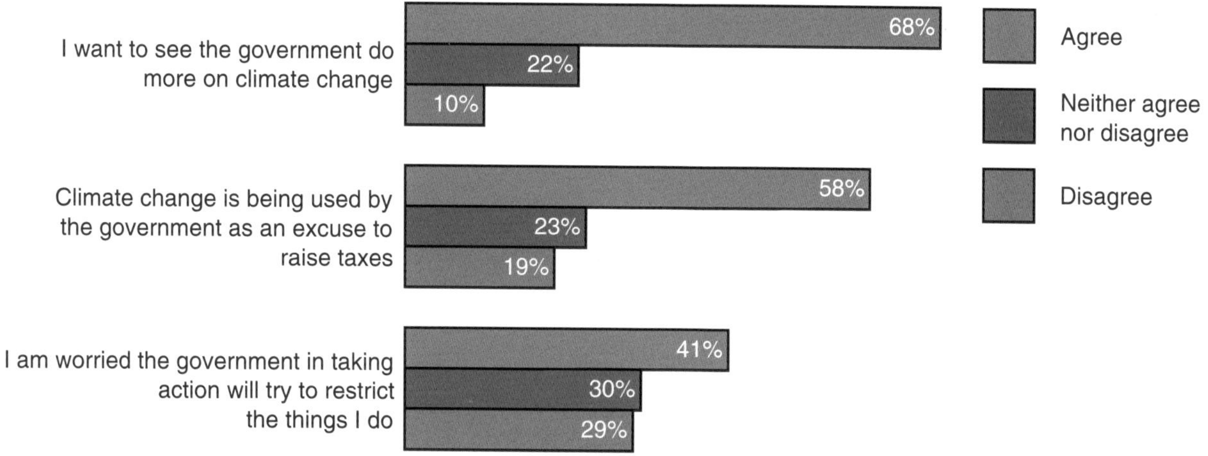
I want to see the government do more on climate change
68%
22%
10%
Climate change is being used by the government as an excuse to raise taxes
58%
23%
19%
I am worried the government in taking action will try to restrict the things I do
41%
30%
29%
Agree
Neither agree nor disagree
Disagree

Personal action

If people are cynical about the government's role they also have doubts about people's own responsibilities.

26% of people believe it's their personal responsibility to make small steps, like recycling more and turning the lights off, but nothing else.

Only 35% of people believe that taking action to reduce their carbon footprint is the 'normal' thing to do, while 77% believe that although people say they're concerned, at the end of the day they're not prepared to make big sacrifices for the environment.

Source: Public attitudes to climate change, 2008, Ipsos-mori
http://www.ipsos-mori.com

Green teens

Young people get radical to save the planet

A survey of 16-19 year olds reveals how far they will go to protect the environment

If global warming continues to get worse, which of the following solutions would you be prepared to support in the future?

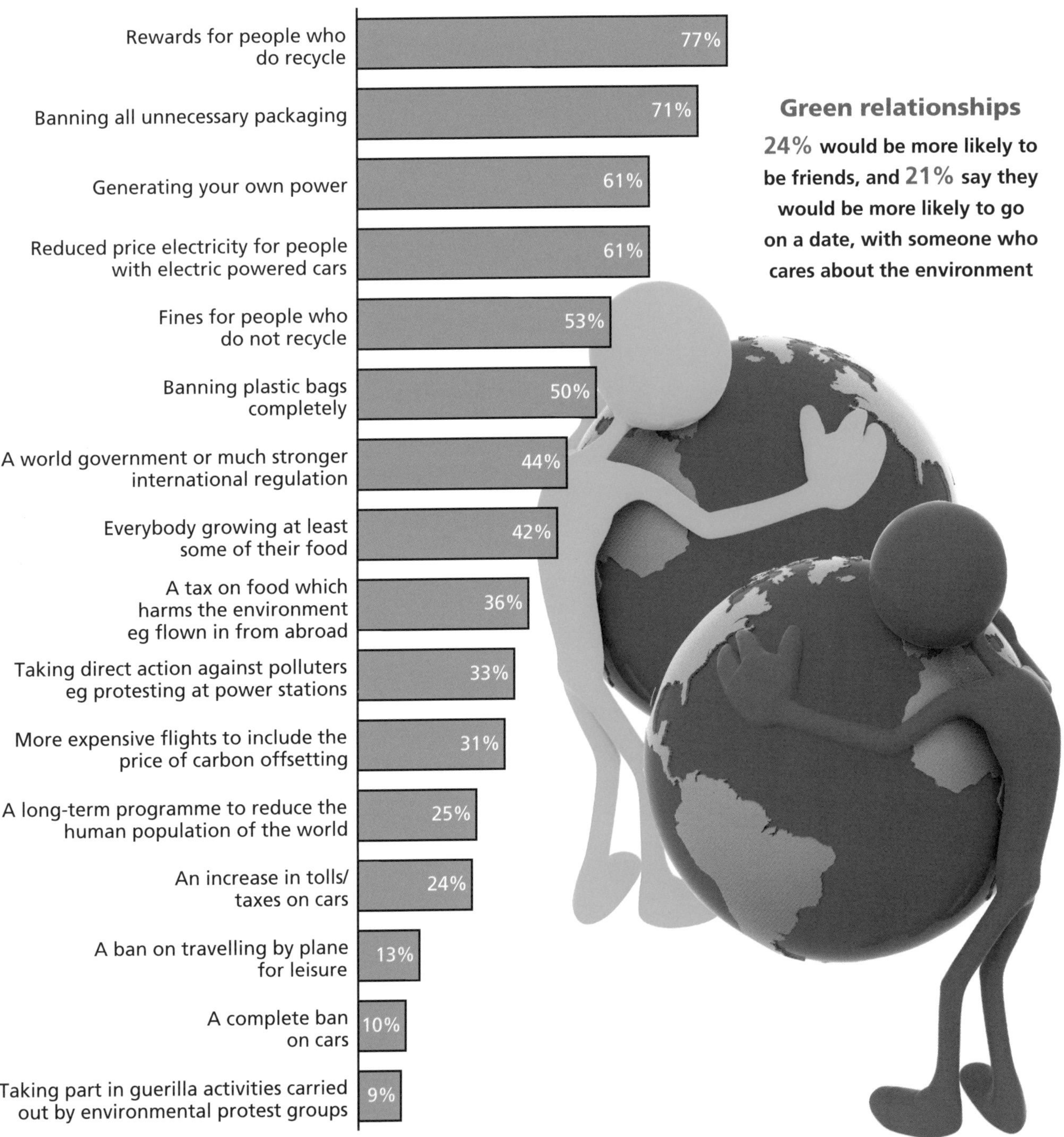

Rewards for people who do recycle 77%
Banning all unnecessary packaging 71%
Generating your own power 61%
Reduced price electricity for people with electric powered cars 61%
Fines for people who do not recycle 53%
Banning plastic bags completely 50%
A world government or much stronger international regulation 44%
Everybody growing at least some of their food 42%
A tax on food which harms the environment eg flown in from abroad 36%
Taking direct action against polluters eg protesting at power stations 33%
More expensive flights to include the price of carbon offsetting 31%
A long-term programme to reduce the human population of the world 25%
An increase in tolls/ taxes on cars 24%
A ban on travelling by plane for leisure 13%
A complete ban on cars 10%
Taking part in guerilla activities carried out by environmental protest groups 9%

Green relationships

24% would be more likely to be friends, and 21% say they would be more likely to go on a date, with someone who cares about the environment

How young people feel about the environment can shape the relationship they have with their parents, friends and potential partners.

48% of young people claim to encourage their parents to recycle and 30% encourage them to buy environmentally friendly products. 45% feel that their parents' generation has not done enough to combat climate change. This may have an impact on what they themselves are prepared to do to help the environment – including direct action in some cases.

Source: Young people and environmental issues, Future Foundation

http://www.futurefoundation.net/

Greenest cities

How do UK cities measure up?

The Sustainable Cities Index ranks Britain's 20 largest cities based on environmental factors. The cities were given a score on each of 3 factors, and then an overall score to discover the greenest cities.

Environmental Impact – impact on the wider environment in terms of resource use & pollution		Quality of Life – what the city is like to live in		Future Proofing – how well the city is preparing itself for a sustainable future	
Top 5 cities	Score	Top 5 cities	Score	Top 5 cities	Score
1 Bradford	61.0	1 Brighton and Hove	74.4	1 Brighton and Hove	57.0
2 Bristol	57.0	2 Edinburgh	62.8	2 Edinburgh	57.0
3 Plymouth	55.5	3 Bristol	56.4	3 Sheffield	56.0
4 Cardiff	50.5	4 Cardiff	55.6	4 Nottingham	52.0
5 Sunderland	49.0	5 Plymouth	52.8	5 Leeds	49.0
This covers air quality, water quality, ecological footprint and household waste per person. Wolverhampton comes bottom of this index		This draws on data such as levels of education and employment, the provision of green space and public transport and life expectancy at 65. Hull comes bottom of this index		This measures the council's response to climate change, the number of 'green businesses' in the area and the trends in composting and recycling. Liverpool is bottom of this index	

Sustainability ranking

1 Brighton and Hove 166.9
2 Edinburgh 156.3
3 Bristol 154.4
4 Plymouth 148.3
5 Leeds 141.1
6 Cardiff 136.1
7 Sheffield 133.5
8 Newcastle 133.3
9 Bradford 129.9
10 London 127.6
11 Nottingham 122.7
12 Manchester 120.2
13 Sunderland 118.6
14 Leicester 109.0
15 Glasgow 104.7
16 Wolverhampton 101.8
17 Coventry 97.5
18 Hull 91.0
19 Birmingham 79.4
20 Liverpool 76.7

Source: The Sustainable Cities Index, Forum for the future
http://www.forumforthefuture.org.uk

Wasteful trade

We import and export the same items!

There is a range of products which the UK both imports and exports. In some cases, like ice cream, almost the same quantities leave the country as come in from abroad. Because of the environmental and fuel costs involved, this has been termed as 'ecologically wasteful trade.'

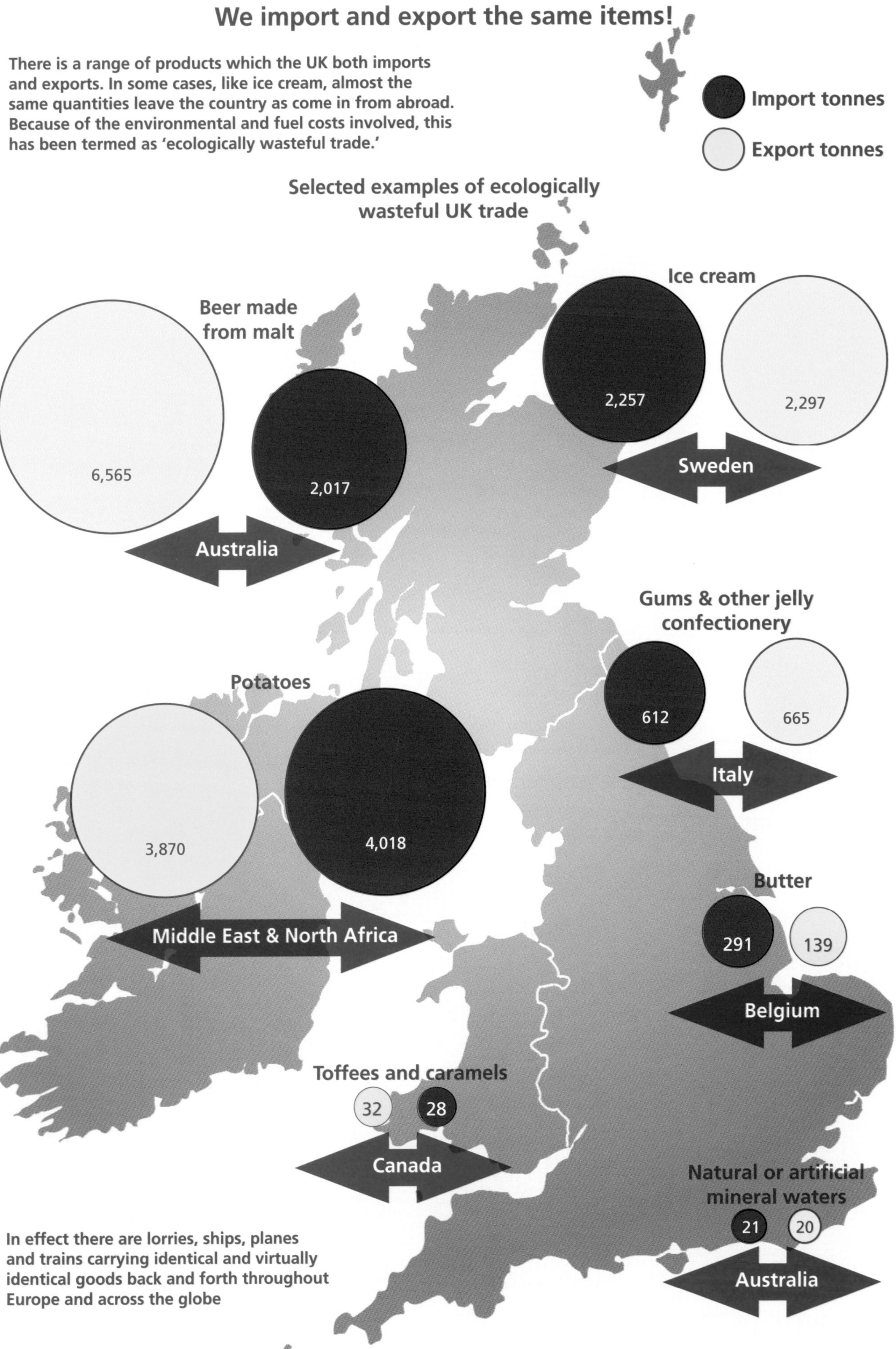
Import tonnes
Export tonnes
Selected examples of ecologically wasteful UK trade
Beer made from malt
6,565
2,017
Australia
Ice cream
2,257
2,297
Sweden
Gums & other jelly confectionery
612
665
Italy
Potatoes
3,870
4,018
Middle East & North Africa
Butter
291
139
Belgium
Toffees and caramels
32
28
Canada
Natural or artificial mineral waters
21
20
Australia

In effect there are lorries, ships, planes and trains carrying identical and virtually identical goods back and forth throughout Europe and across the globe

How our high consuming lifestyles are costing the earth

These examples of trade highlight the nature and scale of the UK's dependence on the rest of the world and the environmentally wasteful nature of the way we trade.

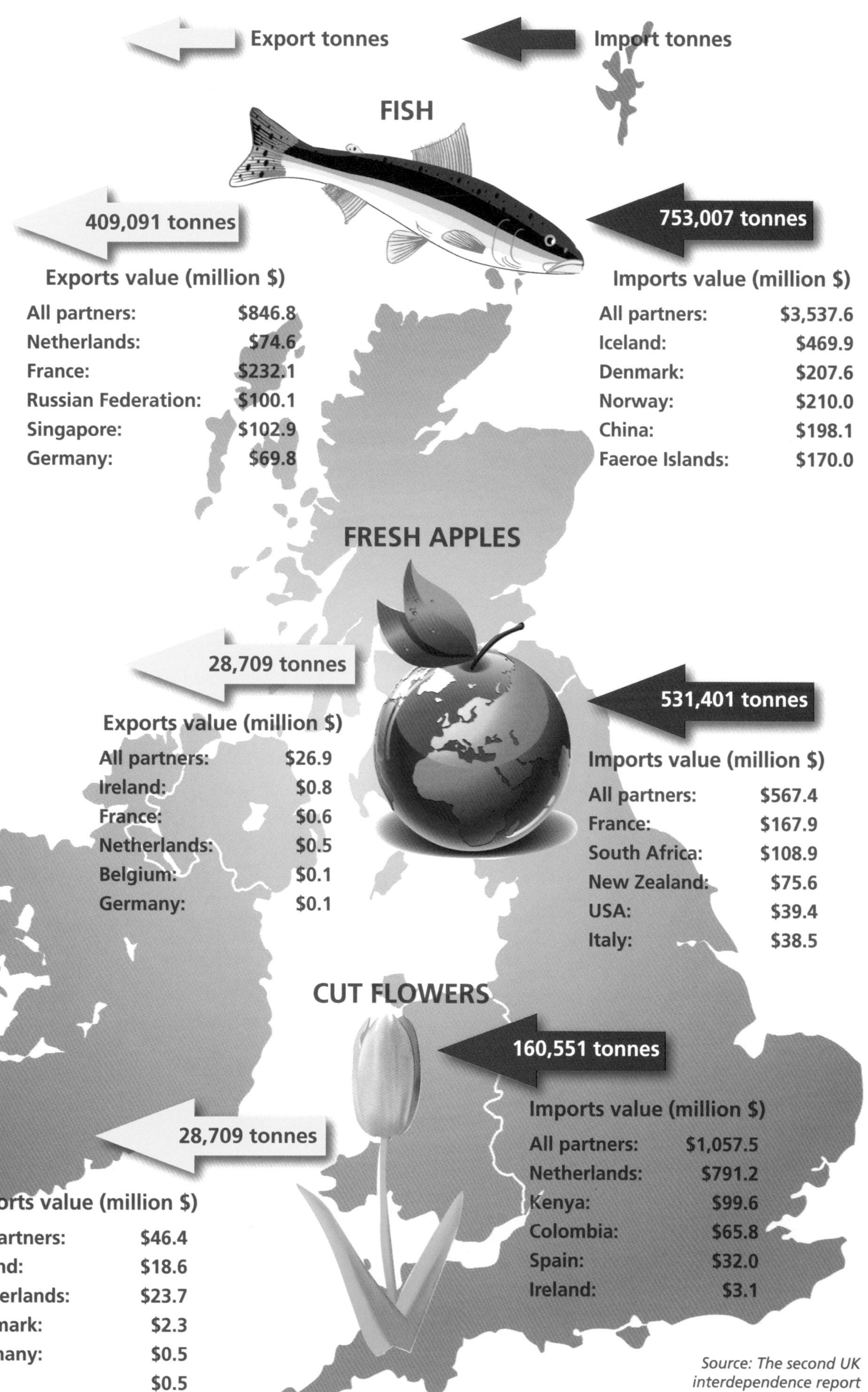

Export tonnes
Import tonnes
FISH
409,091 tonnes
753,007 tonnes
FRESH APPLES
28,709 tonnes
531,401 tonnes
CUT FLOWERS
160,551 tonnes
28,709 tonnes

FISH

Export: 409,091 tonnes

Exports value (million $)	
All partners:	$846.8
Netherlands:	$74.6
France:	$232.1
Russian Federation:	$100.1
Singapore:	$102.9
Germany:	$69.8

Import: 753,007 tonnes

Imports value (million $)	
All partners:	$3,537.6
Iceland:	$469.9
Denmark:	$207.6
Norway:	$210.0
China:	$198.1
Faeroe Islands:	$170.0

FRESH APPLES

Export: 28,709 tonnes

Exports value (million $)	
All partners:	$26.9
Ireland:	$0.8
France:	$0.6
Netherlands:	$0.5
Belgium:	$0.1
Germany:	$0.1

Import: 531,401 tonnes

Imports value (million $)	
All partners:	$567.4
France:	$167.9
South Africa:	$108.9
New Zealand:	$75.6
USA:	$39.4
Italy:	$38.5

CUT FLOWERS

Import: 160,551 tonnes

Imports value (million $)	
All partners:	$1,057.5
Netherlands:	$791.2
Kenya:	$99.6
Colombia:	$65.8
Spain:	$32.0
Ireland:	$3.1

Export: 28,709 tonnes

Exports value (million $)	
All partners:	$46.4
Ireland:	$18.6
Netherlands:	$23.7
Denmark:	$2.3
Germany:	$0.5
USA:	$0.5

Source: The second UK interdependence report
http://www.footprintnetwork.org

Decade of disasters

Scientists warn that climate change will increase natural disasters

The equivalent of a third of the world's population has already been affected by weather-related disasters and this is set to soar because of climate change unless urgent international action is taken.

Natural disasters are grouped into two categories:

Hydrometeorological disasters – those involving weather and/or water, eg floods, windstorms and droughts.

Geophysical disasters – those originating in the earth, eg volcanoes and earthquakes

Natural disasters, 1997-2006

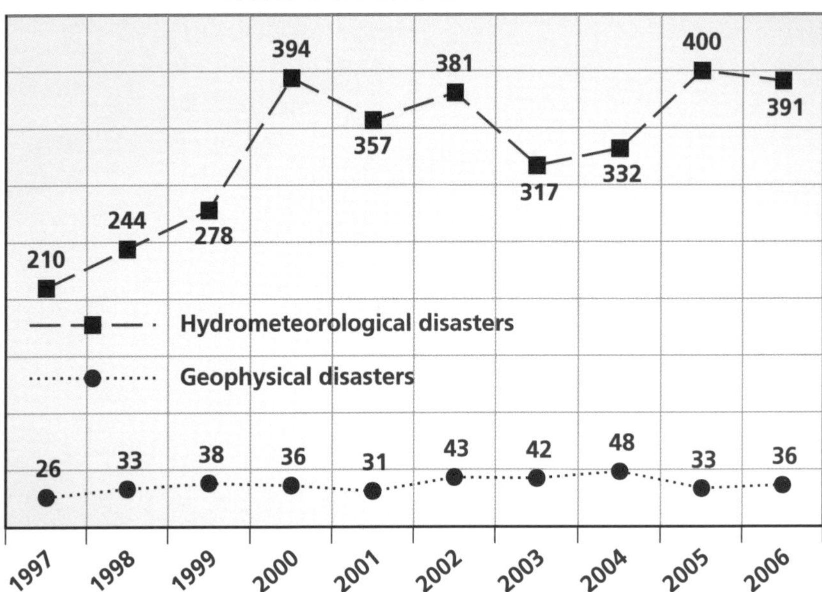

Hydrometeorological disasters
Geophysical disasters
210
244
278
394
357
381
317
332
400
391
26
33
38
36
31
43
42
48
33
36
1997
1998
1999
2000
2001
2002
2003
2004
2005
2006

People affected by natural disasters
(in thousands)

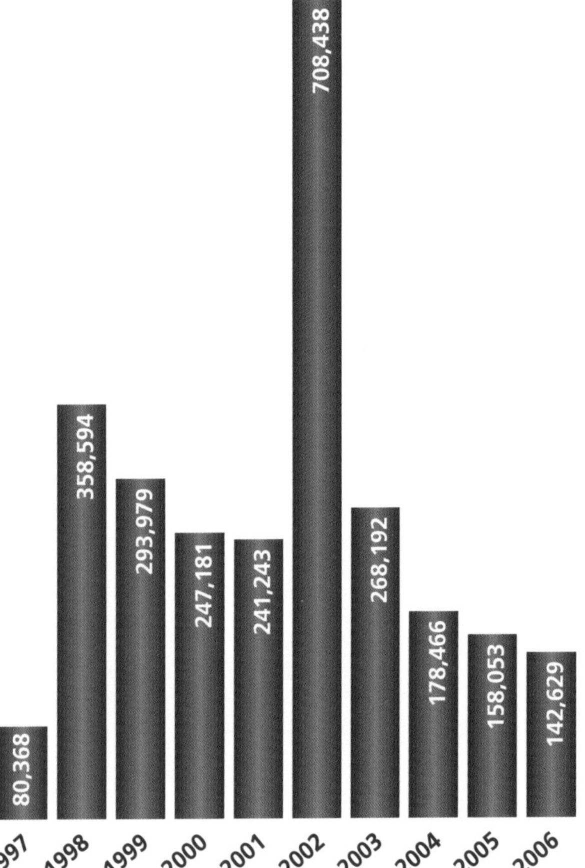

80,368
358,594
293,979
247,181
241,243
708,438
268,192
178,466
158,053
142,629
1997
1998
1999
2000
2001
2002
2003
2004
2005
2006

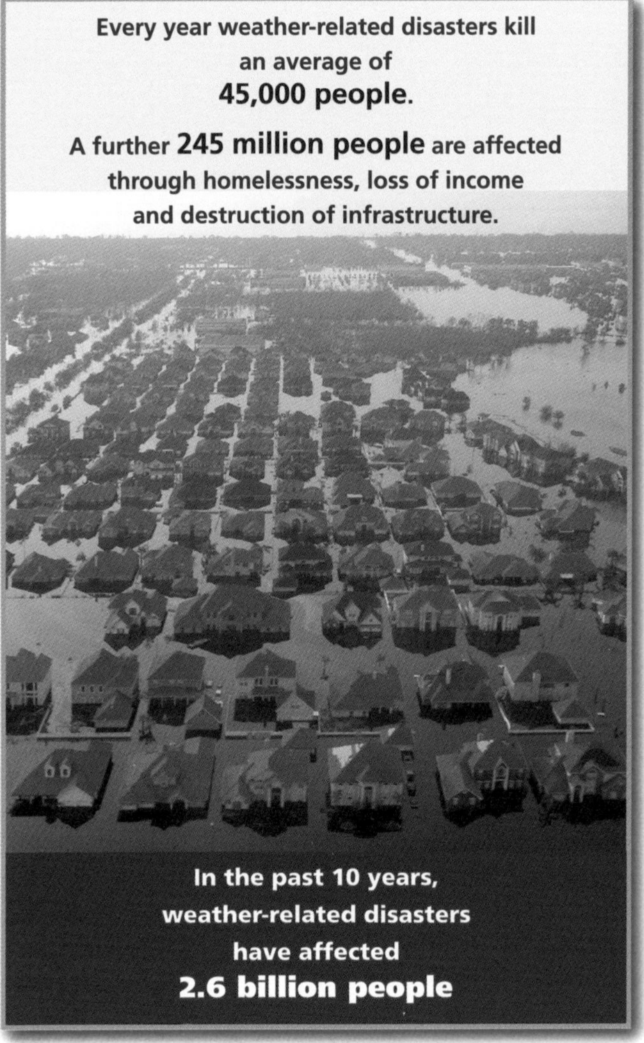

Every year weather-related disasters kill an average of
45,000 people.
A further 245 million people are affected through homelessness, loss of income and destruction of infrastructure.
In the past 10 years, weather-related disasters have affected
2.6 billion people

Source: World Disaster Report 2007 © International Federation of Red Cross and Red Crescent Societies, Climate of Disaster, Tearfund

http://www.ifrc.org
http://www.tearfund.org

Water worldwide

More precious than oil – and supplies are running low

Global distribution of world's water

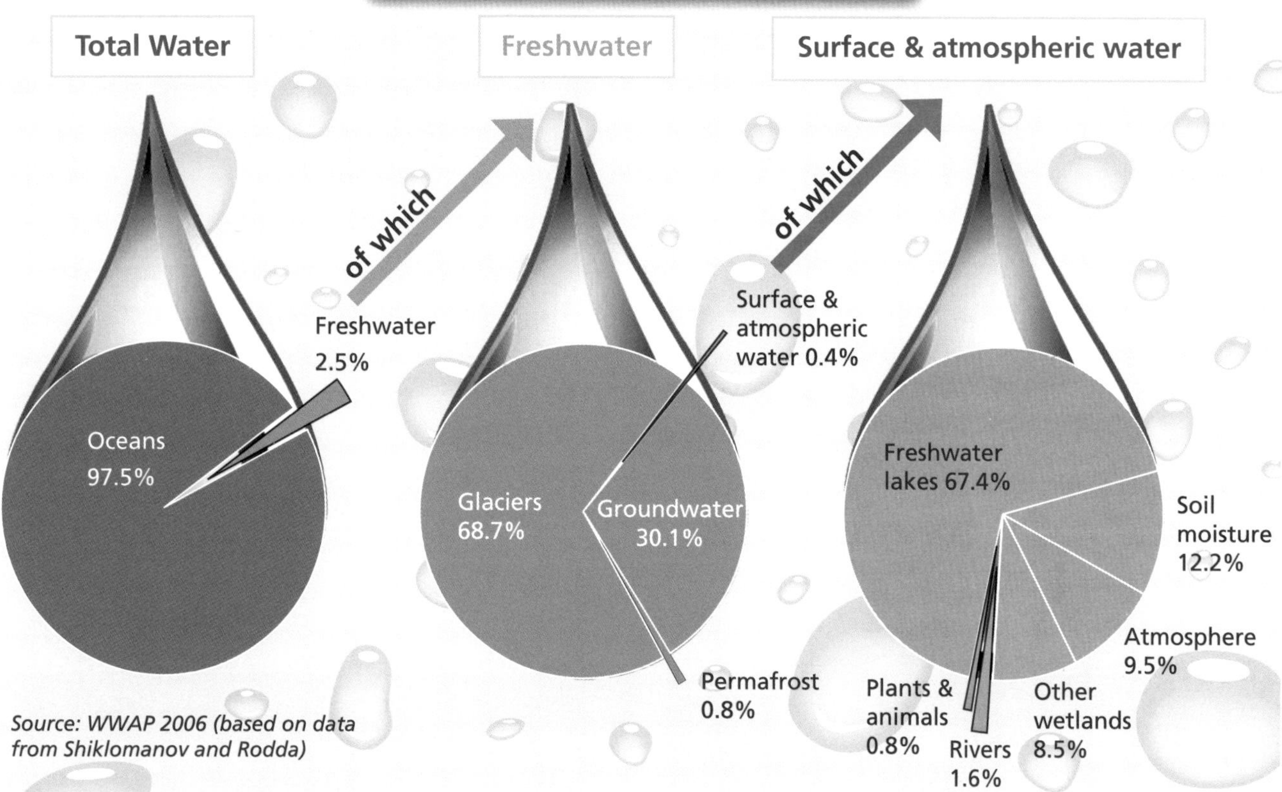

Total Water
Freshwater
Surface & atmospheric water
of which
of which
Oceans 97.5%
Freshwater 2.5%
Glaciers 68.7%
Groundwater 30.1%
Surface & atmospheric water 0.4%
Permafrost 0.8%
Freshwater lakes 67.4%
Soil moisture 12.2%
Atmosphere 9.5%
Other wetlands 8.5%
Rivers 1.6%
Plants & animals 0.8%

Source: WWAP 2006 (based on data from Shiklomanov and Rodda)

The world has plenty of water, but 97.5% of it is saltwater. We depend on the remaining 2.5% – but only a fraction of this is in easily accessible surface water.

In many regions demand for water now outstrips renewable supplies.

Water pollution adds to the challenge of delivering enough good quality water.

Global water consumption rose sixfold between 1900 and 1995 – more than double the rate of population growth – and continues to grow rapidly.

Nearly half the world will live with water scarcity by 2025

Global renewable water supply 1995 and 2025 (projected)
(m³ per person per year)

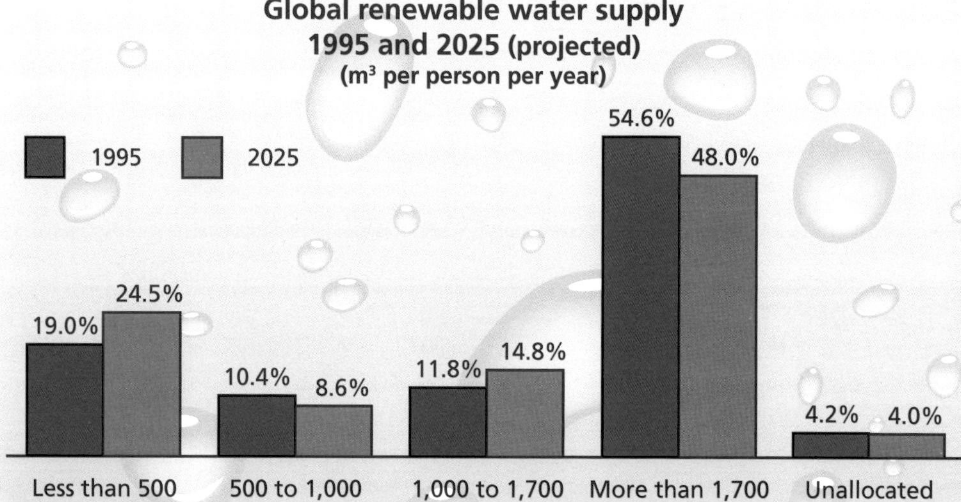

1995
2025
19.0%
24.5%
10.4%
8.6%
11.8%
14.8%
54.6%
48.0%
4.2%
4.0%
Less than 500
500 to 1,000
1,000 to 1,700
More than 1,700
Unallocated

The 2025 estimates are considered conservative because they are based on the United Nations' low-range projections for population growth. A slight mismatch between the water run off and population data means that about 4% of the global population is not accounted for in this analysis.

Areas where water supply per person drops below 1,700m³ per year are experiencing 'water stress' – this means frequent, disruptive water shortages. In areas where the supplies drop below 1,000m³ per person per year, there can be problems with food production and economic development.

Source: World Resources Institute http://www.wri.org/

Ifs and butts

Smokers are banned from buildings, but their litter is filling our streets

Smokers' materials are still the most widespread kind of litter on our streets – found on 78% of sites surveyed by the Local Environment Quality Survey of England.

Smoking related litter is classed as cigarette ends as well as matches, lighters, packaging etc.

In another survey, local authorities were asked how much of a problem smoking-related litter (SRL) is in their area.

98% stated that it is a problem in their area, of which 31% thought it was a major problem.

Asked whether they thought the amount of SRL had changed since the introduction of the smoking ban, 55% of local authorities believed there had been a slight increase, while 30% thought there had been a significant increase.

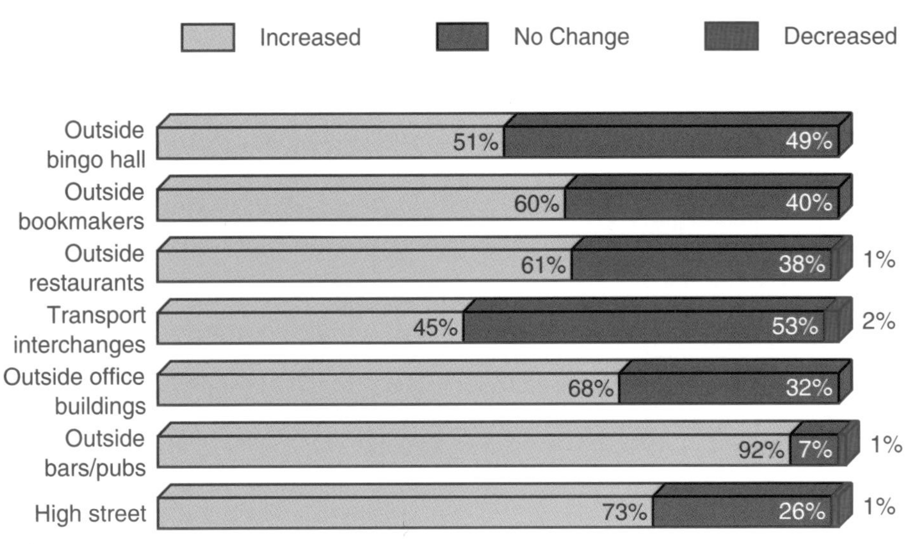
How have the following areas been affected by smoking related litter?
Increased
No Change
Decreased
Outside bingo hall
51%
49%
Outside bookmakers
60%
40%
Outside restaurants
61%
38%
1%
Transport interchanges
45%
53%
2%
Outside office buildings
68%
32%
Outside bars/pubs
92%
7%
1%
High street
73%
26%
1%

Every day UK smokers throw away about 200 million butts. 122 tons of cigarette butts and cigarette related litter is dropped every day in the UK – 70% to 90% of all town centre litter.

It costs the UK government around £370 million a year to remove litter from our streets. A dropped cigarette butt carries a littering fine of at least £50 and can be as much as £2,500.

Many people believe that cigarette filters are biodegradable. They are not!

Cigarette butts are made of cellulose acetate, which takes 12 years to biodegrade

Cigarette butts leak toxins that contaminate water and harm marine life and the environment

Cigarette filters have been found in the stomachs of fish, birds, whales and other marine creatures, who mistake them for food.

Photo courtesy of: ENCAMS

Source: Public Ashtrays; The Impact of the Smoke Free Legislation on Litter, EnCams 2008; Local Environment survey of England, 2006/07, EnCams.
http://www.publicashtrays.com
http://www.encams.org

Family &
relationships

Family first

How do people feel about their families?

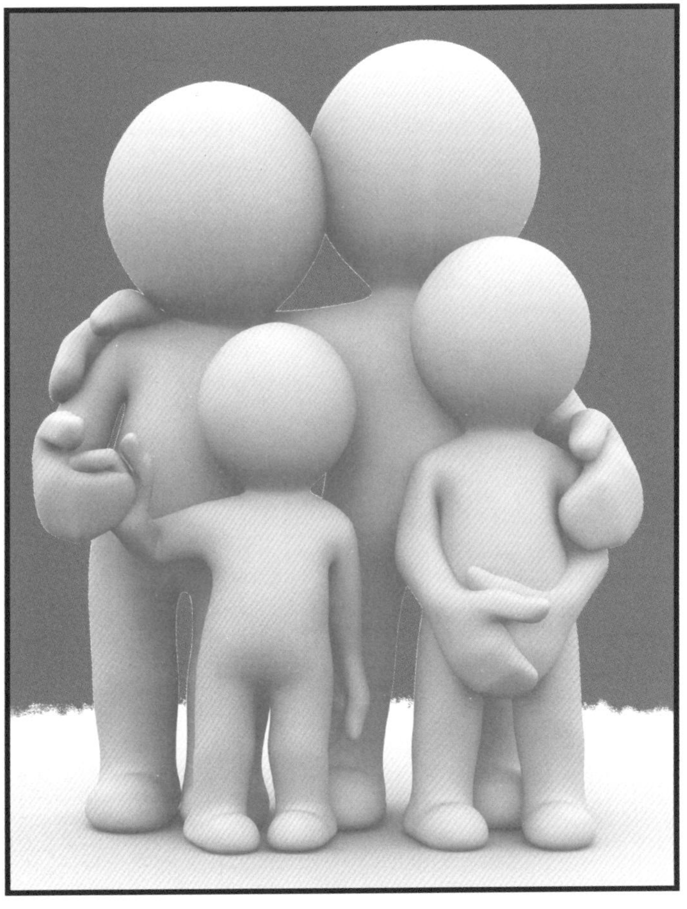

How important is family life to you?

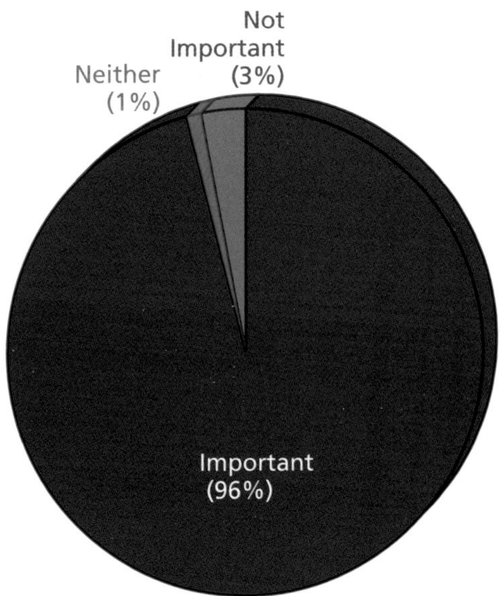
Not Important (3%)
Neither (1%)
Important (96%)

Older people tend to think family life is more important.

Of those aged 65+, **91%** think it is very important, whereas only **78%** of 18-24 year olds do

Who do you feel most happy with?

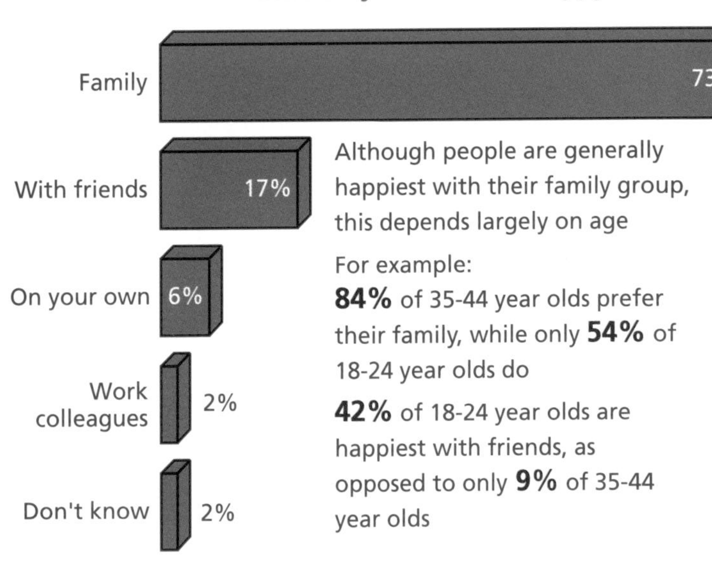
Family 73%
With friends 17%
On your own 6%
Work colleagues 2%
Don't know 2%

Although people are generally happiest with their family group, this depends largely on age

For example:

84% of 35-44 year olds prefer their family, while only **54%** of 18-24 year olds do

42% of 18-24 year olds are happiest with friends, as opposed to only **9%** of 35-44 year olds

How close would you describe your family?

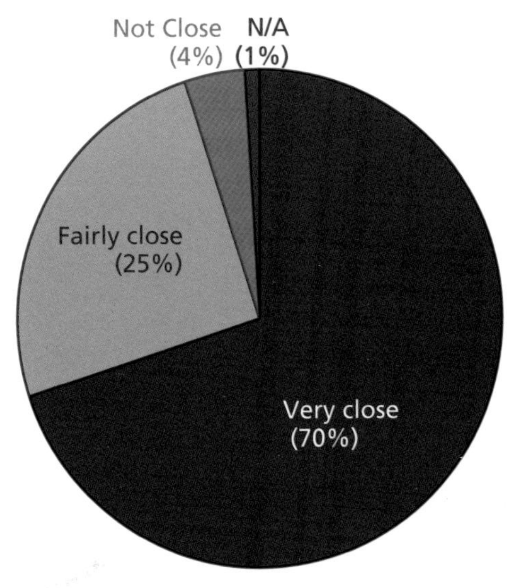
Not Close (4%)
N/A (1%)
Fairly close (25%)
Very close (70%)

How often do you eat a main meal with your family?

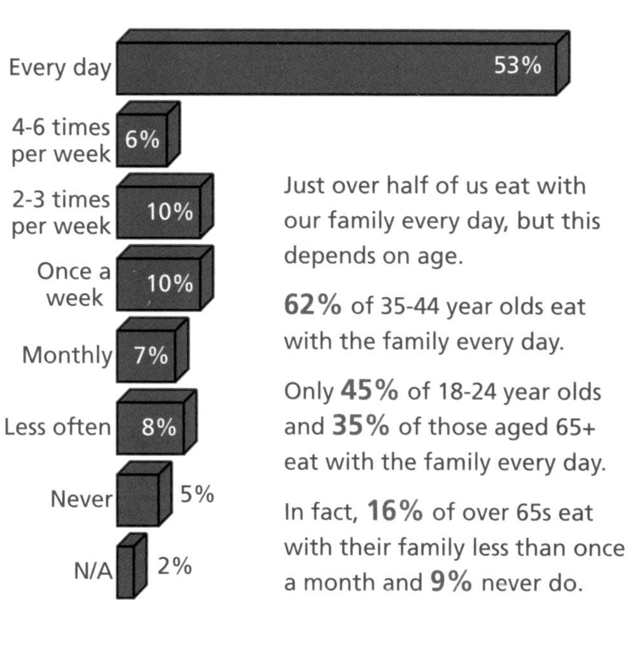

Every day 53%
4-6 times per week 6%
2-3 times per week 10%
Once a week 10%
Monthly 7%
Less often 8%
Never 5%
N/A 2%

Just over half of us eat with our family every day, but this depends on age.

62% of 35-44 year olds eat with the family every day.

Only **45%** of 18-24 year olds and **35%** of those aged 65+ eat with the family every day.

In fact, **16%** of over 65s eat with their family less than once a month and **9%** never do.

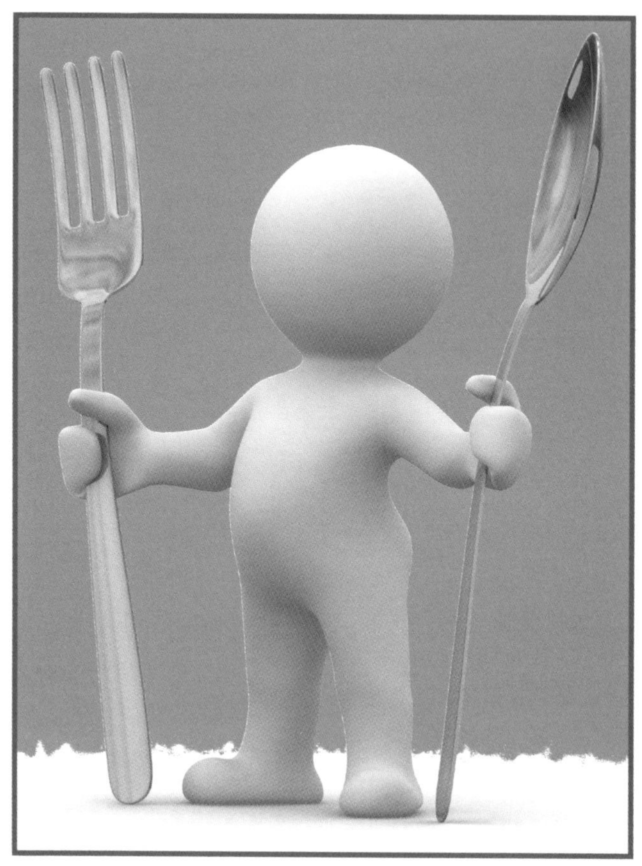

How often does your family argue?

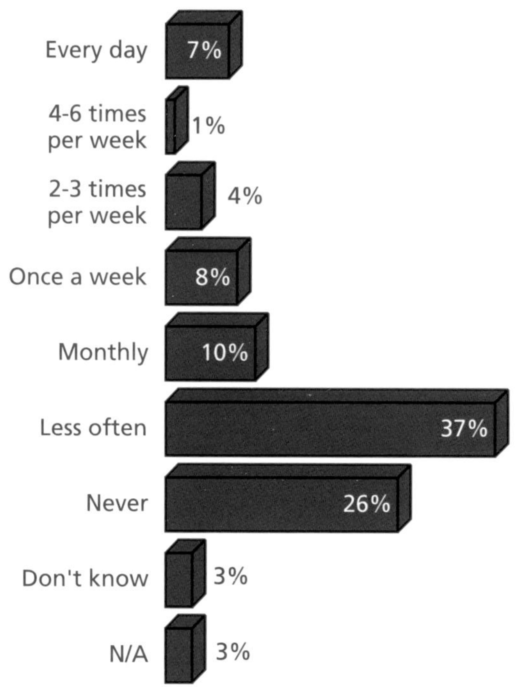

Every day 7%
4-6 times per week 1%
2-3 times per week 4%
Once a week 8%
Monthly 10%
Less often 37%
Never 26%
Don't know 3%
N/A 3%

Younger age groups appear to be involved in more arguments.

For example:
10% of 18-24 year olds argue 2-3 times a week, while only **3%** of 35-44 year olds do.

93% of people say they are happy with family life, yet **70%** feel that family life today is less successful than it was in previous generations.

Are there members of your family that you no longer speak to?

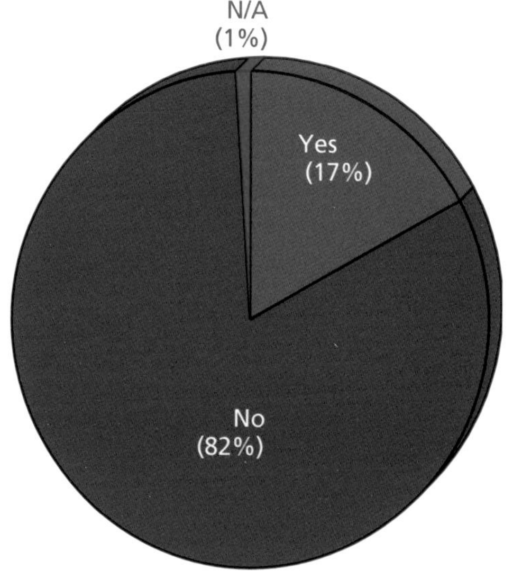

N/A (1%)
Yes (17%)
No (82%)

NB: Figures do not add up to 100% due to rounding
N/A throughout refers to those where it is not applicable because they don't have a family

Source: ICM/BBC
http://www.icmresearch.co.uk/

Family fusion

Families are changing

There are more families now – **17.1 million** in 2006 compared with **16.5 million** in 1996 – and they are more varied than before. The family unit is no longer expected to be a married couple with 2.4 children. Families now take many forms.

Families with children, by family type, GB, 2006

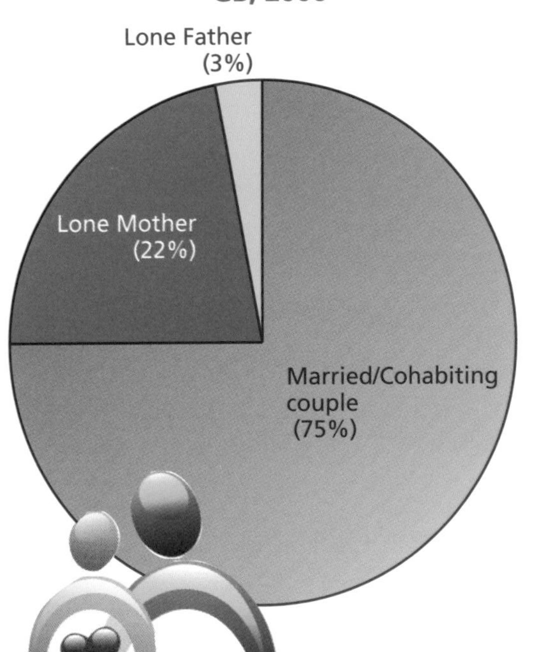

Lone Father (3%)
Lone Mother (22%)
Married/Cohabiting couple (75%)

The structure of the family has changed. In 1971 **92%** of children had parents who were either married or cohabiting compared to **75%** today.

The number of cohabiting couple families in the UK increased by **65%** between 1996 and 2006, from **1.4 million** to **2.3 million**, while married couples fell by **4%** over the same period to **12.1 million**.

Interestingly, men are more likely to think that married couples make better parents, **34%** compared to **23%** of women.

Marriage & parenting, % who agree that...

Marriage gives more financial security than living together	61%
Marriage is still the best kind of relationship	54%
Married couples make better parents than unmarried ones	28%
There is no point in getting married	9%

66% of people think there is little difference socially between being married and living together.

While the heterosexual married couple is no longer the norm, when it comes to bringing up children attitudes are less lenient. When children are involved, alternative family arrangements are seen as less acceptable.

Only four in ten people think that one person can raise a child as well as two.

30% think that it should be harder for couples with children under 16 to get divorced.

While **90%** of people approve of donor insemination for childless couples, this drops to **61%** for single women.

Attitudes to single parents, % who agree that...

There's nothing wrong with a single woman who lives alone having a child	44%
One parent can bring up a child as well as two	42%

Despite the fact that one parent families have increased by **8%** to **2.6 million** since 1996, there still seems to be a preference for two parent families.

There are still doubts over same sex parenting.

42% of people think that a gay male couple are not as capable of being good parents as a man and a woman.

Attitudes to gay men and lesbian couples, % who agree that...

A same sex couple can be just as committed to each other as a man and woman	63%
A lesbian couple are just as capable of being good parents as a man and woman	36%
A gay male couple are just as capable of being good parents as a man and woman	31%

Source: British Social Attitudes 2007/2008; Focus on Families 2007 & General Household Survey 2006, Office for National Statistics

http://www.natcen.ac.uk
http://www.statistics.gov.uk

Teens talk!

How do teenagers rate their parents? And vice versa

Out of 10!

Mums are pretty near perfect, but dads have a bit of catching up according to their adolescent offspring

32% of teenagers give their mothers full marks

73% give them at least 8 out of 10

Only 23% of teenagers think their fathers merit the highest possible score

66% award their dads more than 8 out of 10.

Mummy's boys

Just under half of teenage boys would like to marry someone like their mum, but this is an average and depends on the boy's age

36% of 14-year-old boys want their wives to be like their mothers

This rises to 59% of 15-year-olds who see their mums as a model for their future wives

Only 13% of boys of 18 want to marry someone like their mum

But perhaps maturity brings new appreciation because by the age of 19 this jumps to 32%.

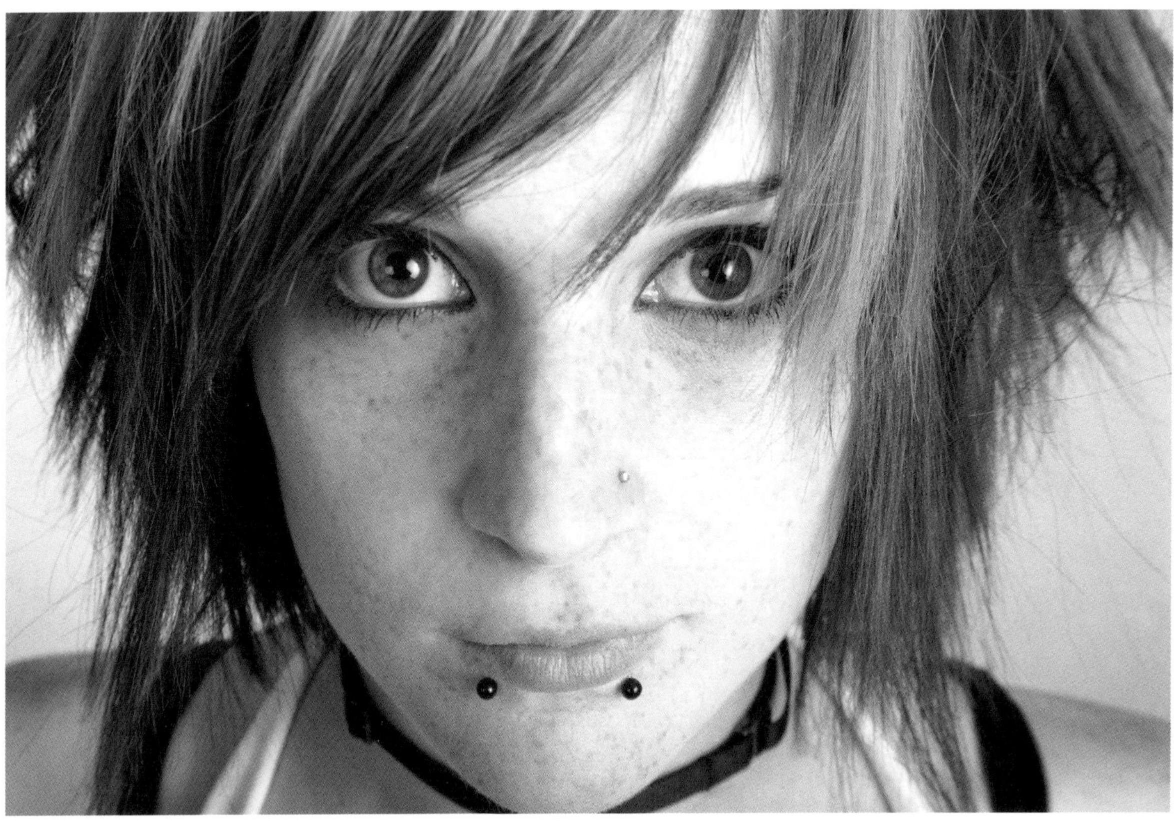

Sibling rivalry

Three-quarters of teenagers get on pretty well with their brothers and sisters, but that leaves a fair percentage who squabble.

Around one-fifth of 15- and 16-year-olds say they don't get on with their siblings

Growing up helps - by the age of 19, only 8% say they don't get on with their brothers and sisters.

Leaving home?

Until 18 most teenagers want to stay with their parents, however girls have a greater urge for independence than boys

40% of all teenage boys said they'd move out of their parents' home if they could

48% of teenage girls said they'd move out

11% of 13-year-olds said they'd leave their parents' home if they had the chance

82% of 19-year-olds would prefer not to be living with their parents.

Teens happy at home?

Only 30% of all teenagers think their parents are unreasonable. The other 70% seem to respect their views.

In answer to the question, **'Do you think your home is a happy one?'** 85% say yes, but there's a bit of a gender divide. 88% of boys say they come from a happy home. Only 81% of girls think their home is happy.

A steady 84-92% of teenagers up to the age of 17 say they have a happy home. But only 77% of 18- and 19-year-olds say their home is happy.

Parents happy at home?

67% of parents say that finances are a source of stress in their lives but only 26% say that their family is a source of stress.

91% of parents would rather spend an evening with their family than with anyone else. 81% of parents say 'I love you' every day to members of their household.

39% say that life as a parent is better than they thought it would be. However, 17% say it's not what they thought it would be and 4% say parenthood is worse than they expected.

Only 4% of parents are happier with their friends than their family.

Pecking order

A child's position in the family has a powerful effect on how they relate to the rest of the family

A quarter of parents reckon their oldest child is the most selfish person in the family
But 28% say the oldest child is the most loved
Out of all the children, 15% of parents say the oldest is the kindest
11% say the oldest child is the meanest of their offspring.

Equality

Asked who wears the trousers, women seem to hold the balance of power

60% of mums say they wear the trousers

But 52% of dads reckon they have the dominant role - or maybe that's what their partners let them think

A hopeful sign is that 17% of parents said that the question 'Who wears the trousers?' does not apply to their family.

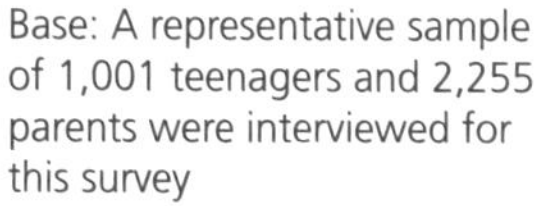

83% of parents say they are happiest with their families.

No need to raise your voice

One-third of parents say they spend an hour a day shouting

But half say they never shout

5% shout for two or more hours every day

Base: A representative sample of 1,001 teenagers and 2,255 parents were interviewed for this survey

Source: Channel 4
http://www.channel4.com

Have you seen...?

One child is reported missing in the UK every five minutes

How many children go missing?

An estimated **210,000** reports of missing people are made to UK police forces each year. Around **two-thirds** of these concern young people under the age of 18. **71%** of 13-17 year olds reported missing to the charity Missing People were female. During 2007/08 the Missing People's Runaway Helpline received **68,000** calls. **77%** of the cases Missing People publicised in 2007-08 were resolved.

Where do runaway children go?

51% of overnight runaways, from a sample of school children, had stayed with friends, **35%** had stayed with relatives, and **16%** had slept rough.

What happens to them while they are away?

9% of young runaways had stolen something, **3%** had begged for money, and **4%** had 'done other things' to survive. **8%** of the young people who ran away overnight had been harmed.

A study of young people who had run away found that **12.5%** reported having been physically hurt and **11%** reported being sexually abused while running away.

Have you run away? Do you need some help?

Runaway Helpline is a 24 hour confidential helpline for runaways operated by the charity Missing People, offering help and advice to young people who have run away from home or care, or who have been forced to leave

You can email:
runawayhelpline@missingpeople.org.uk

Or call the 24 hour confidential Freefone: 0808 800 7070

Are they found?

Most young people who run away do not intend to leave for good, but return to the place they left. Of those who had run away overnight, **52%** stayed away for one night, **27%** stayed away for two to six nights, **11%** stayed away for one to four weeks, and **10%** stayed away for more than four weeks.

Source: Missing People
http://www.missingpeople.org.uk

Lost childhood

Every ten days in England and Wales a child is killed at the hands of a parent

Deadly abuse

There are on average **80** child homicides recorded in England and Wales each year.

In **52%** of all cases of children killed at the hands of another person, the parent is the principal suspect.

Almost **66%** of children killed at the hands of another person are aged **under five**.

The people most likely to die a violent death are **babies under 1 year old**, who are four times more likely to be killed than the average.

Sexual abuse

The NSPCC found that **75%** of sexually abused children they spoke to did not tell anyone about the abuse at the time, and around a third still had not told anyone about their experience(s) by early adulthood. Because of this it is hard to gauge exactly how many children are sexually abused.

However, more than **36%** of all rapes recorded by the police are committed against children **under 16 years of age.**

In total, it is thought that **16%** of children **aged under 16** experienced sexual abuse during childhood.

Of those who spoke about it, **1%** experienced sexual abuse by a parent or carer and another **3%** by another relative during childhood, **11%** by people known but unrelated to them and **5%** of by an adult stranger or someone they had just met.

Who is abused and how?

NSPCC research shows that a significant minority of children suffer serious abuse or neglect. One study of the childhood experiences of 2,869 18-24 year olds found that:

- **6%** experienced frequent and severe emotional maltreatment during childhood.
- **6%** experienced serious absence of care at home during childhood.
- **31%** experienced bullying by their peers during childhood, a further **7%** were discriminated against and **14%** were made to feel different or 'like an outsider'. **43%** experienced at least one of these things during childhood.
- **25%** of children experienced one or more forms of physical violence during childhood. This includes being hit with an implement, being hit with a fist or kicked, shaken, thrown or knocked down, beaten up, choked, burned or scalded on purpose, or threatened with a knife or gun. Of this **25%** of children, the majority had experienced 'some degree of physical abuse' by parents or carers.

If you or a friend has a problem and you need to talk to somebody, call ChildLine on:
0800 1111

Source: NSPCC; ChildLine
http://www.nspcc.org.uk
http://www.childline.org.uk

Missing out

People are confused about the rules for adoption

There are many children in care yet the number being adopted is falling.

Only **53%** of people know that adoption agencies need more adopters. In reality, they are desperately needed.

In 2006 the number of children adopted in England was **3,700** but in 2007 it had fallen to **3,300.**

41% of people think the most common reason a child is adopted is because their parents 'give up' their child. Only **29%** of people know that the main reason is abuse or neglect.

Adopters are urgently needed, particularly for older children.

The reasons why children were in need of care (2007)

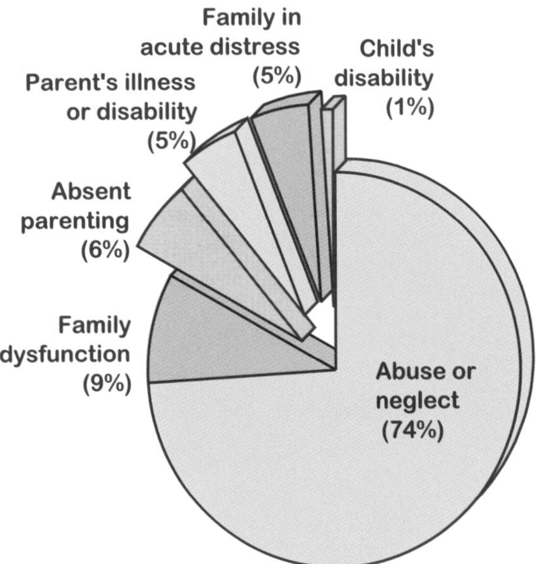

Family in acute distress (5%)
Child's disability (1%)
Parent's illness or disability (5%)
Absent parenting (6%)
Family dysfunction (9%)
Abuse or neglect (74%)

How old were the 3,300 children adopted in 2007?

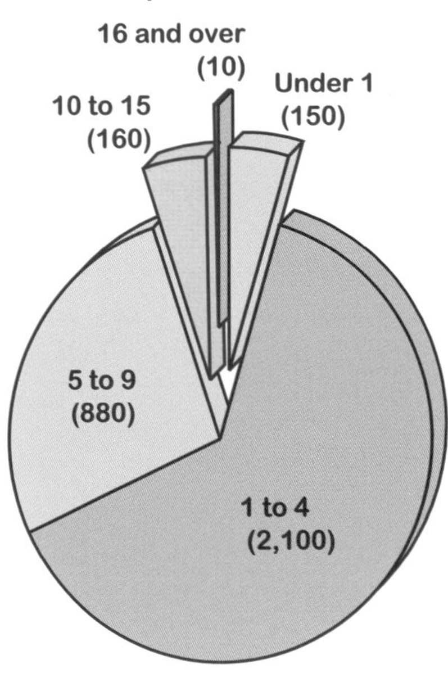

16 and over (10)
Under 1 (150)
10 to 15 (160)
5 to 9 (880)
1 to 4 (2,100)

Many people incorrectly believe the following circumstances stop you adopting:

- **being over 40 (35% believe this)**
- **being unemployed (25%)**
- **being a single man (23%)**
- **being a single woman (14%)**

In fact suitable adopters can come from all backgrounds

(Base: BAAF survey of 2,000 adults)

Source: Department for Children, Schools and Families; British Association for Adoption & Fostering

http://www.dcsf.gov.uk

http://www.baaf.org.uk

Financial issues

From cradle to grave

The cost of key events in life... and death

Raising a child

Total	£ 186,034
Age 19-21	£ 36,746
Age 12-18	£ 43,992
Age 6-11	£ 48,595
Age 2-5	£ 48,517
First year	£ 8,184

Average cost of raising a child from birth to age 21:

£8,859 a year

£738 a month

£24.30 per day

Source: Annual Cost of a Child Survey (2007)

http://www.lv.com

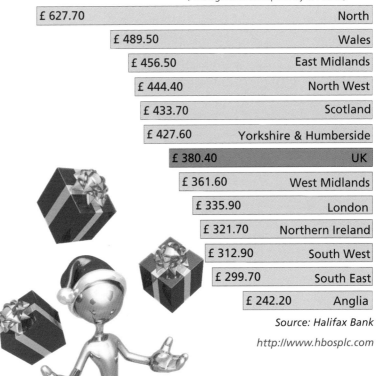

Christmas presents

(Average amount spent by an adult)

North	£ 627.70
Wales	£ 489.50
East Midlands	£ 456.50
North West	£ 444.40
Scotland	£ 433.70
Yorkshire & Humberside	£ 427.60
UK	£ 380.40
West Midlands	£ 361.60
London	£ 335.90
Northern Ireland	£ 321.70
South West	£ 312.90
South East	£ 299.70
Anglia	£ 242.20

Source: Halifax Bank

http://www.hbosplc.com

Running a car

Depreciation	£ 2,357
Fuel	£ 1,129
Cost of Finance	£ 1,160
Insurance	£ 446
Maintenance	£ 273
Tax	£ 129
RAC membership	£ 133
Total cost (per year)	**£ 5,627**
Total cost (per week)	**£ 108.20**

Source: RAC

http://www.aviva.com

Getting married

Insurance	£ 110
The service	£ 520
Reception	£ 4,000
Evening reception	£ 1,700
Entertainment	£ 850
Flowers	£ 685
Decorations	£ 460
Bride's outfit	£ 1,590
Hair and beauty	£ 170
Groom's outfit	£ 200
Attendants' outfits	£ 575
Photography	£ 905
Videography	£ 905
Transport	£ 480
Stationery	£ 465
Wedding cake	£ 370
Wedding rings	£ 630
Gifts	£ 205
Stag & hen nights	£ 280
Honeymoon & first night hotel	£ 3,400
Total	**£ 18,500**

http://www.weddingsday.co.uk

The cost of a UK wedding is anywhere between £15,000 and a staggering £25,000, with the average around £18,500

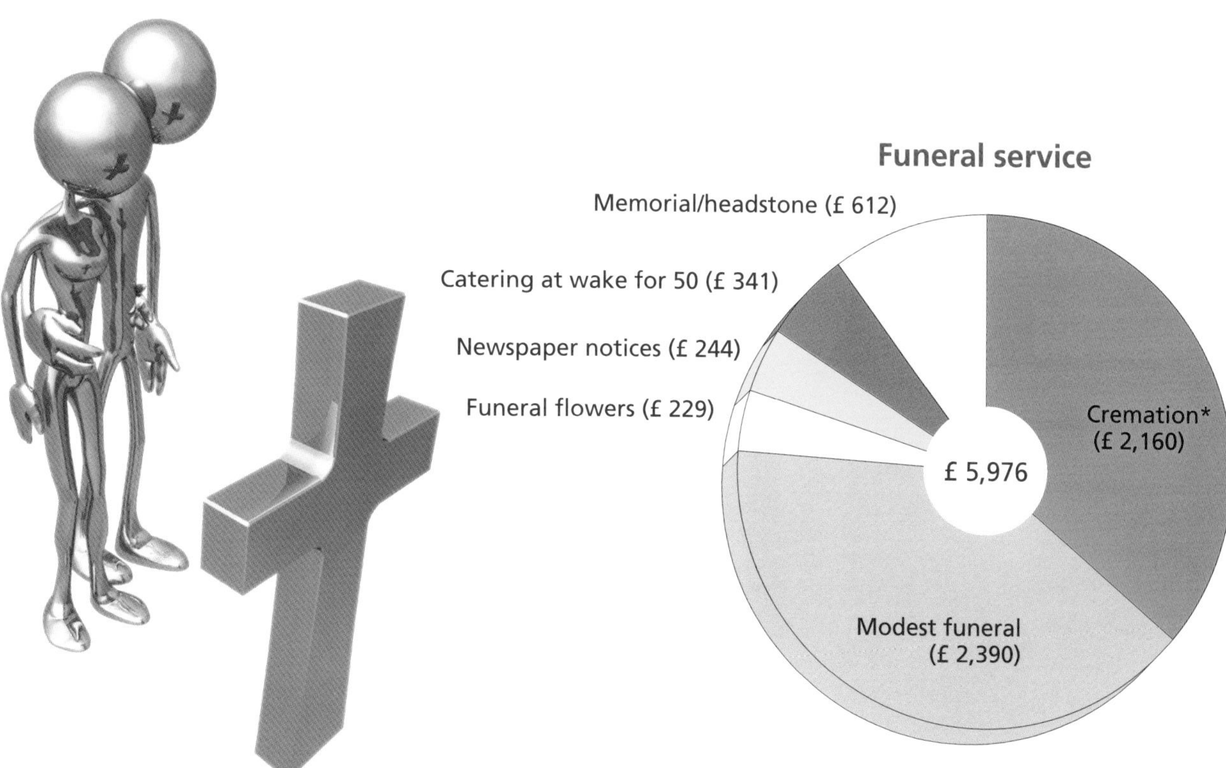
Funeral service
Memorial/headstone (£ 612)
Catering at wake for 50 (£ 341)
Newspaper notices (£ 244)
Funeral flowers (£ 229)
Cremation* (£ 2,160)
£ 5,976
Modest funeral (£ 2,390)

* 72% of funerals are cremations, a burial costs £2,620

Source: AXA
http://www.axa.co.uk

There are considerable regional variations in costs with London having the highest cost of dying £8,020 compared to £4,573 in the North East

Is it worth it?

54% of graduates are leaving university with debts of over £10,000

The maximum student loan for 2007/08 was approximately £4,510 per year

How much do you know about student money issues?

1. **How much does the average student outside London spend in a year?**

   a) £2,210 b) £4,508 c) £6,300 d) £8,810 e) £11,710 f) £12,500

2. **How much of this goes on books?**

   a) £24 b) £47 c) £79 d) £101 e) £112 f) £136

3. **What percentage of students has a part-time job while at university?**

   a) 9% b) 21% c) 44% d) 58% e) 67% f) 85%

4. **What was the average starting salary for graduates in 2007?**

   a) £14,515 b) £15,700 c) £17,549 d) £19,050 e) £21,520 f) £23,350

Answers: 1.d 2.f 3.c 4.a

Weekly student spend (Based on 8 month term time)

Rent	£ 77.30
Alcohol	£ 15.40
Books	£ 8.20
Supermarket food	£ 18.40
Cigarettes	£ 13.90
Going out	£ 10.60
Buying clothes	£ 11.10
Transport	£ 12.30
Utility bills	£ 14.30
Telephone bills	£ 9.00
Eating out	£ 11.60
Total	**£ 202.10**

Tuition fees not included

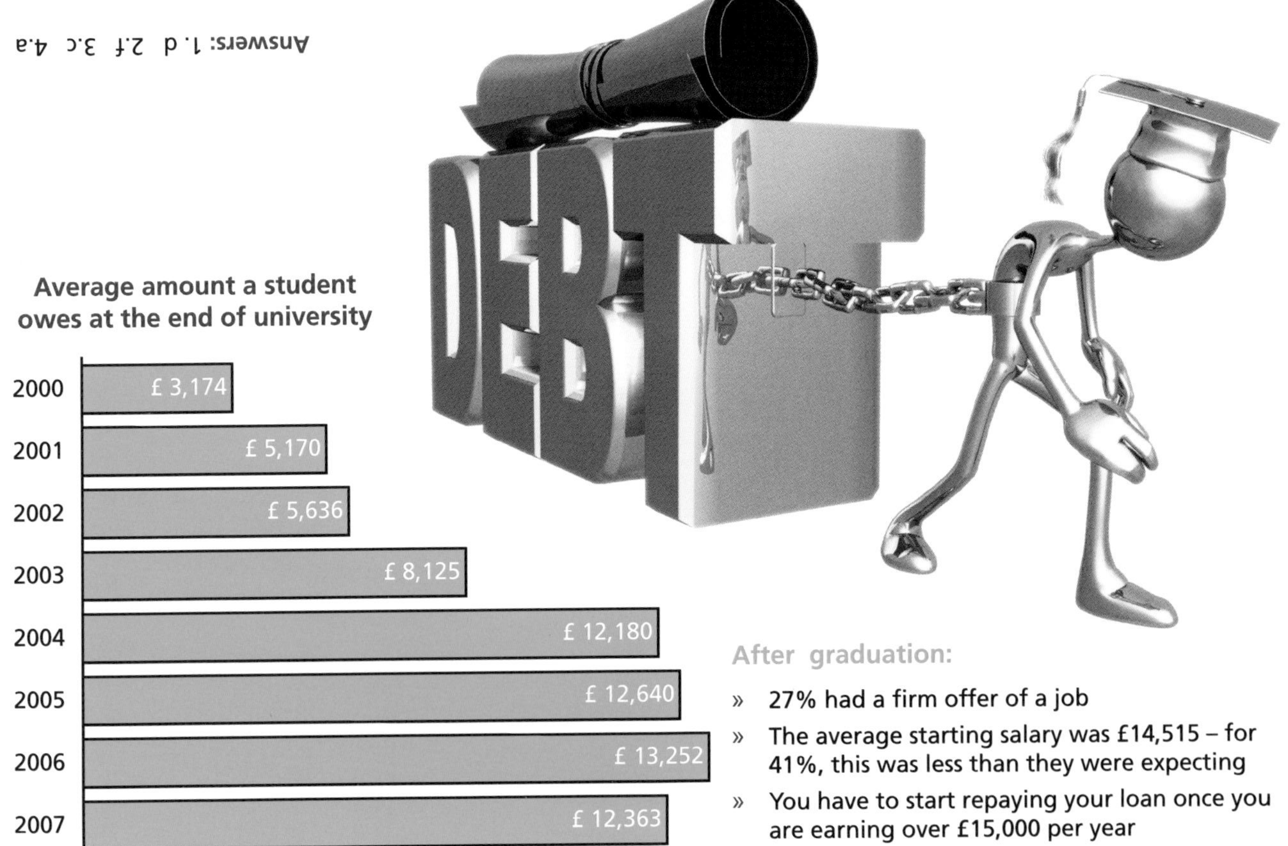
DEBT
Average amount a student owes at the end of university
2000 £ 3,174
2001 £ 5,170
2002 £ 5,636
2003 £ 8,125
2004 £ 12,180
2005 £ 12,640
2006 £ 13,252
2007 £ 12,363

After graduation:

- 27% had a firm offer of a job
- The average starting salary was £14,515 – for 41%, this was less than they were expecting
- You have to start repaying your loan once you are earning over £15,000 per year

Source: NatWest Student Money Matters 2007, creditaction

http://www.natwest.com

http://www.creditaction.org.uk

Life on loan

Debt has become 'a fact of life' amongst young adults

There was a clear feeling amongst the young people interviewed that credit was just a normal part of modern life. It was viewed as a legitimate way to be able to afford more.

" If there is something you really need and you can just pay a bit every week then you're going to buy it"
Damien, South of England

Amount currently owed by 18-24 year olds who had experienced debt

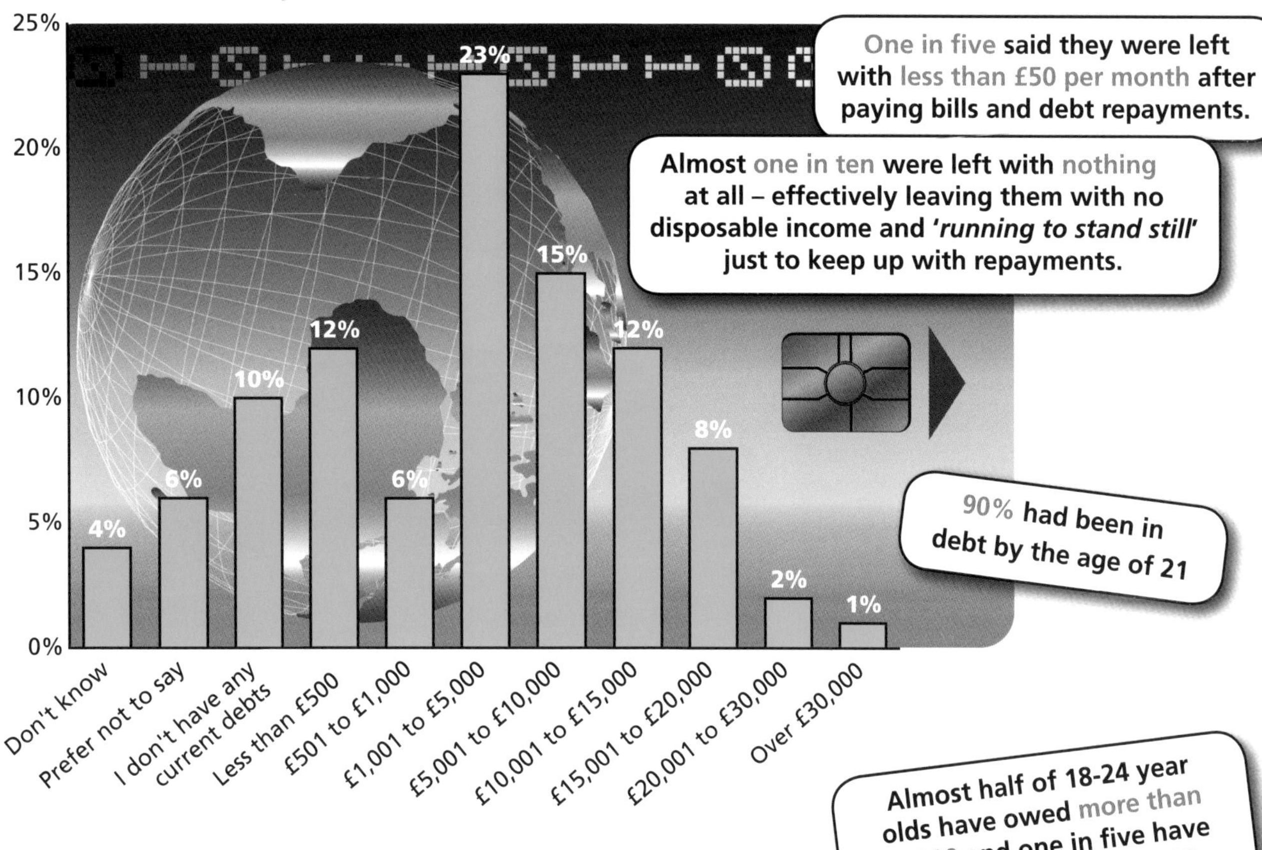

25%
20%
15%
10%
5%
0%
4%
6%
10%
12%
6%
23%
15%
12%
8%
2%
1%
Don't know
Prefer not to say
I don't have any current debts
Less than £500
£501 to £1,000
£1,001 to £5,000
£5,001 to £10,000
£10,001 to £15,000
£15,001 to £20,000
£20,001 to £30,000
Over £30,000

One in five said they were left with less than £50 per month after paying bills and debt repayments.

Almost one in ten were left with nothing at all – effectively leaving them with no disposable income and *'running to stand still'* just to keep up with repayments.

90% had been in debt by the age of 21

Almost half of 18-24 year olds have owed more than £2,000 and one in five have owed more than £10,000

Almost two thirds of those who had borrowed from relatives said that this had led to arguments about money.

" I didn't think it would be such a big deal. I didn't realise how much my mother needed the money back."
Ceri, South East

Most common forms of debt

(respondents were asked to list their main source of debt, and could select up to three categories)

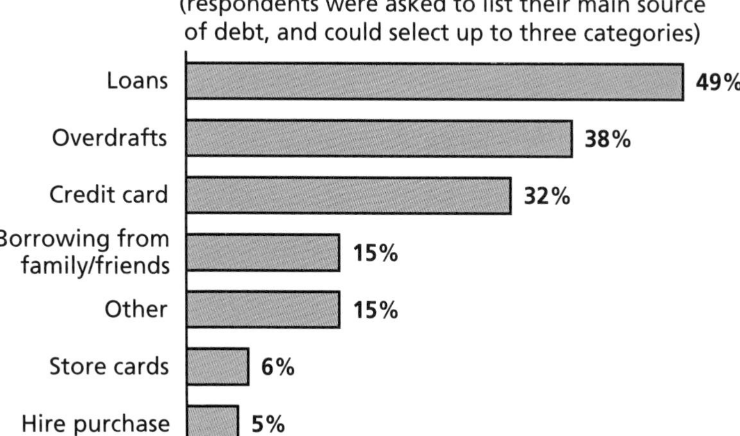

Loans 49%
Overdrafts 38%
Credit card 32%
Borrowing from family/friends 15%
Other 15%
Store cards 6%
Hire purchase 5%

A representative sample of 4,000 18-24 year olds were interviewed in England and Wales in 2 waves in 2008 to provide a picture of debt

Source: Why do the young pay more? Rainer
http://www.raineronline.org

Bare necessities

Many people cannot afford what they really need to live

What is acceptable?

Currently, the Government defines poverty as having an income less than 60% of the national average (median). The MIS (minimum income standard), in contrast, represents what is needed to have a socially acceptable standard of living. It includes items such as dvd players, computers and money to spend socially, the things you need in order to be part of society.

How is it measured?

Individuals from each type of household and all income backgrounds took part in discussions and workshops. The group also included experts such as a nutritionist and a heating engineer. The standards were developed from these discussions.

To afford the basic minimum standard on top of rent, a single person would need to earn £13,400 a year before tax and a couple with two children £26,800. The MIS is above the official "poverty line" for nearly all household groups. This shows that almost everybody classified as being in poverty has an income too low to pay for a standard of living regarded as "adequate" by all members of the public who took part in this research.

"Food and shelter keeps you alive, it doesn't make you live"
Survey participant

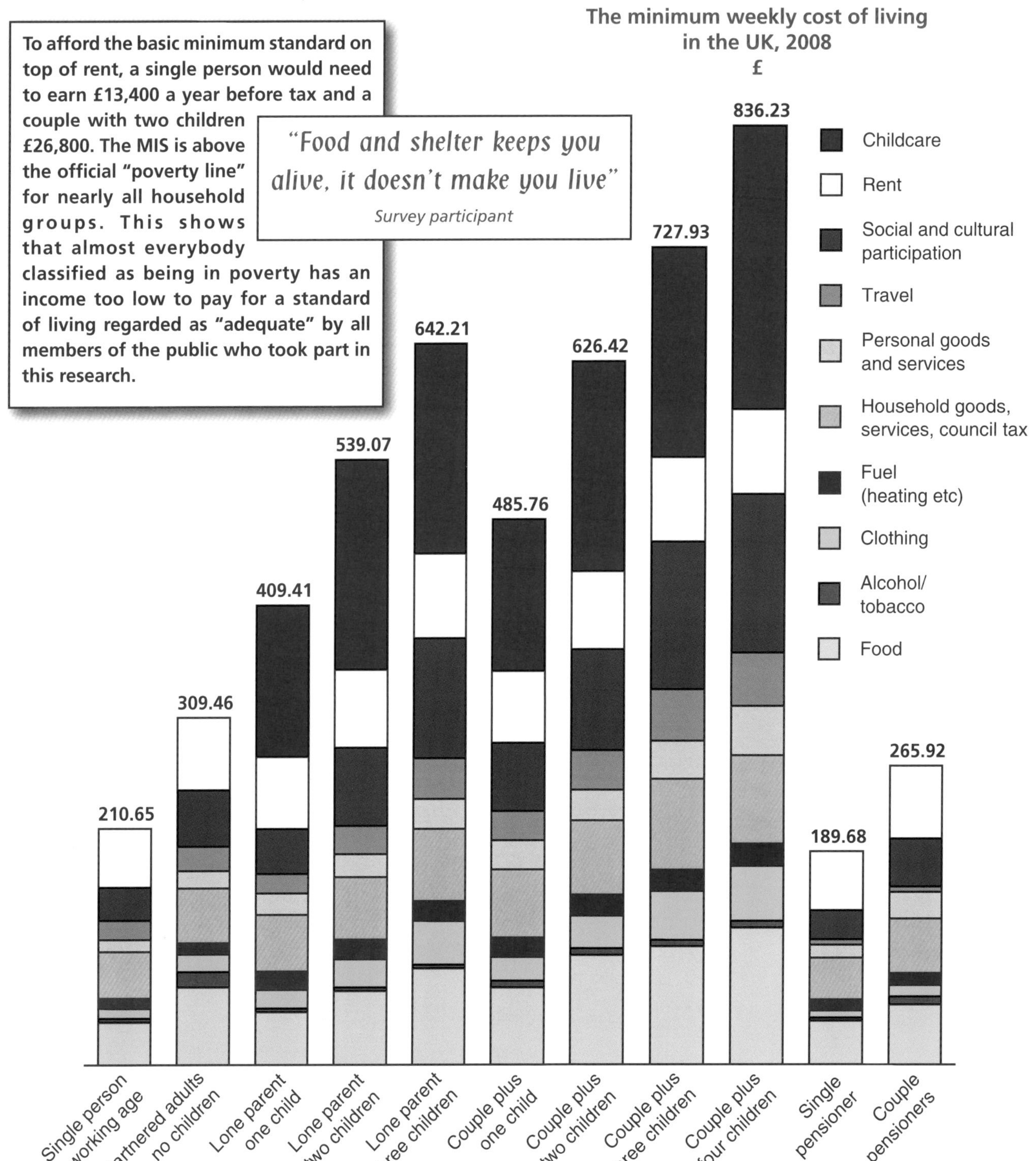

The minimum weekly cost of living in the UK, 2008
£
210.65
309.46
409.41
539.07
642.21
485.76
626.42
727.93
836.23
189.68
265.92
Childcare
Rent
Social and cultural participation
Travel
Personal goods and services
Household goods, services, council tax
Fuel (heating etc)
Clothing
Alcohol/ tobacco
Food
Single person working age
Partnered adults no children
Lone parent one child
Lone parent two children
Lone parent three children
Couple plus one child
Couple plus two children
Couple plus three children
Couple plus four children
Single pensioner
Couple pensioners

Source: Minimum Income Standard, Joseph Rowntree Foundation

http://www.minimumincomestandard.org
http://www.jrf.org.uk

Pricey places

London is the second most expensive place to live

An annual international study by a price comparison site has highlighted the different costs of items around the world, for example a DVD which costs £4.25 in Shanghai is priced at £17.50 in Paris

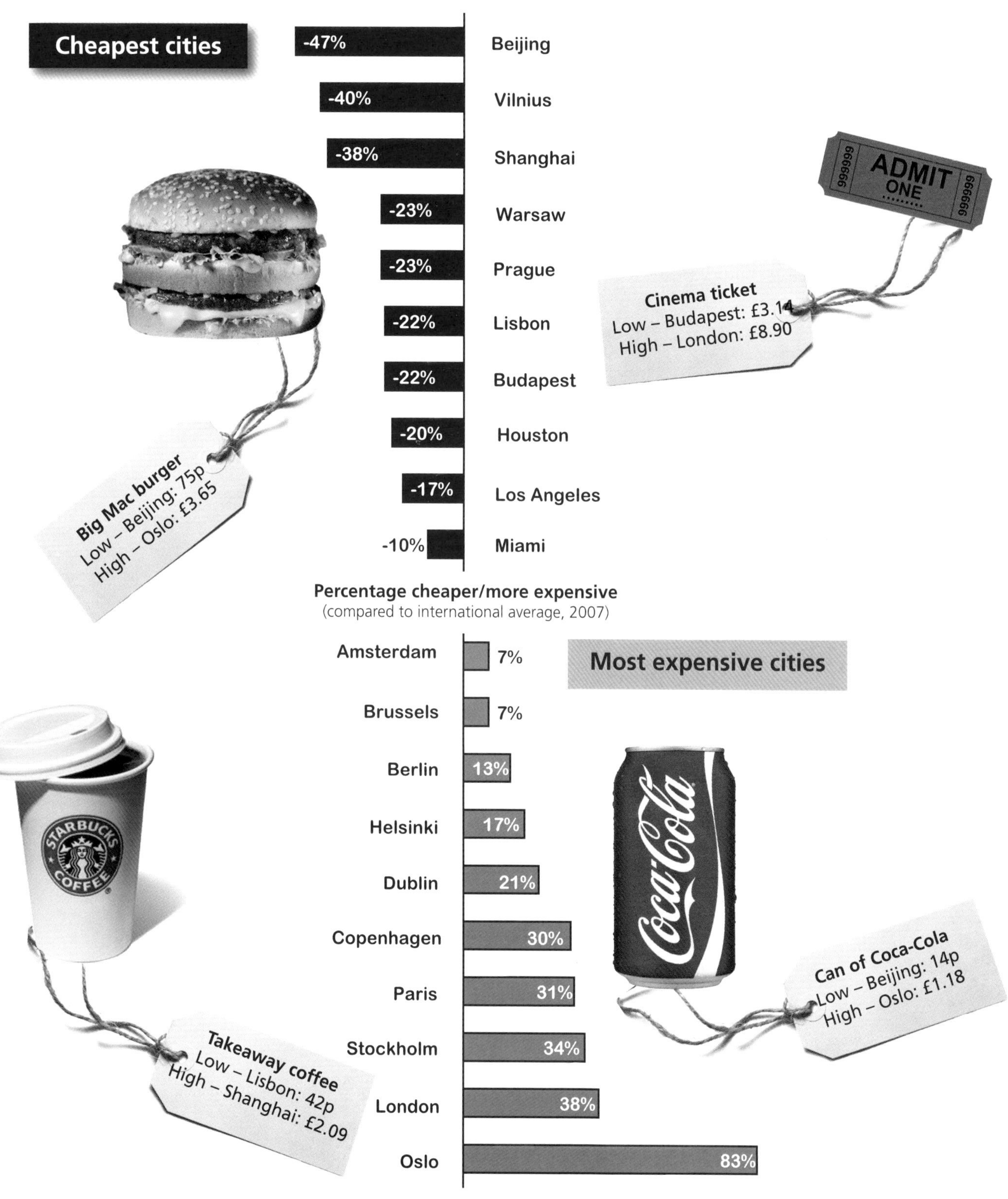

Cities cheaper or more expensive than international average
Cheapest cities
-47% Beijing
-40% Vilnius
-38% Shanghai
-23% Warsaw
-23% Prague
-22% Lisbon
-22% Budapest
-20% Houston
-17% Los Angeles
-10% Miami
Percentage cheaper/more expensive
(compared to international average, 2007)
Most expensive cities
Amsterdam 7%
Brussels 7%
Berlin 13%
Helsinki 17%
Dublin 21%
Copenhagen 30%
Paris 31%
Stockholm 34%
London 38%
Oslo 83%
Big Mac burger
Low – Beijing: 75p
High – Oslo: £3.65
Cinema ticket
Low – Budapest: £3.14
High – London: £8.90
ADMIT ONE
Takeaway coffee
Low – Lisbon: 42p
High – Shanghai: £2.09
Can of Coca-Cola
Low – Beijing: 14p
High – Oslo: £1.18

Base: 29 cities worldwide, surveyed in 2007

Source: http://www.pricerunner.co.uk

The price isn't right

Consumers are facing higher prices for basic goods

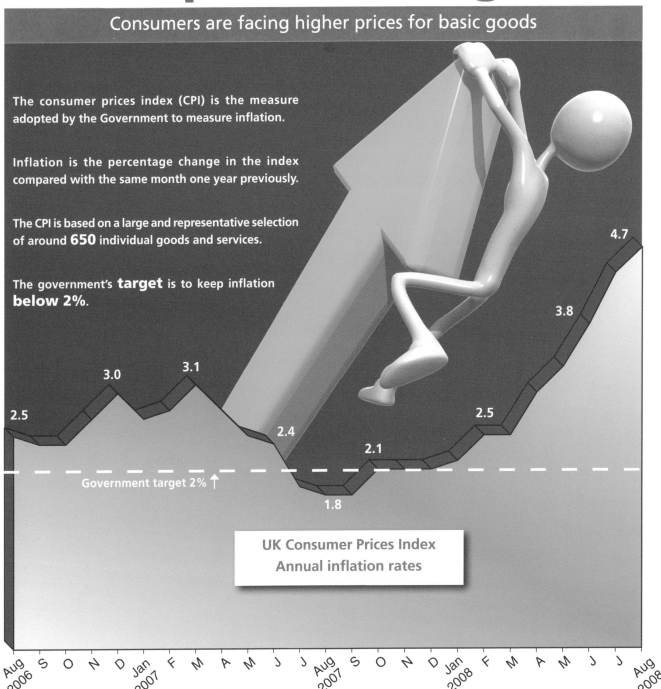

The consumer prices index (CPI) is the measure adopted by the Government to measure inflation.

Inflation is the percentage change in the index compared with the same month one year previously.

The CPI is based on a large and representative selection of around **650** individual goods and services.

The government's **target** is to keep inflation **below 2%**.

12 month % change

2.5 3.0 3.1 2.4 1.8 2.1 2.5 3.8 4.7

Government target 2%

UK Consumer Prices Index
Annual inflation rates

Aug 2006 S O N D Jan 2007 F M A M J J Aug 2007 S O N D Jan 2008 F M A M J J Aug 2008

The most useful way to think about the consumer prices index (CPI) is to imagine a shopping basket containing those goods and services on which people typically spend their money. As the prices of the various items in the basket change over time, so does the total cost of the basket.

The largest upward move came from a rise in average gas and electricity bills this year.

Another large upward move was in the price of bread and cereals mainly because of increases in the price of breakfast cereals and pizzas. Meat prices also rose by more than last year.

There was a further large upward move in miscellaneous good and services, particularly banking services and products for personal care (eg hairdryers and toilet rolls).

There were large downward effects from transport costs and communication.

A Cost of Living Index has been produced by the media. It looks at a smaller basket of essentials than the CPI. It found higher increases than the government's inflation rate as measured by CPI.

The increasing price of food plus increases in the cost of heat, light and petrol is likely to push up the total for 'must pay' bills.

Shopping basket (selected items)	Actual % increase since last year	CPI average
Dairy		19%
6 pints semi-skimmed milk	26.1%	
250g Mild Cheddar cheese	37.2%	
Dozen medium free-range eggs	32.3%	
Bread & cereals		17.4%
800g thick sliced white loaf	50%	
24 biscuits Weetabix	78%	
500g fusilli pasta	113.5%	
Oils & fats		30.1%
1ltr pure corn oil	181.6%	
Coffee, tea & cocoa		8.7%
Nescafé original coffee 200g	12.8%	
80 premium teabags	30.3%	
Meat		17.1%
500g British beef mince	57.1%	
1.55kg fresh chicken	131.5%	
454g – eight thick pork sausages	40.9%	
Vegetables		10.2%
1kg frozen garden peas	68.8%	
2.5kg bag Maris Piper potatoes	25.3%	
Loose iceberg lettuce	15.3%	

Source: Office for National Statistics © Crown copyright 2008 & various
http://www.statistics.gov.uk

Poorer sex

In the EU, single mothers are at greater risk of poverty...

Women living alone with a dependent child are especially vulnerable. In 2005, some **32%** of lone parents in EU-25 countries, almost all of whom were women, had an income which placed them at risk of poverty – defined as having a disposable income below 60% of the national median

Lone parents at risk of poverty in Europe

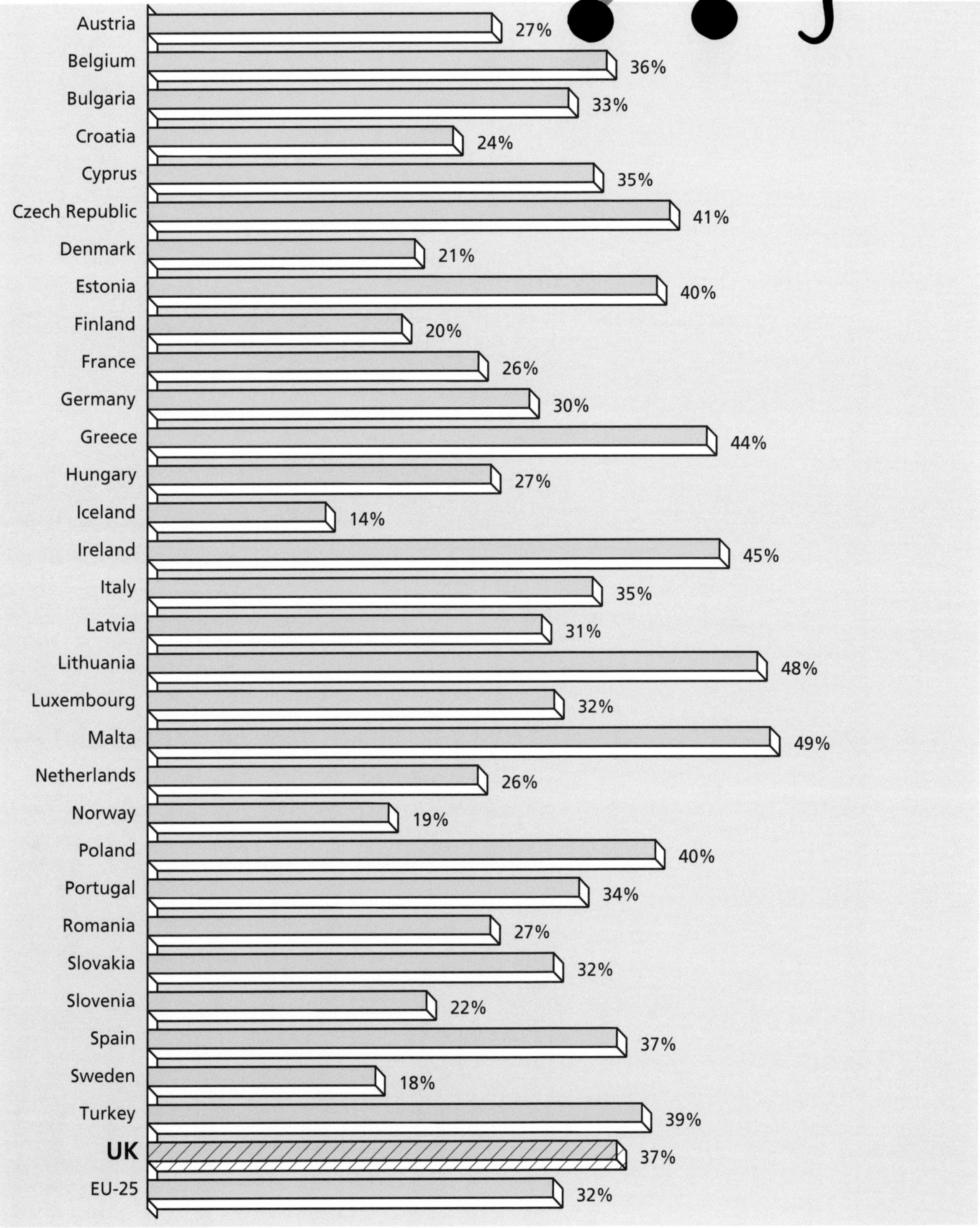

Austria	27%
Belgium	36%
Bulgaria	33%
Croatia	24%
Cyprus	35%
Czech Republic	41%
Denmark	21%
Estonia	40%
Finland	20%
France	26%
Germany	30%
Greece	44%
Hungary	27%
Iceland	14%
Ireland	45%
Italy	35%
Latvia	31%
Lithuania	48%
Luxembourg	32%
Malta	49%
Netherlands	26%
Norway	19%
Poland	40%
Portugal	34%
Romania	27%
Slovakia	32%
Slovenia	22%
Spain	37%
Sweden	18%
Turkey	39%
UK	37%
EU-25	32%

...at retirement age too, women are more likely to be poor

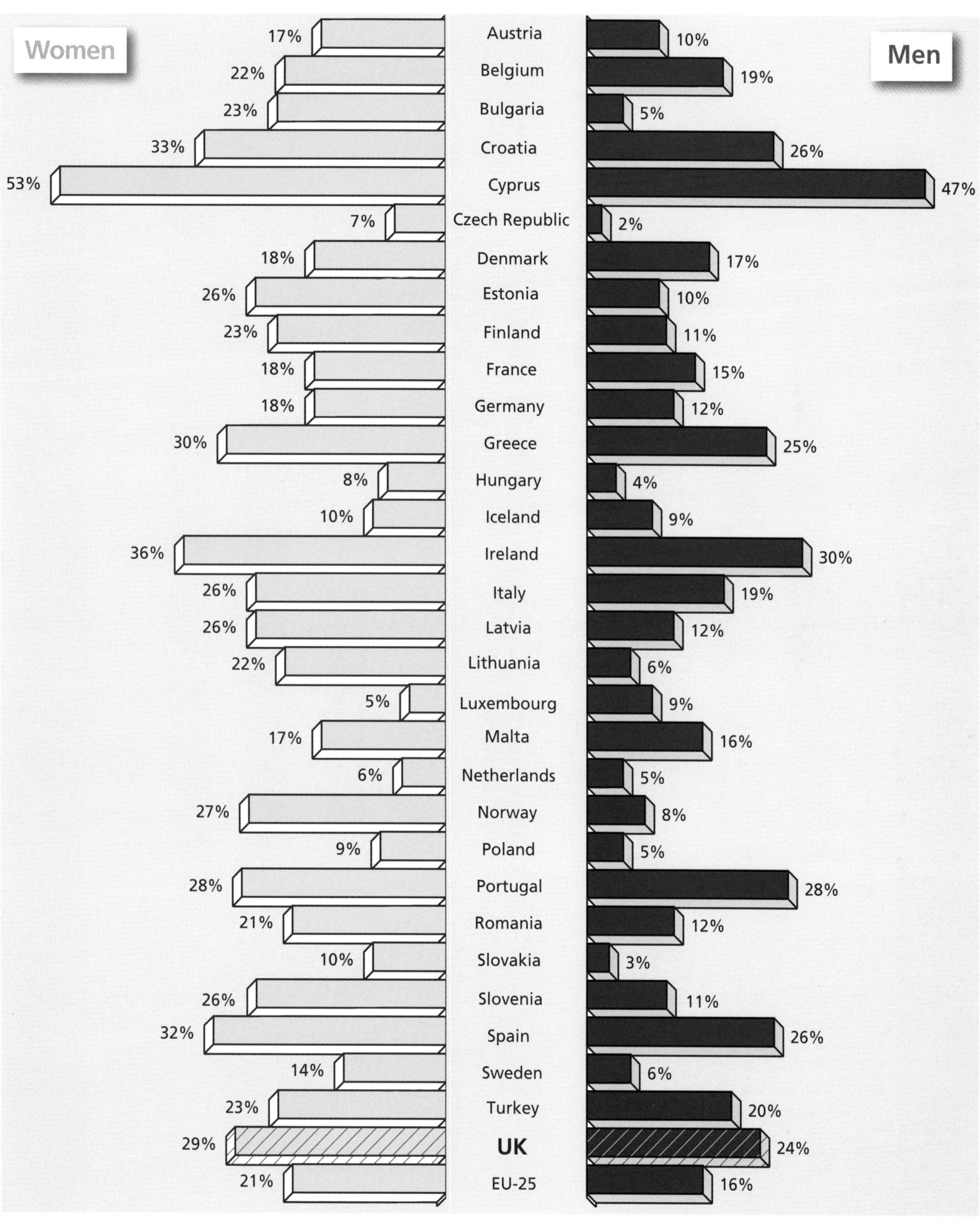

Men and women aged 65 and over living in households at risk of poverty in Europe
Women
Men
Austria 17% 10%
Belgium 22% 19%
Bulgaria 23% 5%
Croatia 33% 26%
Cyprus 53% 47%
Czech Republic 7% 2%
Denmark 18% 17%
Estonia 26% 10%
Finland 23% 11%
France 18% 15%
Germany 18% 12%
Greece 30% 25%
Hungary 8% 4%
Iceland 10% 9%
Ireland 36% 30%
Italy 26% 19%
Latvia 26% 12%
Lithuania 22% 6%
Luxembourg 5% 9%
Malta 17% 16%
Netherlands 6% 5%
Norway 27% 8%
Poland 9% 5%
Portugal 28% 28%
Romania 21% 12%
Slovakia 10% 3%
Slovenia 26% 11%
Spain 32% 26%
Sweden 14% 6%
Turkey 23% 20%
UK 29% 24%
EU-25 21% 16%

Source: Eurostat © European Communities 2008
http://www.europa.eu

Repossessions

Lenders repossessed 21% more homes in 2007

The number of repossessions across the UK rose to 18,900 in the first six months of 2008 – up 48% on the same period the previous year. However, repossessions are a tiny proportion of all loans

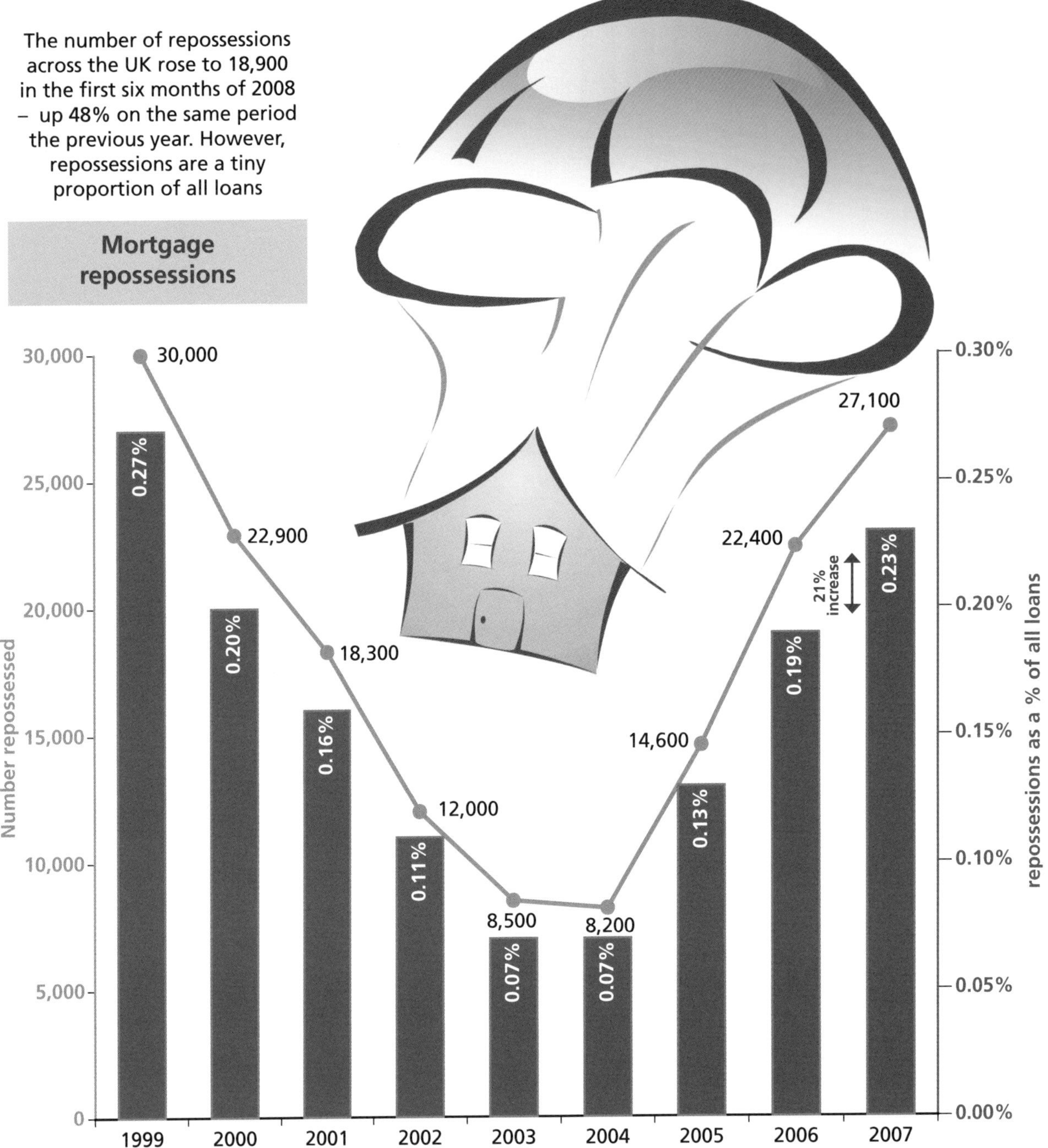

Mortgage repossessions
Number repossessed
repossessions as a % of all loans
30,000
25,000
20,000
15,000
10,000
5,000
0
0.30%
0.25%
0.20%
0.15%
0.10%
0.05%
0.00%
1999
2000
2001
2002
2003
2004
2005
2006
2007
30,000
22,900
18,300
12,000
8,500
8,200
14,600
22,400
27,100
0.27%
0.20%
0.16%
0.11%
0.07%
0.07%
0.13%
0.19%
0.23%
21% increase

In the future:-

- **80% of mortgage lenders believe repossessions will continue to increase**
- **First-time buyers are the most likely to be repossessed followed by those with 100% mortgages and sub-prime mortgage customers**
- **Sub-prime mortgages are those offered to people with inferior credit records or unpredictable incomes, usually at a high rate of interest**
- **32% of lenders anticipate that there will be an increase in cases where the sale of the house doesn't raise enough to pay off the mortgage**
- **The main causes (69%) of repossessions are: couples splitting up, redundancy or business failure**
- **Homeowners can expect added pressures owing to higher energy bills, food costs and more than a million people coming off fixed-rate mortgages**

Source: Council of Mortgage Lenders
http://www.cml.org.uk

Pensioner poverty

Older people are making themselves ill worrying about the future

> **"When older people live on a fixed income it is virtually impossible for them to pull themselves out of poverty. Pensioners often have to cut back on essential household items, just to survive. This is a disgrace."**
>
> ***Mervyn Kohler, special adviser for Help the Aged***

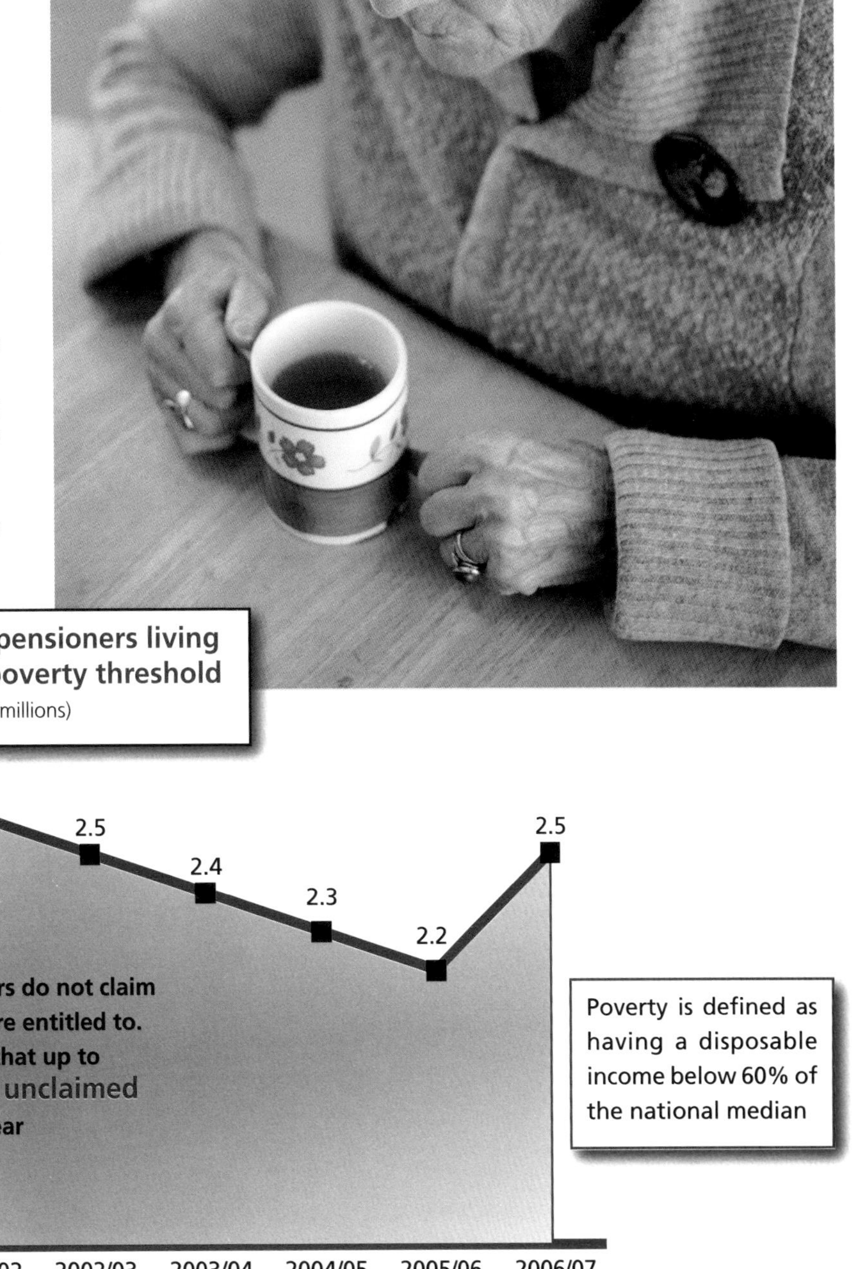

9% of people over 65 feel their general quality of life has improved in the last year while **20%** say it has worsened

23% of people aged 65 and over avoid heating their bedroom, bathroom or living room because they are worried about the cost

Pensioners who are most likely to live in poverty are:

- single and living alone
- owner-occupiers who own their homes outright
- those living in a household headed by someone from an ethnic minority group

The older the pensioners, the greater the likelihood of low income

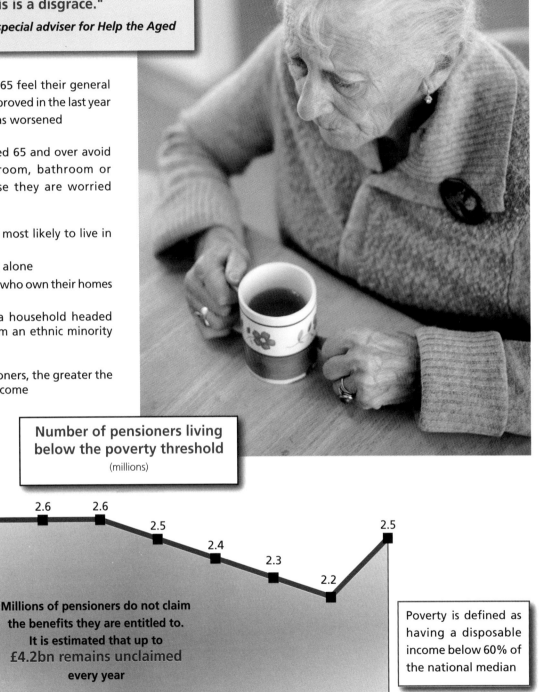

Number of pensioners living below the poverty threshold
(millions)

	Millions
1998/99	2.8
1999/00	2.6
2000/01	2.6
2001/02	2.6
2002/03	2.5
2003/04	2.4
2004/05	2.3
2005/06	2.2
2006/07	2.5

Millions of pensioners do not claim the benefits they are entitled to. It is estimated that up to £4.2bn remains unclaimed every year

Poverty is defined as having a disposable income below 60% of the national median

NB before housing costs

Source: Department for Work & Pensions © Crown copyright 2008, Help the Aged
http://www.dwp.gov.uk
http://www.helptheaged.org.uk

Worthy cause

What does our giving say about our values?

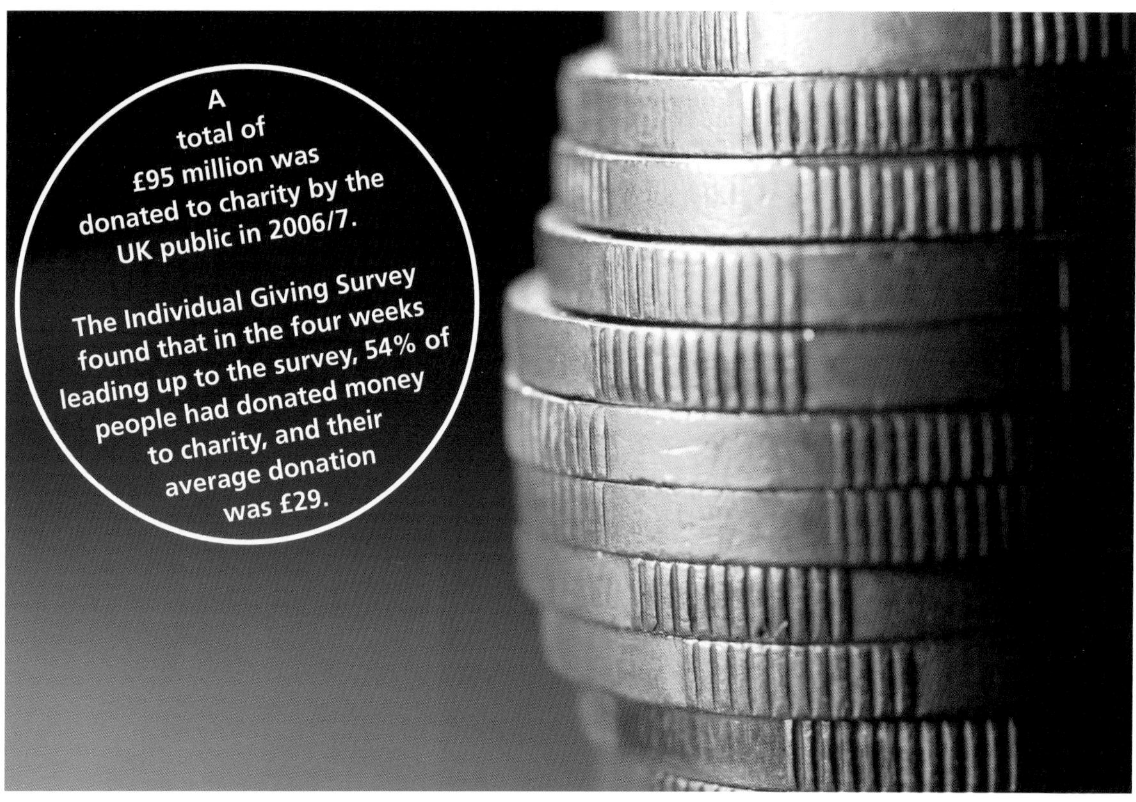
A total of £95 million was donated to charity by the UK public in 2006/7.
The Individual Giving Survey found that in the four weeks leading up to the survey, 54% of people had donated money to charity, and their average donation was £29.

The survey found that more money is being donated to charity by regular giving than by spontaneous donation.

The amount donated through regular giving increased from 22% in 2004/05 to 29% in 2006/07.

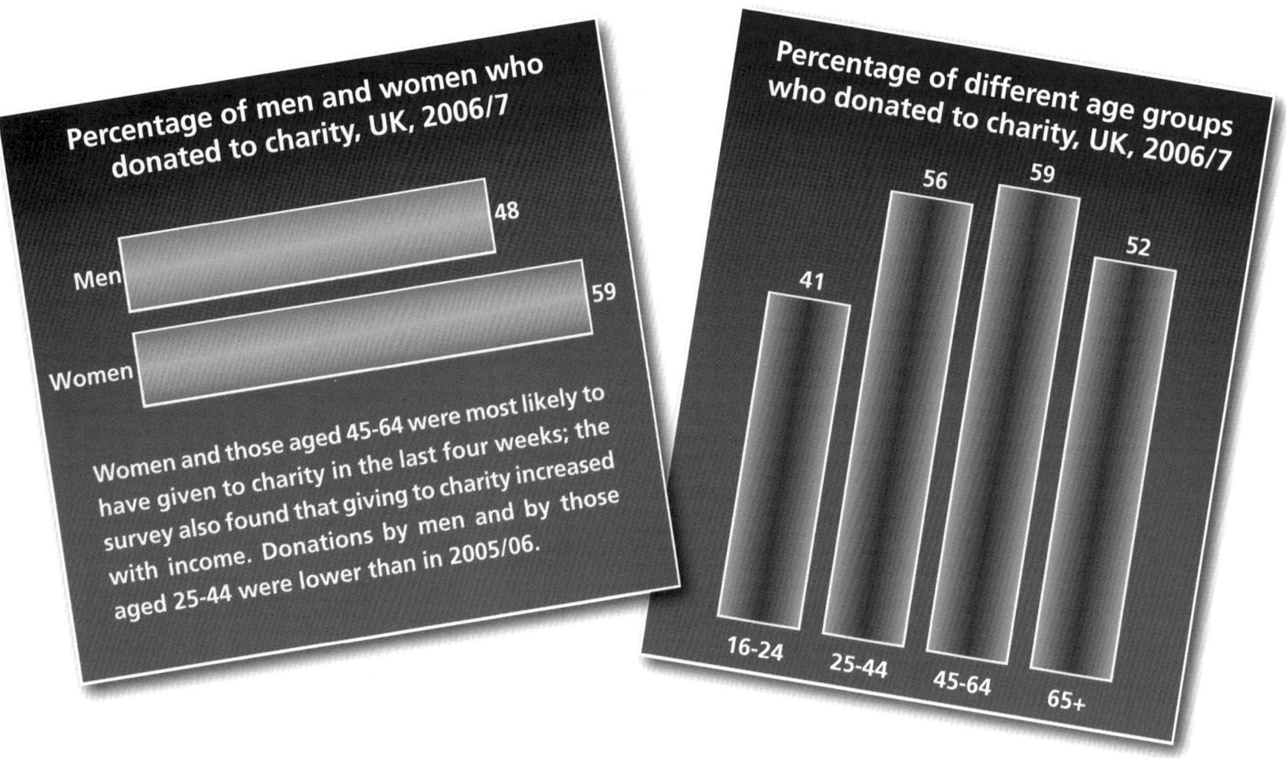
Percentage of men and women who donated to charity, UK, 2006/7
Men
48
Women
59
Women and those aged 45-64 were most likely to have given to charity in the last four weeks; the survey also found that giving to charity increased with income. Donations by men and by those aged 25-44 were lower than in 2005/06.
Percentage of different age groups who donated to charity, UK, 2006/7
41
56
59
52
16-24
25-44
45-64
65+

Which charities receive the largest share? UK, 2006/07

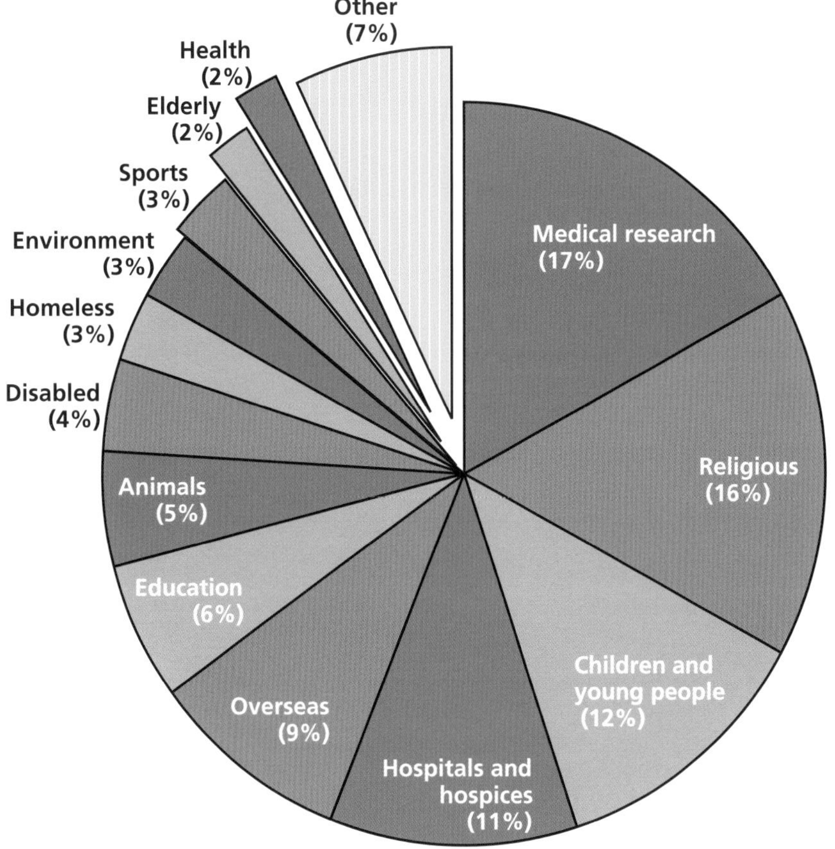
Other (7%)
Health (2%)
Elderly (2%)
Sports (3%)
Environment (3%)
Homeless (3%)
Disabled (4%)
Animals (5%)
Education (6%)
Overseas (9%)
Hospitals and hospices (11%)
Children and young people (12%)
Religious (16%)
Medical research (17%)

Medical research received the largest share of the total UK donations in 2006/07, as it has done in previous years.

The share of the total given to religious causes has decreased since 2005/06, while the share given to educational charities has increased.

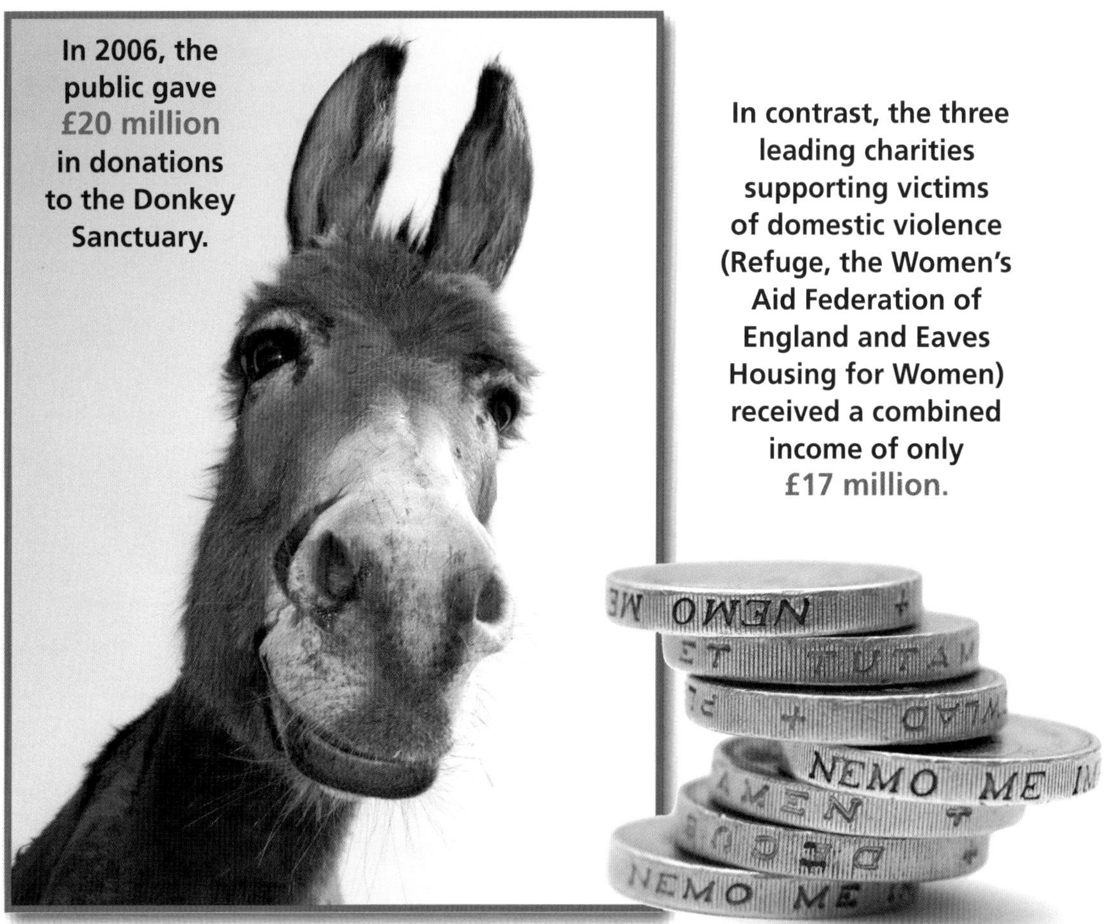
In 2006, the public gave £20 million in donations to the Donkey Sanctuary.
NEMO ME

In contrast, the three leading charities supporting victims of domestic violence (Refuge, the Women's Aid Federation of England and Eaves Housing for Women) received a combined income of only £17 million.

Source: UK Giving Report 2007 © Charities Aid Foundation and National Council for Voluntary Organisations.

https://www.cafonline.org

Fraud abroad

Chip and pin has shifted fraud overseas

Credit and debit card fraud losses on UK issued cards

Fraud Type	2004	2005	2006	2007
Phone, internet and mail order (card-not-present fraud)	£150.8m	£183.2m	£212.7m	£290.5m
Counterfeit (skimmed/cloned) card fraud	£129.7m	£96.8m	£98.6m	£144.3m
Fraud on lost or stolen cards	£114. 4m	£89.0m	£68.5m	£56.2m
Card ID theft	£36.9m	£30.5m	£31.9m	£34.1m
Mail non-receipt	£72.9m	£40.0m	£15.4 m	£10.2m
Total	£504.7m	£439.5m	£427.1m	£535.3m

The rise in overall card fraud is being mainly driven by criminals working overseas using stolen UK card details.

A report by web security company Symantec revealed that bank account details were selling for as little as £5 as part of a thriving trade in stolen information on the internet.

Chip and PIN

Chip and PIN was introduced on 14/2/06

Fraud abroad now accounts for 39% of total card fraud losses in 2007. There was a £90.5 million rise in fraud abroad as more UK card details are being stolen for use in countries yet to upgrade to chip and PIN.

Banks throughout Europe have agreed to bring in chip and PIN cards by 2010.

Card-not-present fraud losses have to be seen in the context of huge increases in the amount of people shopping online and over the phone, and the numbers of shops offering telephone or online shopping. From 2001 to 2006 card-not-present fraud losses rose by 122%; over the same time period, the total value of online shopping transactions alone increased by 358% (up from £6.6 billion in 2001 to £30.2 billion in 2006).

Percentage change +/- (2006/2007)

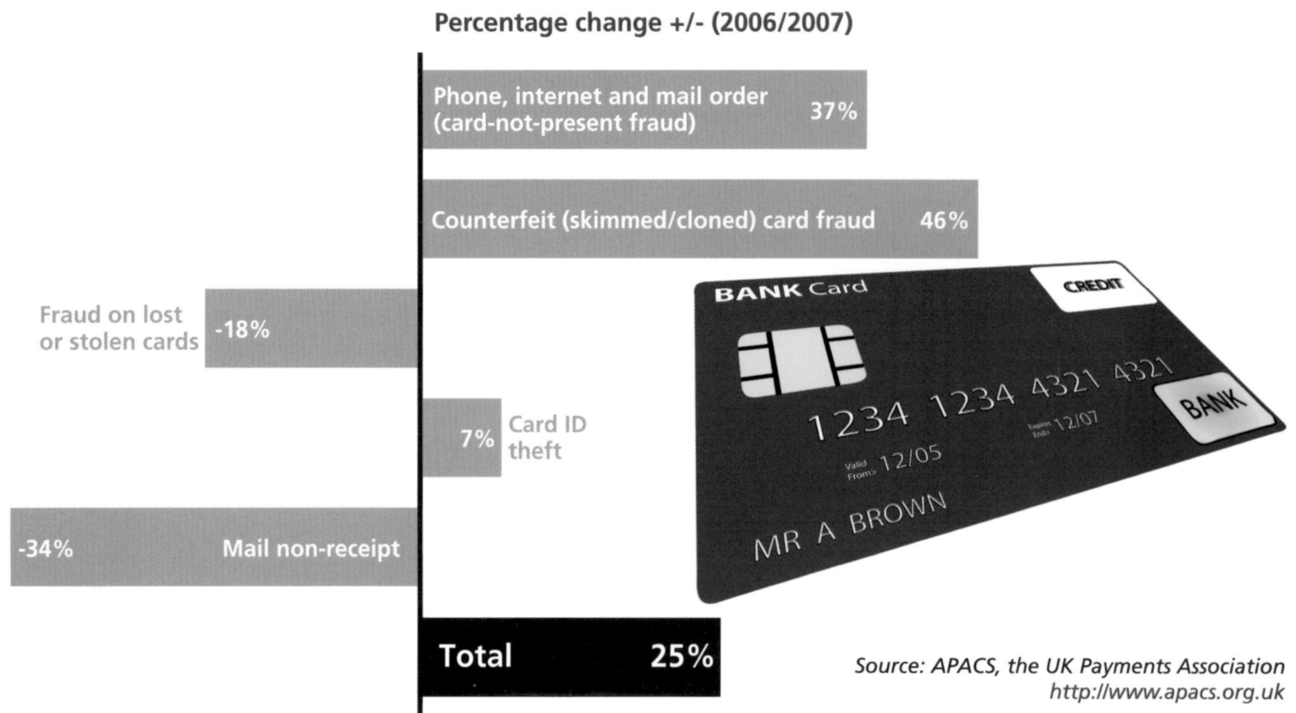
Phone, internet and mail order (card-not-present fraud) 37%
Counterfeit (skimmed/cloned) card fraud 46%
Fraud on lost or stolen cards -18%
7% Card ID theft
-34% Mail non-receipt
Total 25%
BANK Card
CREDIT
1234 1234 4321 4321
BANK
Valid From> 12/05
12/07
MR A BROWN

Source: APACS, the UK Payments Association http://www.apacs.org.uk

Food & drink

An apple a day? More like 4 million!

A quarter of the food we throw away is unopened or untouched

In the UK we throw away **6.7 million tonnes** of food every year, roughly a third of everything we buy. Most of this is avoidable and could have been eaten if only we had planned, stored and managed it better. Less than a fifth is truly unavoidable – things like bones, cores and peelings.

Nearly one quarter of the **4.1 million tonnes** of avoidable food waste is thrown away whole, untouched or unopened. Of this, at least **340,000 tonnes** is still in date when thrown away. A further **1.2 million** tonnes is simply left on our plates. This all adds up to a story of staggering wastefulness.

Number of avoidable pieces of food wasted per day in the UK

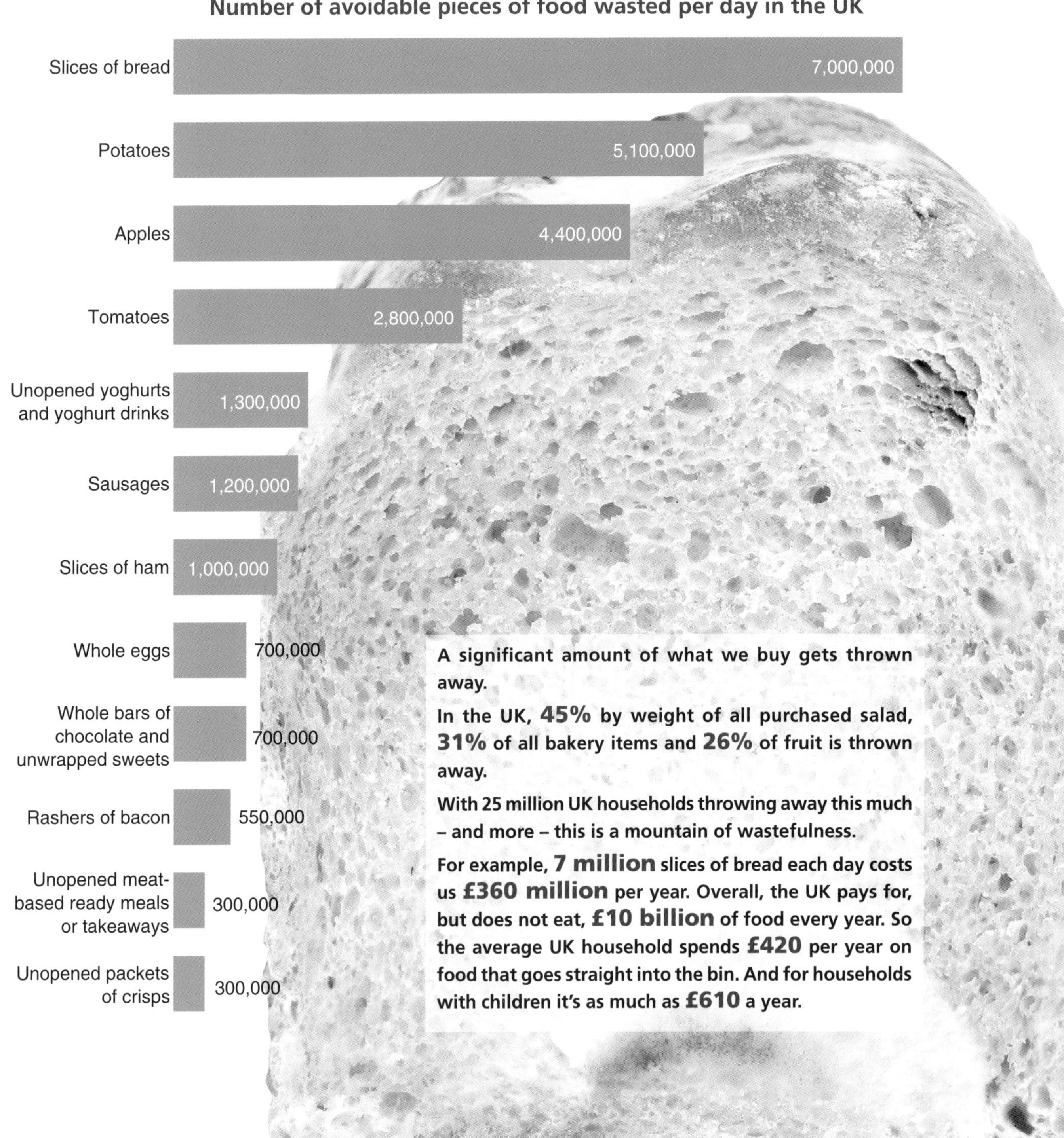
Slices of bread 7,000,000
Potatoes 5,100,000
Apples 4,400,000
Tomatoes 2,800,000
Unopened yoghurts and yoghurt drinks 1,300,000
Sausages 1,200,000
Slices of ham 1,000,000
Whole eggs 700,000
Whole bars of chocolate and unwrapped sweets 700,000
Rashers of bacon 550,000
Unopened meat-based ready meals or takeaways 300,000
Unopened packets of crisps 300,000

A significant amount of what we buy gets thrown away.

In the UK, 45% by weight of all purchased salad, 31% of all bakery items and 26% of fruit is thrown away.

With 25 million UK households throwing away this much – and more – this is a mountain of wastefulness.

For example, 7 million slices of bread each day costs us £360 million per year. Overall, the UK pays for, but does not eat, £10 billion of food every year. So the average UK household spends £420 per year on food that goes straight into the bin. And for households with children it's as much as £610 a year.

Every tonne of food waste is responsible for 4.5 tonnes of CO_2

Food waste
=
CO2
CO2
CO2
CO2
CO2

Not only is throwing away food a waste of money, but the environment and our climate also suffer as a result. Food waste sent to landfill generates methane, a greenhouse gas far more powerful than carbon dioxide (CO_2), that accelerates the problem of global warming. But that's only a small part of the environmental damage we cause by wasting food. More important are the significant amounts of greenhouse gases emitted by producing, processing and transporting food to us – that's senseless if the food isn't even used.

You only need to look at the graph above to imagine how much CO_2 we produce in the UK alone. This all leads to a significant environmental impact. Stopping this waste of good food could avoid 18 million tonnes of CO_2 being emitted each year, the equivalent of taking one in five cars off the road.

Estimated annual weight of the top 10 items of avoidable food waste (tonnes)

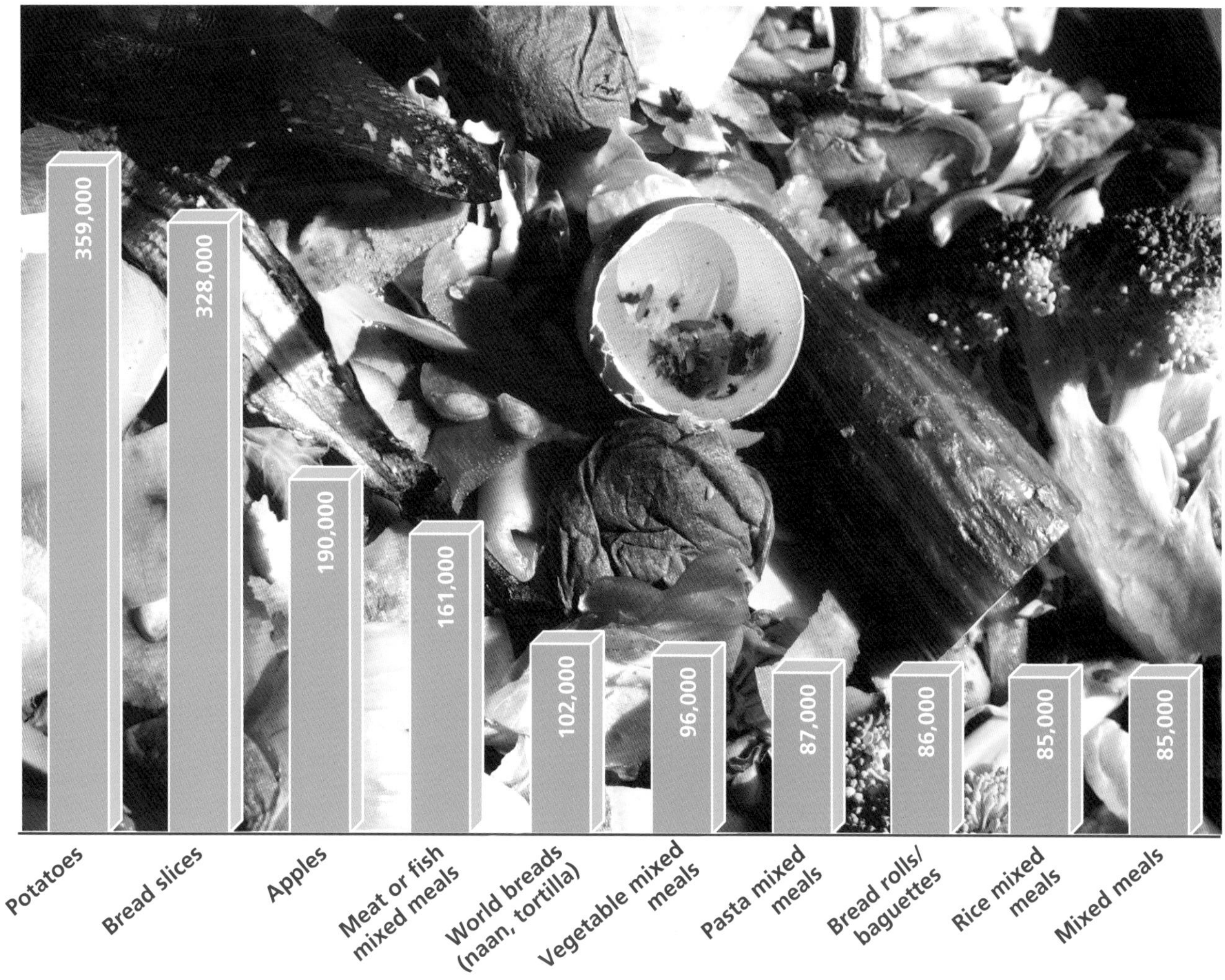

Potatoes	359,000
Bread slices	328,000
Apples	190,000
Meat or fish mixed meals	161,000
World breads (naan, tortilla)	102,000
Vegetable mixed meals	96,000
Pasta mixed meals	87,000
Bread rolls/ baguettes	86,000
Rice mixed meals	85,000
Mixed meals	85,000

Source: The Food We Waste, Wrap

http://www.wrap.org.uk/

Organic obstacles

'Going organic' may not be so simple

- In 2006, retail sales of organic products in the UK were worth an estimated £1,937 million – representing a **22% increase** since 2005.
- The retail market for organic products has grown by an average of **27%** a year over the last decade.
- The UK organic market is now the **third largest** in Europe after Germany and Italy.

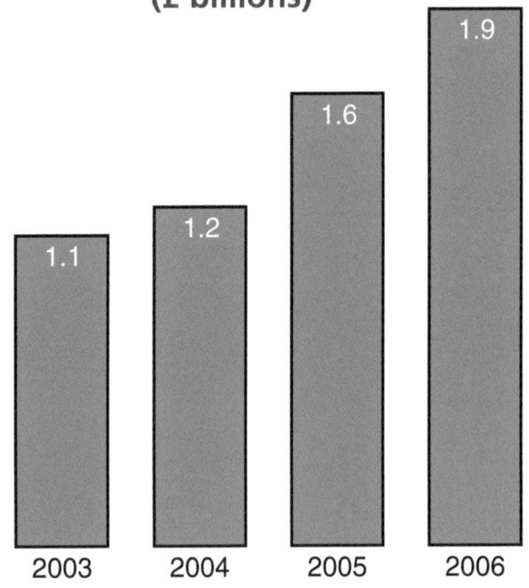
Annual organic sales figures
(£ billions)
1.1
1.2
1.6
1.9
2003
2004
2005
2006

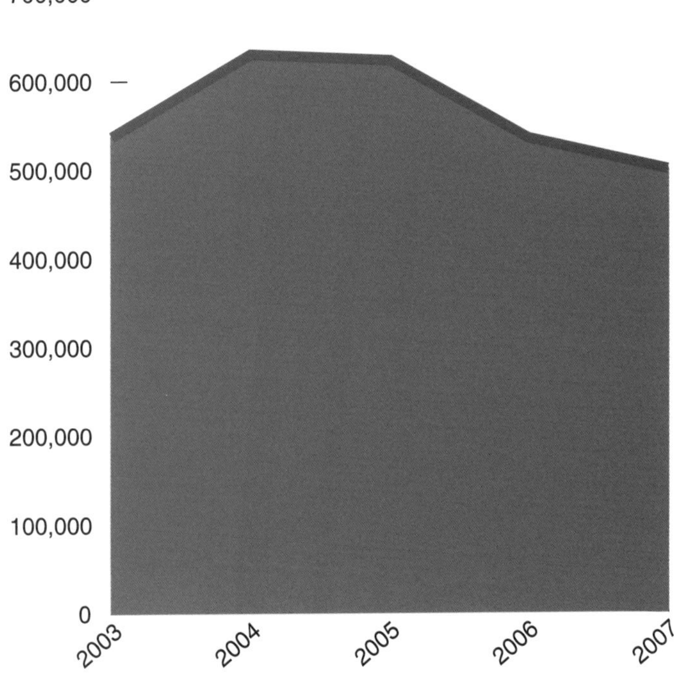
Hectares of organic land UK
700,000
600,000
500,000
400,000
300,000
200,000
100,000
0
2003
2004
2005
2006
2007

- The organic poultry market continues to increase rapidly, showing no signs of slowing down.
- An estimated **12.4 million** organic table birds were consumed in 2006 – an increase of **39%** since 2005.
- The combined sales value of free range and organic eggs exceeded that of cage eggs for the first time in 2006.
- The amount of land producing organic food in the UK increased dramatically from **69,000** hectares in 1998 following the introduction of aid to organic farmers. However, many of the farmers encouraged to convert their land found they didn't make the profit they expected.
- Organically managed land only accounts for approximately **3.5%** of the UK's total agricultural land area and approximately **1.6%** of all farms in the UK.

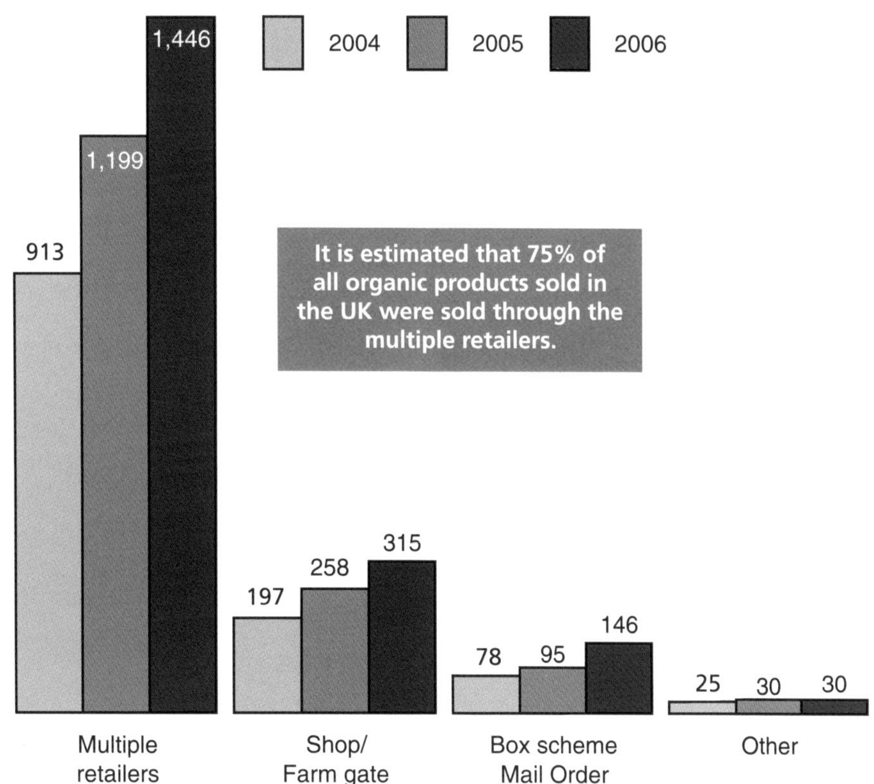
Retail sales of organic products by outlets
(£ millions)
2004
2005
2006
913
1,199
1,446
197
258
315
78
95
146
25
30
30
Multiple retailers
Shop/ Farm gate
Box scheme Mail Order
Other
It is estimated that 75% of all organic products sold in the UK were sold through the multiple retailers.

If organic sales continue to increase, yet the amount of organic land in the UK continues to decline, where are the organic products we are buying coming from?

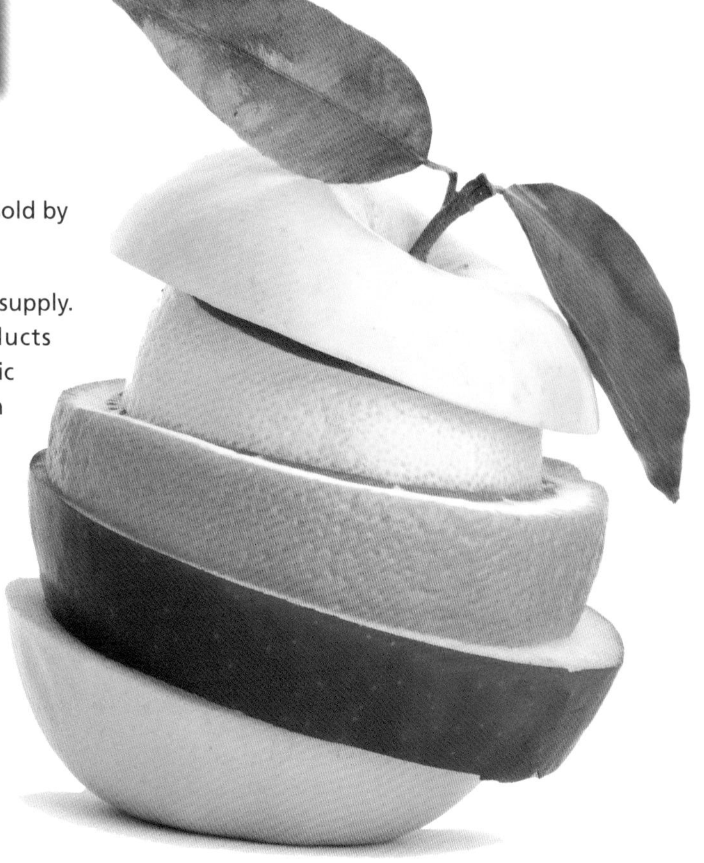

In 2006, an average of 66% of the organic produce sold by the multiple retailers was sourced in the UK.

However, retailers always try to maintain a constant supply. While demand for organic pork and pork products continued to increase in 2006, the number of organic pigs being produced in the UK declined, due to high production costs. As a result, some multiple retailers imported organic pork from Europe mainly Denmark and the Netherlands.

UK consumers are used to having a year round supply of products, including out of season and exotic foods. Some examples of organic products imported to meet demand in UK supermarkets are pears from Italy, avocados and oranges from South Africa, apples and kiwi fruit from New Zealand.

Such imports reduce the environmental credentials of organic food since they involve transport - often by air.

Source: Organic Market Report 2007; Defra
http://www.soilassociation.org

Healthy choice

Could consumers influence how animals are treated?

60 billion animals are farmed for food worldwide every year and the vast majority are reared intensively. EU consumers are increasingly concerned about animal welfare when they shop.

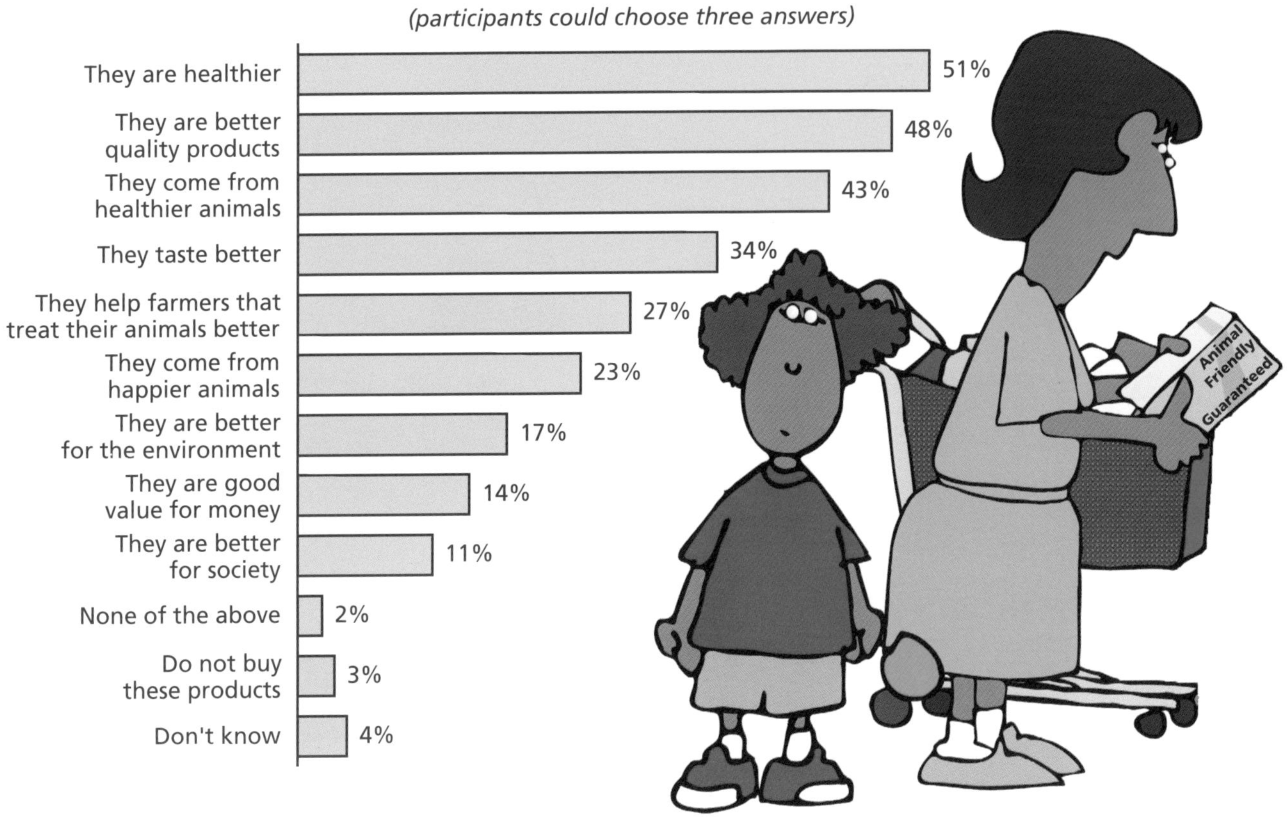

From the following list, what would be your main reasons why you would buy food products produced in a more animal friendly way (eg free-range systems)?
(participants could choose three answers)
They are healthier 51%
They are better quality products 48%
They come from healthier animals 43%
They taste better 34%
They help farmers that treat their animals better 27%
They come from happier animals 23%
They are better for the environment 17%
They are good value for money 14%
They are better for society 11%
None of the above 2%
Do not buy these products 3%
Don't know 4%
Animal Friendly Guaranteed

Across the range of EU countries, the pattern of results changes. In Greece and Cyprus, the healthy nature of these products was mentioned by **78%** and **84%** of respondents respectively.

In the Netherlands and Sweden, less than one third of those polled mentioned healthier products. Instead the emphasis is more on the well-being of farmed animals. At least **4 out of every 10** in both these countries mentioned the view that such products come from happier animals.

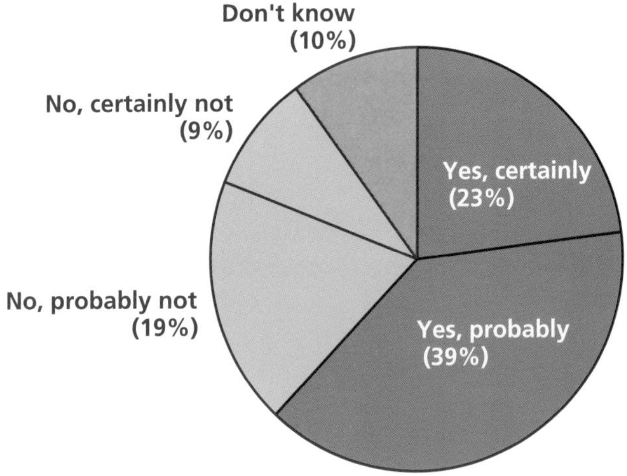

Would you be willing to change your usual place of shopping in order to be able to buy more animal welfare friendly food products?
Don't know (10%)
No, certainly not (9%)
Yes, certainly (23%)
No, probably not (19%)
Yes, probably (39%)

Source: Supermarkets and Farm Animal Welfare, Compassion in World Farming, Attitudes of EU citizens towards Animal Welfare, Eurobarometer

http://ec.europa.eu/public_opinion/index_en.htm, http://www.ciwf.org.uk

Decade of trade

Fair trade goes from strength to strength

Fair trade focuses particularly on exports from developing countries to developed countries.

More than 2,000 products in the UK from 58 developing countries now carry the FAIRTRADE mark.

Food and drink products that are now available with the FAIRTRADE mark include: bananas, cocoa, coffee, dried fruit, fresh fruit and fresh vegetables, honey, juices, nuts/oil seeds and purees, quinoa, rice, spices, sugar, tea, wine.

While the sale of the most popular food and drink items totalled £336 million, sales of FAIRTRADE flowers, wine, cotton and other items have also increased.

In 2007 wine sales reached £8.2 million and flowers reached £24 million. The most impressive increase was in FAIRTRADE cotton sales which increased 1,655% by volume and 658% by retail value, totalling £34.8 million.

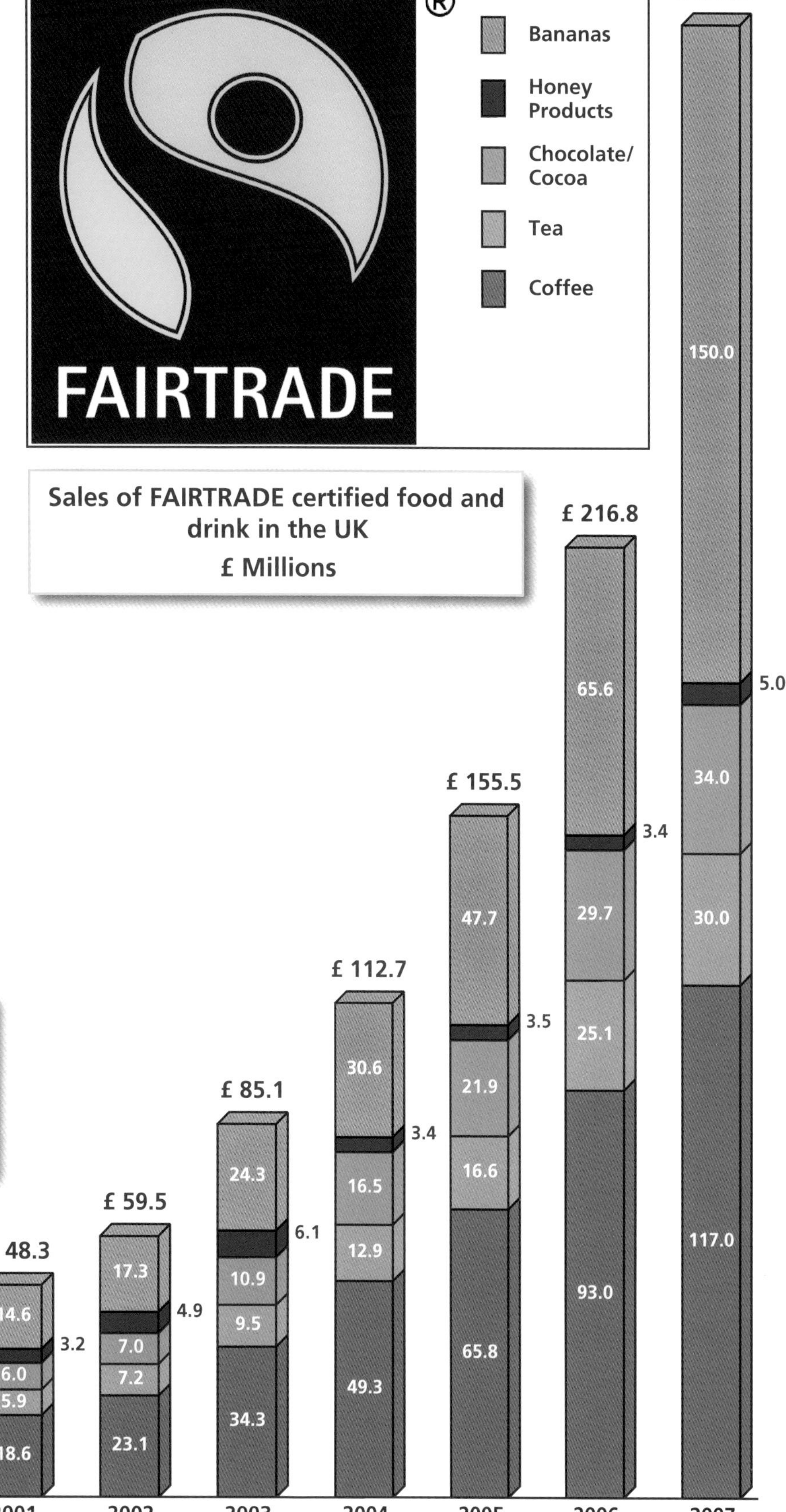
FAIRTRADE
®
Bananas
Honey Products
Chocolate/ Cocoa
Tea
Coffee
Sales of FAIRTRADE certified food and drink in the UK
£ Millions
£ 16.7
1.0
2.0
13.7
£ 21.8
2.3
4.5
15.0
£ 32.9
7.8
0.9
3.6
5.1
15.5
£ 48.3
14.6
3.2
6.0
5.9
18.6
£ 59.5
17.3
4.9
7.0
7.2
23.1
£ 85.1
24.3
6.1
10.9
9.5
34.3
£ 112.7
30.6
3.4
16.5
12.9
49.3
£ 155.5
47.7
3.5
21.9
16.6
65.8
£ 216.8
65.6
3.4
29.7
25.1
93.0
£ 336.0
150.0
5.0
34.0
30.0
117.0
1998
1999
2000
2001
2002
2003
2004
2005
2006
2007

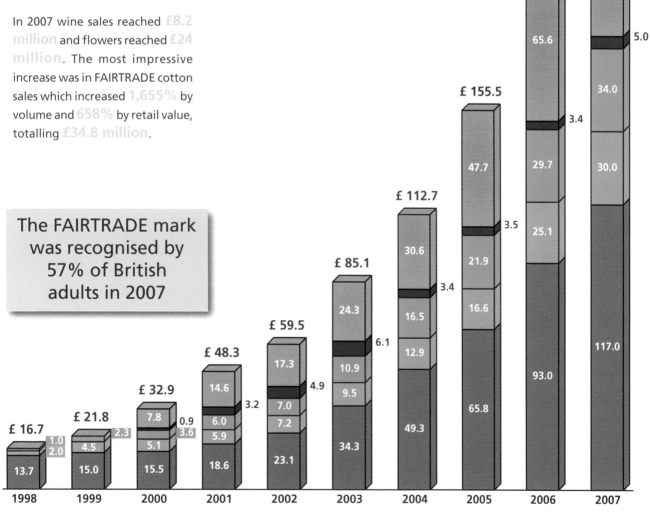

The FAIRTRADE mark was recognised by 57% of British adults in 2007

Source: The Fairtrade Foundation

http://www.fairtrade.org.uk

Kitchen concerns

Some of our biggest restaurants are lacking in hygiene

Almost 70% of us eat out every month, yet only 22% of us showed concern about the hygiene in restaurants.

Q. Have you been concerned about hygiene in any of the following places in the last 12 months?

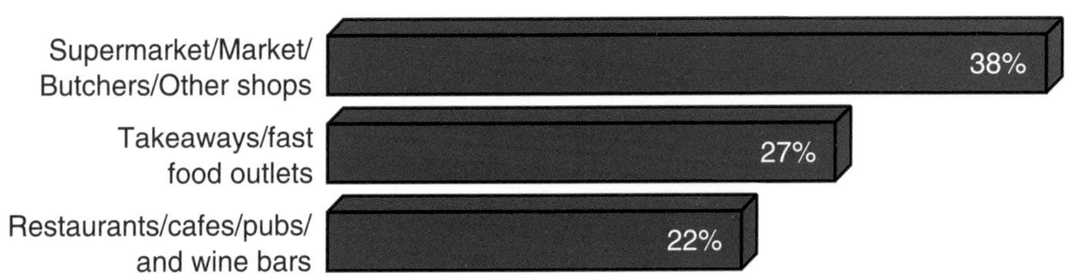

Supermarket/Market/ Butchers/Other shops
38%
Takeaways/fast food outlets
27%
Restaurants/cafes/pubs/ and wine bars
22%

Of those who were concerned about the hygiene at a restaurant 21% complained to the staff, 5% to the council and 1% to someone else, however an astounding 73% didn't complain at all.

Under the law, all restaurants are inspected every two years by environmental health officers and most hand out star ratings of between five and zero.

Restaurants with no stars are "very poor" with a general failure to comply with legal requirements.

One-star establishments have poor compliance with hygiene standards.

Those with two stars need to make more effort to hit all the legal requirements, however some health experts have said that a two star score restaurant is unsafe.

The Independent newspaper analysed the star rating of 1,270 outlets run by 10 of Britain's best-known restaurant chains. All of the companies had at least one branch, and in some cases dozens, failing fully to comply with food safety legislation.

Percentage of surveyed restaurants that achieved two stars or fewer when inspected by environmental health officers

Yo! Sushi
34.8%
Pizza Hut
17.7%
Pizza Express
13.3%
Nandos
12.3%
Wagamama
11.1%
Burger King
9.3%
McDonald's
8.2%
KFC
6.1%
Gourmet Burger Kitchen
4.5%
Pret a Manger
1.9%
£3

Photo: Ferris

Source: Consumer attitudes to food standards, Food Standards Agency, 2008. The Independent.
http://www.independent.co.uk
http://food.gov.uk.

What's on the menu?

67% of us in the UK eat out at least once a month, yet do we know what we're getting?

How often do you buy a meal out?

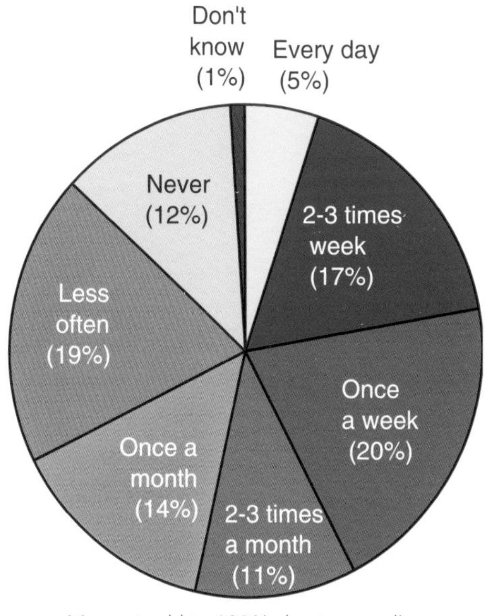
Don't know (1%)
Every day (5%)
2-3 times week (17%)
Once a week (20%)
2-3 times a month (11%)
Once a month (14%)
Less often (19%)
Never (12%)

May not add to 100% due to rounding

How easy do you think it is at the moment to make healthy choices when eating out?

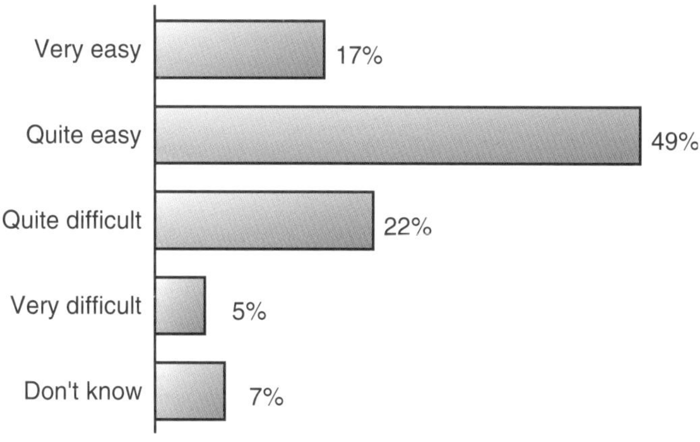
Very easy 17%
Quite easy 49%
Quite difficult 22%
Very difficult 5%
Don't know 7%

How much do you agree with the following statement: Restaurants, pubs, canteens and cafes have a responsibility to make clear what is in their food to help people make healthier choices if they want to?

Strongly agree 38%
Agree 48%
Disagree 8%
Strongly disagree 2%
Don't know 5%

Photo by Askpang

What is it that people want then when eating out? 41% say they want the food they eat out to be made healthier and to taste as good and they would like information about what's in it, but 15% want healthier food without the information. 22% said they want the food to stay the same and would like information also, while 14% want the same without the information.

Source: Catering Omnibus Survey, 2008, Food Standards Agency http://www.food.gov.uk

Bad taste

While concern about food has decreased, fat, salt and sugar are still top issues

Concerns about specific food issues 2007, %
(2006 figures in brackets)

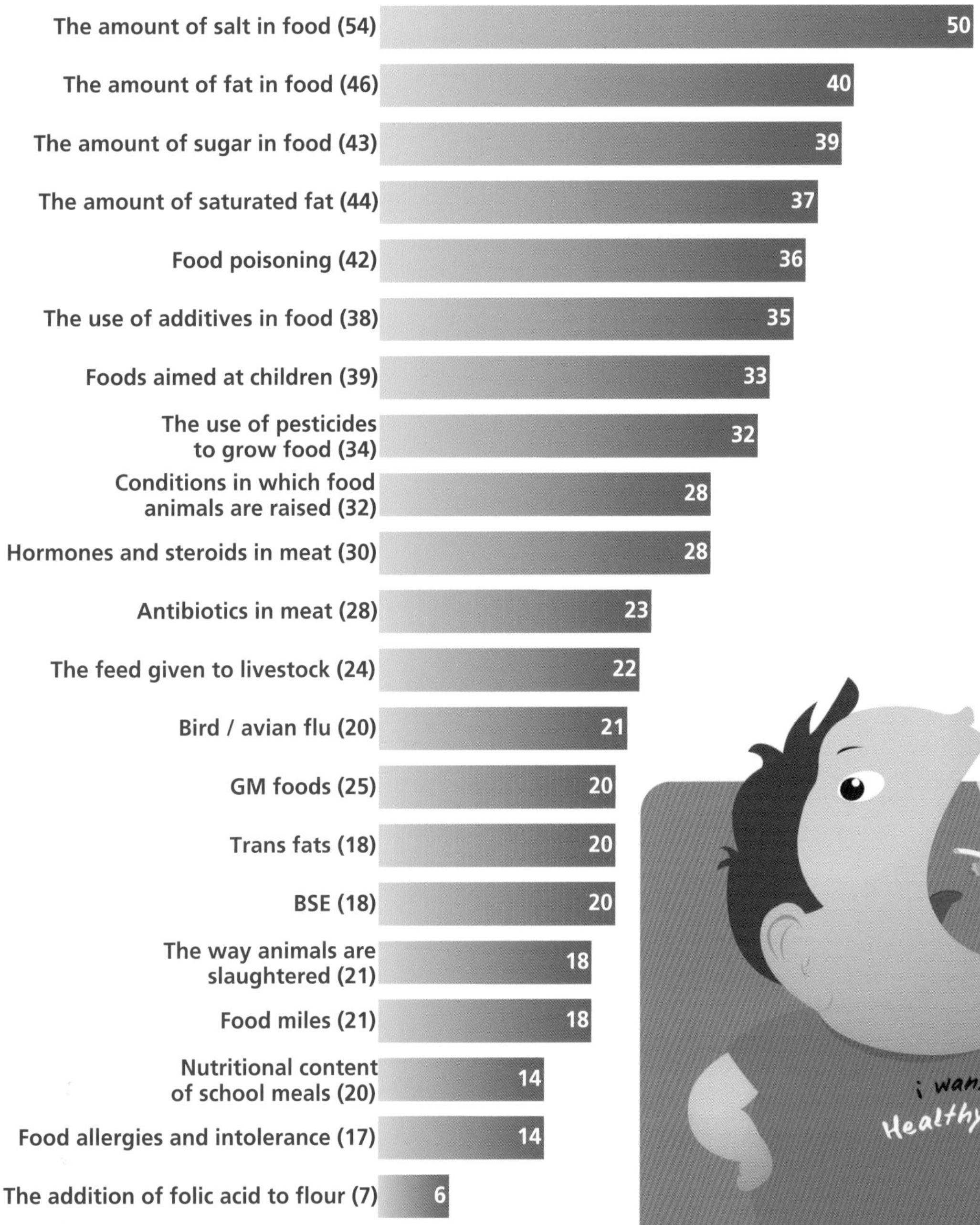

The amount of salt in food (54)	50
The amount of fat in food (46)	40
The amount of sugar in food (43)	39
The amount of saturated fat (44)	37
Food poisoning (42)	36
The use of additives in food (38)	35
Foods aimed at children (39)	33
The use of pesticides to grow food (34)	32
Conditions in which food animals are raised (32)	28
Hormones and steroids in meat (30)	28
Antibiotics in meat (28)	23
The feed given to livestock (24)	22
Bird / avian flu (20)	21
GM foods (25)	20
Trans fats (18)	20
BSE (18)	20
The way animals are slaughtered (21)	18
Food miles (21)	18
Nutritional content of school meals (20)	14
Food allergies and intolerance (17)	14
The addition of folic acid to flour (7)	6

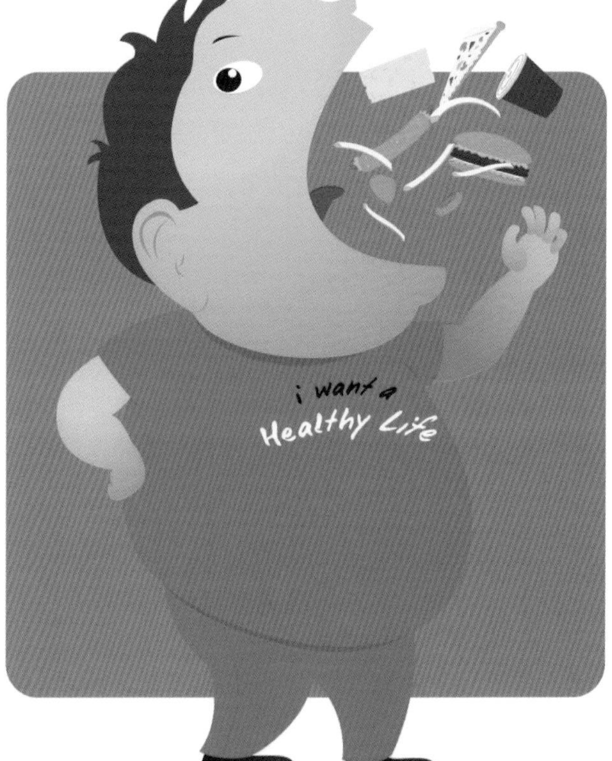

i want a
Healthy Life

Trans fats were mentioned by a significantly greater number of people this year. This issue was the subject of some media coverage and some manufacturers publicised the removal of trans fats from their products in 2007.

Base: 2,627 adults in the UK

Source: Consumer attitudes to food standards 2008, Food Standards Agency
http://www.food.gov.uk

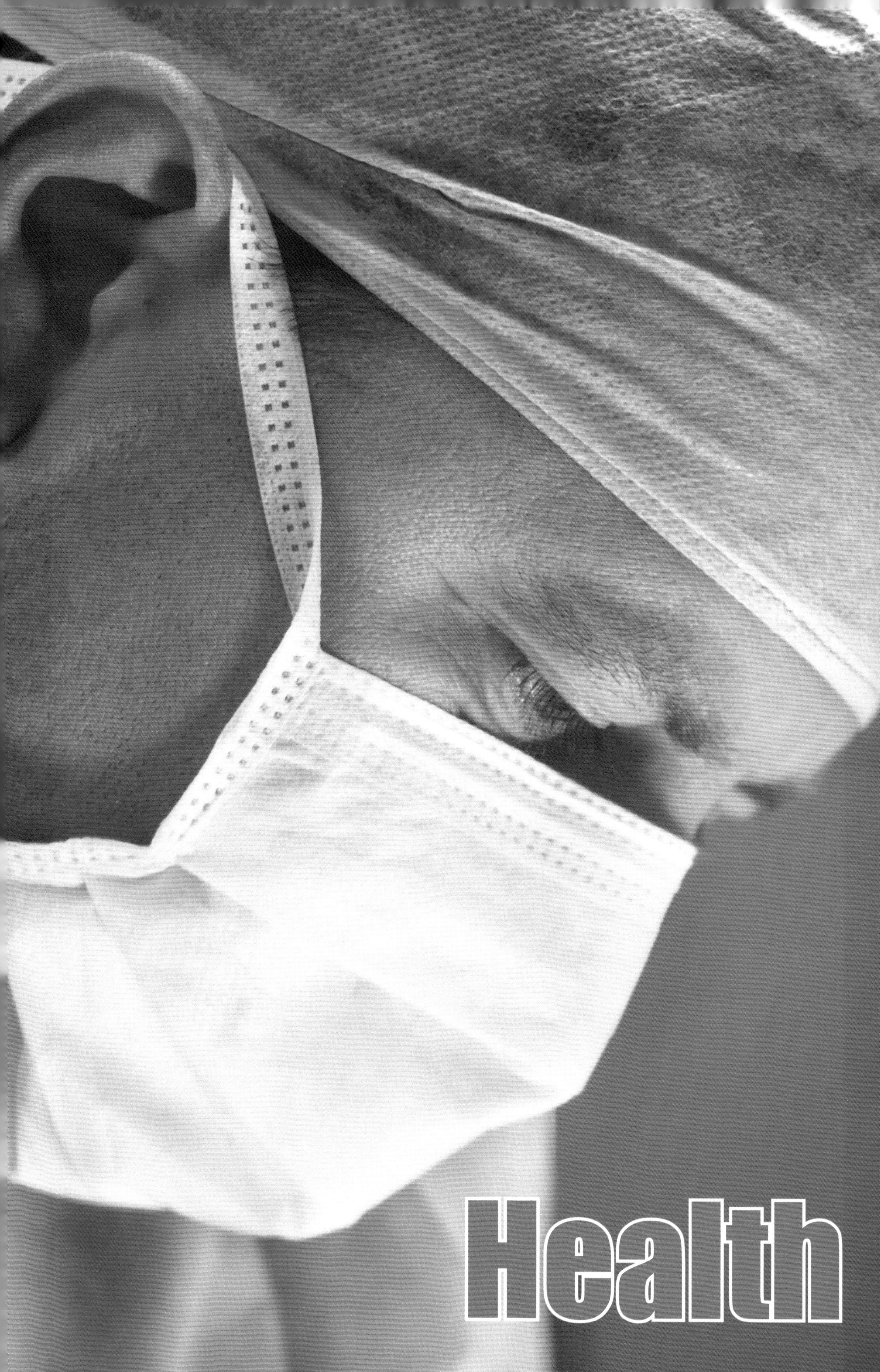
Health

Excess waist

Obesity in young people may be even worse than we think

Body mass index (BMI) is the most widely used measure of obesity. It calculates weight against height.
A desirable BMI is 18 to 25, overweight is more than 25 to 30 and obese is over 30.

Percentage of overweight and/or obese adults and children in England
using BMI as measurement

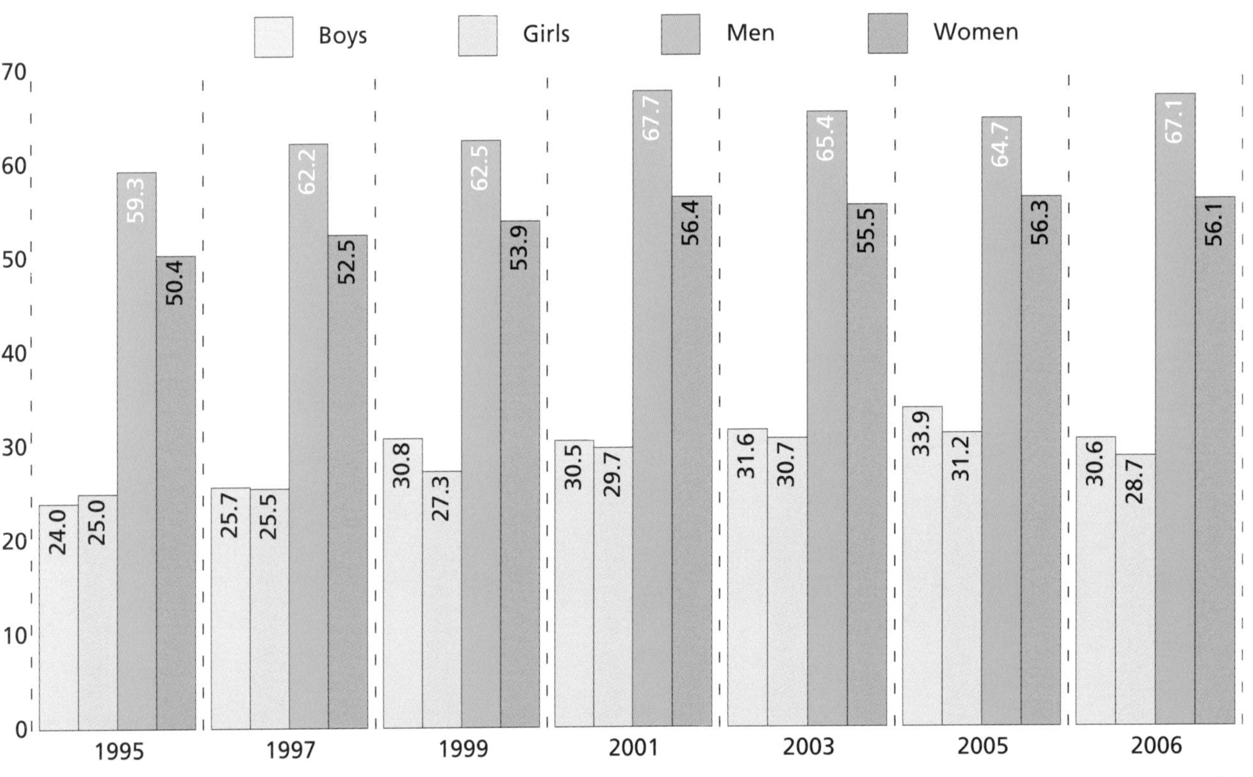

Boys
Girls
Men
Women
70
60
50
40
30
20
10
0
1995: 24.0 25.0 59.3 50.4
1997: 25.7 25.5 62.2 52.5
1999: 30.8 27.3 62.5 53.9
2001: 30.5 29.7 67.7 56.4
2003: 31.6 30.7 65.4 55.5
2005: 33.9 31.2 64.7 56.3
2006: 30.6 28.7 67.1 56.1

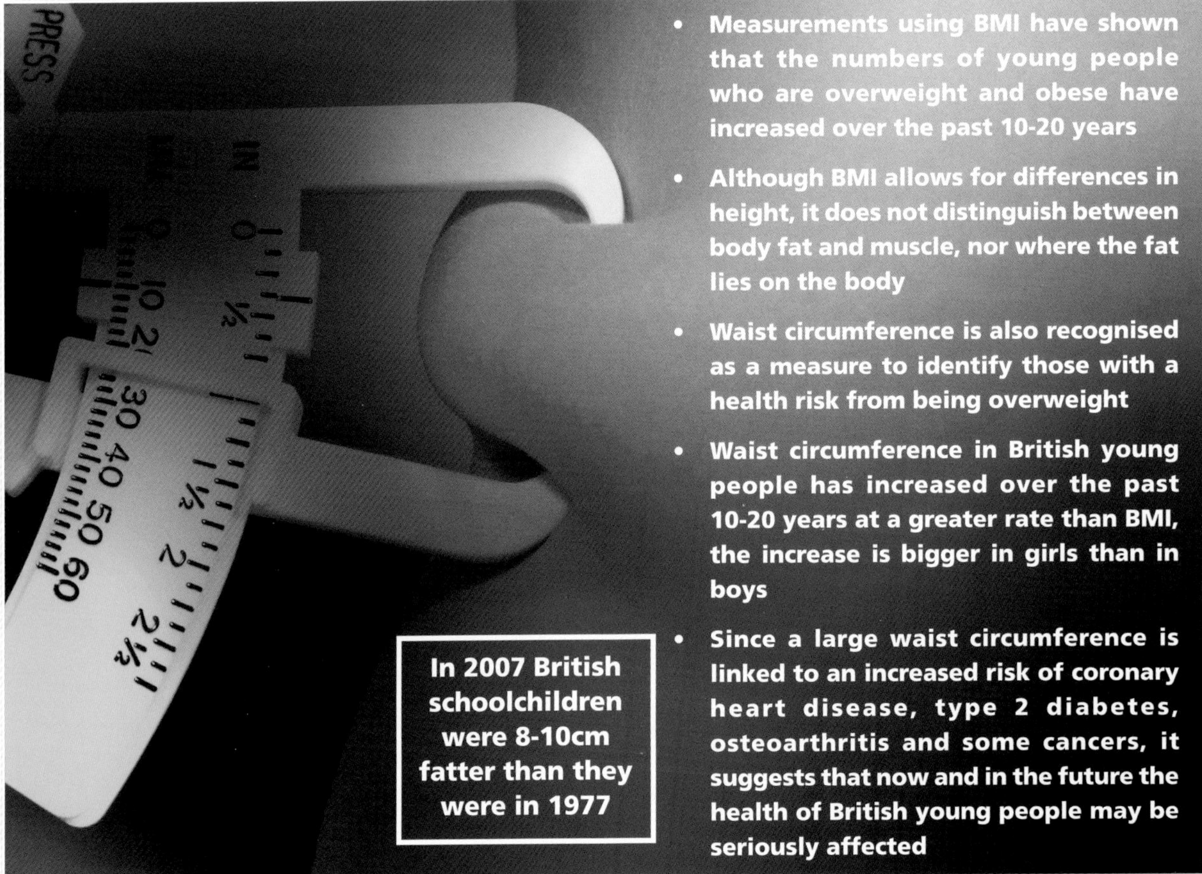

- Measurements using BMI have shown that the numbers of young people who are overweight and obese have increased over the past 10-20 years
- Although BMI allows for differences in height, it does not distinguish between body fat and muscle, nor where the fat lies on the body
- Waist circumference is also recognised as a measure to identify those with a health risk from being overweight
- Waist circumference in British young people has increased over the past 10-20 years at a greater rate than BMI, the increase is bigger in girls than in boys
- Since a large waist circumference is linked to an increased risk of coronary heart disease, type 2 diabetes, osteoarthritis and some cancers, it suggests that now and in the future the health of British young people may be seriously affected

In 2007 British schoolchildren were 8-10cm fatter than they were in 1977

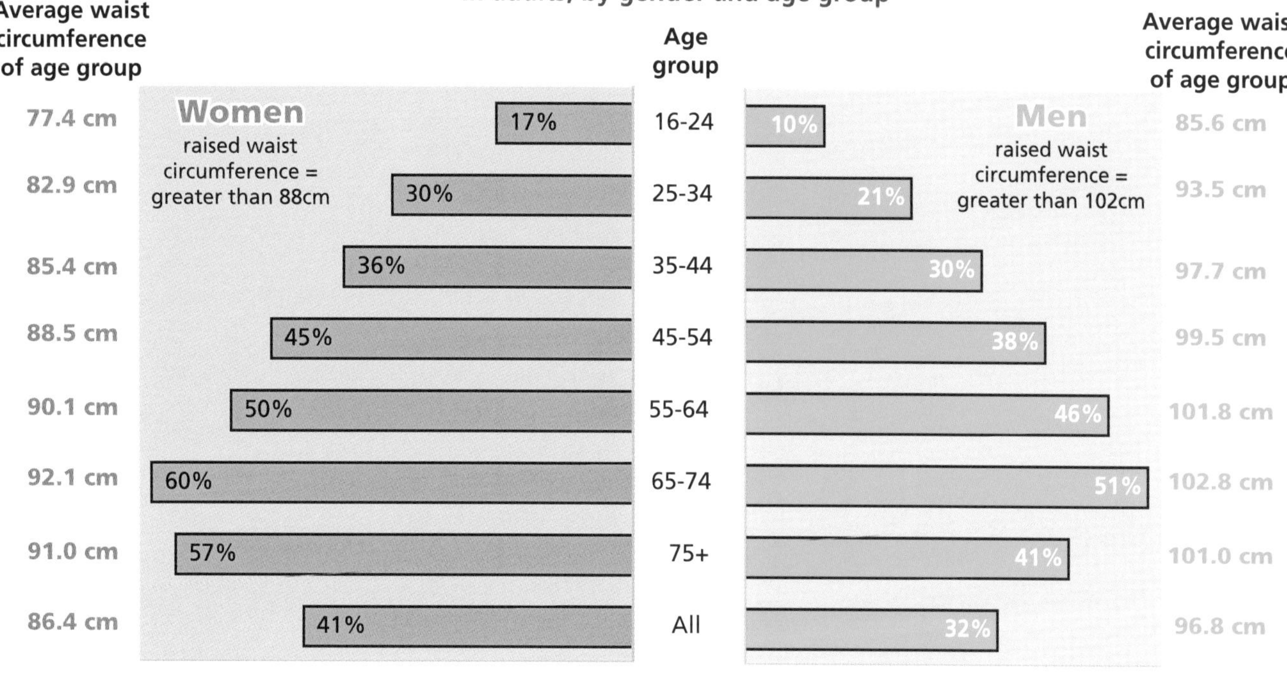
Percentage of raised waist circumferences, in adults, by gender and age group
Average waist circumference of age group
Age group
Average waist circumference of age group
Women
raised waist circumference = greater than 88cm
Men
raised waist circumference = greater than 102cm
77.4 cm | 17% | 16-24 | 10% | 85.6 cm
82.9 cm | 30% | 25-34 | 21% | 93.5 cm
85.4 cm | 36% | 35-44 | 30% | 97.7 cm
88.5 cm | 45% | 45-54 | 38% | 99.5 cm
90.1 cm | 50% | 55-64 | 46% | 101.8 cm
92.1 cm | 60% | 65-74 | 51% | 102.8 cm
91.0 cm | 57% | 75+ | 41% | 101.0 cm
86.4 cm | 41% | All | 32% | 96.8 cm

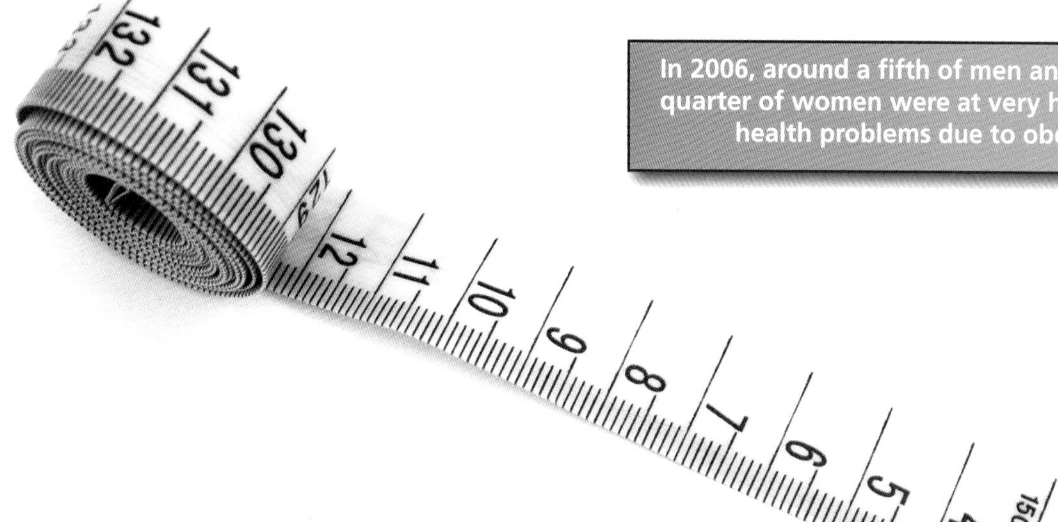
150 cm

In 2006, around a fifth of men and almost a quarter of women were at very high risk of health problems due to obesity

Increased risk of health problems
(using the combined categories of BMI and waist circumference)

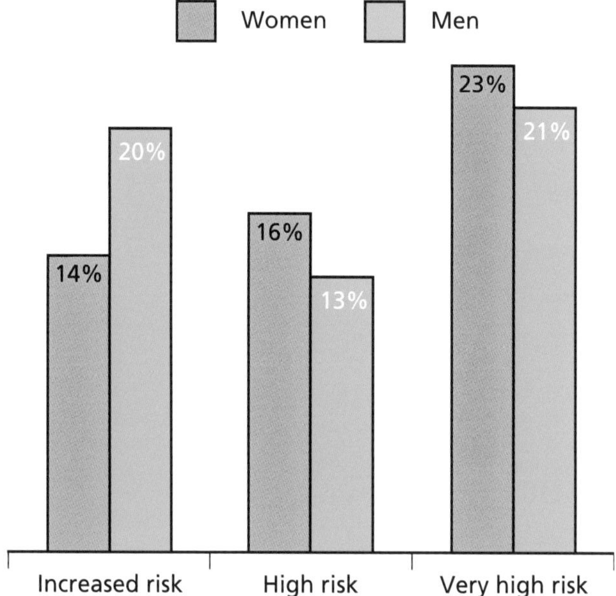
Women
Men
Increased risk: Women 14%, Men 20%
High risk: Women 16%, Men 13%
Very high risk: Women 23%, Men 21%

The proportion of both men and women at very high risk of the health effects of obesity increased with age, peaking in the 65 to 74 age group, where 30% of men and 34% of women were in this category

Source: The Information Centre, Lifestyles Statistics © 2008
Central overweight and obesity in British youth, British Medical Journal, Vol 326

http://www.ic.nhs.uk
http://www.bmj.com

Gift of life

More than 7,000 people in the UK are waiting for a transplant

In 2007 over **1.07 million** more people pledged to help others after their death by registering their wishes on the NHS Organ Donor Register

ORGANS from **793** people who died were used to save or dramatically improve many people's lives through **2,339** transplants.

7,570 patients were listed as actively waiting for a transplant: a **7%** increase compared to the previous year and the highest number on record. The vast majority of those were waiting for a kidney transplant.

CORNEAS
2,393 had their sight restored in 2007, **4%** fewer than in 2006

CARDIOTHORACIC
258 received transplants of which:

129 received a **HEART**

120 received **LUNGS** (**90** double **30** single)

8 HEART & LUNG

1 HEART & KIDNEY

KIDNEYS
2,218 received a transplant

804 of these were given their kidney by a living donor – **797** given by a friend or relative and, for the first time, **7** given by strangers

PANCREAS
253 received a pancreas or combined kidney/ pancreas transplant – an increase of **53%** over 2006

LIVERS
644 received a transplant

Source: UK Transplant, National Health Service Blood and Transplant

http://www.uktransplant.org.uk
http://www.giveandletlive.co.uk/en/

All figures are for 2007 calendar year

Weaker sex?

Men have more ill health and die younger

Are boys born unhealthy?

At the very beginning men outnumber women – about 125 males are conceived for every 100 females.

Problems that happen in the womb – cerebral palsy, premature birth, stillbirth, deformities – are all more common in males, so by birth, the male lead has reduced to 105 for every 100 females.

Through the childhood years, males notch up higher scores in hyperactivity, reading and behavioural problems, autism, clumsiness and stammering. The chief suspect is testosterone – too much and the risk of developmental disorders soars.

A testosterone boost in adolescence is also linked with a rise in violence and accidents.

5,000 people are severely injured in accidents every year in the UK – 75% of them are men. Testosterone has also been linked with higher blood pressure, raising the risk of heart disease and damping down the immune system.

41% of all male deaths under the age of 75 (almost 60,000 a year in the UK) are caused by circulatory diseases – the largest single cause of death.

Of these deaths, over two-thirds – 41,000 – are due to coronary heart disease.

Nearly 22,000 men in the UK are newly diagnosed with prostate cancer each year and about 9,500 die. The number of new cases diagnosed is expected to treble over the next 20 years.

The majority of men are too heavy for their health: around 45% are medically defined as overweight and around an additional 17% as obese.

The average man can expect to be seriously or chronically ill for 15 years of his life

The average life expectancy of a male born in the UK in 1997 is still less than 75 years

Women on average live five years longer than men and men are twice as likely to die before age 65

Advice for men:

DON'T smoke
that can take six years off your life

DON'T do reckless things
like drinking and driving or fighting on the way back from the pub

DON'T drink alcohol to excess
keep consumption to a reasonable level

DO have regular health check ups
older men are well known for leaving things until it's too late to do much about it

Source: Malehealth
http://www.malehealth.co.uk

The cost of a drink

Alcohol is a part of social life for many, but it is harmful for some

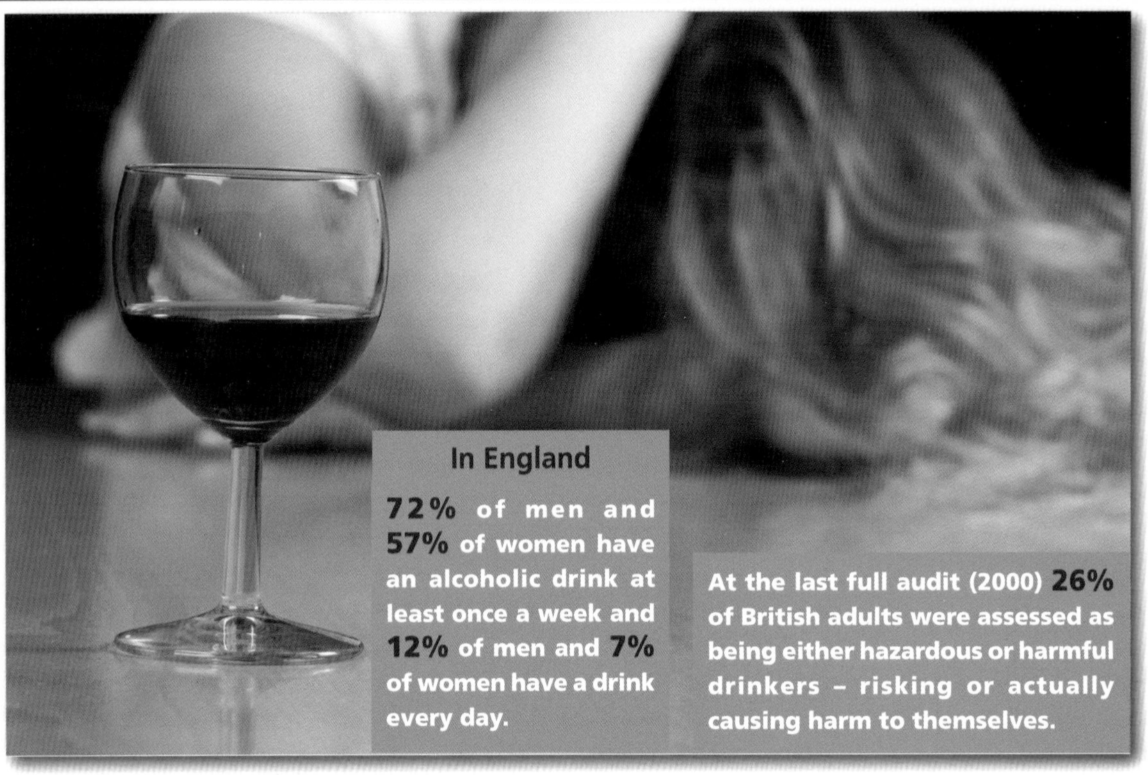
In England
72% of men and 57% of women have an alcoholic drink at least once a week and 12% of men and 7% of women have a drink every day.
At the last full audit (2000) 26% of British adults were assessed as being either hazardous or harmful drinkers - risking or actually causing harm to themselves.

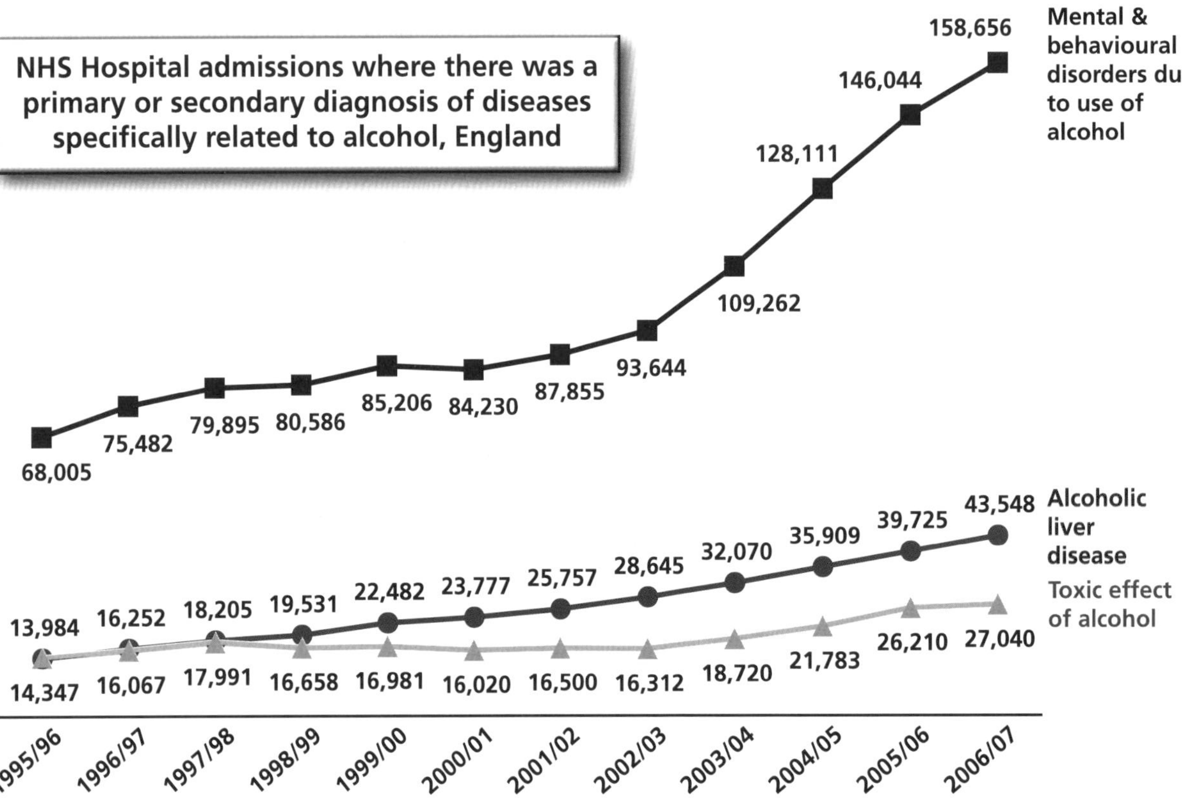
NHS Hospital admissions where there was a primary or secondary diagnosis of diseases specifically related to alcohol, England
Mental & behavioural disorders due to use of alcohol
68,005
75,482
79,895
80,586
85,206
84,230
87,855
93,644
109,262
128,111
146,044
158,656
Alcoholic liver disease
13,984
16,252
18,205
19,531
22,482
23,777
25,757
28,645
32,070
35,909
39,725
43,548
Toxic effect of alcohol
14,347
16,067
17,991
16,658
16,981
16,020
16,500
16,312
18,720
21,783
26,210
27,040
1995/96
1996/97
1997/98
1998/99
1999/00
2000/01
2001/02
2002/03
2003/04
2004/05
2005/06
2006/07

Some drinkers become dependant on alcohol, losing control of their drinking and eventually neglecting health and other aspects of their lives.

In 2007 there were **112,267** prescriptions for drugs for the treatment of alcohol dependency. This is an increase of **20%** since 2003.

Source: NHS Information Centre, Lifestyle statistics © Crown copyright
http://www.ic.nhs.uk/

Drug deaths

There were more than 13,000 drug-related deaths between 2003-2007

Drug deaths include accidents and suicides involving drug poisoning, as well as poisonings due to drug abuse and drug dependence whether intentional or accidental. They also include deaths due to mental or behavioural disorders caused by drug use.

The range of substances involved is wide, including legal and illegal drugs, prescription drugs and over-the-counter medications.

In 2007 the number of **male** deaths related to drug poisoning increased by **7%** compared to 2006.

The number of **female** deaths decreased by **8%** compared to 2006. This is the lowest recorded annual number since 1993 (the first year held within the database).

Numbers of deaths from drug-related poisoning, by gender, England & Wales

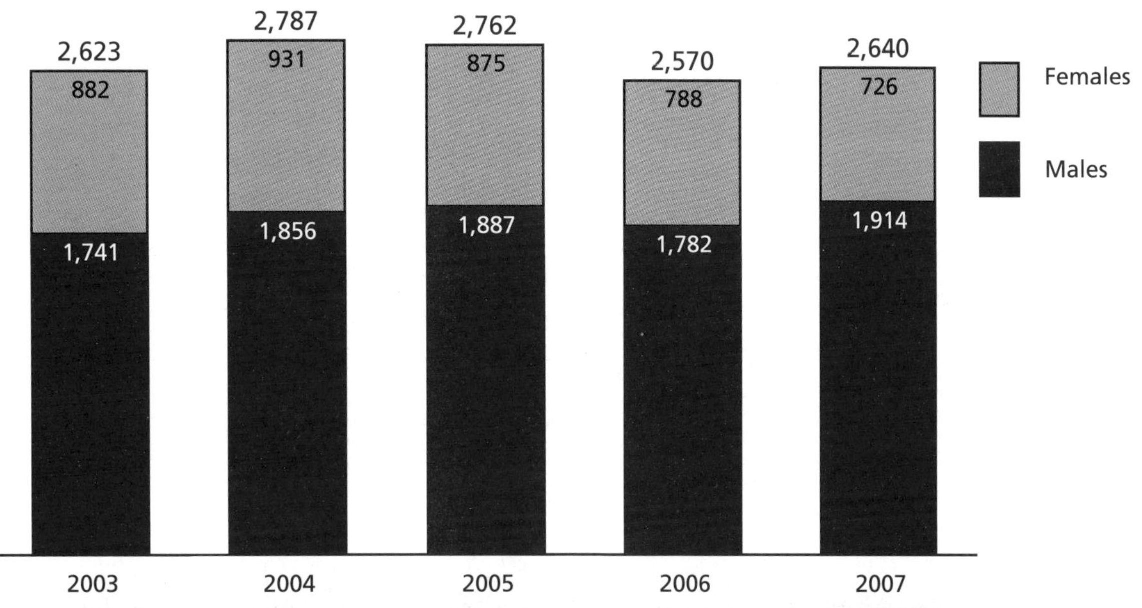

2,623
882
1,741
2,787
931
1,856
2,762
875
1,887
2,570
788
1,782
2,640
726
1,914
Females
Males
2003
2004
2005
2006
2007

In 2007 29% of drug-related poisoning deaths mentioned more than one drug, or a 'multiple drug overdose':

31% contained a mention of **alcohol** in addition to a drug

829 deaths involved **heroin** or **morphine**, a **16%** rise compared to 2006

35% increase in deaths since 2006 involving **methadone**, a **62%** increase compared to 2003

196 deaths involved **cocaine**. This was the **highest** number of deaths involving cocaine since 1993 (11 deaths).

97 deaths involved **amphetamines** – nearly half of these being accounted for by deaths mentioning **ecstasy**.

6 deaths involved barbiturates (prescribed to calm people down or help them to sleep). This is the **lowest** recorded number since 1993.

335 deaths involved **antidepressants** – the **lowest** recorded number since 1993.

242 deaths involved **paracetamol** and its compounds. This has continued a long-term downward trend since 1997 and has **nearly halved** since 2003.

12 deaths involved **aspirin** – the lowest recorded number since 1993

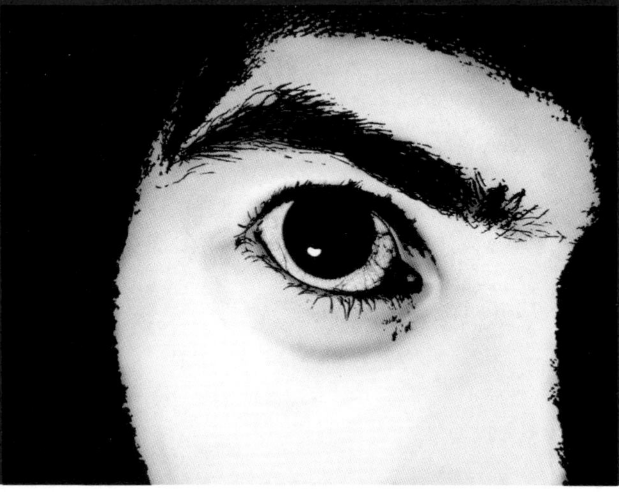

Source: Health Statistics Autumn 2008, Office for National Statistics © Crown copyright

http://www.statistics.gov.uk

Suicide

There is one suicide attempt by a young person every 20 minutes

UK adult suicide rates, aged 15 and over

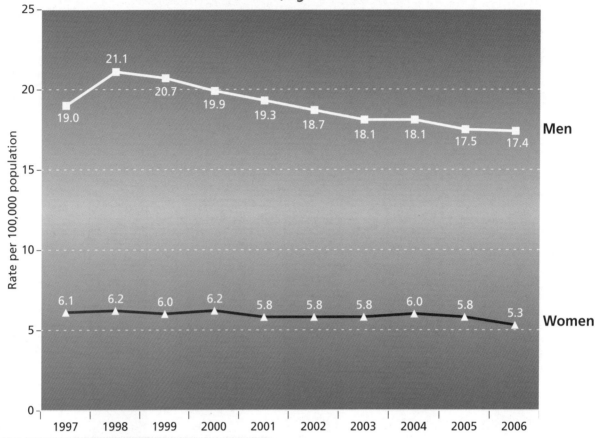

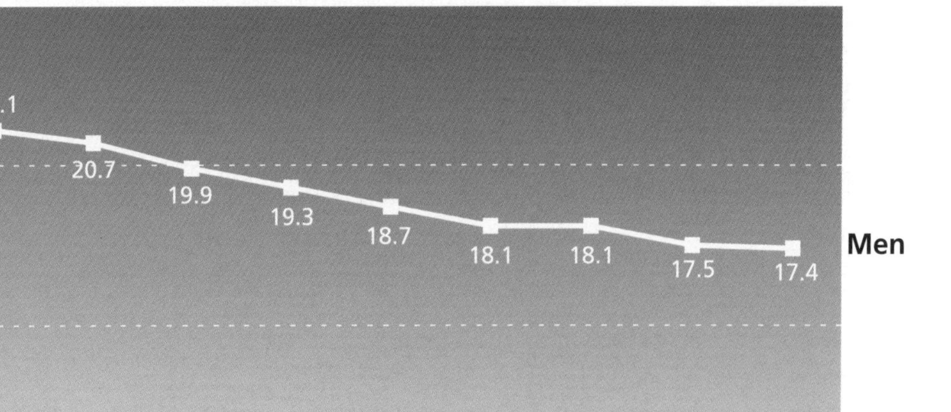
Rate per 100,000 population
25
20
15
10
5
0
21.1
19.0
20.7
19.9
19.3
18.7
18.1
18.1
17.5
17.4
Men
6.1
6.2
6.0
6.2
5.8
5.8
5.8
6.0
5.8
5.3
1997
1998
1999
2000
2001
2002
2003
2004
2005
2006

Women

Annual suicides	Men	Women
1997	4,320	1,496
1998	4,799	1,555
1999	4,749	1,506
2000	4,581	1,543
2001	4,469	1,463
2002	4,347	1,479
2003	4,267	1,464
2004	4,288	1,562
2005	4,192	1,479
2006	4,196	1,358

In 2008 there was much media reporting of young people and internet suicide, in particular the supposed Bridgend cluster and speculation about a link via the internet and chat rooms – the coroner dismissed this link.

How common is suicide?

- Every year there are about **24,000** cases of attempted suicide by young people aged 10-19 years in England and Wales alone.
- In the UK for people aged 15-24, suicide is the second biggest cause of death after road accidents.
- One in three adolescents who died by suicide was under the influence of alcohol.
- Suicidal young men are **10 times** more likely than other young men to use a drug to relieve stress. They are also more likely to feel that they had been pressurised into taking drugs.
- This group also spends far more on drugs than the non-suicidal group.
- Suicidal young men are significantly more likely to have a father who is absent.

Papyrus – the national charity dedicated to the prevention of young suicide – is campaigning for it to be illegal to 'groom' young people for suicide via internet sites

Deaths from suicides ages 12-17 in England and Wales

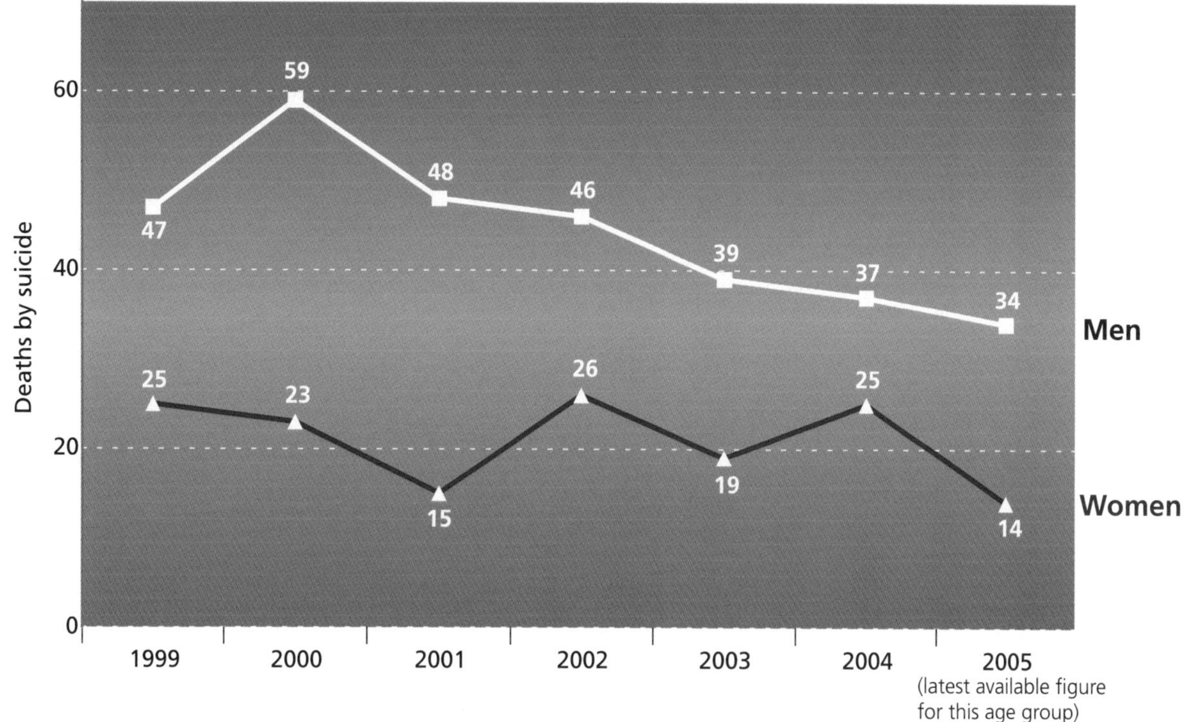

Deaths by suicide
60
40
20
0
59
47
48
46
39
37
34
Men
25
23
15
26
19
25
14
Women
1999
2000
2001
2002
2003
2004
2005
(latest available figure for this age group)

Source: BMJ research, Office for National Statistics © Crown copyright

http://www.bmj.com
http://www.samaritans.org
http://www.statistics.gov.uk
http://www.papyrus-uk.org

Teething troubles

Access to NHS dentistry is still a problem

Respondents were asked:

Q Which, if any, of the following are the main reasons why you have not been to an NHS dentist since April 2006?

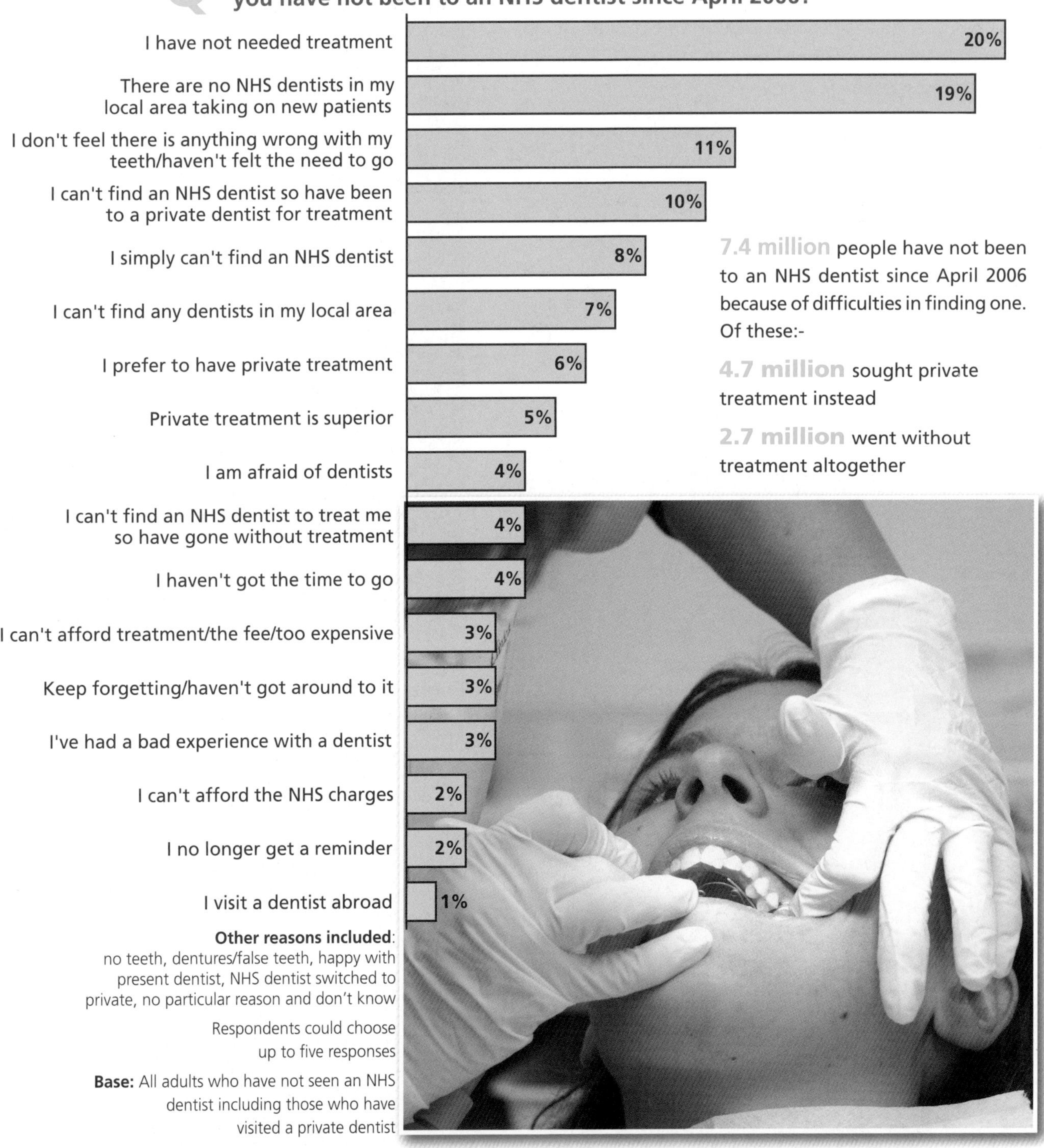

I have not needed treatment 20%
There are no NHS dentists in my local area taking on new patients 19%
I don't feel there is anything wrong with my teeth/haven't felt the need to go 11%
I can't find an NHS dentist so have been to a private dentist for treatment 10%
I simply can't find an NHS dentist 8%
I can't find any dentists in my local area 7%
I prefer to have private treatment 6%
Private treatment is superior 5%
I am afraid of dentists 4%
I can't find an NHS dentist to treat me so have gone without treatment 4%
I haven't got the time to go 4%
I can't afford treatment/the fee/too expensive 3%
Keep forgetting/haven't got around to it 3%
I've had a bad experience with a dentist 3%
I can't afford the NHS charges 2%
I no longer get a reminder 2%
I visit a dentist abroad 1%

7.4 million people have not been to an NHS dentist since April 2006 because of difficulties in finding one. Of these:-

4.7 million sought private treatment instead

2.7 million went without treatment altogether

Other reasons included: no teeth, dentures/false teeth, happy with present dentist, NHS dentist switched to private, no particular reason and don't know

Respondents could choose up to five responses

Base: All adults who have not seen an NHS dentist including those who have visited a private dentist

Latest figures for England (2007/08) show that although there were 655 more NHS dentists, 1.1m fewer patients were being seen than in the previous two years. Costs increased by £56m. There were more extractions and dentures but fewer crowns and fillings leading the British Dental Association to conclude:

"...the system discourages modern preventative care..."

Source: © Citizens Advice, NHS Information Centre
http://www.citizensadvice.org.uk
http://www.ic.nhs.uk

Base: Over 1,800 representative adults were interviewed in England and Wales on behalf of Citizens Advice

Internet &
media

Trust in the media

Despite recent scandals, the BBC is one of the most trusted organisations

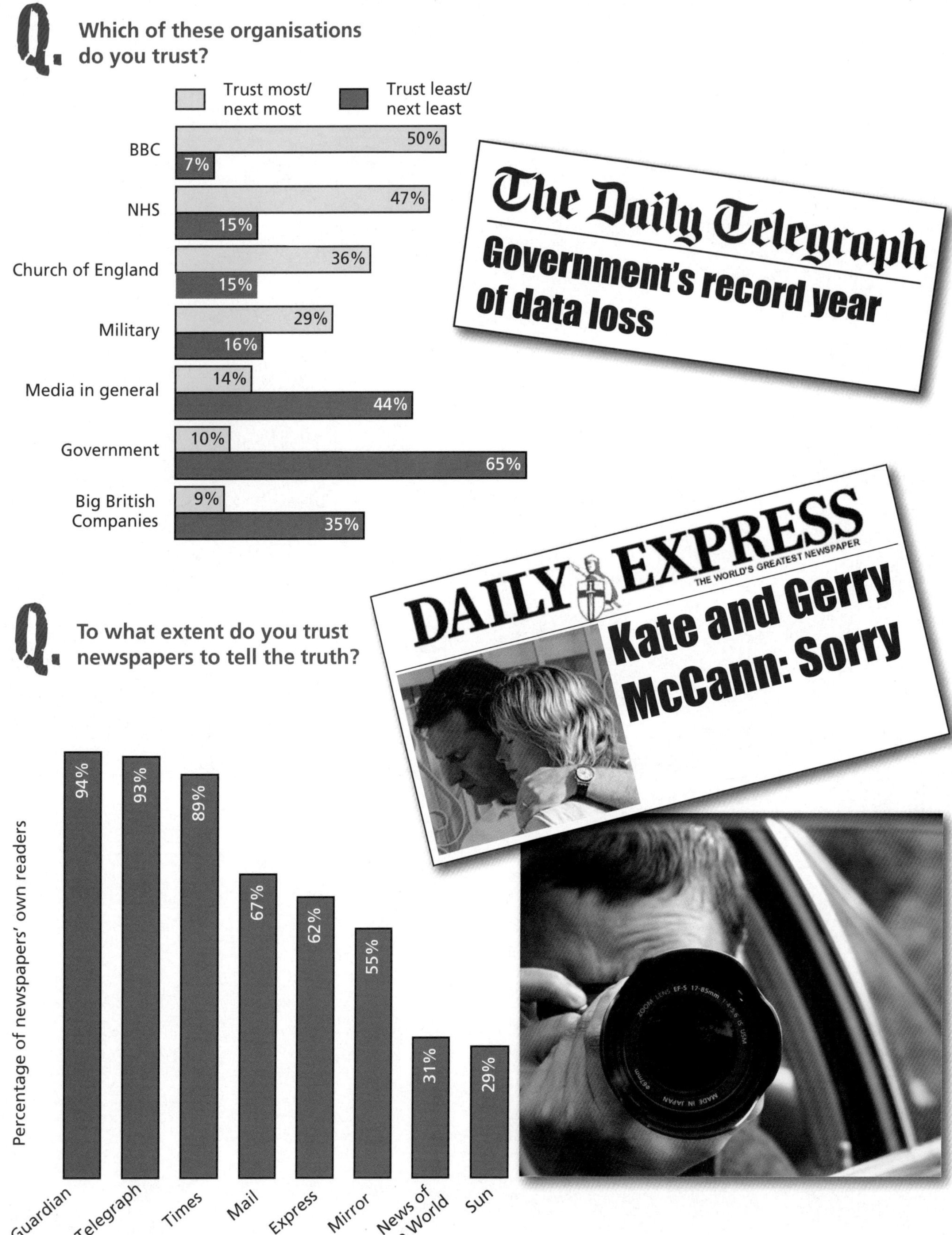

Q. Which of these organisations do you trust?
Trust most/ next most
Trust least/ next least
BBC 50% 7%
NHS 47% 15%
Church of England 36% 15%
Military 29% 16%
Media in general 14% 44%
Government 10% 65%
Big British Companies 9% 35%
The Daily Telegraph
Government's record year of data loss
DAILY EXPRESS
THE WORLD'S GREATEST NEWSPAPER
Kate and Gerry McCann: Sorry
Q. To what extent do you trust newspapers to tell the truth?
Percentage of newspapers' own readers
Guardian 94%
Telegraph 93%
Times 89%
Mail 67%
Express 62%
Mirror 55%
News of the World 31%
Sun 29%

NB includes Daily and Sunday editions

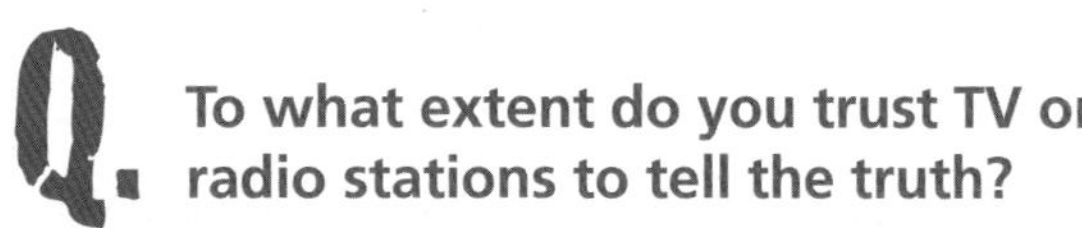
Q.
To what extent do you trust TV or radio stations to tell the truth?

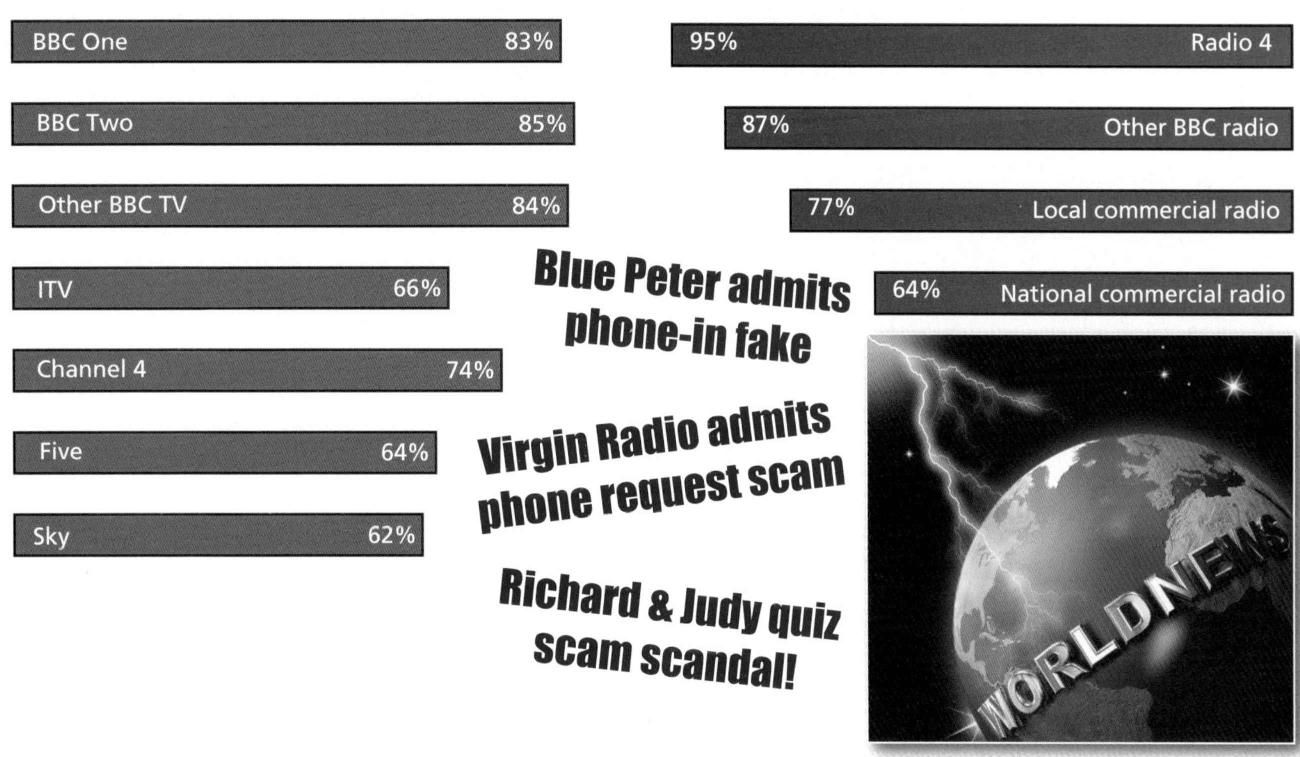
BBC One 83%
BBC Two 85%
Other BBC TV 84%
ITV 66%
Channel 4 74%
Five 64%
Sky 62%
95% Radio 4
87% Other BBC radio
77% Local commercial radio
64% National commercial radio
Blue Peter admits phone-in fake
Virgin Radio admits phone request scam
Richard & Judy quiz scam scandal!
WORLDNEWS

Q. Which of the following has the most and least powerful influence on your day to day life?

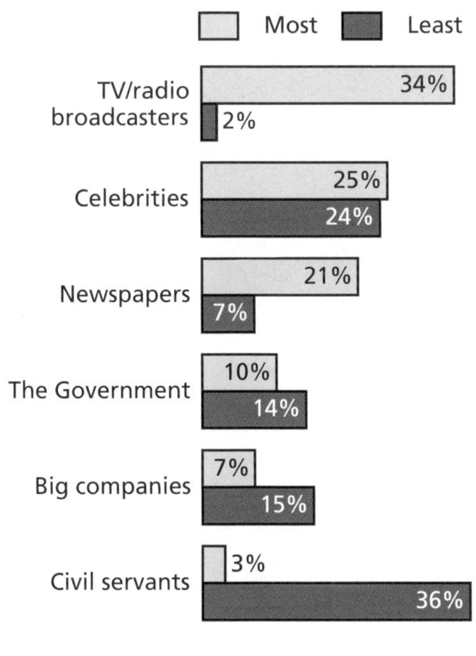
Most
Least
TV/radio broadcasters 34% 2%
Celebrities 25% 24%
Newspapers 21% 7%
The Government 10% 14%
Big companies 7% 15%
Civil servants 3% 36%

LATEST NEWS

Source: BBC Survey on Trust 2008
http://www.ipsos-mori.com

Base: Survey of over 1,000 adults in the UK

Life online

Do parents know what's really happening?

The rapid growth of social networking sites (SNS) such as MySpace, Facebook & Bebo indicates that they are now a mainstream communication method for many people. But are children aware of the potential dangers involved in such sites?

Only 37% of parents thought their child had a site, in fact 49% of those aged 8-17 have one.

Percentage of parents and children who have a profile on a social networking site

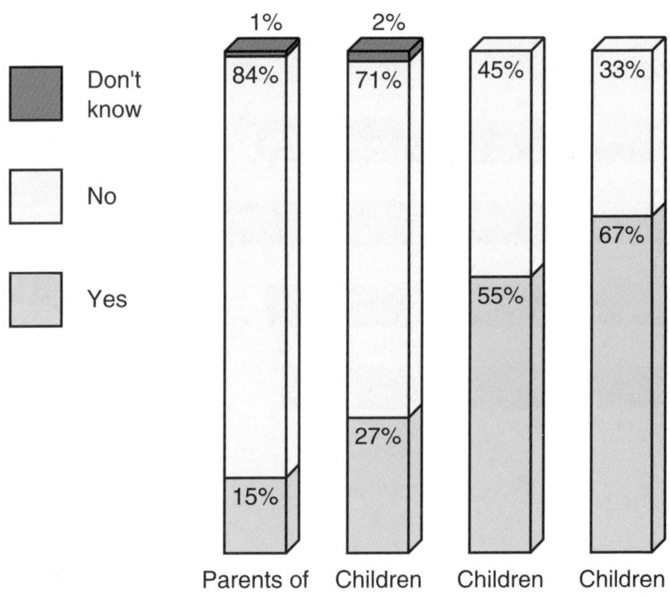

Don't know
No
Yes
1%
84%
15%
Parents of 8-17s
2%
71%
27%
Children 8-11
45%
55%
Children 12-15
33%
67%
Children 16-17

Features people use on social networking sites

Talk to friends/ family I talk to a lot	69%
Talk to friends/ family I rarely see	65%
Look for old friends I have lost touch with	47%
Look at other people's sites without leaving a message	40%
Talk to people who are friends of friends	35%
Listen to music/ find out about bands	29%
Talk to people I don't know	17%
Look at campaigns and petitions	6%
Other uses	4%

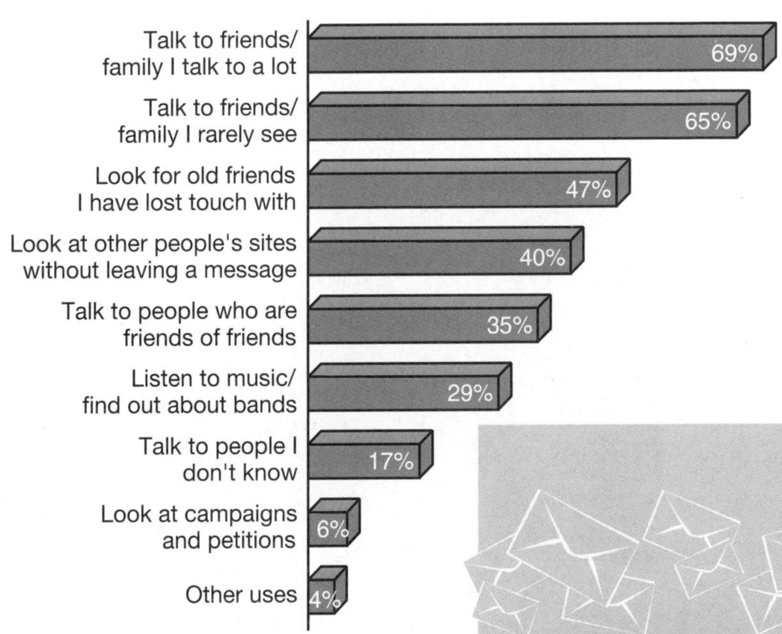

The majority of all children (59%) reported that they had used social networking sites to make new 'friends'.

Source: Social Networking, a quantitative and qualitative research report into attitudes, behaviours and use, Ofcom, 2008
http://www.ofcom.org.uk

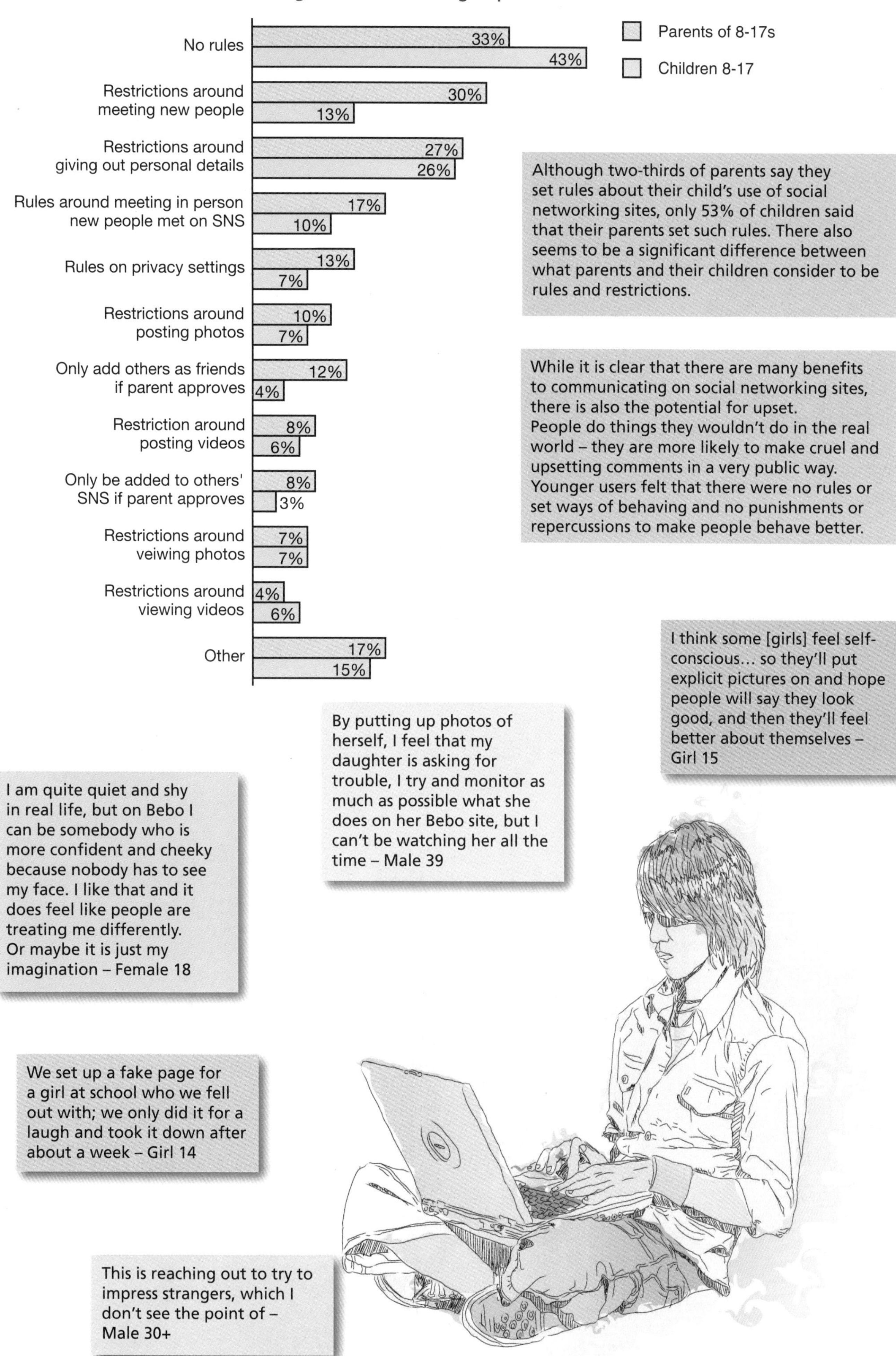

Rules and restrictions on what children use social networking sites for, according to parents and children

	Parents of 8-17s	Children 8-17
No rules	33%	43%
Restrictions around meeting new people	30%	13%
Restrictions around giving out personal details	27%	26%
Rules around meeting in person new people met on SNS	17%	10%
Rules on privacy settings	13%	7%
Restrictions around posting photos	10%	7%
Only add others as friends if parent approves	12%	4%
Restriction around posting videos	8%	6%
Only be added to others' SNS if parent approves	8%	3%
Restrictions around veiwing photos	7%	7%
Restrictions around viewing videos	4%	6%
Other	17%	15%

Although two-thirds of parents say they set rules about their child's use of social networking sites, only 53% of children said that their parents set such rules. There also seems to be a significant difference between what parents and their children consider to be rules and restrictions.

While it is clear that there are many benefits to communicating on social networking sites, there is also the potential for upset.
People do things they wouldn't do in the real world – they are more likely to make cruel and upsetting comments in a very public way.
Younger users felt that there were no rules or set ways of behaving and no punishments or repercussions to make people behave better.

I think some [girls] feel self-conscious... so they'll put explicit pictures on and hope people will say they look good, and then they'll feel better about themselves – Girl 15

By putting up photos of herself, I feel that my daughter is asking for trouble, I try and monitor as much as possible what she does on her Bebo site, but I can't be watching her all the time – Male 39

I am quite quiet and shy in real life, but on Bebo I can be somebody who is more confident and cheeky because nobody has to see my face. I like that and it does feel like people are treating me differently. Or maybe it is just my imagination – Female 18

We set up a fake page for a girl at school who we fell out with; we only did it for a laugh and took it down after about a week – Girl 14

This is reaching out to try to impress strangers, which I don't see the point of – Male 30+

Mixed media

Consumers are experimenting with new technology

Take-up of new communication technology in UK 2008
% of adults

Use of social networking sites

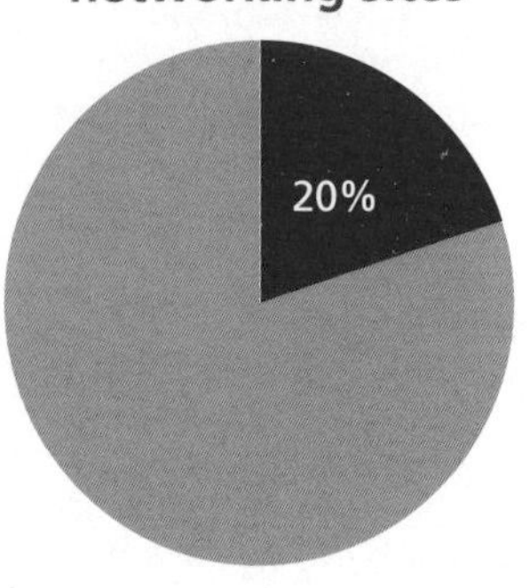
20%

Internet access with a mobile phone

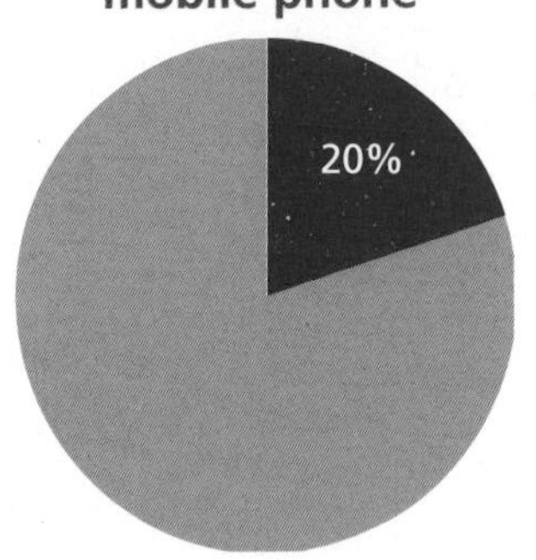
20%

Listening to audio content on a mobile phone

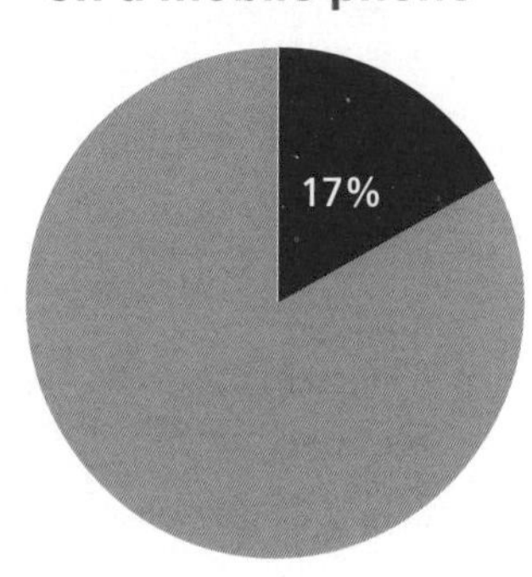
17%

Watching video content online

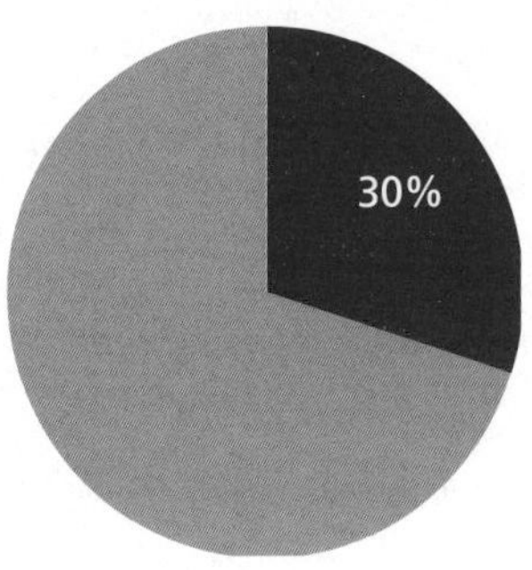
30%

Listening to the radio online

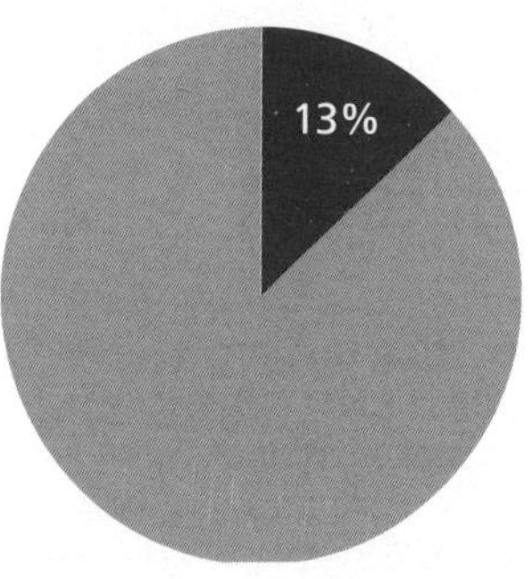
13%

Use of VoIP at home

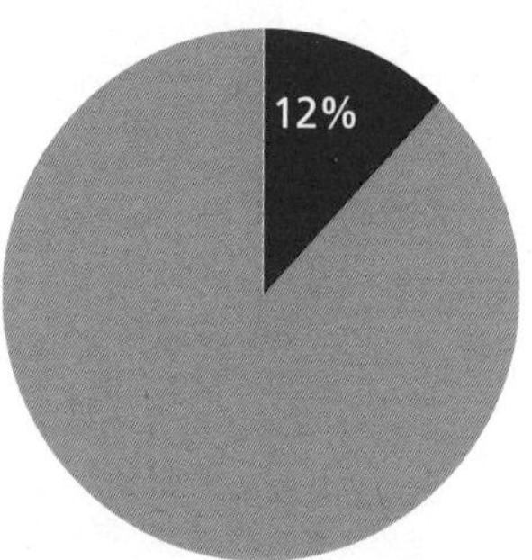
12%

Voice over Internet Protocol (VoIP), such as Skype allows you to make voice calls using a broadband internet connection instead of a regular (or analog) phone line

Watching video on a mobile phone
4%

In January 2008:-

- **17.31 million** people accessed the internet on their phones
- **6.3 billion** text messages were sent – **5,000 every second**
- **42.52 million** picture messages were sent

Source: Ofcom – The Nations & Regions Communications Market 2008, Q1 2008 UK Mobile Trends Report Mobile Data Association

http://www.ofcom.org.uk
http://www.themda.org

Take a gamble

Online gambling proves attractive to younger men

A nationally representative sample of 8,000 adults are surveyed annually about their gambling habits

LOTTO
£
Gala
BINGO

8.8% of those surveyed gamble remotely

The remote methods used were:

6.9%	Internet through PC, laptop or handheld device
2.3%	WAP/internet or text (SMS) on mobile phone
2.0%	Interactive/digital TV

NB percentages add up to more than 8.8% as multiple responses permitted

The most popular types of remote gambling were:

National Lottery	6.2%
Betting	2.2%
Poker	1.4%
Other lotteries	1.3%
Casino type games	0.9%
Bingo	0.9%

Q Have you gambled (including on the National Lottery or other lotteries) for money using any of the remote methods in the last month?

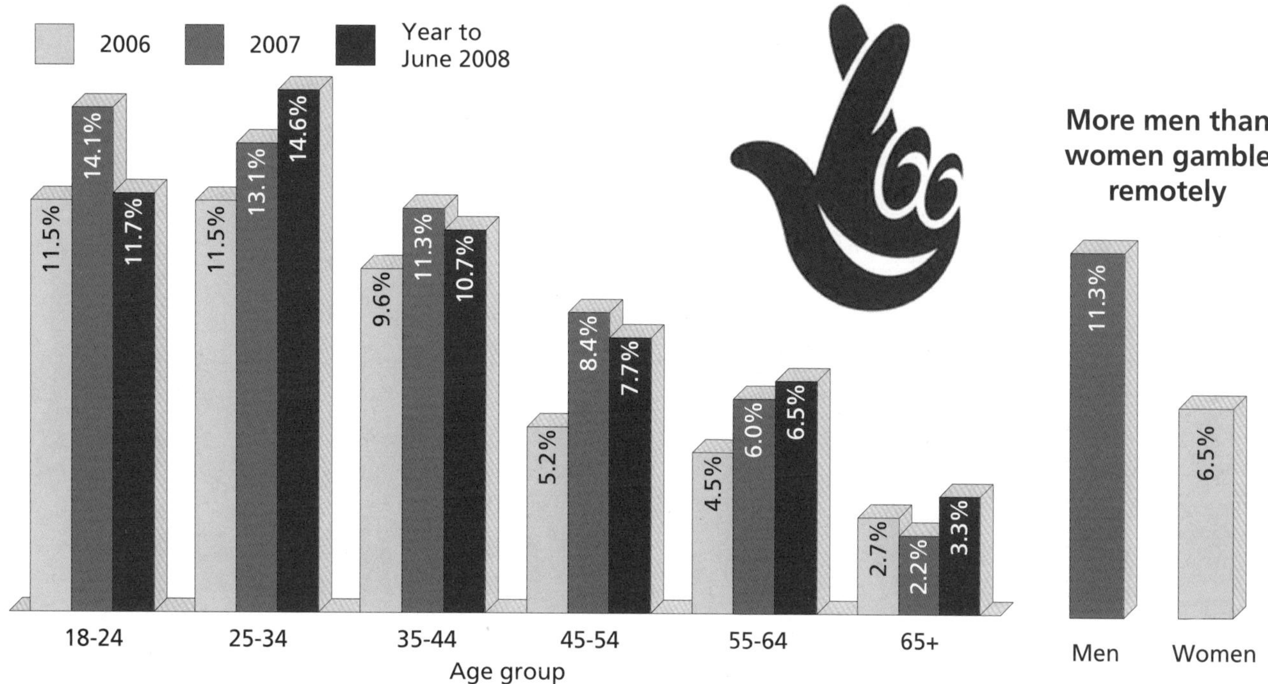

2006
2007
Year to June 2008
11.5%
14.1%
11.7%
11.5%
13.1%
14.6%
9.6%
11.3%
10.7%
5.2%
8.4%
7.7%
4.5%
6.0%
6.5%
2.7%
2.2%
3.3%
18-24
25-34
35-44
45-54
55-64
65+
Age group
More men than women gamble remotely
11.3%
6.5%
Men
Women

Source: Gambling Commission
http://www.gamblingcommission.gov.uk

Transmission transition

The under 25s are leading the way to a TV change

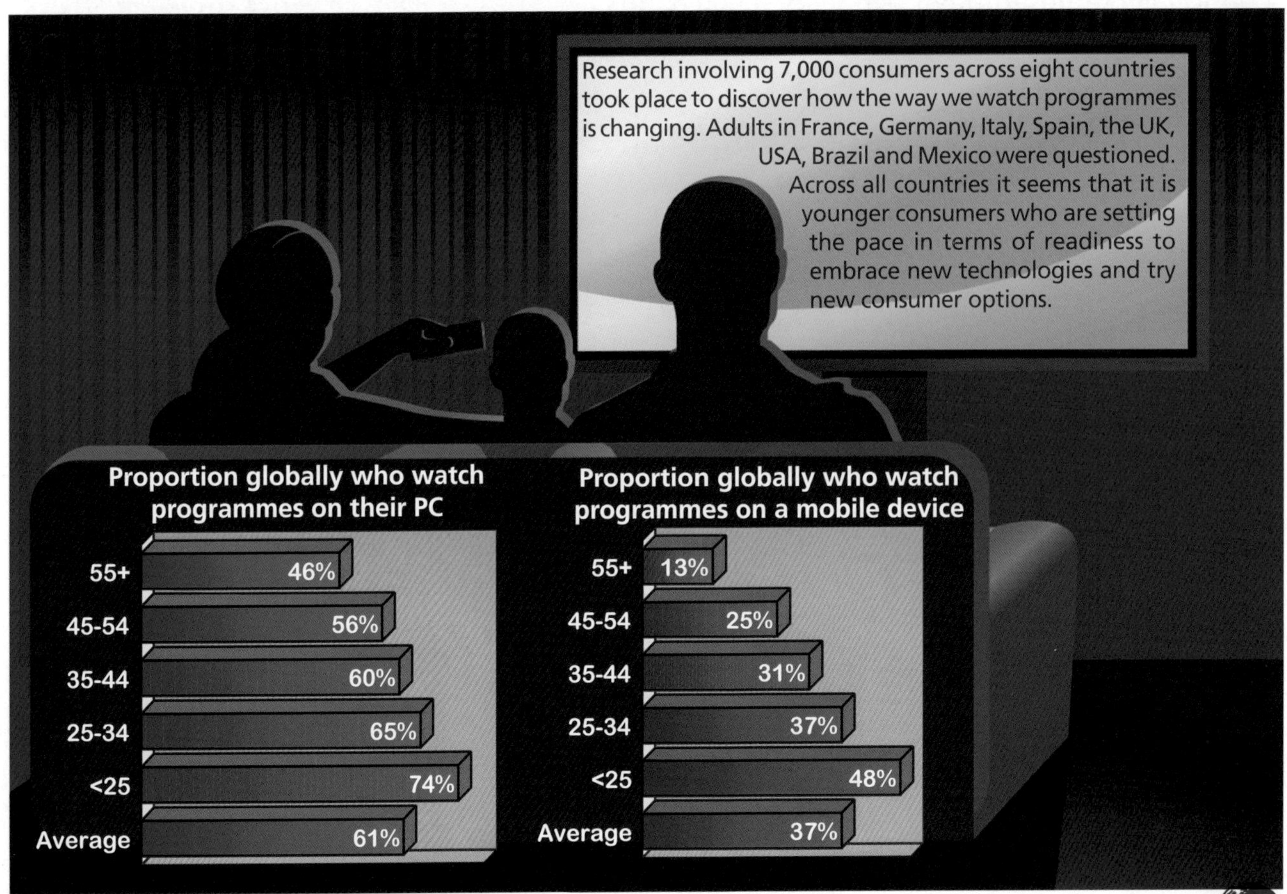

Research involving 7,000 consumers across eight countries took place to discover how the way we watch programmes is changing. Adults in France, Germany, Italy, Spain, the UK, USA, Brazil and Mexico were questioned. Across all countries it seems that it is younger consumers who are setting the pace in terms of readiness to embrace new technologies and try new consumer options.
Proportion globally who watch programmes on their PC
55+ 46%
45-54 56%
35-44 60%
25-34 65%
<25 74%
Average 61%
Proportion globally who watch programmes on a mobile device
55+ 13%
45-54 25%
35-44 31%
25-34 37%
<25 48%
Average 37%

Consumers worldwide increasingly regard the traditional television set as just one option for consuming video content as the boundaries among TV, mobile handsets and PCs blur by the day.

While all consumers are joining the move toward new modes of consuming content, younger consumers are spearheading this shift, especially those under 25. These consumers are more dissatisfied with current television options and more likely to watch content on alternative devices, and more likely to prefer watching content on demand.

This behavioural shift among younger adults represents the beginnings of an impending wave of change.

What consumers dislike about watching 'live' TV

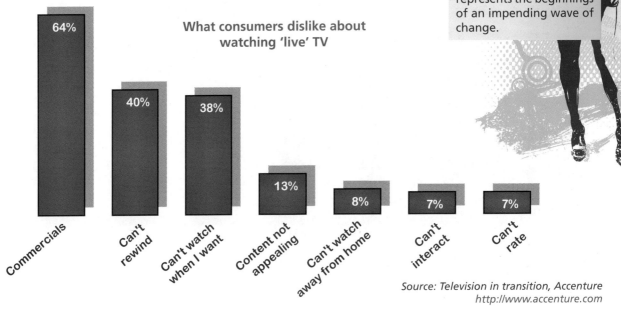

Commercials	Can't rewind	Can't watch when I want	Content not appealing	Can't watch away from home	Can't interact	Can't rate
64%	40%	38%	13%	8%	7%	7%

Source: Television in transition, Accenture
http://www.accenture.com

Ads effect

Can advertising affect drinking behaviour?

Advertising changes

New rules for television advertising came into force in 2005 aimed at preventing alcohol advertising having a strong appeal to under 18s and, in particular, being associated with youth culture.

Has it changed us?

A research study has contrasted attitudes and behaviour before and after the new rules, among 11-21 year olds in the UK.

Alcohol consumption by category, 2005 and 2007

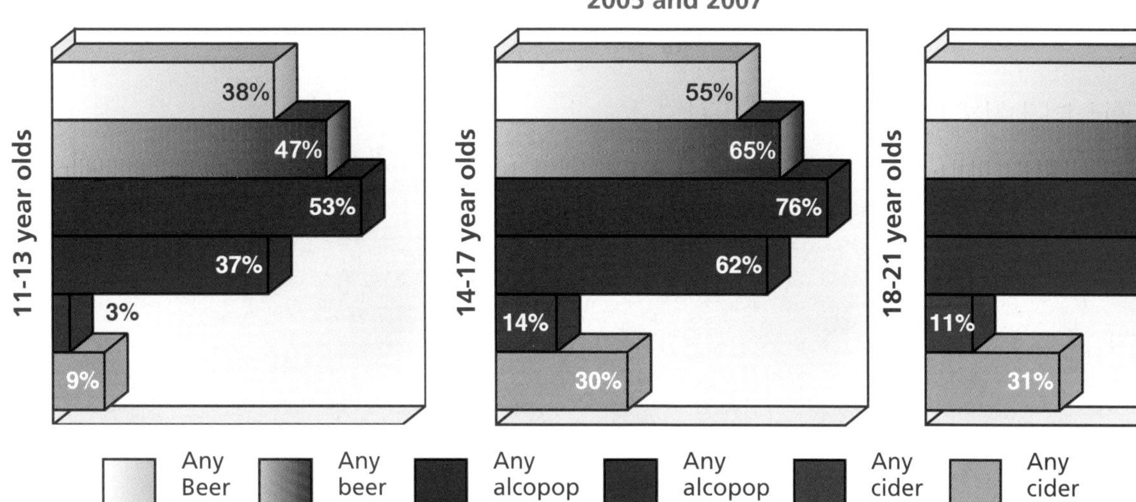
11-13 year olds
38%
47%
53%
37%
3%
9%
14-17 year olds
55%
65%
76%
62%
14%
30%
18-21 year olds
67%
71%
69%
61%
11%
31%
Any Beer 2005
Any beer 2007
Any alcopop 2005
Any alcopop 2007
Any cider 2005
Any cider 2007

Base: All those who had a drink in the last six months

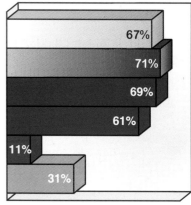

Advertising spots aired on TV (thousands)

	2004	2006
Lager	130	134
Cider	25	79
Alcopops	34	15

It can clearly be seen that the types of alcohol drunk in each age group changed as did the amount of advertisements aired for different alcoholic drinks.

Number of adverts

Alcopop advertisements, which had previously been blamed for being aimed directly at teenagers, more than halved while the number of adverts for cider more than trebled.

Spend on adverts

The amount of money that companies spent on advertising also mirrored this. There was **-37.7%** spend on alcopops yet an increase of **233.8%** on cider advertising.

Recollection of adverts

When young people were asked which alcohol adverts they recalled seeing recently, the change was similar. In 2007 **42%** recalled seeing alcopop adverts compared to **50%** in 2005. Recollection of cider adverts increased from **6%** in 2005 to **19%** in 2007.

Source: Young people & alcohol advertising
http://www.ofcom.org.uk

Textaholics

We send 8.9 million messages every hour

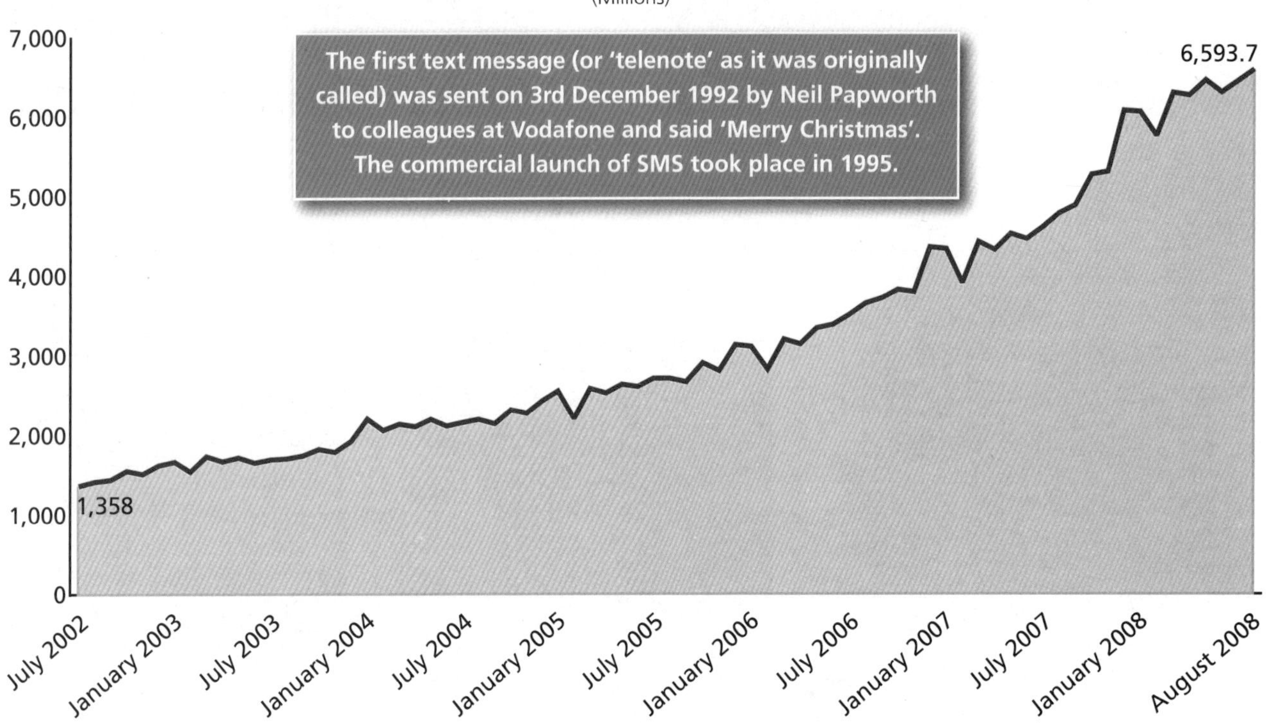

Text messages sent monthly
(Millions)
7,000
6,000
5,000
4,000
3,000
2,000
1,000
0
The first text message (or 'telenote' as it was originally called) was sent on 3rd December 1992 by Neil Papworth to colleagues at Vodafone and said 'Merry Christmas'. The commercial launch of SMS took place in 1995.
6,593.7
1,358
July 2002
January 2003
July 2003
January 2004
July 2004
January 2005
July 2005
January 2006
July 2006
January 2007
July 2007
January 2008
August 2008

Number of person to person **text messages (SMS)** sent in the UK:

Per month	**6,467,070,000**
Per week	**1,492,400,769**
Per day	**212,616,000**

Number of person to person **picture and video messages (MMS)** sent in the UK:

Per month (during May 2008)	**46,516,405**
Per week	**10,734,555**
Per day	**1,529,306**

Annual SMS totals:

1999	**1 billion**
2000	**6.2 billion**
2001	**12.2 billion**
2002	**16.8 billion**
2003	**20.5 billion**
2004	**26 billion**
2005	**32 billion**
2006	**41 billion**

The peak time for texting is between 10.30pm and 11.00pm

The first recorded monthly text message total was 5.4 million in April 1998

What happens next?

New pricing systems and highly desirable, multi-function devices such as the iPhone and Nokia N95, will drive forward the adoption of mobile internet access.

The Mobile Data Association predicts that mobile internet will become a true rival for traditional desktop Internet access, with growth of around **20%** being seen in 2009.

A recent US study indicated that iPhone owners were responsible for 1 in 1,000 web page views in June 2008.

Source: The Mobile Data Association
http://www.themda.org

METROPOLITAN
POLICE

Law & order

Police force

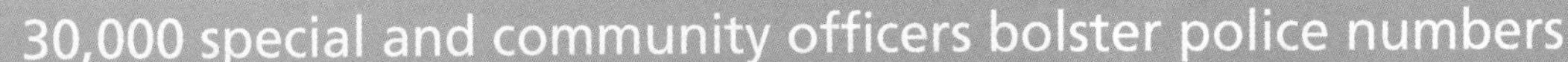
30,000 special and community officers bolster police numbers

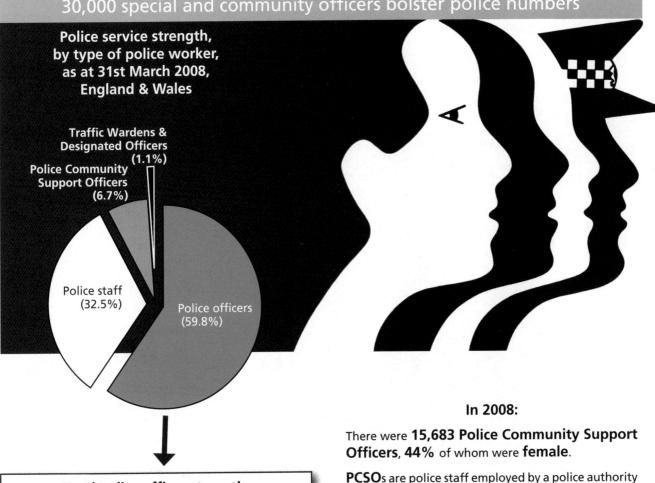

Police service strength, by type of police worker, as at 31st March 2008, England & Wales

Traffic Wardens & Designated Officers (1.1%)

Police Community Support Officers (6.7%)

Police staff (32.5%)

Police officers (59.8%)

Total police officer strength, England & Wales

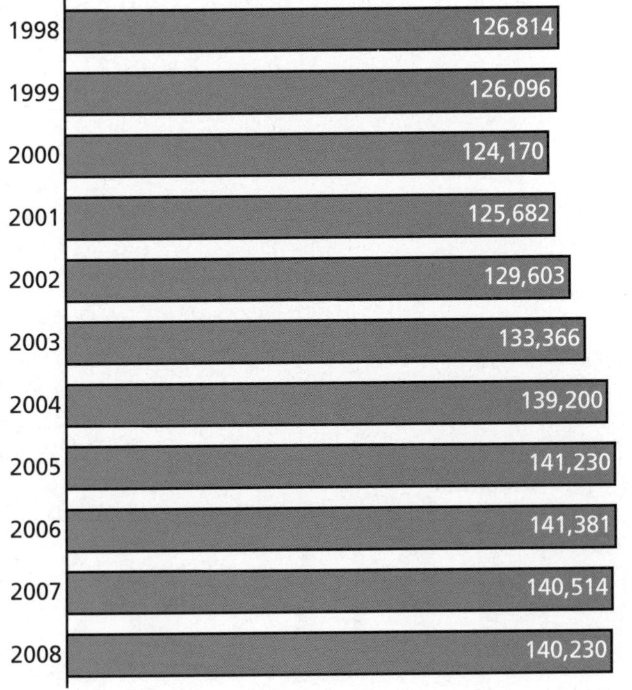
1998
126,814
1999
126,096
2000
124,170
2001
125,682
2002
129,603
2003
133,366
2004
139,200
2005
141,230
2006
141,381
2007
140,514
2008
140,230

In 2008:

There were **15,683 Police Community Support Officers, 44%** of whom were **female**.

PCSOs are police staff employed by a police authority in a highly visible, patrolling role.

They complement the work of police officers by focusing on lower level crime, disorder and anti-social behaviour.

They free up police officer time by taking on those policing functions that do not require the full expertise of a police officer.

They do not have the power of arrest, though they can detain suspects for half an hour.

Traffic warden numbers have **decreased by 23%** since 2007. The continued decline in the number of traffic wardens reflects the increasing role of local authorities in parking control.

There were **1,903 Designated Officers** employed by the police authority who were chosen by Chief Officers to exercise specified powers which would otherwise only be available to police officers such as detention, escort and investigation.

In addition there were **14,547 Special Constables** providing a voluntary police resource to police forces and local communities in England and Wales.

Source: Home Office © Crown copyright
http://www.homeoffice.gov.uk

Hold fire

Armed police were called out 18,000 times but they only fired on 3 occasions

Use of firearms by Police in England and Wales

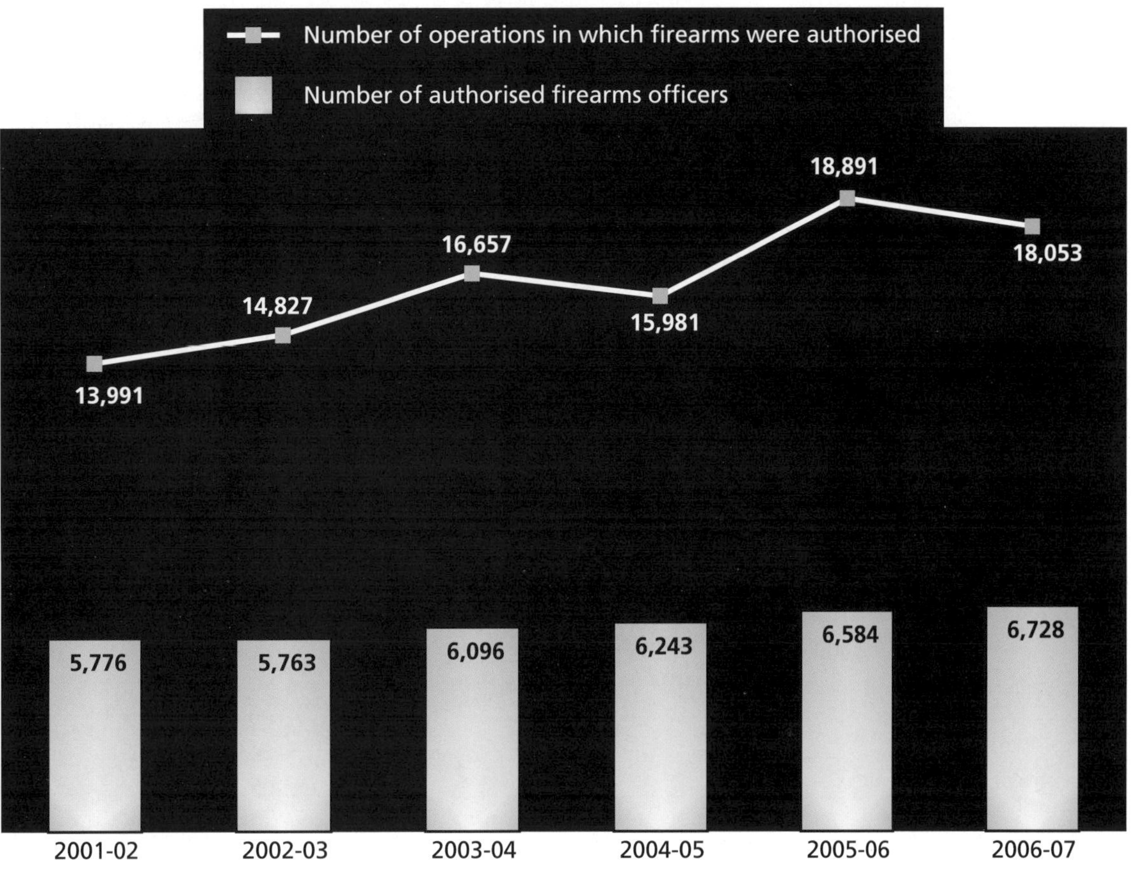

Number of operations in which firearms were authorised
Number of authorised firearms officers
13,991
14,827
16,657
15,981
18,891
18,053
5,776
5,763
6,096
6,243
6,584
6,728
2001-02
2002-03
2003-04
2004-05
2005-06
2006-07

Number of operations involving armed response vehicles

2001-02	11,574
2002-03	11,848
2003-04	13,218
2004-05	13,137
2005-06	14,355
2006-07	14,530

Top 5 Police Forces authorising use of fire arms, 2006/07

Metropolitan	3,878
West Yorkshire	1,272
West Midlands	1,557
South Yorkshire	737
Merseyside	727

Taser use

Tasers deliver powerful electric shocks and are intended to be a 'less lethal' alternative to regular police weapons.

Police figures reveal that between 2004 (when they were introduced) and 2007, Tasers were used 424 times in the UK. This figure excludes North Wales and Merseyside Police who did not give figures.

Cleveland Police and Durham Constabulary have the highest figures for the number of times they have fired Tasers – 23 times each. When population sizes are taken into account this is more than five times the national average. In Scotland the Taser has only been fired six times.

Source: Police Review, Home Office © Crown copyright 2008
http://www.policereview.com
http://www.homeoffice.gov.uk

Hate crime

Crimes of prejudice are being reported more than ever before

On 22 April 1993 a black teenager, Stephen Lawrence, was murdered in South East London. After vigorous campaigning by his parents there was an enquiry into the way the police had handled the investigation. This resulted in a new definition of racist incidents which was taken up by all police forces: "A racist incident is any incident which is perceived to be racist by the victim or any other person." (*The Macpherson Report, 1999*)

Racist incidents reported to the police, England and Wales

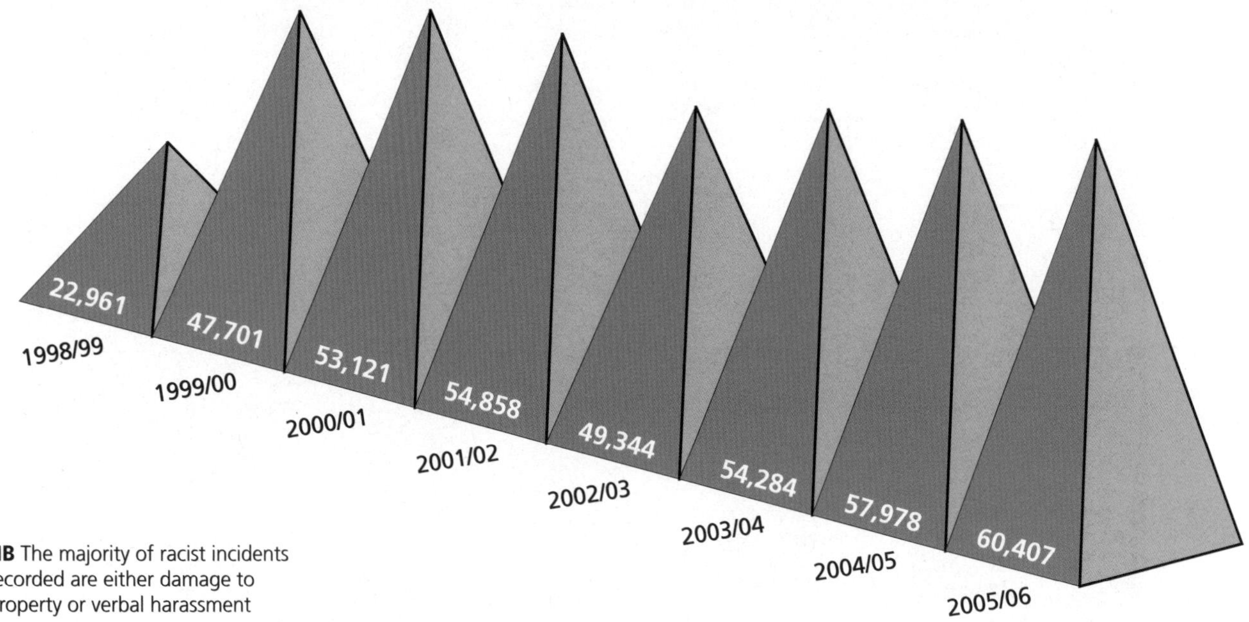

22,961
1998/99
47,701
1999/00
53,121
2000/01
54,858
2001/02
49,344
2002/03
54,284
2003/04
57,978
2004/05
60,407
2005/06

NB The majority of racist incidents recorded are either damage to property or verbal harassment

Racially or religiously aggravated offences reported to the police

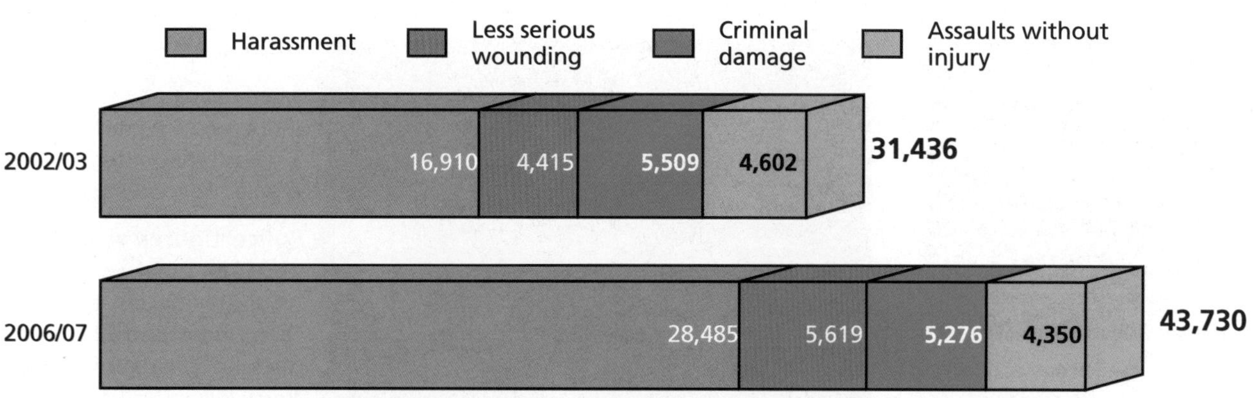

Harassment
Less serious wounding
Criminal damage
Assaults without injury
2002/03
16,910
4,415
5,509
4,602
31,436
2006/07
28,485
5,619
5,276
4,350
43,730

An offence may be defined as racially or religiously aggravated if:

- **at the time of committing the offence, or immediately before or after doing so, the offender demonstrates towards the victim of the offence hostility based on the victim's membership (or presumed membership) of a racial or religious group; or**
- **the offence is motivated (wholly or partly) by hostility towards members of a racial or religious group based on their membership of that group**

Source: Recorded Crime Statistics , Home Office © Crown copyright 2007, Statistics on Race and the Criminal Justice System © Crown copyright 2007

http://www.homeoffice.gov.uk
http://www.justice.gov.uk

The British Crime Survey records people's experiences and perceptions of crime including whether victims of crime perceived the incident to be racially motivated. It is estimated that there were around **139,000** racially motivated incidents in 2005/06

The attrition* rate for racist crime in England and Wales: from British Crime Survey estimates through to prosecuted defendants in 2005-06

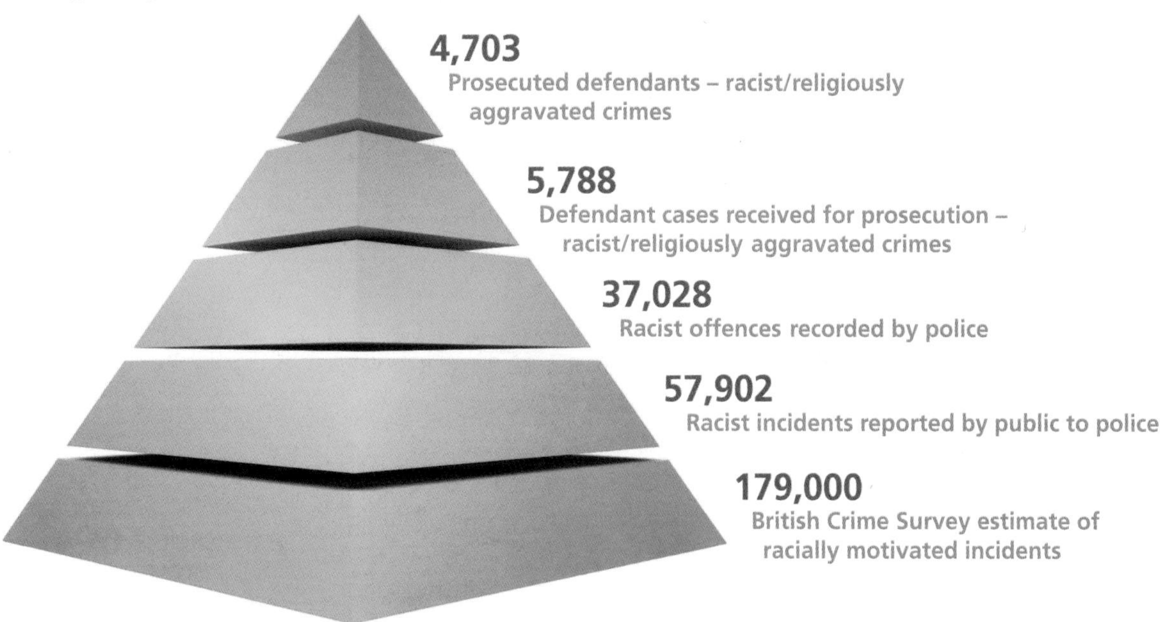

4,703
Prosecuted defendants – racist/religiously aggravated crimes
5,788
Defendant cases received for prosecution – racist/religiously aggravated crimes
37,028
Racist offences recorded by police
57,902
Racist incidents reported by public to police
179,000
British Crime Survey estimate of racially motivated incidents

Source: Report on racism and xenophobia in the Member States of the EU
http://www.europa.eu

*Attrition rate: the gradual reduction in numbers between the number of crimes and successful prosecution

In Scotland:

There were **5,124** racist incidents recorded by the police in 2005-06, an increase of **588** (13%) from 2004-05

The number of racist related crimes recorded by the police in Scotland was 6,439, up 12% on the previous year

Most incidents took place in the street, and most commonly occurred on Friday or Saturday night

Two specific crimes - racially aggravated harassment and racially aggravated conduct - accounted for over half of all racist related crimes recorded by the police

The majority of victims were of Asian origin (Indian, Pakistani, Bangladeshi or other Asian), with the majority being Pakistani. (The largest visible minority ethnic group in the Scotland)

Over 20% of victims had experience of one or more previous racist incidents

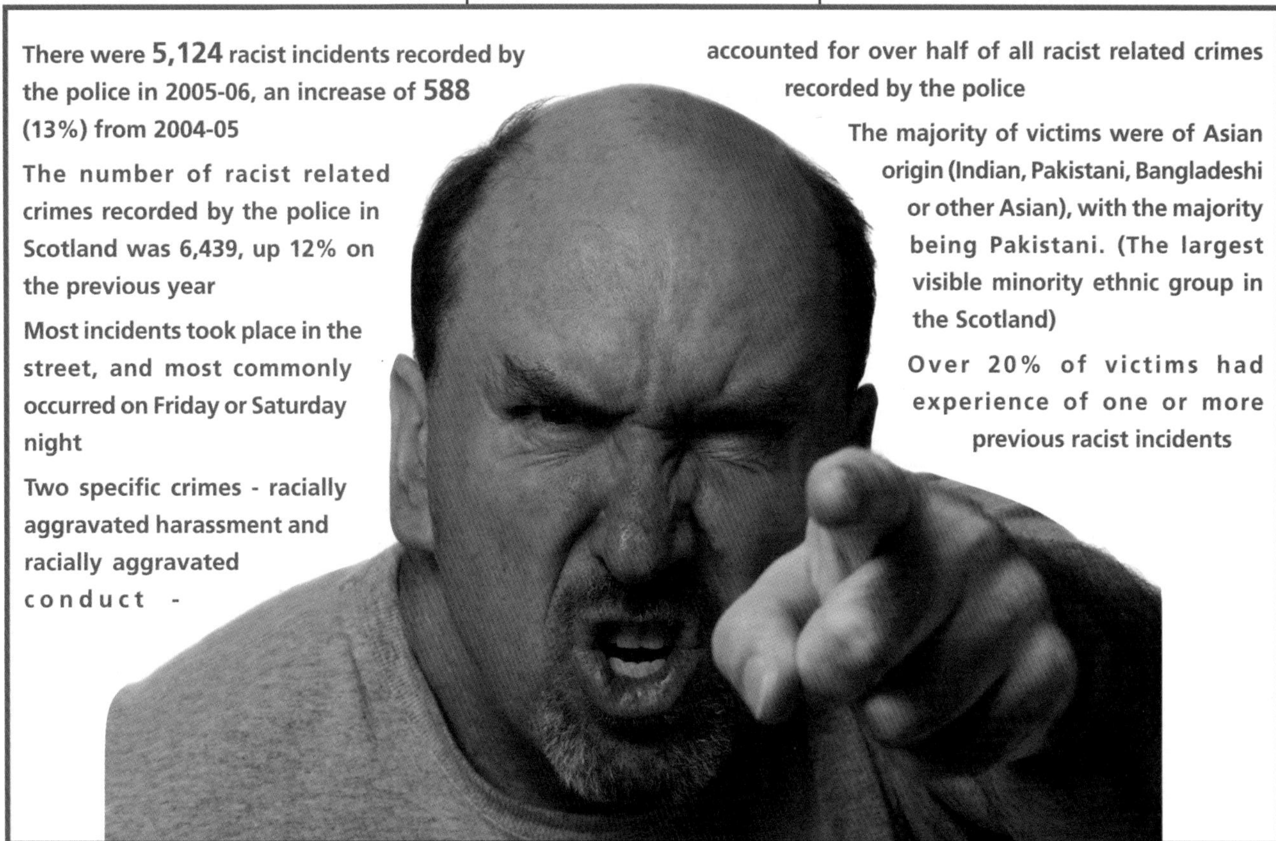

Source:
The Scottish Government news release
http://www.scotland.gov.uk

Knife edge

There is a knife attack every 24 minutes in England & Wales

Knife crime map of England & Wales 2007/08 – Serious offences involving a knife

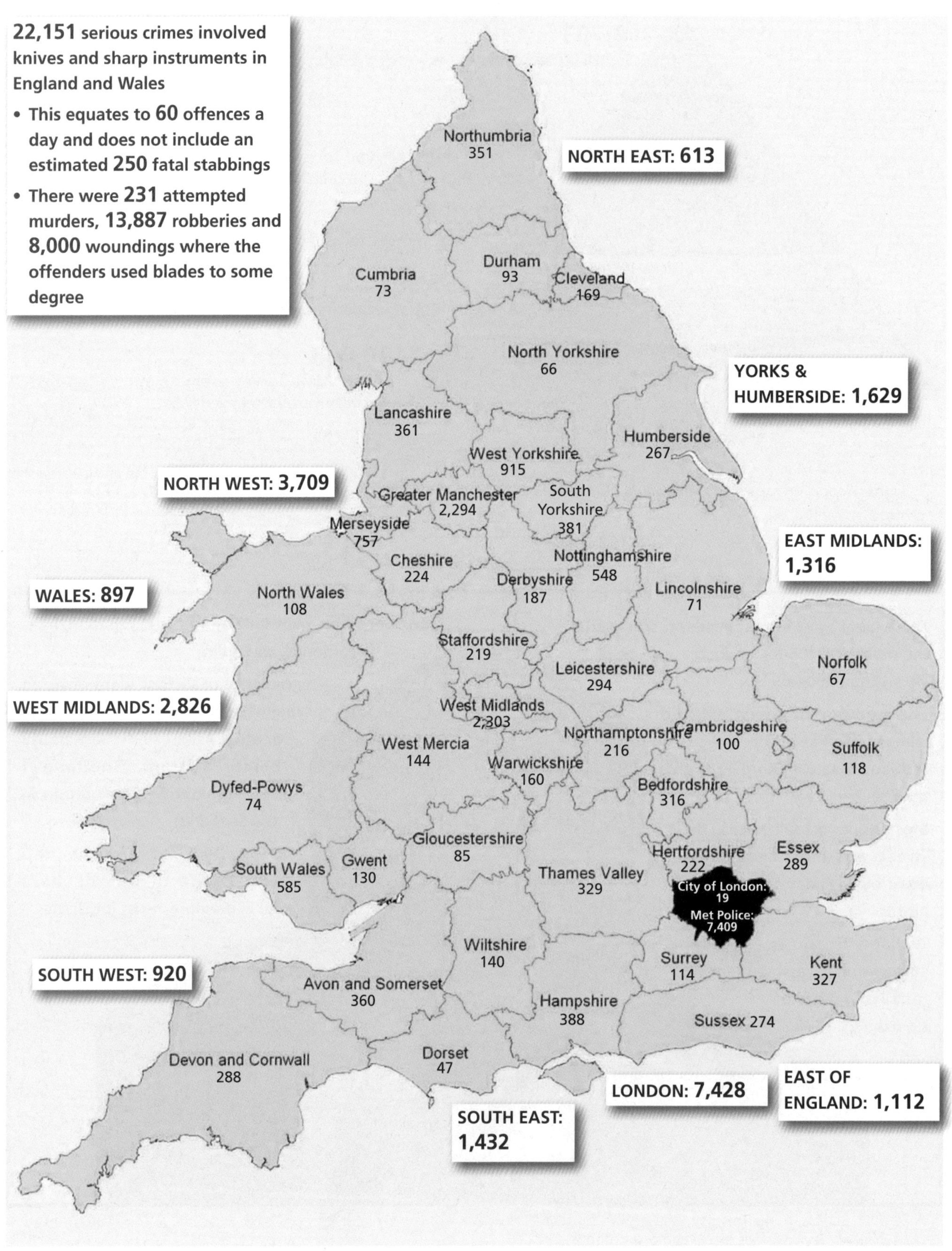

22,151 serious crimes involved knives and sharp instruments in England and Wales
• This equates to 60 offences a day and does not include an estimated 250 fatal stabbings
• There were 231 attempted murders, 13,887 robberies and 8,000 woundings where the offenders used blades to some degree
NORTH EAST: 613
YORKS & HUMBERSIDE: 1,629
NORTH WEST: 3,709
EAST MIDLANDS: 1,316
WALES: 897
WEST MIDLANDS: 2,826
SOUTH WEST: 920
LONDON: 7,428
EAST OF ENGLAND: 1,112
SOUTH EAST: 1,432
Northumbria 351
Cumbria 73
Durham 93
Cleveland 169
North Yorkshire 66
Lancashire 361
West Yorkshire 915
Humberside 267
Greater Manchester 2,294
South Yorkshire 381
Merseyside 757
Cheshire 224
Nottinghamshire 548
Derbyshire 187
Lincolnshire 71
North Wales 108
Staffordshire 219
Leicestershire 294
Norfolk 67
West Midlands 2,303
Northamptonshire 216
Cambridgeshire 100
West Mercia 144
Suffolk 118
Warwickshire 160
Bedfordshire 316
Dyfed-Powys 74
Gloucestershire 85
Hertfordshire 222
Essex 289
Gwent 130
South Wales 585
Thames Valley 329
City of London: 19
Met Police: 7,409
Wiltshire 140
Surrey 114
Kent 327
Avon and Somerset 360
Hampshire 388
Sussex 274
Devon and Cornwall 288
Dorset 47

Q In the last 12 months, have you carried a knife with you for your own protection, for use in crimes or in case you got into a fight?

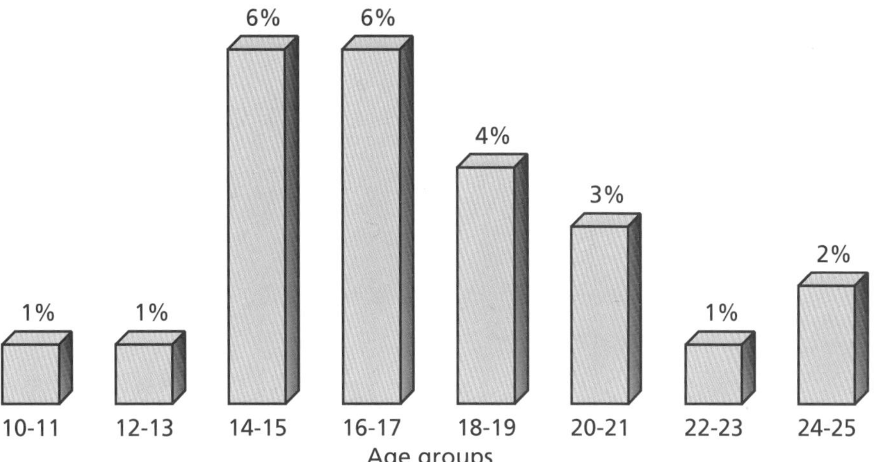

1%
1%
6%
6%
4%
3%
1%
2%
10-11
12-13
14-15
16-17
18-19
20-21
22-23
24-25
Age groups

> **There is now a need for radical, short-term solutions... introducing a minimum prison sentence for carrying a knife... would have a dramatic impact.**
>
> *Ian Johnston, president of the Police Superintendents' Association*

In a special initiative against knives between June and August 2008, the government said more than **2,500 arrests** were made and **1,600 knives** were seized. Over **55,000** people were **stopped and searched** under the measures.

Of those who had carried knives:

85% said it was for their **own protection**

8% in case they got into a **fight**

7% carried them for **other reasons**

54% had carried knives once or twice

18% three or four times

11% between five and ten times

17% more than ten times

46% had carried a **penknife**

20% a **flick knife**

12% a **kitchen knife**

22% another type of knife

More than 5,000 10 to 25 year olds completed a self-report survey about their offending. This type of survey is designed to provide a better measure of the extent and nature of offending than can be obtained through official records.

Source: Home Office statistical bulletins 07/08 & 09/08 © Crown copyright 2008
http://www.homeoffice.gov.uk

Homicide

Around 65% of victims know their killer

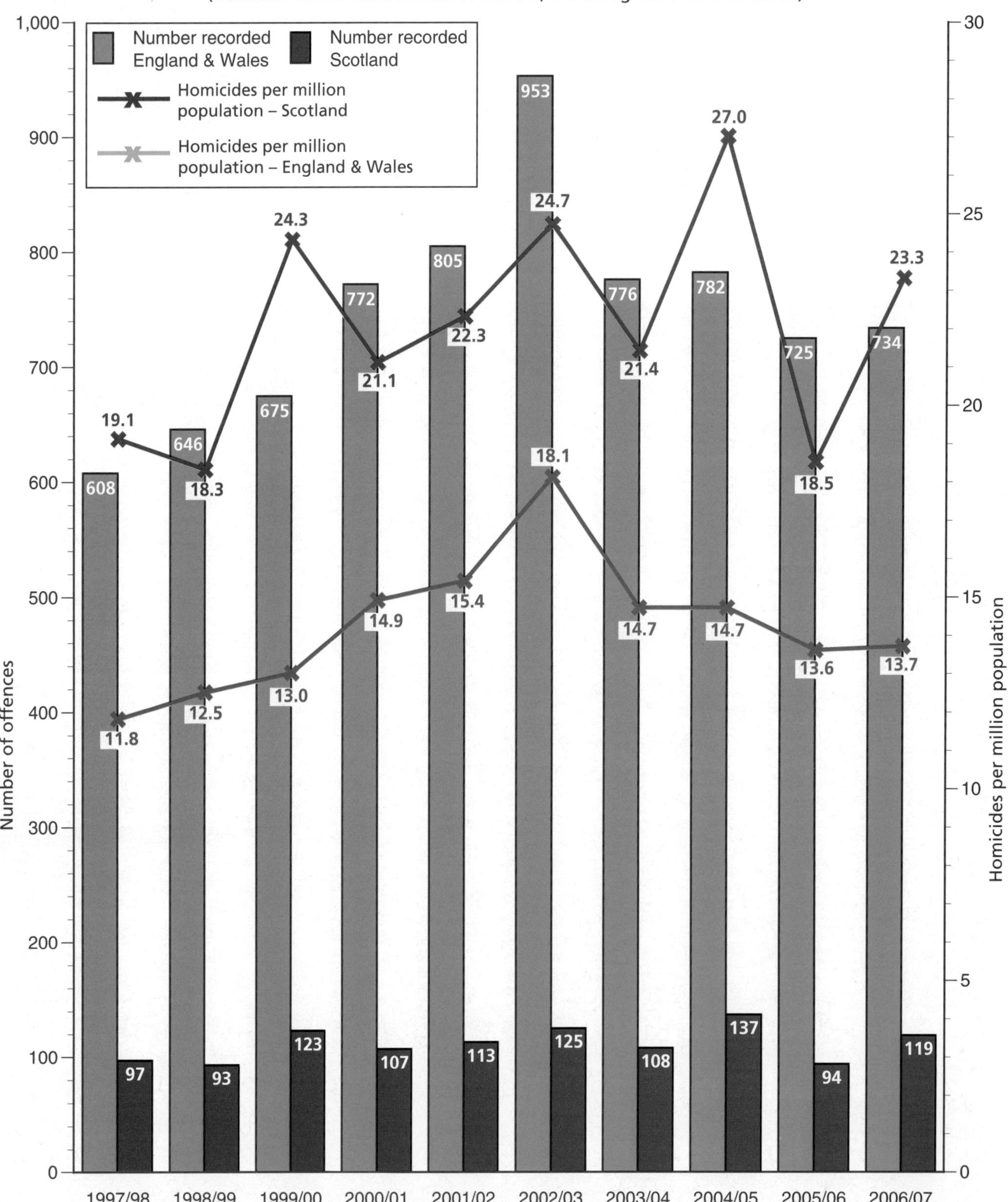

Homicides recorded by the police
(Homicide covers the offences of murder, manslaughter and infanticide)
Number recorded England & Wales
Number recorded Scotland
Homicides per million population – Scotland
Homicides per million population – England & Wales
Number of offences
Homicides per million population
1,000
900
800
700
600
500
400
300
200
100
0
30
25
20
15
10
5
0
1997/98
1998/99
1999/00
2000/01
2001/02
2002/03
2003/04
2004/05
2005/06
2006/07
608
646
675
772
805
953
776
782
725
734
97
93
123
107
113
125
108
137
94
119
19.1
18.3
24.3
21.1
22.3
24.7
21.4
27.0
18.5
23.3
11.8
12.5
13.0
14.9
15.4
18.1
14.7
14.7
13.6
13.7

In England & Wales:

2000/01 includes **58** Chinese nationals who collectively suffocated in a lorry en route in the UK

2002/03 includes **172** victims of Dr Harold Shipman

2003/04 includes **20** cockle pickers who drowned in Morecambe Bay

2005/06 includes **52** victims of the 7th July London bombings

The relationship between victim and suspect

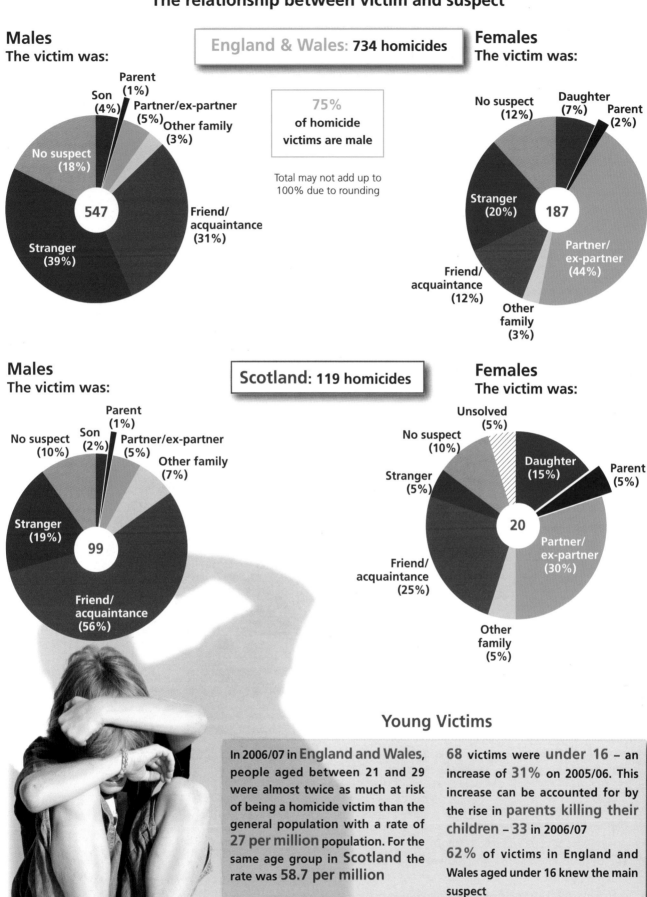

England & Wales: 734 homicides

75%
of homicide victims are male

Total may not add up to 100% due to rounding

Males
The victim was:

547

- Son (4%)
- Parent (1%)
- Partner/ex-partner (5%)
- Other family (3%)
- Friend/acquaintance (31%)
- Stranger (39%)
- No suspect (18%)

Females
The victim was:

187

- Daughter (7%)
- Parent (2%)
- Partner/ex-partner (44%)
- Other family (3%)
- Friend/acquaintance (12%)
- Stranger (20%)
- No suspect (12%)

Scotland: 119 homicides

Males
The victim was:

99

- Son (2%)
- Parent (1%)
- Partner/ex-partner (5%)
- Other family (7%)
- Friend/acquaintance (56%)
- Stranger (19%)
- No suspect (10%)

Females
The victim was:

20

- Unsolved (5%)
- Daughter (15%)
- Parent (5%)
- Partner/ex-partner (30%)
- Other family (5%)
- Friend/acquaintance (25%)
- Stranger (5%)
- No suspect (10%)

Young Victims

In 2006/07 in England and Wales, people aged between 21 and 29 were almost twice as much at risk of being a homicide victim than the general population with a rate of 27 per million population. For the same age group in Scotland the rate was 58.7 per million

68 victims were under 16 – an increase of 31% on 2005/06. This increase can be accounted for by the rise in parents killing their children – 33 in 2006/07

62% of victims in England and Wales aged under 16 knew the main suspect

Source: Homicides, Firearm Offences and Intimate Violence 2006/07, The Scottish Government © Crown copyright 2008

http://www.homeoffice.gov.uk/rds
http://www.scotland.gov.uk

Drunk & disorderly

Numbers of drunken women soar

Female arrests for drunk and disorderly behaviour in selected police force areas in England and Wales
Percentage change between 2003/04 and 2007/08
West Midlands 1,138
Gwent 578
Leicestershire 450
West Yorkshire 86
Dyfed-Powys 84
Essex 82
Norfolk 73
Durham 57
North Yorkshire 55
Northumbria 48
Devon and Cornwall 9
Cambridgeshire -13
Northamptonshire -14
Dorset -36
Gloucestershire -56

Medical experts warn that binge drinking among young women has reached epidemic proportions, with some in their 20s and 30s suffering liver conditions which doctors expect to see among far older, hardened drinkers.

Police chiefs believe that there is "clear need" for tough action, particularly to tackle under-age drinking. They suggest:

- a total ban on alcopops
- ban on all alcohol advertising
- pricing alcohol according to strength
- end of discounted drinks, such as two-for-one deals, and happy hours
- stop supermarkets selling alcohol below cost price

Figures requested from Police Forces were revealed following a request by Channel 4 news under the Freedom of Information Act, although not all forces were able to provide full details.

Source: Channel 4 news
http://www.channel4.com

Number of arrests by each police force

Police Forces	2007/08*
West Midlands	731
Gwent	190
Leicestershire	77
West Yorkshire	981
Dyfed-Powys	120
Essex	204
Norfolk	78
Durham	299
North Yorkshire	209
Northumbria	2,101
Devon and Cornwall	375
Cambridgeshire	90
Northamptonshire	56
Dorset	74
Gloucestershire	29

NB Figures for 2007/08 include the part year April 2007 to the end of February 2008

Under the influence

75% of Class A drug users support their habits through crime

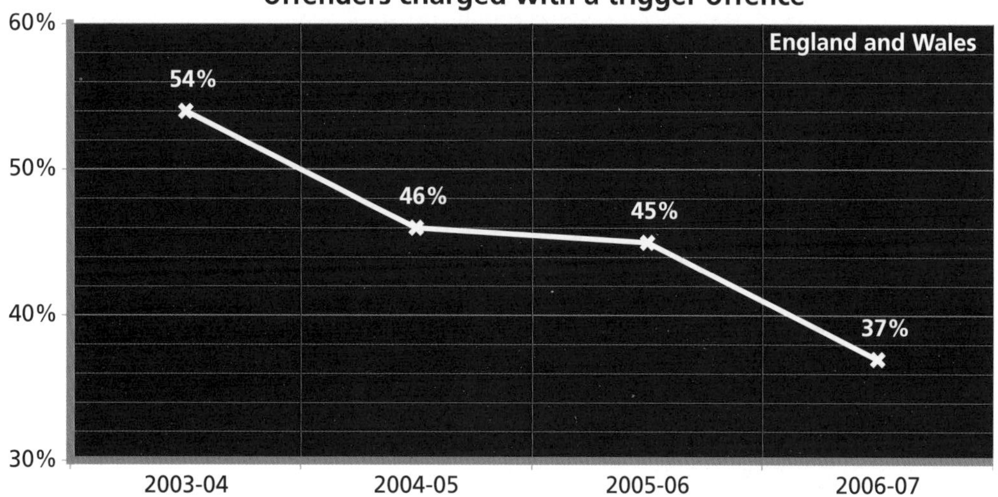

Positive tests for heroin and cocaine/crack for offenders charged with a trigger offence
England and Wales
60%
50%
40%
30%
54%
46%
45%
37%
2003-04
2004-05
2005-06
2006-07

NB Only offenders arrested or charged with a 'trigger offence' – offences which include all kinds of theft, handling stolen goods, possession of drugs, fraud and begging – are required to provide a sample to be tested for specified Class A drugs

A survey of over 7,500 17-year-old arrestees found:

- **57% had taken one or more drugs in the last month**
- **46% cannabis**
- **18% heroin**
- **15% crack**
- **10% cocaine**

General criminal offences routinely recorded by the police do not contain information on the offenders' drug habits. It is therefore not possible to provide an accurate estimate of the number of offences that are drug related but research provides the link between drug use, particularly use of heroin and crack cocaine, and acquisitive crime.

Top ten criminal activities that are drug-related

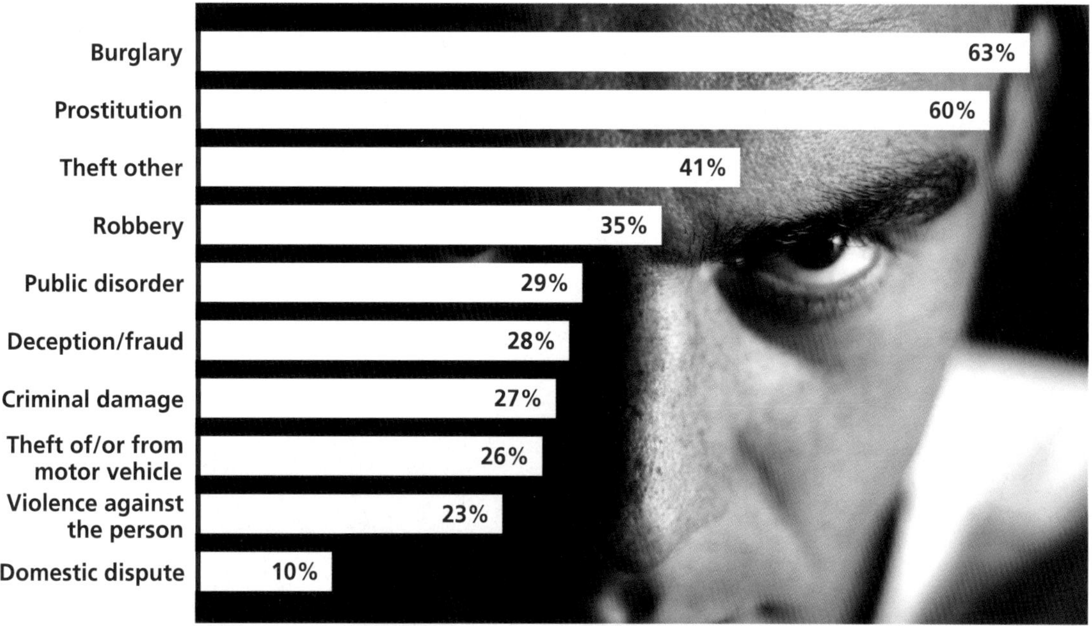

Burglary 63%
Prostitution 60%
Theft other 41%
Robbery 35%
Public disorder 29%
Deception/fraud 28%
Criminal damage 27%
Theft of/or from motor vehicle 26%
Violence against the person 23%
Domestic dispute 10%

These figures are estimates based on a variety of surveys, and when no information was available a subjective estimate was made by senior police officers

Source: European Monitoring Centre for Drugs and Drug Addiction
http:// www.emcdda.europa.eu

Source: Hansard © Parliamentary copyright 2008
http://www.parliament.uk

Cannabis confusion

50% of people are unsure about the status of cannabis

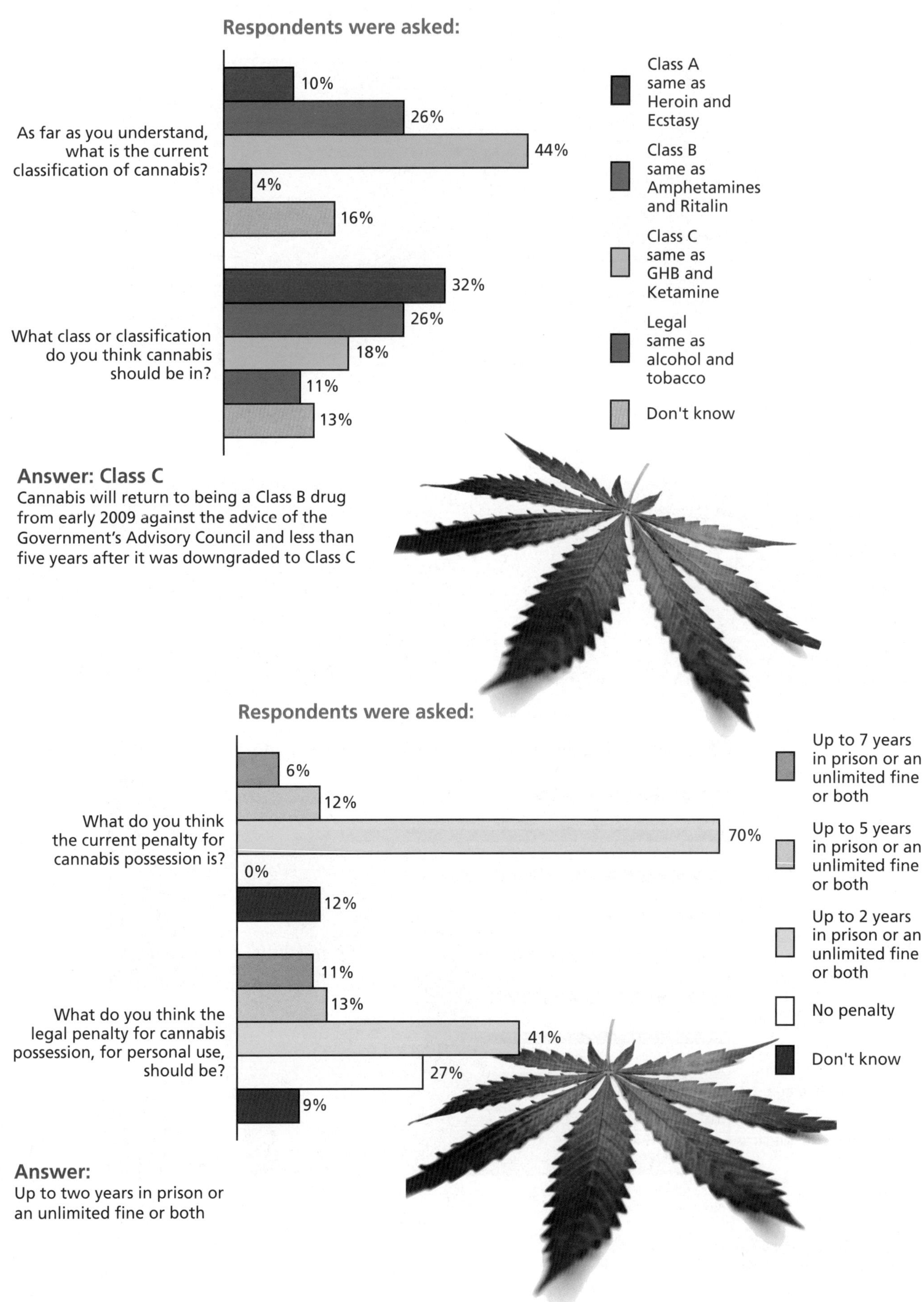
Respondents were asked:
As far as you understand, what is the current classification of cannabis?
10%
26%
44%
4%
16%
What class or classification do you think cannabis should be in?
32%
26%
18%
11%
13%
Class A same as Heroin and Ecstasy
Class B same as Amphetamines and Ritalin
Class C same as GHB and Ketamine
Legal same as alcohol and tobacco
Don't know
Respondents were asked:
What do you think the current penalty for cannabis possession is?
6%
12%
70%
0%
12%
What do you think the legal penalty for cannabis possession, for personal use, should be?
11%
13%
41%
27%
9%
Up to 7 years in prison or an unlimited fine or both
Up to 5 years in prison or an unlimited fine or both
Up to 2 years in prison or an unlimited fine or both
No penalty
Don't know

Answer: Class C

Cannabis will return to being a Class B drug from early 2009 against the advice of the Government's Advisory Council and less than five years after it was downgraded to Class C

Answer:

Up to two years in prison or an unlimited fine or both

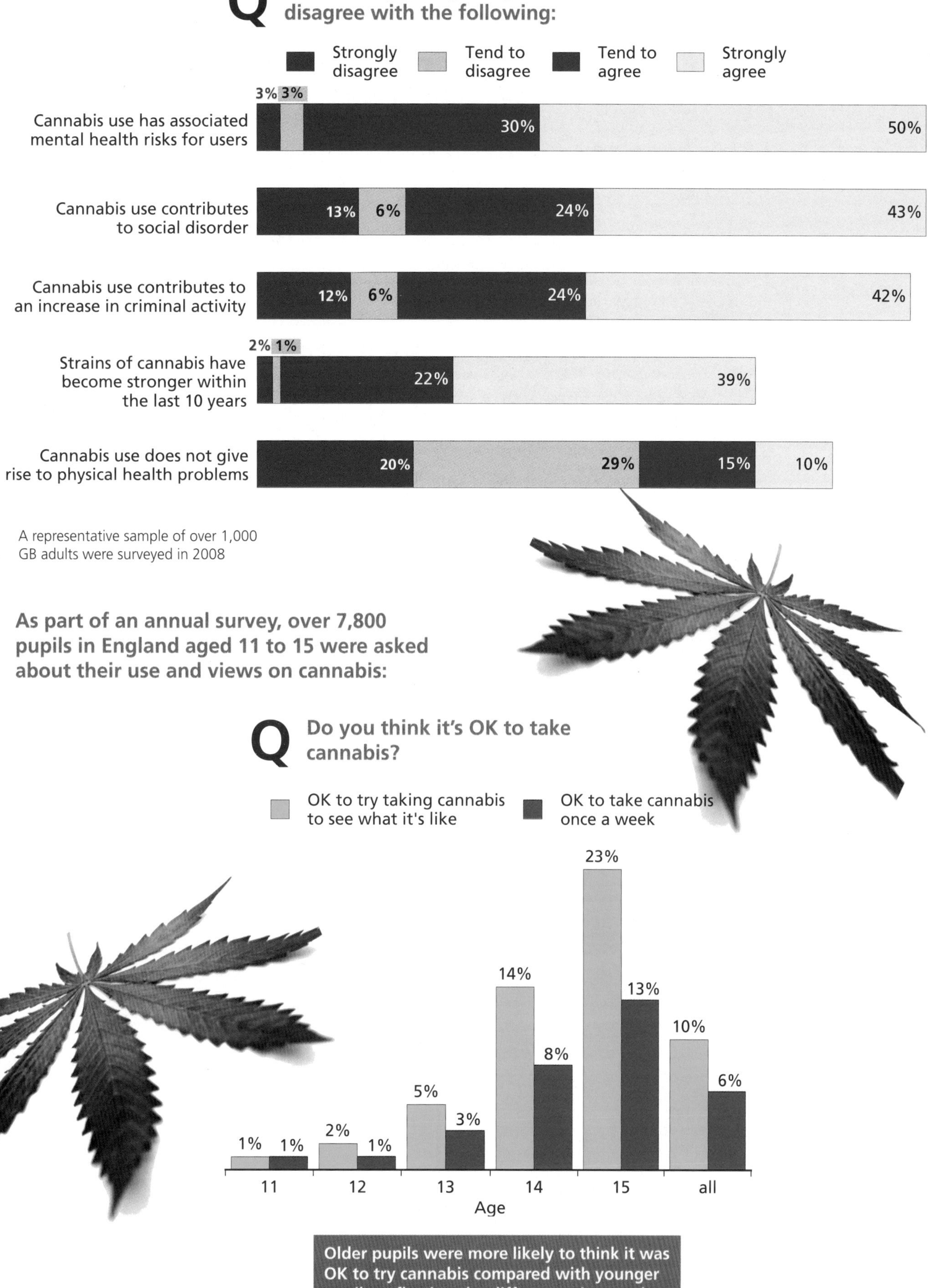
Q How strongly do you agree or disagree with the following:
Strongly disagree
Tend to disagree
Tend to agree
Strongly agree
Cannabis use has associated mental health risks for users
3% 3% 30% 50%
Cannabis use contributes to social disorder
13% 6% 24% 43%
Cannabis use contributes to an increase in criminal activity
12% 6% 24% 42%
Strains of cannabis have become stronger within the last 10 years
2% 1% 22% 39%
Cannabis use does not give rise to physical health problems
20% 29% 15% 10%
A representative sample of over 1,000 GB adults were surveyed in 2008
As part of an annual survey, over 7,800 pupils in England aged 11 to 15 were asked about their use and views on cannabis:
Q Do you think it's OK to take cannabis?
OK to try taking cannabis to see what it's like
OK to take cannabis once a week
11: 1% 1%
12: 2% 1%
13: 5% 3%
14: 14% 8%
15: 23% 13%
all: 10% 6%
Age
Older pupils were more likely to think it was OK to try cannabis compared with younger pupils, reflecting the differences in actual behaviour among pupils of different ages.

Source: Ipsos MORI; Drink use, smoking and drinking among young people in England in 2007, NHS Information Centre
http://www.ipsos-mori.com
http://www.ic.nhs.uk

Awaiting justice

"Remand prisoners are often held for excessively long periods in conditions that are worse than for sentenced prisoners"

Rob Allen, Director of the International Centre for Prison Studies

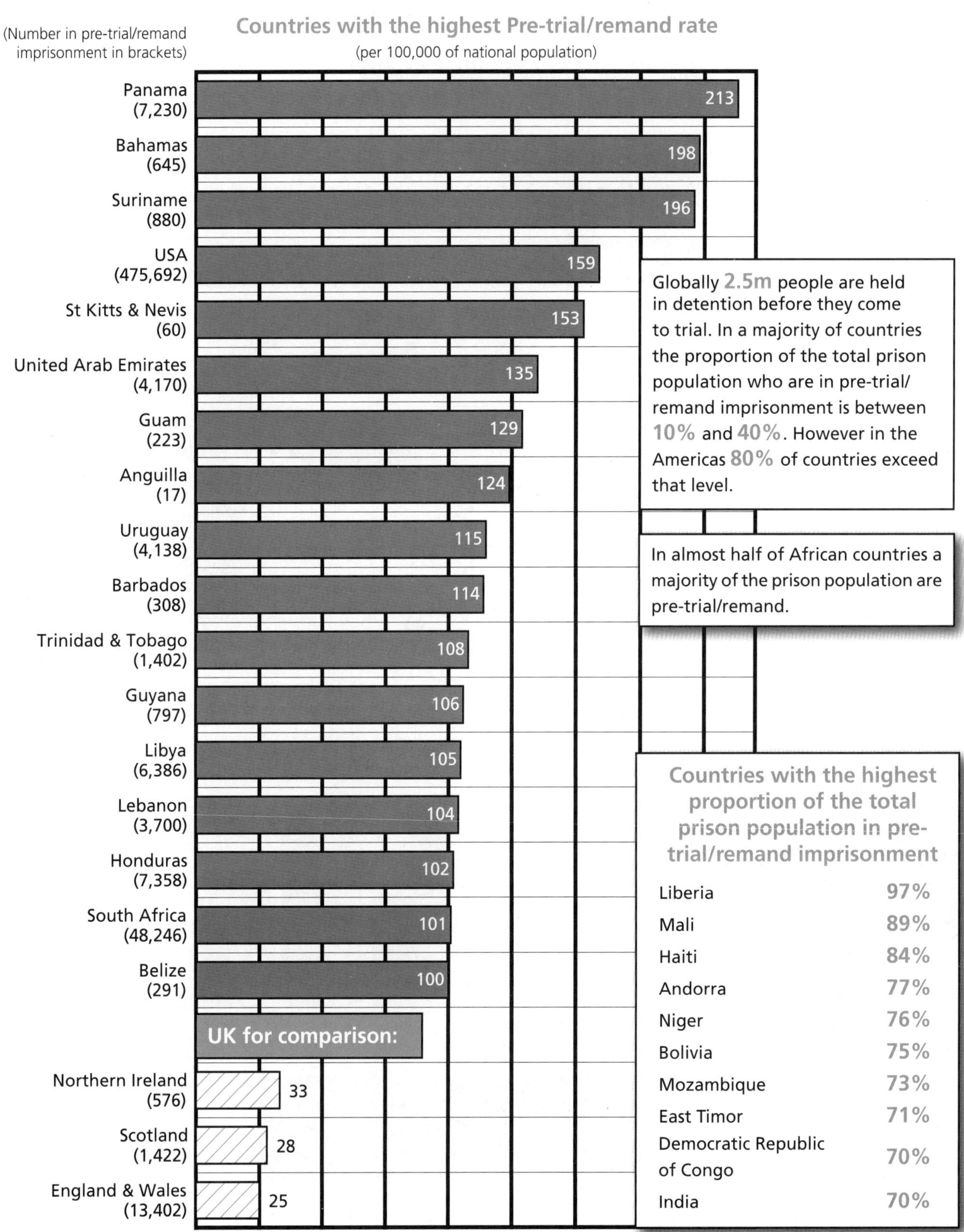

Countries with the highest Pre-trial/remand rate
(per 100,000 of national population)
(Number in pre-trial/remand imprisonment in brackets)
Panama (7,230) 213
Bahamas (645) 198
Suriname (880) 196
USA (475,692) 159
St Kitts & Nevis (60) 153
United Arab Emirates (4,170) 135
Guam (223) 129
Anguilla (17) 124
Uruguay (4,138) 115
Barbados (308) 114
Trinidad & Tobago (1,402) 108
Guyana (797) 106
Libya (6,386) 105
Lebanon (3,700) 104
Honduras (7,358) 102
South Africa (48,246) 101
Belize (291) 100
UK for comparison:
Northern Ireland (576) 33
Scotland (1,422) 28
England & Wales (13,402) 25

Globally 2.5m people are held in detention before they come to trial. In a majority of countries the proportion of the total prison population who are in pre-trial/remand imprisonment is between 10% and 40%. However in the Americas 80% of countries exceed that level.

In almost half of African countries a majority of the prison population are pre-trial/remand.

Countries with the highest proportion of the total prison population in pre-trial/remand imprisonment

Liberia	97%
Mali	89%
Haiti	84%
Andorra	77%
Niger	76%
Bolivia	75%
Mozambique	73%
East Timor	71%
Democratic Republic of Congo	70%
India	70%

Source: International Centre for Prison Studies
www.kcl.ac.uk/icps

Behind bars

Titan prisons are being built to house record numbers

The total prison population in England and Wales has increased significantly since the mid-1990s, rising from **61,470** in June 1997 to **83,495** in July 2008 (**79,046** Males **4,449** Females)

The number of prisoners in England and Wales **increased by 25,000** in the decade from 1996 to 2006

The number of women in prison has nearly doubled over the past decade.

In 1996 the mid year figure for women in prison was **2,305**

In 2000 it was **3,355**

In May 2008 the women's prison population stood at **4,458**

On 5th December 2007 in its response to Lord Carter's review of prisons the government announced an additional **10,500** prison places to be built by 2014.

A new building programme will take the rate of imprisonment in England and Wales to **178 per 100,000** of population. That is beyond Bulgaria (148), Slovakia (155), Romania (155) and Hungary (156).

Highest projected prison population, England & Wales

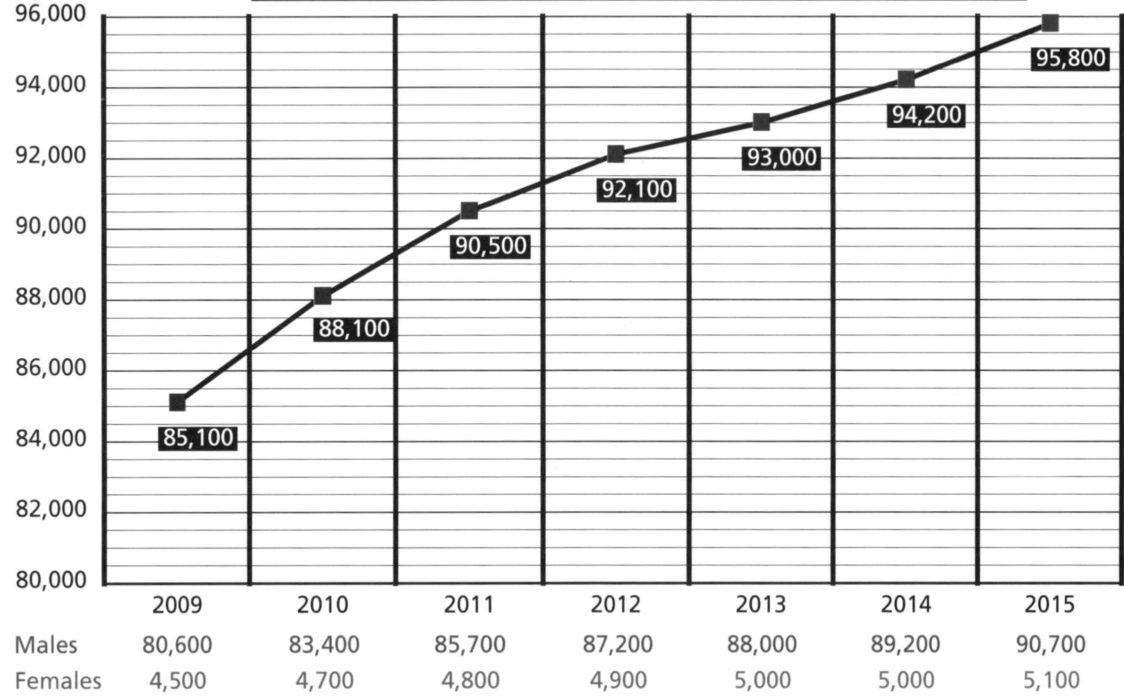

96,000
94,000
92,000
90,000
88,000
86,000
84,000
82,000
80,000
85,100
88,100
90,500
92,100
93,000
94,200
95,800

	2009	2010	2011	2012	2013	2014	2015
Males	80,600	83,400	85,700	87,200	88,000	89,200	90,700
Females	4,500	4,700	4,800	4,900	5,000	5,000	5,100

Source: Ministry of Justice, Scottish Prison Service, Northern Ireland Prison Service © Crown copyright
http:// www.justice.gov.uk
http://www.sps.gov.uk
http://www.niprisonservice.gov.uk

NB Totals may not add up due to rounding

Rape reports

In some areas reported rapes are five times more likely to result in a conviction than in others

Regional rape conviction rates, England and Wales 2006

- In Leicestershire, fewer than one in every 35 women who report rape secures a conviction.
- In Cleveland, one in seven reported rapes are convicted.
- The conviction rate has got worse in 18 out of 43 police areas since 2004

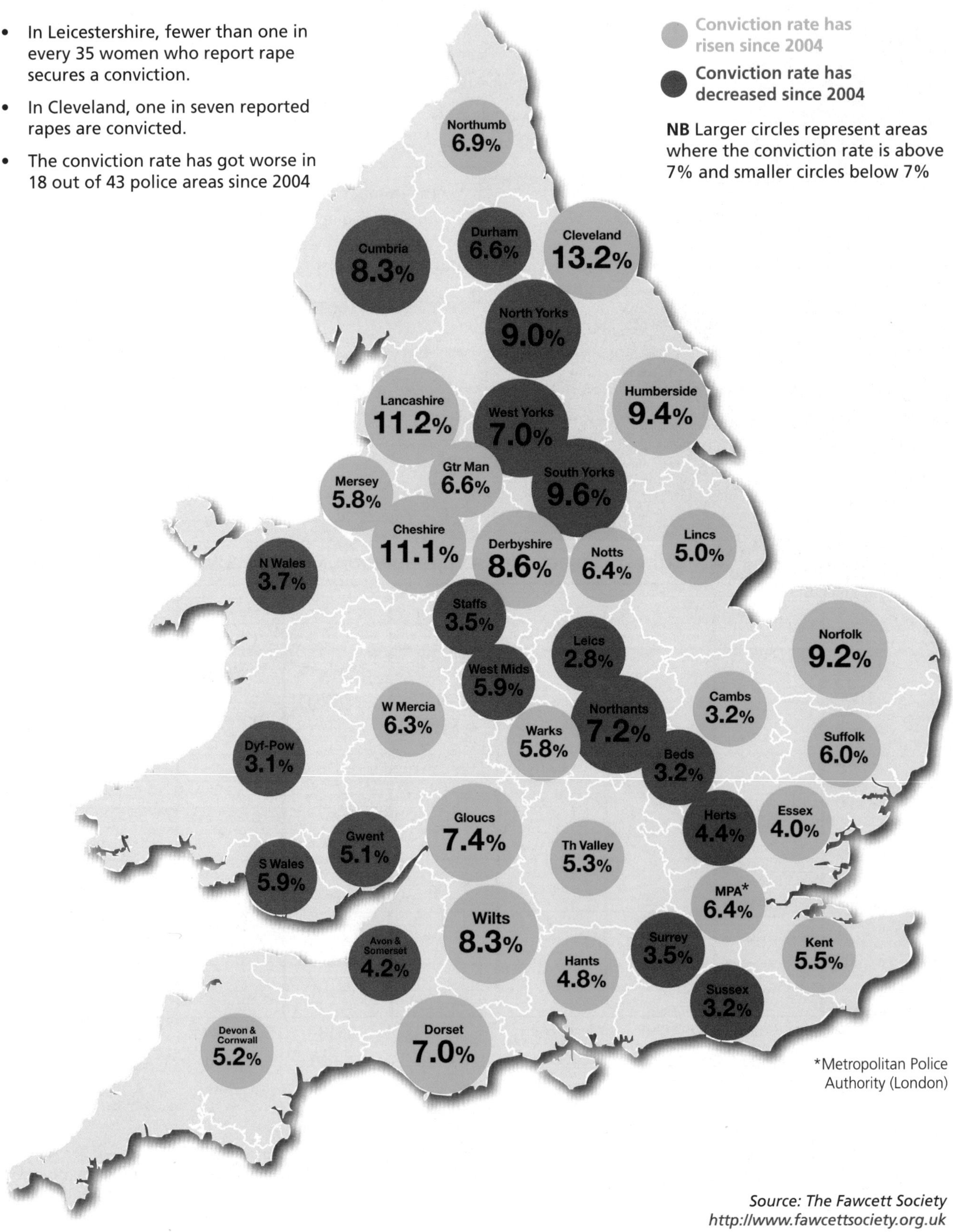
Conviction rate has risen since 2004
Conviction rate has decreased since 2004
NB Larger circles represent areas where the conviction rate is above 7% and smaller circles below 7%
Northumb 6.9%
Cumbria 8.3%
Durham 6.6%
Cleveland 13.2%
North Yorks 9.0%
Lancashire 11.2%
West Yorks 7.0%
Humberside 9.4%
Mersey 5.8%
Gtr Man 6.6%
South Yorks 9.6%
Cheshire 11.1%
Derbyshire 8.6%
Notts 6.4%
Lincs 5.0%
N Wales 3.7%
Staffs 3.5%
Leics 2.8%
Norfolk 9.2%
West Mids 5.9%
W Mercia 6.3%
Northants 7.2%
Cambs 3.2%
Warks 5.8%
Suffolk 6.0%
Dyf-Pow 3.1%
Beds 3.2%
Gloucs 7.4%
Herts 4.4%
Essex 4.0%
Gwent 5.1%
Th Valley 5.3%
S Wales 5.9%
MPA* 6.4%
Wilts 8.3%
Avon & Somerset 4.2%
Surrey 3.5%
Kent 5.5%
Hants 4.8%
Sussex 3.2%
Devon & Cornwall 5.2%
Dorset 7.0%
*Metropolitan Police Authority (London)

Source: The Fawcett Society
http://www.fawcettsociety.org.uk

Sport & leisure

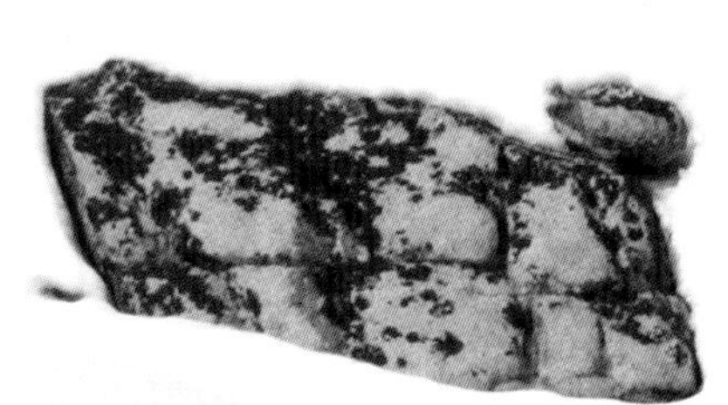
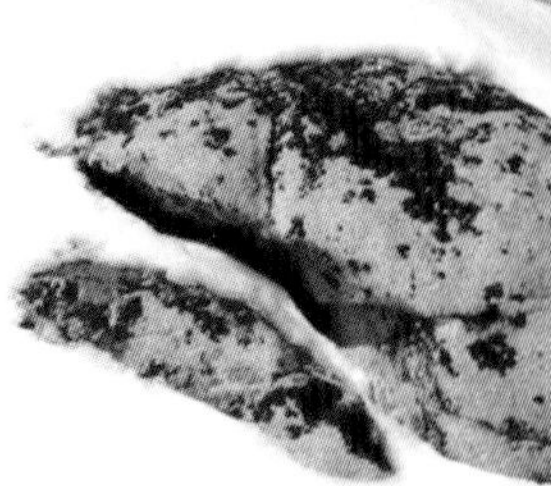

Olympics 2008

Who really won? It all depends on the way you count

The official medal rankings, which count only GOLD medals, look like this:

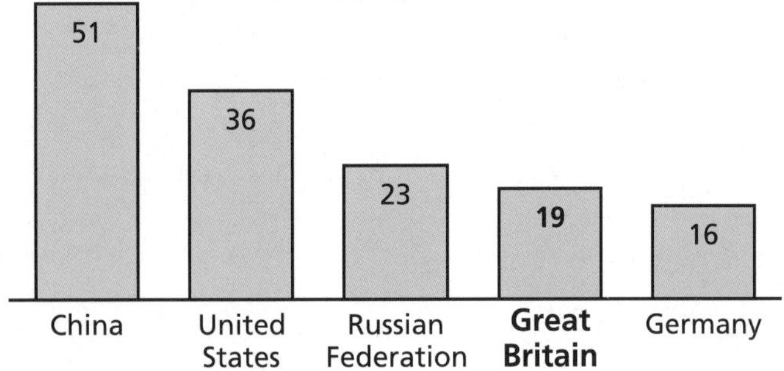
51
36
23
19
16
China
United States
Russian Federation
Great Britain
Germany

It hardly seems fair to discount all the medals below gold so other lists (particularly in the US) prefer to count all medals won. Then the rankings look like this:

United States **110** medals, China **100**, Russia **72**, GB **47**, Australia **46**.

An even fairer system might be to give the medals a value:

3 points for **GOLD** **2** for **SILVER** **1** for **BRONZE**

This would give China top ranking at **223** points, US 2nd with **220**, Russia 3rd with **139**, Great Britain would still be 4th with **98** points and Australia 5th with **89**.

Medals per head of population

(population in brackets)

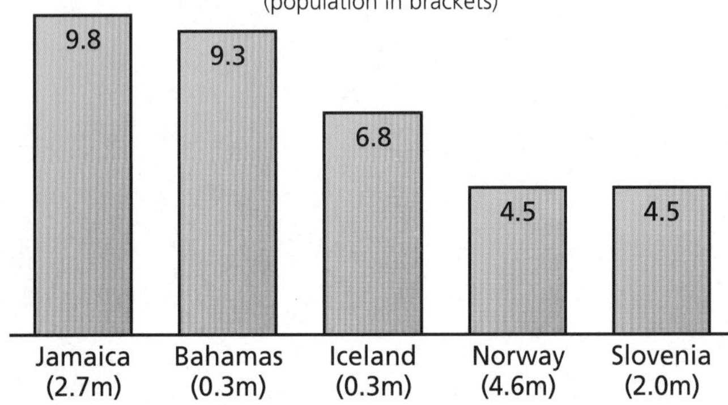
9.8
9.3
6.8
4.5
4.5
Jamaica (2.7m)
Bahamas (0.3m)
Iceland (0.3m)
Norway (4.6m)
Slovenia (2.0m)

But some countries have a much bigger **population** to draw on – so perhaps we should look at how many medals (weighted as above) per head of population.

On this count the US has **0.12** medals per million people and ranks 44th out of 197 countries and China with **0.04**, ranks 66th. GB at **1.6** medals per person, ranks 22nd.

A wealthy country might be expected to win a lot of medals. In contrast the sporting achievements of a country with a low **Gross Domestic Product** (GDP) might be considered to be both a more efficient use of money and to have more merit.

With GDP taken into account a medal table would look like this:

Ranking	Country	GDP 2007 $US millions	Million GDP per weighted medals
1	North Korea	2,220	608
2	Zimbabwe	3,418	1,147
3	Mongolia	3,894	1,173
4	Jamaica	10,739	1,243
5	Georgia	10,176	2,550
44	China	3,280,053	44,265
54	GB	2,727,806	83,855
72	US	13,811,200	189,298

The problem with this method is that certain countries arrive at the top of the rankings simply because their economies have been ruined.

The conclusion must be that there is no ultimately fair way to rank sporting achievement

Source: Beijing 2008, Sports Illustrated, Bill Mitchell's Alternative Olympic Games
http://en.beijing2008.cn
http://sportsillustrated.cnn.com/olympics/2008/medals/tracker/
www.billmitchell.org/sport/medal_tally_2008.html

Team GB

Can money 'buy' Olympic success?

Past Olympic Games – Team GB Statistics

At the Atlanta Olympics in 1996, Britain's squad won only one gold medal and finished 36th in the medals table. It was the worst GB team performance in the 100 year history of the games.

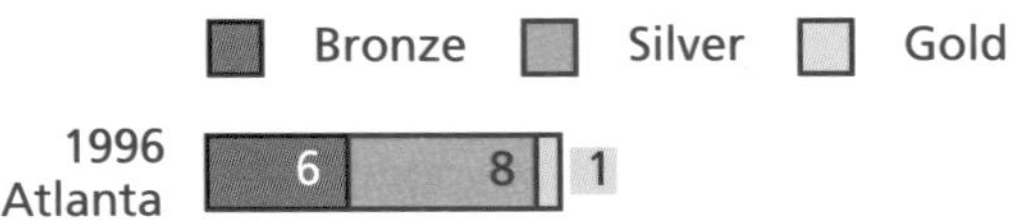

Bronze
Silver
Gold
1996 Atlanta
6
8
1

After Atlanta the rules of national lottery funding were changed, allowing money to be used to help individual athletes and governing bodies.

The results were seen more quickly than expected

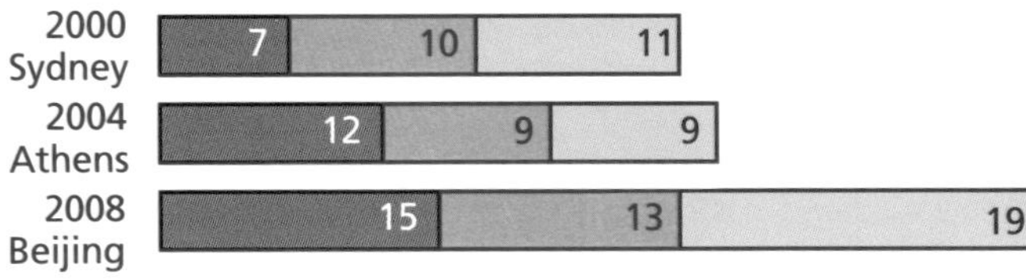

2000 Sydney
7
10
11
2004 Athens
12
9
9
2008 Beijing
15
13
19

Eight of cycling's medals were gold – a return for the £22m spent since Athens and a contrast to the grant of £22,750 given to cycling before the Atlanta games.

GREAT BRITAIN

Great Britain's Chris Hoy celebrates winning the Gold Medal in the Men's Sprint Final at the Laoshan Velodrome at the 2008 Beijing Olympics

Photo: John Giles PA/PA Photos

Team GB targets, achievements and funding

Sport (medal target in brackets)	**Funding since Athens**	**Medals achieved**
Cycling (6)	£ 22,151,000	14
Rowing (4)	£ 26,042,000	6
Sailing (4)	£ 22,292,000	6
Swimming (3)	£ 20,659,000	6
Athletics (5)	£ 26,513,000	4
Canoeing/kayaking (2)	£ 13,622,000	3
Boxing (2)	£ 5,005,000	3
Equestrian (3)	£ 11,727,000	2
Gymnastics (1)	£ 9,036,000	1
Modern pentathlon (1)	£ 5,920,000	1
Taekwondo (1)	£ 2,637,000	1

Rebecca Adlington – double gold in swimming and Sarah Stevenson – bronze in taekwondo, are both on the Advanced Apprenticeship in Sporting Excellence (AASE). This funding allows athletes much more coaching than they would otherwise get and at the same time to study for their wider career.

But money cannot be the only predictor of success. A combined figure of £32.2m was spent for Beijing on archery, badminton, diving, fencing, judo and shooting, which failed to deliver a medal between them when they were expected to win at least five. Athletics is a relatively rich sport since it has sponsorship income as well as funding yet fewer medals were achieved than was expected.

Source: Beijing 2008 http://en.beijing2008.cn

Sports mad world

Sport is popular around the world – especially football

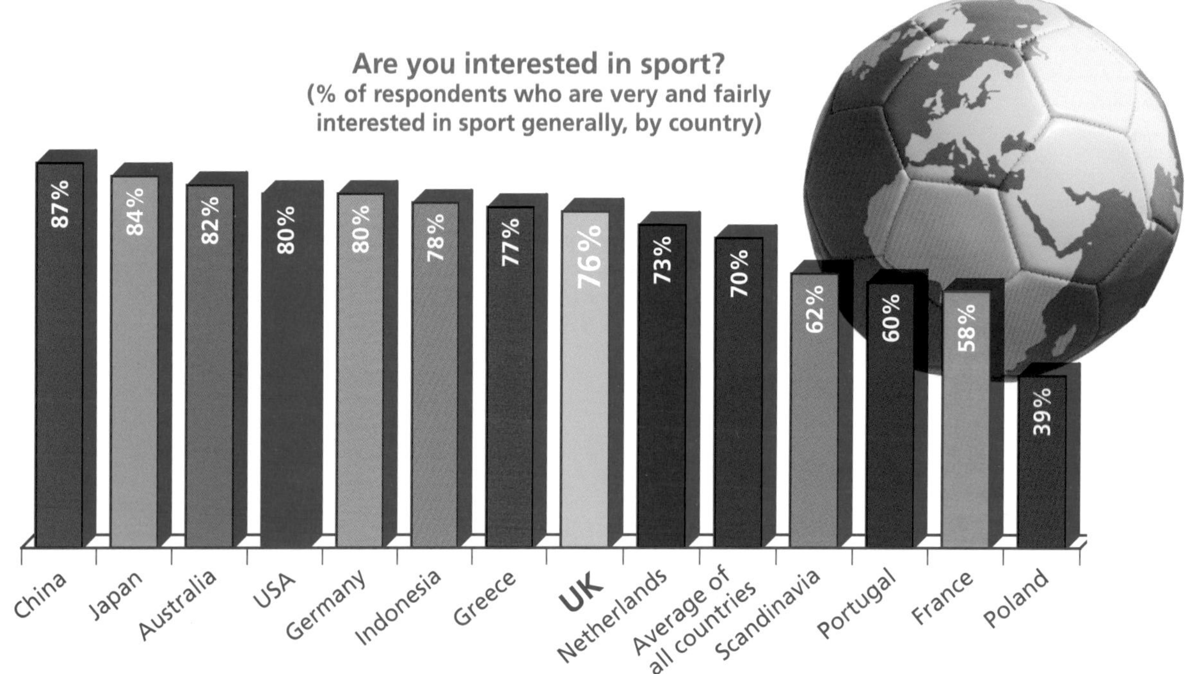

Are you interested in sport?
(% of respondents who are very and fairly interested in sport generally, by country)
87%
84%
82%
80%
80%
78%
77%
76%
73%
70%
62%
60%
58%
39%
China
Japan
Australia
USA
Germany
Indonesia
Greece
UK
Netherlands
Average of all countries
Scandinavia
Portugal
France
Poland

What do you watch?

(All sports scoring more than 1% in past 12 months across all countries)

Football	22.6%
Basketball	4.7%
Volleyball	3.1%
Athletics/marathon	2.7%
Cycling	1.8%
Cricket	1.7%
Speedway	1.6%
Rugby	1.4%
Lawn tennis	1.2%
American football league	1.2%

715 million people watched the last FIFA World Cup Final

In all, more than 50 different sports were named by respondents as sports they had spectated at in the past year, but very few attracted significant numbers of spectators at a 'global' level. Just 10 sports had been seen by more than 1% of the total sample.

What do you take part in?

(All sports scoring more than 1% in past 12 months across all countries)

Football	12.1%	Volleyball	2.7%
Swimming	10.8%	Bodybuilding/weightlifting	2.7%
Athletics/jogging	7.9%	Cross-country skiing	2.7%
Cycling	7.1%	Alpine skiing	2.4%
Badminton	5.7%	Snooker/billiards	2.1%
Basketball	4.4%	Martial arts (any)	2.0%
Aerobics	4.2%	Chess	1.6%
Golf	3.9%	Squash	1.3%
Lawn tennis	3.9%	Rugby	1.2%
Table tennis	3.2%	Snowboarding	1.0%

Research was carried out among nationally representative samples of countries across Europe, Asia, North America and Australasia

Source: Supporting Sport © FDS International Ltd 2008
http://www.fds.co.uk

Man of the world

Becks – still the universal sporting hero

Which international sportsmen or sportswomen are you familiar with?
(all personalities scoring more than a 1% mention)
David Beckham 18.3%
Michael Schumacher 8.5%
Ronaldo* 8.5%
Ronaldinho 8.4%
Tiger Woods 5.7%
Luis Figo 5.5%
Roger Federer 5.1%
Zinedine Zidane 4.6%
Serena Williams 3.2%
Michael Jordan 2.9%
Ian Thorpe 2.7%
Fernando Alonso 2.7%
Valentino Rossi 2.5%
Andre Agassi 2.5%
Venus Williams 2.4%
Yao Ming 2.2%
Liu Xiang 2.1%
Maria Sharapova 2.1%
Diego Maradona 1.9%
Steffi Graf 1.6%
Thierry Henry 1.6%
Mike Tyson 1.6%
Martina Hingis 1.4%
Pele 1.4%
Muhammad Ali 1.2%
Lance Armstrong 1.1%
Research was carried out among nationally representative samples in 16 countries worldwide

Top 10 international sportsmen or sportswomen mentioned by respondents in the UK

David Beckham 39.6%

Thierry Henry 6.6%, Ronaldo* 5.2%, Michael Schumacher 4.2%, Tiger Woods 4.2%, Roger Federer 2.6%, Ronaldinho 2.2%, Fernando Alonso 2.2%, Valentino Rossi 1.6%, Venus Williams 1.6%

Why is David Beckham an international star?

Although he has captained the England football team, Beckham has never dominated his sport in the same way as outstanding achievers like Michael Schumacher or Tiger Woods. Yet he is the sports star whose name is known in almost every country.

The Beckham 'brand' is associated with a far wider set of values than most sports stars. Those values include the skill, fitness and determination which form part of all sporting achievement. But people also see David Beckham as likeable, fashionable, caring and a good family man. His image is associated with being responsible rather than aggressive and is also international – as shown by his various ethnic tattoos and his work with the UN.

While David Beckham gives an image to the brands he advertises, marketing has certainly contributed to his fame.

NB Scoring based on first three mentioned stars only (in order to counteract the tendency for some countries to name more sportspeople than others)

*Unfortunately, in the vast majority of cases, the survey could not distinguish between mentions of Ronaldo, the Brazilian star, and Cristiano Ronaldo, of Portugal and Manchester United

Source: Supporting Sport © Copyright FDS International Ltd 2008
http://www.fds.co.uk

Club v country

Does foreign domination of the Premier League harm the national team?

The Football Association's stated ambition is a semi-final appearance (at least) at the next World Cup or European Championships. It might not seem too demanding for a nation which has dominated the Champions League in 2008. However the number of Englishmen playing top-flight football in their own country has never been lower.

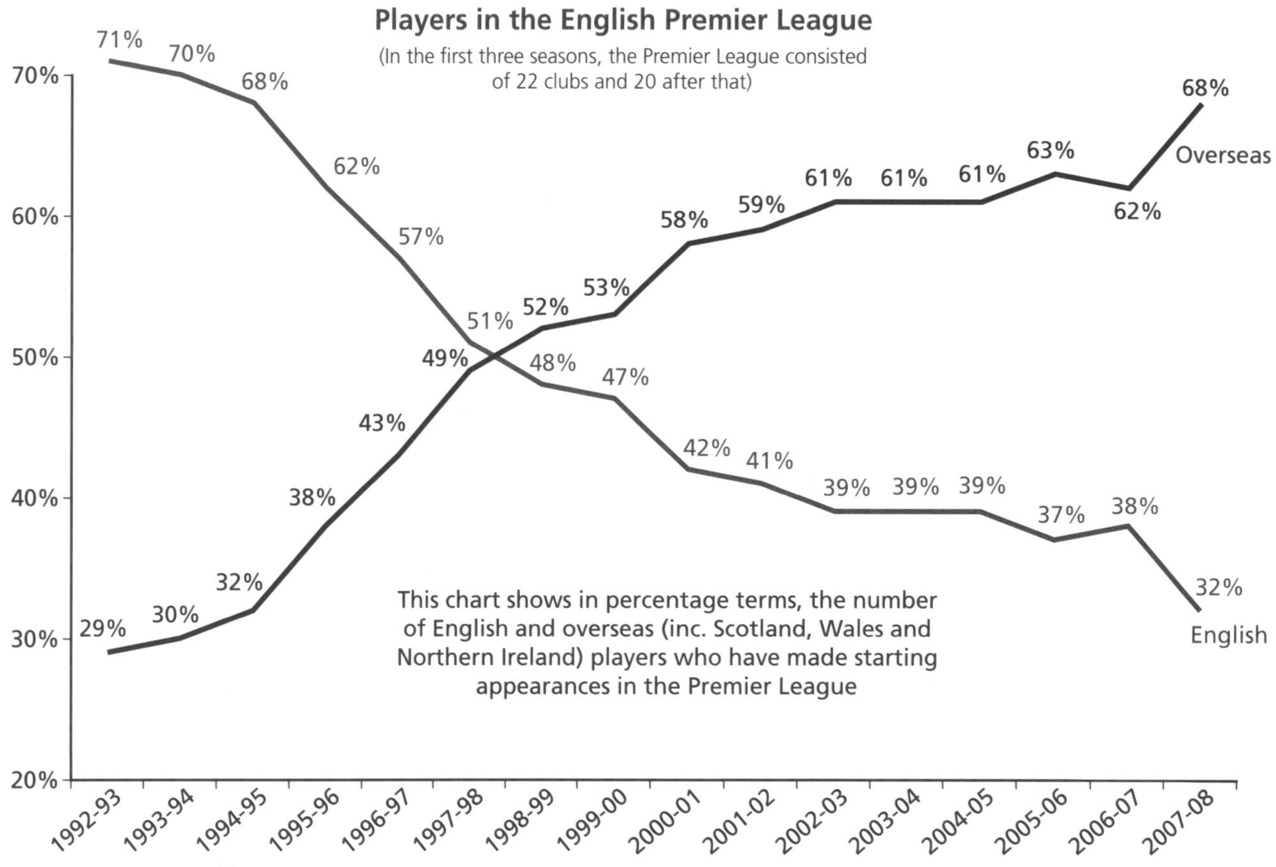

Players in the English Premier League
(In the first three seasons, the Premier League consisted of 22 clubs and 20 after that)
70%
60%
50%
40%
30%
20%
71%
70%
68%
62%
57%
51%
48%
47%
42%
41%
39%
39%
39%
37%
38%
32%
29%
30%
32%
38%
43%
49%
52%
53%
58%
59%
61%
61%
61%
63%
62%
68%
Overseas
English
This chart shows in percentage terms, the number of English and overseas (inc. Scotland, Wales and Northern Ireland) players who have made starting appearances in the Premier League
1992-93
1993-94
1994-95
1995-96
1996-97
1997-98
1998-99
1999-00
2000-01
2001-02
2002-03
2003-04
2004-05
2005-06
2006-07
2007-08

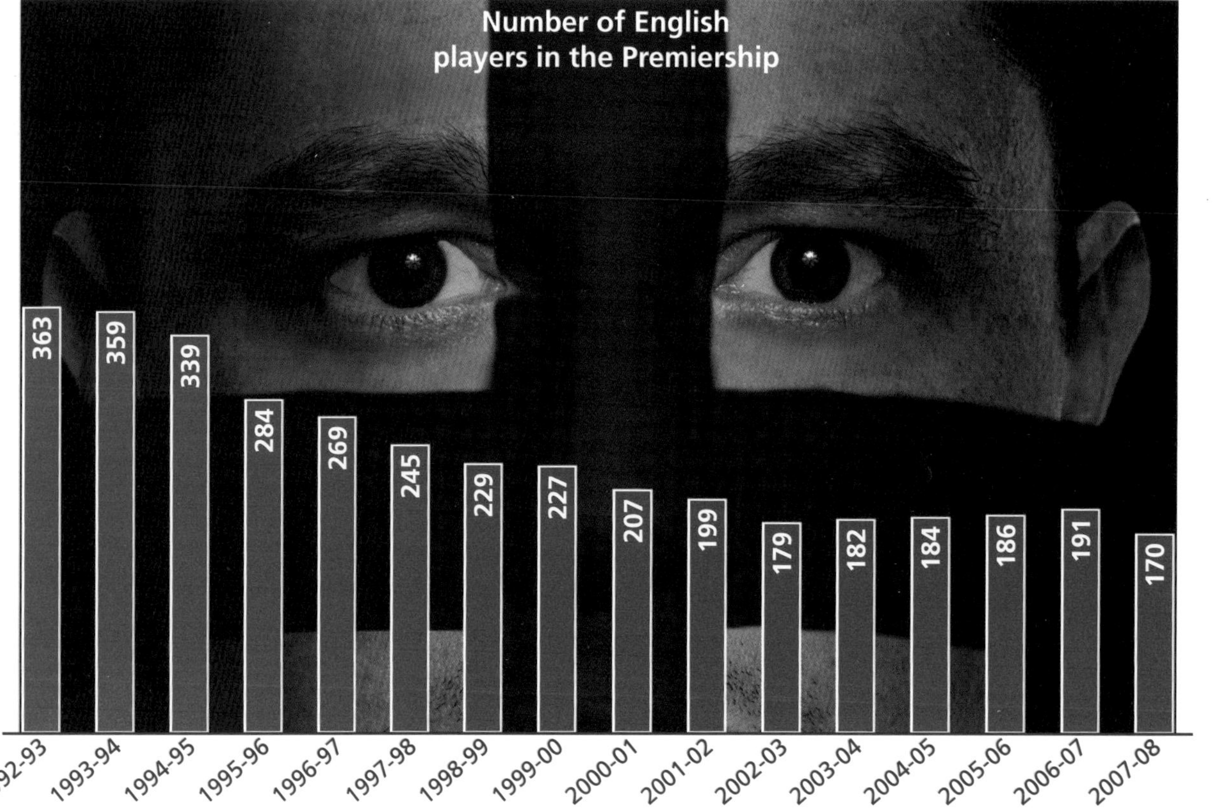

Number of English players in the Premiership
363
359
339
284
269
245
229
227
207
199
179
182
184
186
191
170
1992-93
1993-94
1994-95
1995-96
1996-97
1997-98
1998-99
1999-00
2000-01
2001-02
2002-03
2003-04
2004-05
2005-06
2006-07
2007-08

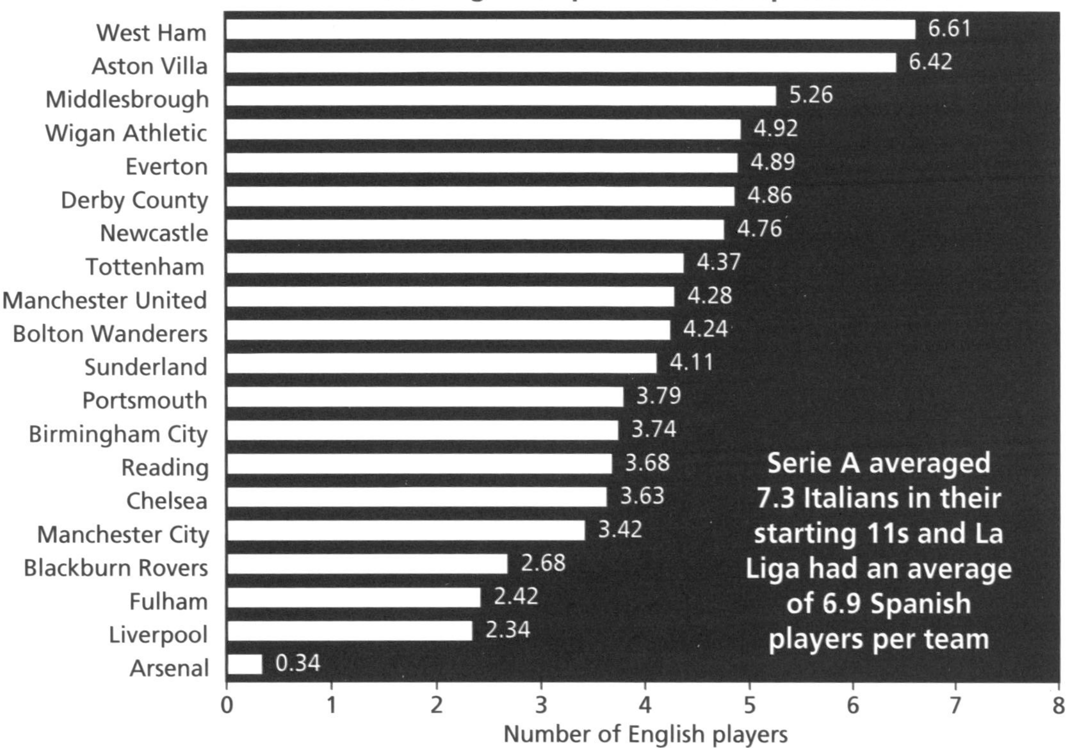

Average number of Englishmen in starting line-up in Premiership 2007/08
West Ham 6.61
Aston Villa 6.42
Middlesbrough 5.26
Wigan Athletic 4.92
Everton 4.89
Derby County 4.86
Newcastle 4.76
Tottenham 4.37
Manchester United 4.28
Bolton Wanderers 4.24
Sunderland 4.11
Portsmouth 3.79
Birmingham City 3.74
Reading 3.68
Chelsea 3.63
Manchester City 3.42
Blackburn Rovers 2.68
Fulham 2.42
Liverpool 2.34
Arsenal 0.34
0
1
2
3
4
5
6
7
8
Number of English players
Serie A averaged 7.3 Italians in their starting 11s and La Liga had an average of 6.9 Spanish players per team

When over 3,000 English football supporters of all Premier and Football League clubs were surveyed, it was found that the club v country debate is often central to discussions about the national side

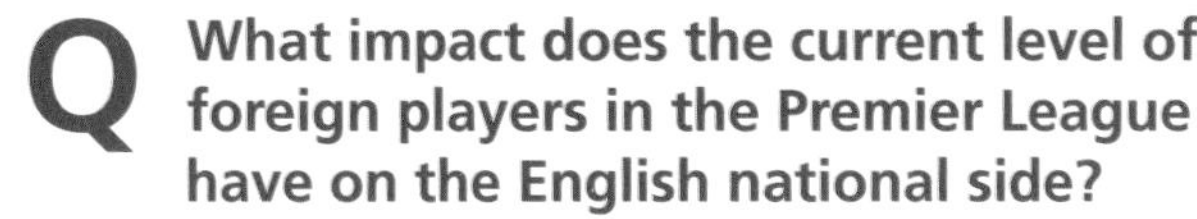

Q What impact does the current level of foreign players in the Premier League have on the English national side?

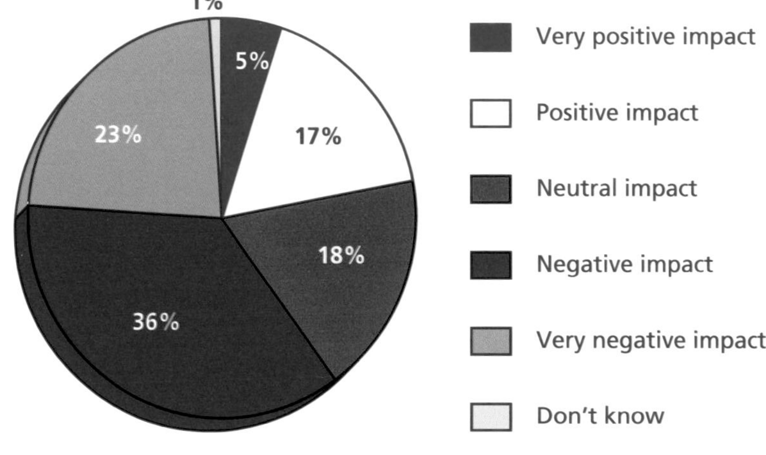

1%
5%
17%
18%
36%
23%
Very positive impact
Positive impact
Neutral impact
Negative impact
Very negative impact
Don't know

Q Which is most important to you?

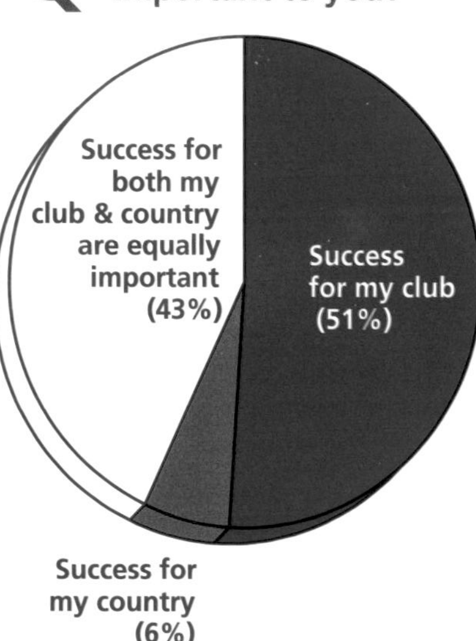

Success for both my club & country are equally important (43%)
Success for my club (51%)
Success for my country (6%)

Football's governing body FIFA has endorsed president Sepp Blatter's 'six-plus-five' principle, which would limit a team's foreign players to five.

He wants to bring in the proposal by 2012/2013 – but the European Commission says it is discriminatory and illegal.

Source: Professional Footballers Association, The Football Fans Census © Crown copyright 2007

http://www.givemefootball.com
http://www.footballfanscensus.com

Popularity contest

Can you measure the popularity of a team?

Fanbase

Fanbase is a direct measure of the popularity of a club, in its domestic market or around the world.

How do you measure fanbase or even define a 'fan'?

There is no single methodology, and true comparisons are difficult. The most accessible measure is the club's average matchday attendance.

Popularity contest

Man U has estimated its current fanbase at 333 million (including 139 million 'active supporters') 5% of the world's population

They also have the largest club ground in the UK and had the highest domestic league attendance in Europe at 75,800 in 2006/07

Top 20 European club attendances

Average attendance domestic league, home matches only 2002/03-2006/07

Borussia Dortmund	74,000
FC Barcelona	70,900
Real Madrid	70,700
Manchester United	69,500
Schalke 04	61,100
Bayern Munich	59,300
AC Milan	59,200
Celtic	57,900
Internazionale	55,400
Newcastle United	51,700
Olympique de Marseille	50,400
Hamburger SV	50,200
Rangers	49,100
Ajax	48,100
Hertha Berlin	45,200
AS Roma	44,300
Valencia	43,500
Liverpool	43,300
Athletico Madrid	42,800
Arsenal	42,500

Source: Deloitte Football Money League 2008
http://www.deloitte.com

AIG
7

Photo: John Walton/EMPICS Sport/PA Photos

Cotton wool kids

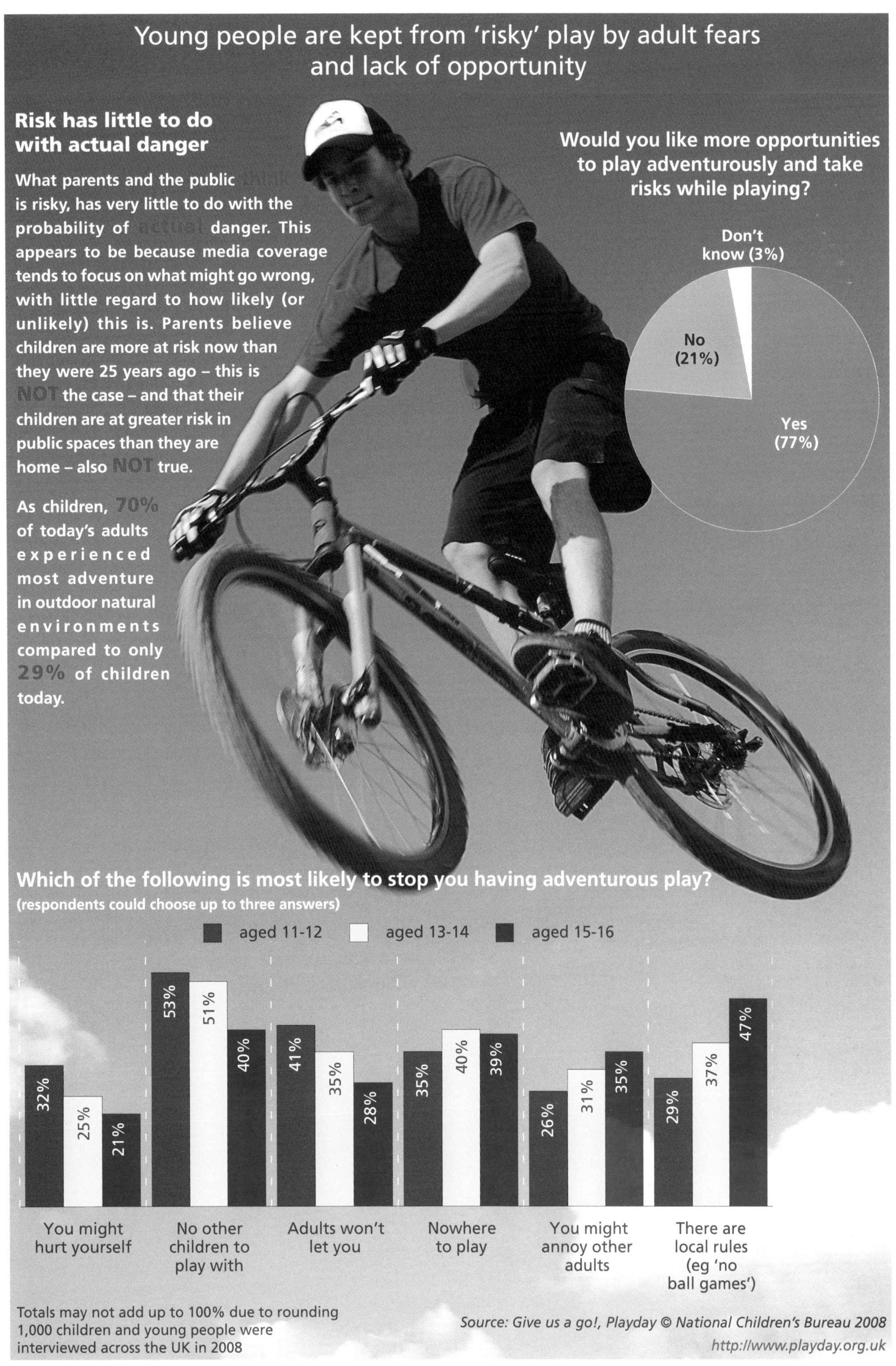
Young people are kept from 'risky' play by adult fears and lack of opportunity
Risk has little to do with actual danger
What parents and the public think is risky, has very little to do with the probability of actual danger. This appears to be because media coverage tends to focus on what might go wrong, with little regard to how likely (or unlikely) this is. Parents believe children are more at risk now than they were 25 years ago – this is NOT the case – and that their children are at greater risk in public spaces than they are home – also NOT true.
As children, 70% of today's adults experienced most adventure in outdoor natural environments compared to only 29% of children today.
Would you like more opportunities to play adventurously and take risks while playing?
Don't know (3%)
No (21%)
Yes (77%)
Which of the following is most likely to stop you having adventurous play?
(respondents could choose up to three answers)
aged 11-12
aged 13-14
aged 15-16
32%
25%
21%
53%
51%
40%
41%
35%
28%
35%
40%
39%
26%
31%
35%
29%
37%
47%
You might hurt yourself
No other children to play with
Adults won't let you
Nowhere to play
You might annoy other adults
There are local rules (eg 'no ball games')
Totals may not add up to 100% due to rounding
1,000 children and young people were interviewed across the UK in 2008
Source: Give us a go!, Playday © National Children's Bureau 2008
http://www.playday.org.uk

Keep on running

Taking part makes all the difference

There is a big contrast between the number of calories burnt in passive and active tasks. While it may be fun watching football, it's not half as healthy as playing it. Just a little bit of effort can make the difference. For example, you'd burn less than one calorie using a lift to go up 3 floors, but you'd use up 15 calories if you took the stairs.

Next time you have to spend half an hour tidying your room or helping with the housework, just think of the health benefits – you'd burn 75-125 calories depending how hard you cleaned!

Although video games have always been seen as unenergetic, some, like Mario & Sonic at the Olympic Games, do burn calories, approximately 120 in half an hour. However, this doesn't come close to actually playing the sports:

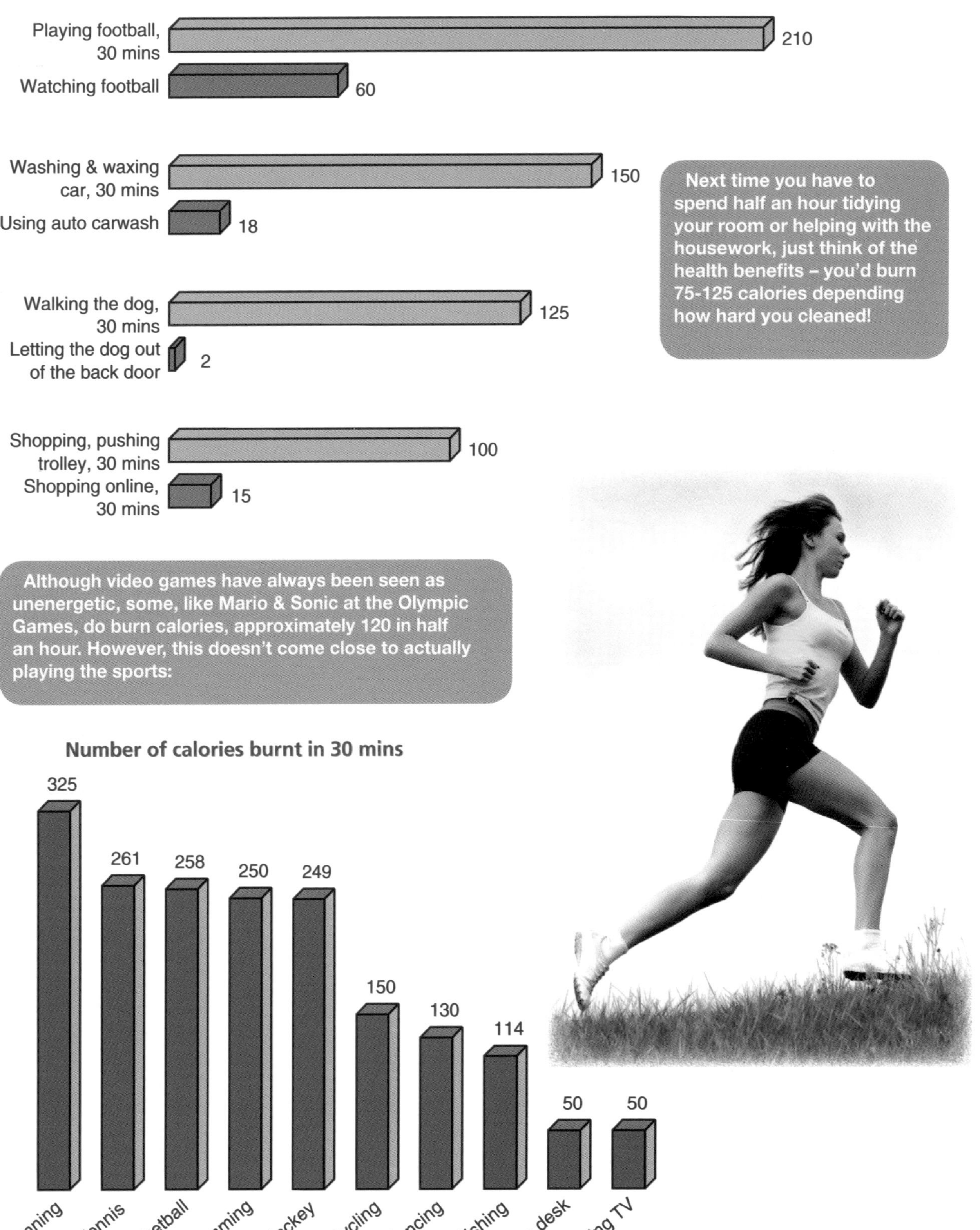

Amount of calories burnt
Playing football, 30 mins
210
Watching football
60
Washing & waxing car, 30 mins
150
Using auto carwash
18
Walking the dog, 30 mins
125
Letting the dog out of the back door
2
Shopping, pushing trolley, 30 mins
100
Shopping online, 30 mins
15
Number of calories burnt in 30 mins
Running
325
Tennis
261
Basketball
258
Swimming
250
Hockey
249
Cycling
150
Dancing
130
Fishing
114
Sitting at a desk
50
Watching TV
50

Source: Food Magazine & Various
http://www.foodcomm.org.uk

Gameboy

The average UK gamer is a male aged 33

In 2007:

- There were more outlets selling games (7,385 stores) than either DVD (5,586 stores) or music (5,026 stores)
- Internet sales now account for **16.4%** of computer games sales
- Despite the flurry of new formats and technical innovation, computer games have increased in price over the year by just **1.7%** – less than inflation – to an average **£21.31**

In the first 6 months of 2008:

- Sales of games showed unprecedented **growth** of **42%** thanks to Wii, Xbox 360 and PS3, plus Nintendo DS
- **3.1million** consoles were sold, an increase of **41%** over 2007
- PC games software suffered a **decline** of **29%**
- Revenue from games, hardware and accessories totalled **£1,452 million**

Retail values of games in UK (excluding rentals) £m

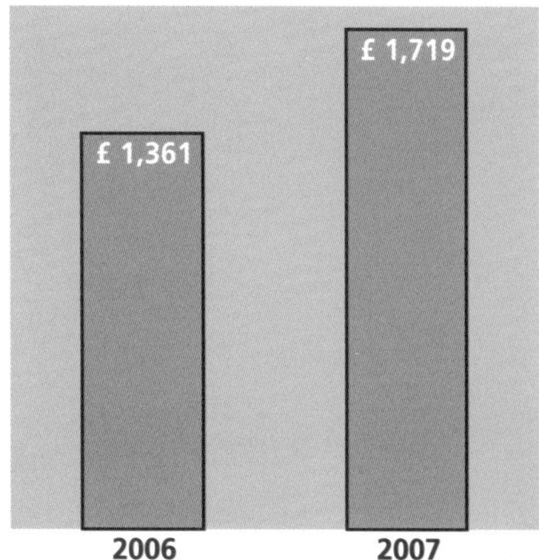

£ 1,361
£ 1,719
2006
2007

UK gamers buy more than any other European gamers, with **18%** purchasing **10 or more** games annually

The average number of video games **owned** by a gamer in the UK is **40+**

Q: In a typical week, how many hours do you spend playing video games?

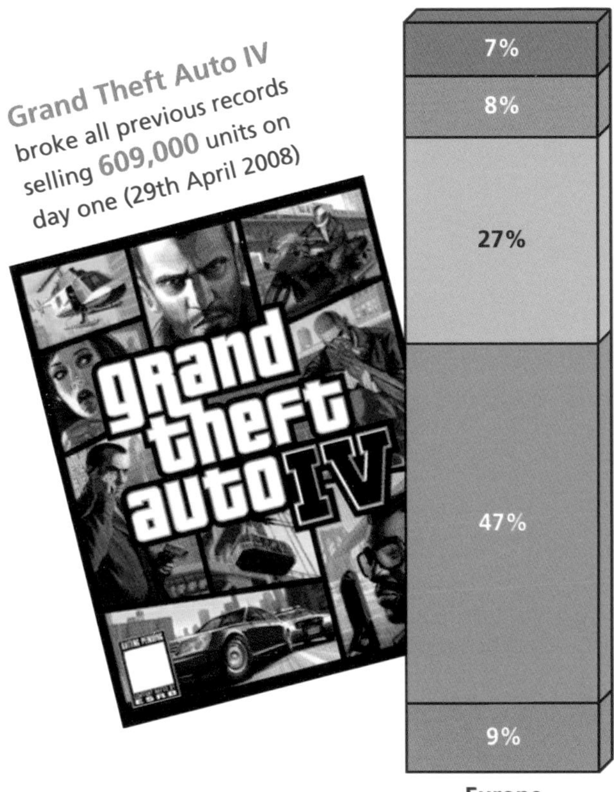

Grand Theft Auto IV broke all previous records selling 609,000 units on day one (29th April 2008)
grand theft auto IV
7%
8%
27%
47%
9%
Europe (inc. UK)

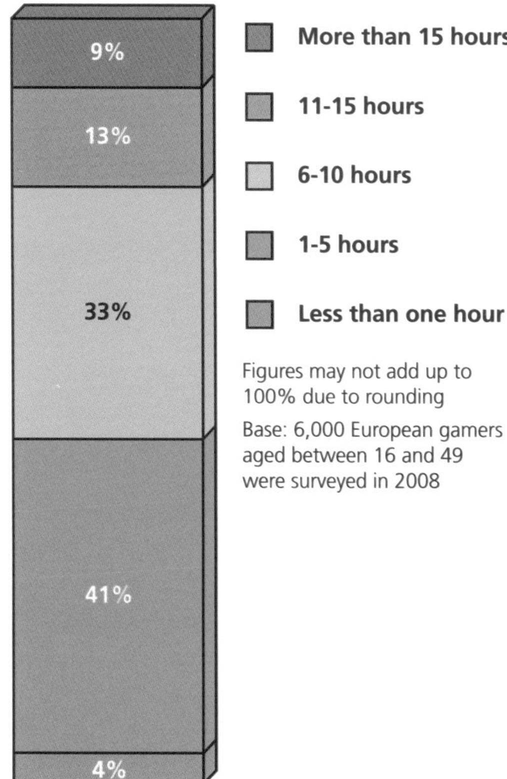

9%
13%
33%
41%
4%
UK only
More than 15 hours
11-15 hours
6-10 hours
1-5 hours
Less than one hour

Figures may not add up to 100% due to rounding

Base: 6,000 European gamers aged between 16 and 49 were surveyed in 2008

Source: Entertainment and Leisure Software Publishers Association © elspa 2008; The Interactive Software Federation of Europe; Entertainment Retailers Association (ERA)

http://www.elpsa.com
http://www.isfe-eu.org
http://www.bardltd.org

Art attack

While a lot of kids attend arts events, sport is still more popular

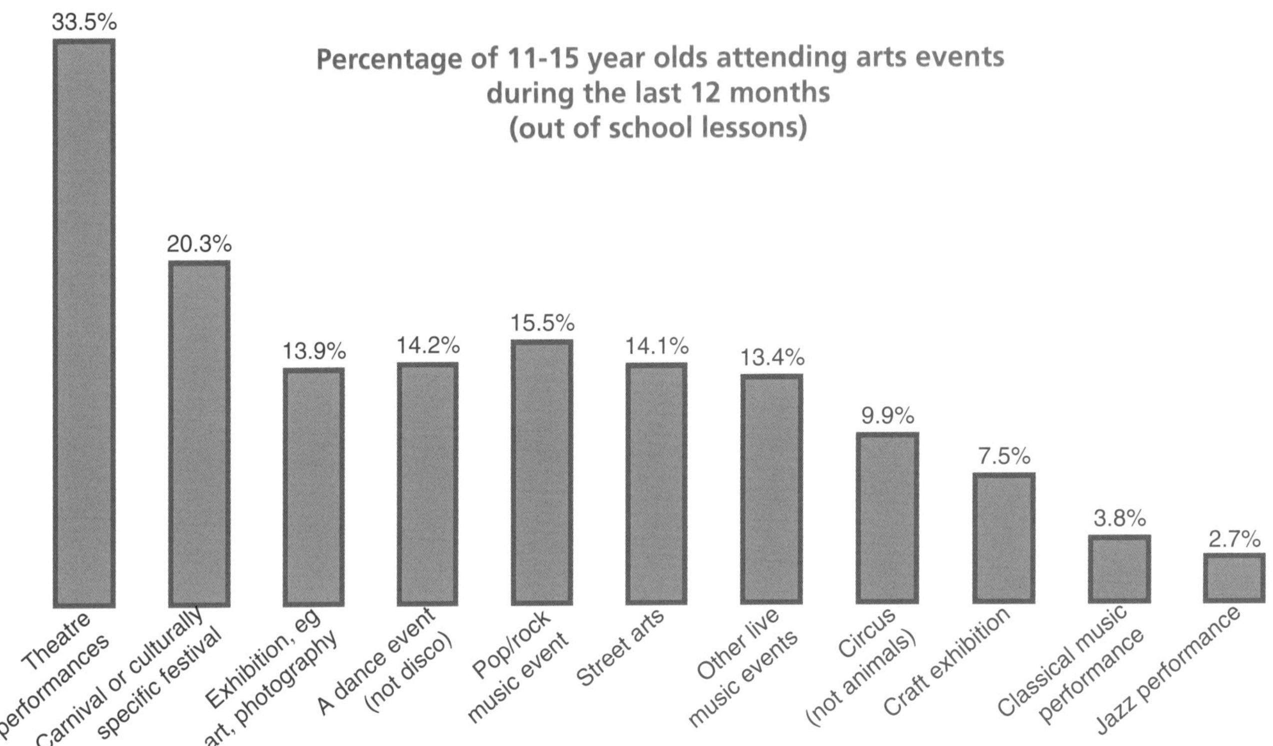
Percentage of 11-15 year olds attending arts events during the last 12 months (out of school lessons)
33.5%
Theatre performances
20.3%
Carnival or culturally specific festival
13.9%
Exhibition, eg art, photography
14.2%
A dance event (not disco)
15.5%
Pop/rock music event
14.1%
Street arts
13.4%
Other live music events
9.9%
Circus (not animals)
7.5%
Craft exhibition
3.8%
Classical music performance
2.7%
Jazz performance

How often they attended

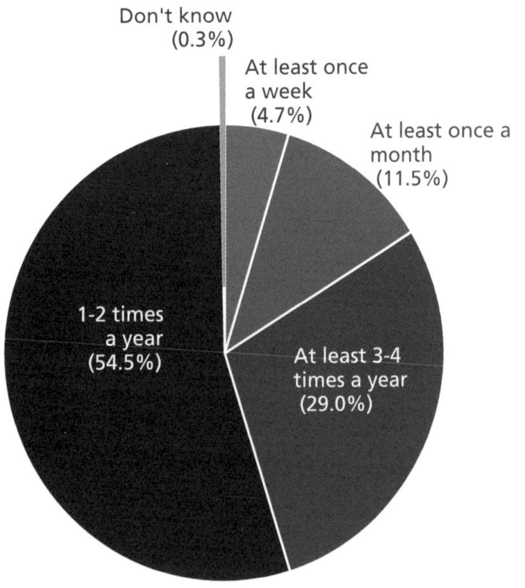
Don't know (0.3%)
At least once a week (4.7%)
At least once a month (11.5%)
At least 3-4 times a year (29.0%)
1-2 times a year (54.5%)

While most kids only attend arts events a couple of times a year, many take part in artistic activities on a regular basis. **70.3%** participated in an arts activity at least once a week.

The most common activities were:

- painting, drawing, printmaking, sculpture or model-making (**38.2%**)
- playing a musical instrument for pleasure (**29.3%**)
- creating original artworks using a computer (**28.0%**)

Percentage of 11-15 year olds taking part in sports (out of school) during the last four weeks

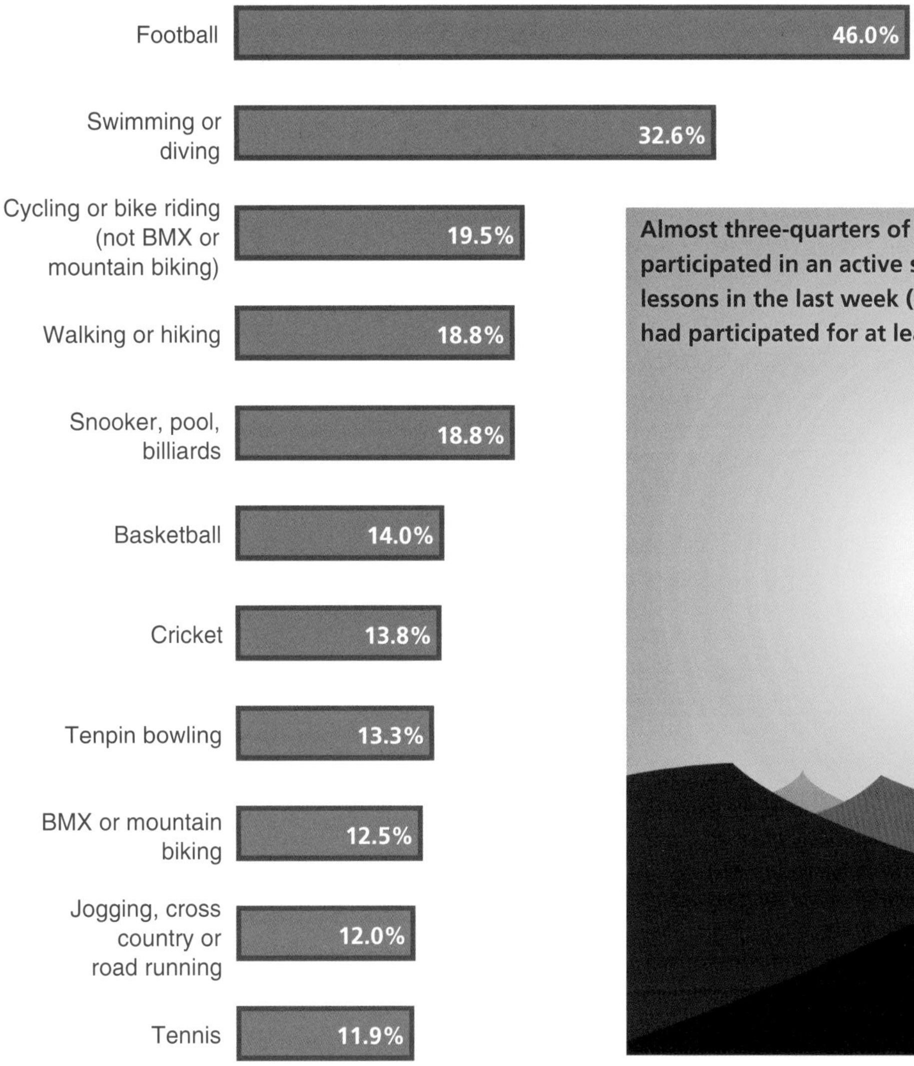

Football	46.0%
Swimming or diving	32.6%
Cycling or bike riding (not BMX or mountain biking)	19.5%
Walking or hiking	18.8%
Snooker, pool, billiards	18.8%
Basketball	14.0%
Cricket	13.8%
Tenpin bowling	13.3%
BMX or mountain biking	12.5%
Jogging, cross country or road running	12.0%
Tennis	11.9%

Almost three-quarters of all children had participated in an active sport outside school lessons in the last week (74%), of those 23% had participated for at least an hour on one day

Of those participating in sport out of school lessons in the last week, number of days they participated for at least an hour

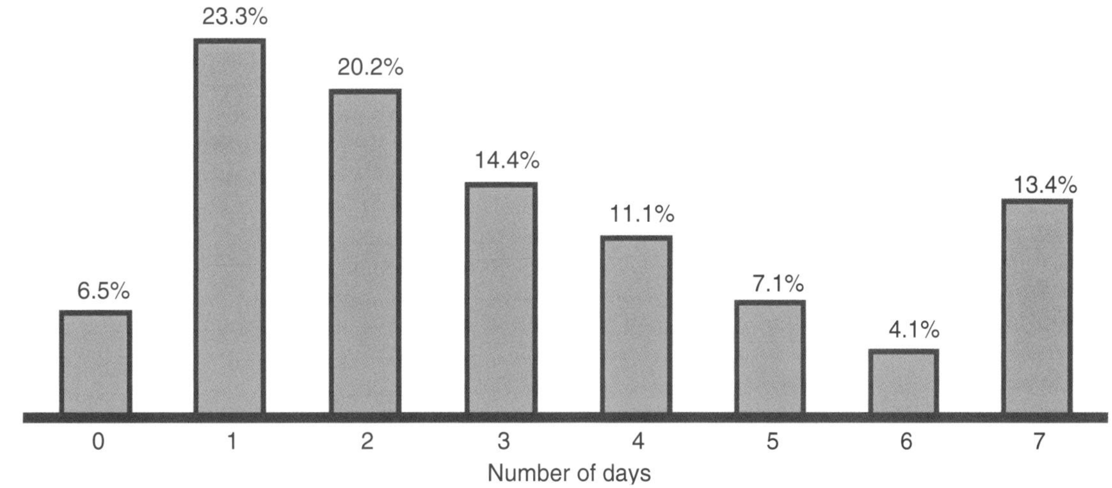

6.5%
23.3%
20.2%
14.4%
11.1%
7.1%
4.1%
13.4%
0
1
2
3
4
5
6
7
Number of days

Source: Taking Part: The National Survey of Culture, Leisure and Sport, DCHS
http://www.culture.gov.uk

Culture fix

Money and time is an issue, but we're still getting our culture fix

Frequency of attendance at arts events during the past 12 months (Adults)

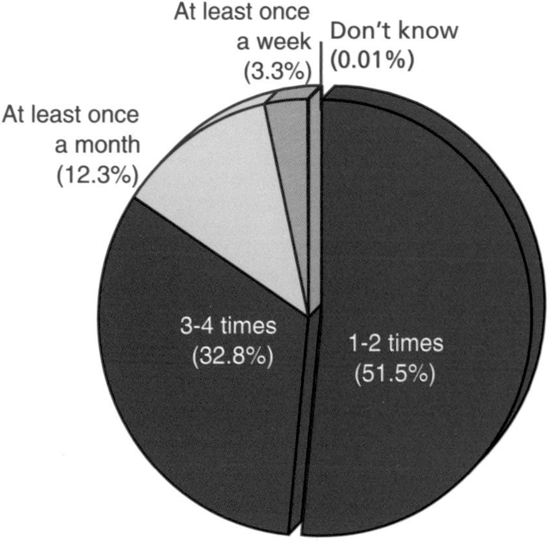

At least once a week (3.3%)
Don't know (0.01%)
At least once a month (12.3%)
3-4 times (32.8%)
1-2 times (51.5%)

Artless wonder

The top five reasons for not having attended an arts event in the last 12 months were the following:

32.5% said they weren't really interested

28.9% think it's difficult to find the time

15.7% said their health isn't good enough

5.2% think it costs too much

3.9% said it never really occurred to them

Money matters

If cost is an issue it's interesting to see what percentage of each income group attended an arts event within the last 12 months. Of those from a hard pressed neighbourhood, **50.3%** had attended an arts event compared to **77.5%** of those identified as wealthy achievers

Types of arts events attended during the past 12 months

Other theatre performance, eg musical, pantomime	26.2%
Live music event (excluding jazz or classical)	24.9%
Play or drama	21.7%
Exhibition of art, photography or sculpture	21.4%
Carnival	17.2%
Craft exhibition	14.3%
Street arts	13.6%
Classical music performance	7.7%
Culturally specific festival	5.4%
Jazz performance	5.6%
Event connected with books or writing	4.6%
Opera or operetta	3.8%
Video or electronic art event	4.2%
Ballet	3.5%
Other live dance event	3.4%
African people's dance or South Asian and Chinese dance	2.3%
Contemporary dance	2.0%

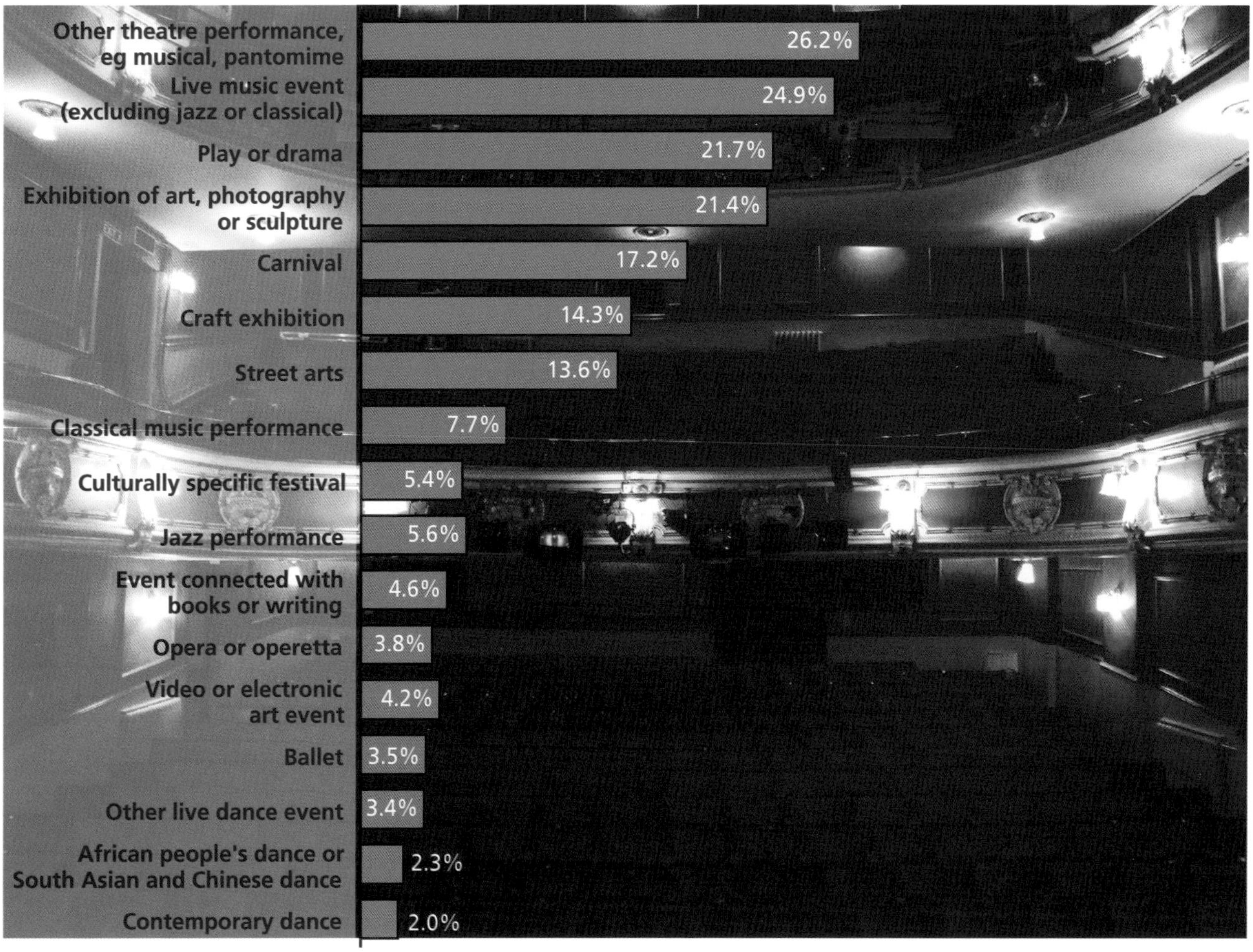

Source: England's Survey of Culture, Leisure and Sport Annual data 2006/07, Department for culture, media and sport http://www.culture.gov.uk

Music lover

In the UK we may spend more on mobiles, but music is what we love

What do you spend your monthly entertainment budget on?

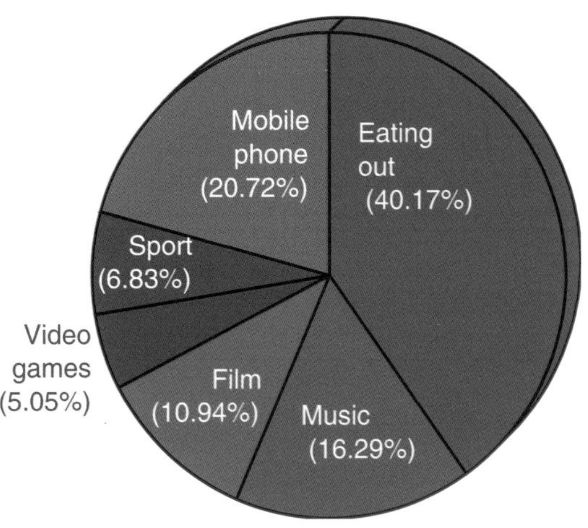

Mobile phone (20.72%)
Eating out (40.17%)
Sport (6.83%)
Video games (5.05%)
Film (10.94%)
Music (16.29%)

What item would you take with you on a desert island
(respondents could choose three items)

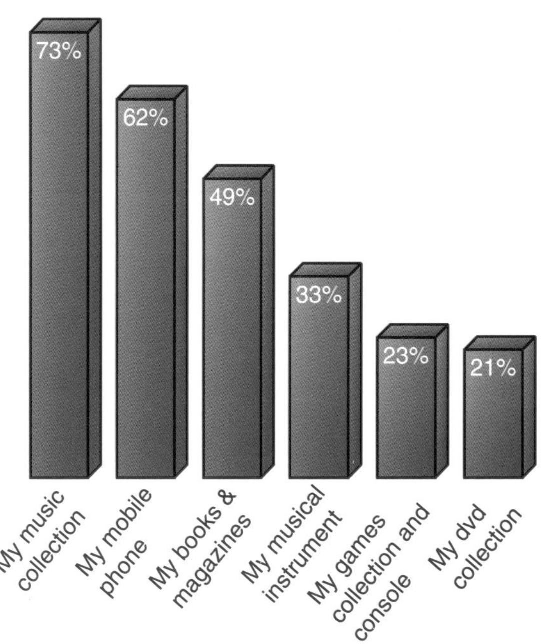

73%
62%
49%
33%
23%
21%
My music collection
My mobile phone
My books & magazines
My musical instrument
My games collection and console
My dvd collection

Other possessions that people were asked about included Designer outfits, jewellery, posters and paintings and make-up, though these were far less important to them than any of their entertainment items.

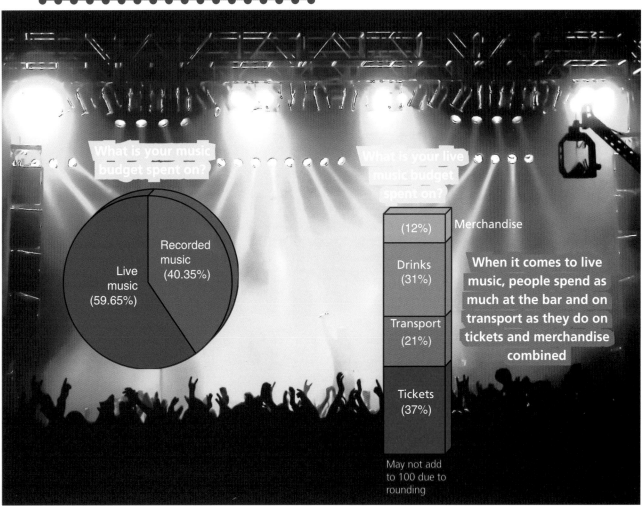

What is your music budget spent on?

Live music (59.65%)
Recorded music (40.35%)

What is your live music budget spent on?

Merchandise (12%)
Drinks (31%)
Transport (21%)
Tickets (37%)

May not add to 100 due to rounding

When it comes to live music, people spend as much at the bar and on transport as they do on tickets and merchandise combined

Source: Music Experience & Behaviour in Young People Spring, 2008
http://www.bmr.org

Libraries online

There are more visitors but they are borrowing less

Public library visits (millions), UK

318.15
337.32
2001-02
2006-07

Items borrowed from public libraries (millions), UK

Audio-visual

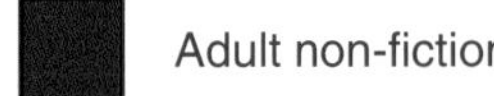
Adult non-fiction

Adult fiction

Children's

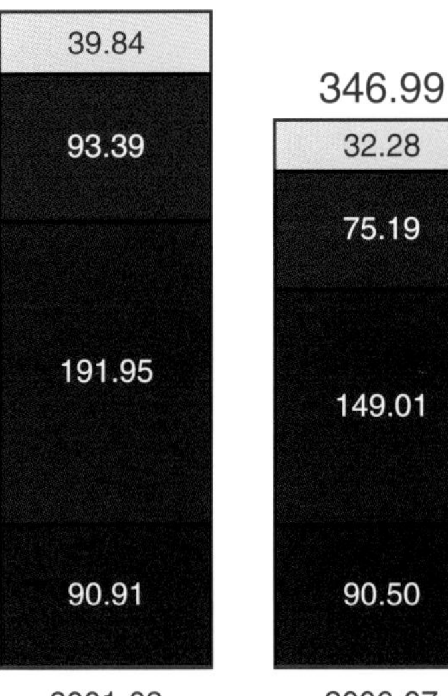
416.10
39.84
93.39
191.95
90.91
346.99
32.28
75.19
149.01
90.50
2001-02
2006-07

The UK's 4,567 public libraries received over 330 million visits in 2006-7, an increase of 6% from 2001-2.

However, in the same period, the number of items borrowed from public libraries has decreased. Only the borrowing of children's books has remained relatively stable.

Computer workstations in public libraries (thousands), UK

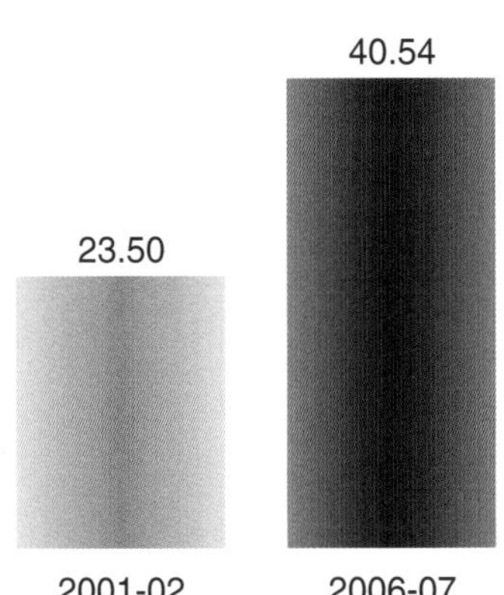
40.54
23.50
2001-02
2006-07

Since 2002, the People's Network initiative has installed more than 30,000 computer workstations in public libraries, and nearly all UK public libraries have an internet connection, providing over 68 million hours' worth of broadband internet use every year.

Case studies suggest that the People's Network project has attracted new groups of users to the library, including young people aged 16-25, refugees and asylum seekers, people with a disability and black & minority ethnic groups.

Source: Museums, Libraries and Archives Council

Source: LISU Libraries, Archives, Museums and Publishing Online Statistical Tables © Loughborough University, 2008 http://www.lboro.ac.uk/departments/is/lisu/lampost.htm

Travel &
Transport

Walking distance

Do you really have to go by car?

More of us have cars and often more than one, but are journeys really necessary when most people live close to local facilities?

Urban areas have better access to more frequent public transport so it is easier for people to manage without a car. In London in 2007, 43% of households did not have access to a car, compared with 31% in Metropolitan built-up areas and 10% in rural areas.

In rural areas, 51% of households had access to two or more cars compared with 16% in London.

Household car availability, GB

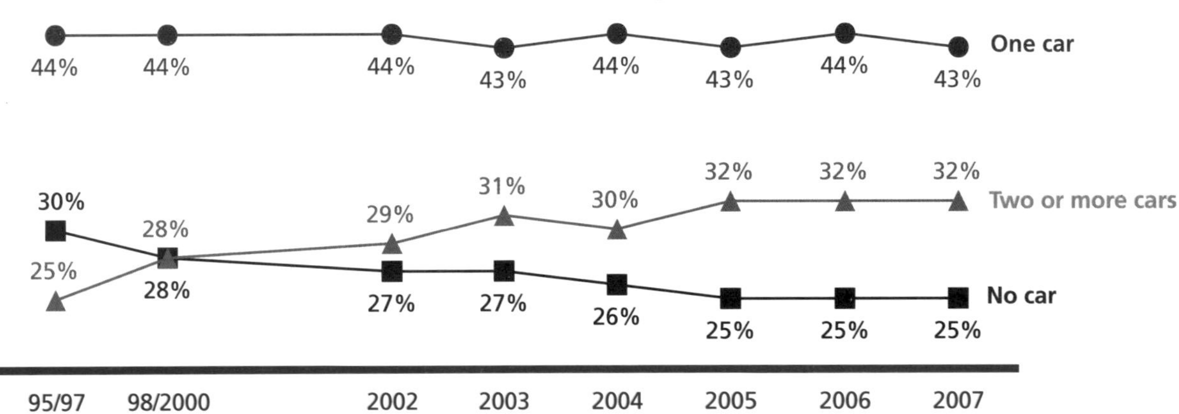

One car
44%
44%
44%
43%
44%
43%
44%
43%
Two or more cars
25%
28%
29%
31%
30%
32%
32%
32%
No car
30%
28%
27%
27%
26%
25%
25%
25%
95/97
98/2000
2002
2003
2004
2005
2006
2007

Shortest journey time to local facilities on foot or by public transport, GB
(% of households)

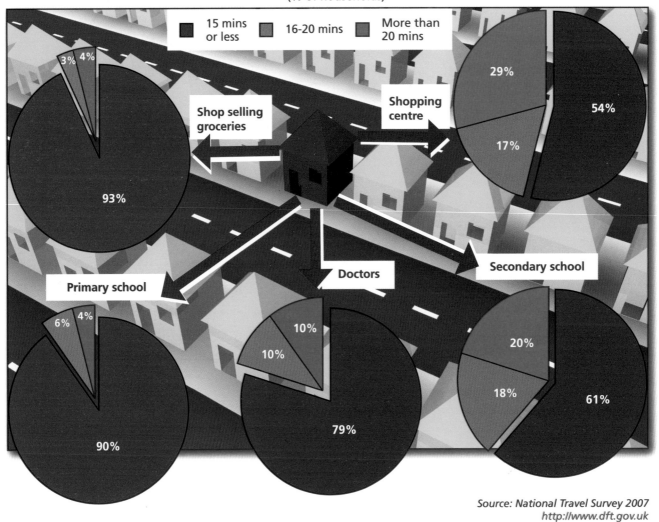

15 mins or less
16-20 mins
More than 20 mins

Shop selling groceries: 93%, 3%, 4%

Shopping centre: 54%, 17%, 29%

Primary school: 90%, 6%, 4%

Doctors: 79%, 10%, 10%

Secondary school: 61%, 18%, 20%

Source: National Travel Survey 2007
http://www.dft.gov.uk

Travel to school

11 to 16 year olds travel an average of 3.4 miles to school

For 11-16 year olds the proportion of trips to school made **on foot** decreased from **48%** in 1989–91 to **41%** in 2006, with a corresponding increase in the proportion made **by car**, from **14%** to **20%**.

How do 11-16 year olds get to school?

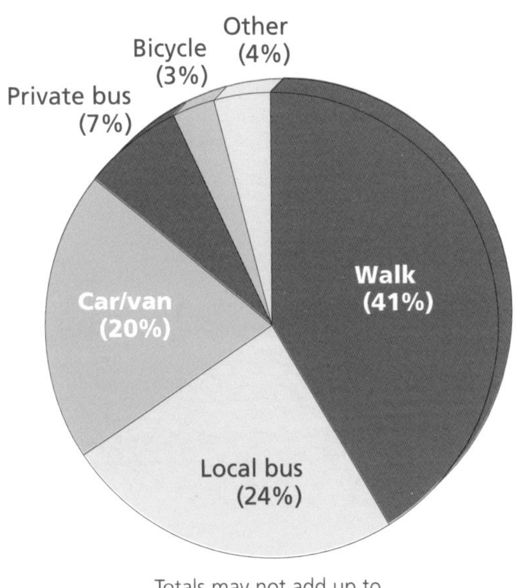

Other (4%)
Bicycle (3%)
Private bus (7%)
Car/van (20%)
Walk (41%)
Local bus (24%)

Totals may not add up to 100% due to rounding

Are 11-13 year olds accompanied to school by an adult?

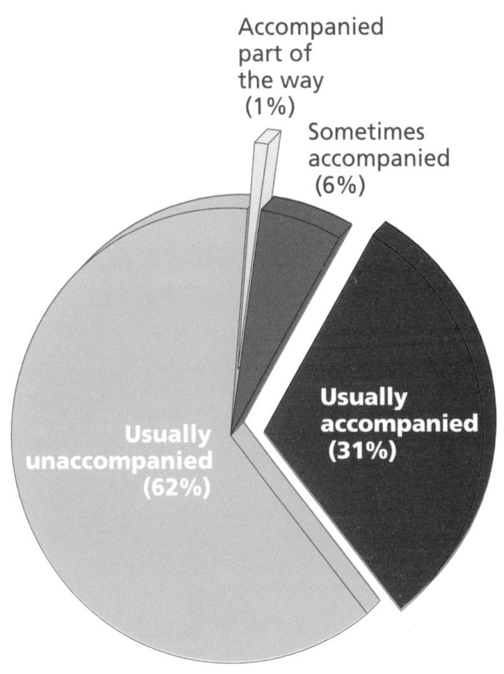

Accompanied part of the way (1%)
Sometimes accompanied (6%)
Usually unaccompanied (62%)
Usually accompanied (31%)

Why are 11-13 year olds accompanied to school by an adult?

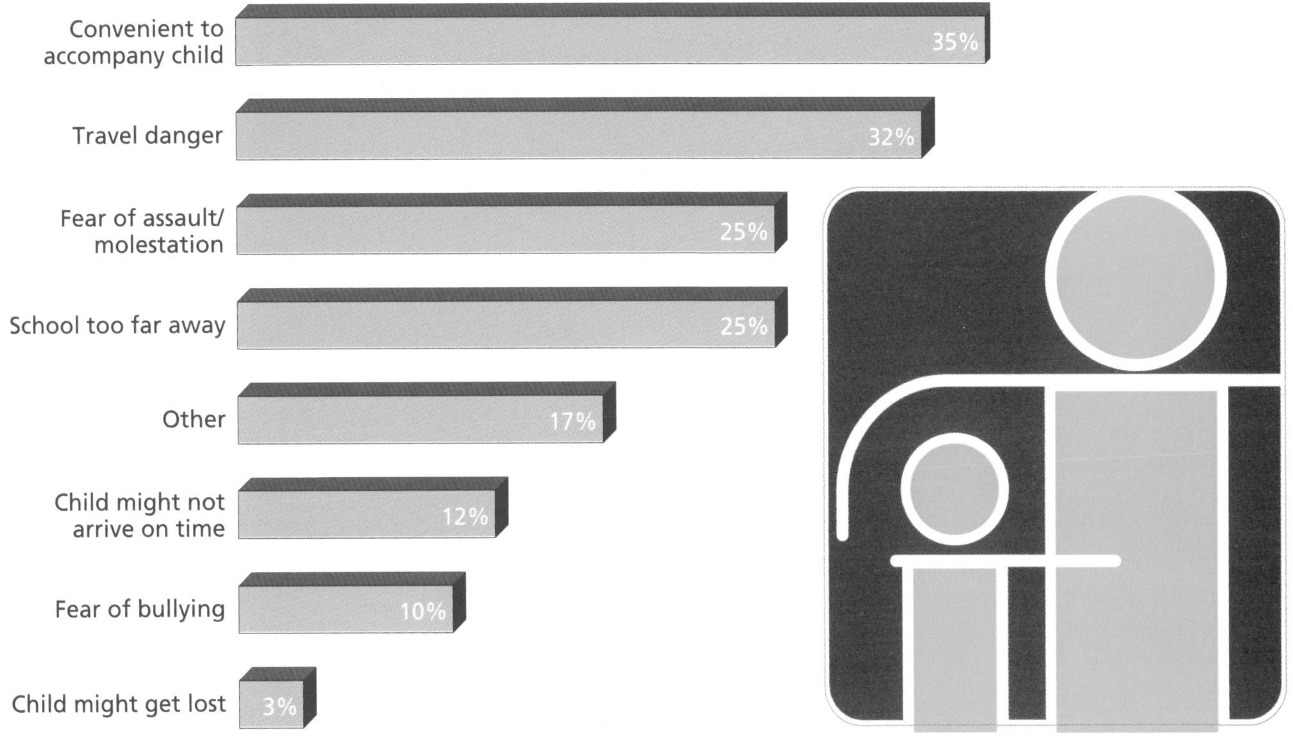

Convenient to accompany child 35%
Travel danger 32%
Fear of assault/ molestation 25%
School too far away 25%
Other 17%
Child might not arrive on time 12%
Fear of bullying 10%
Child might get lost 3%

8,300 GB households provided personal travel diaries for a week's travel in 2006

Source: Personal Travel Factsheet - March 2008, Department for Transport © Crown copyright 2008
http://www.dft.gov.uk

Road flow

Although peak times vary, Britain's roads are busy throughout the day

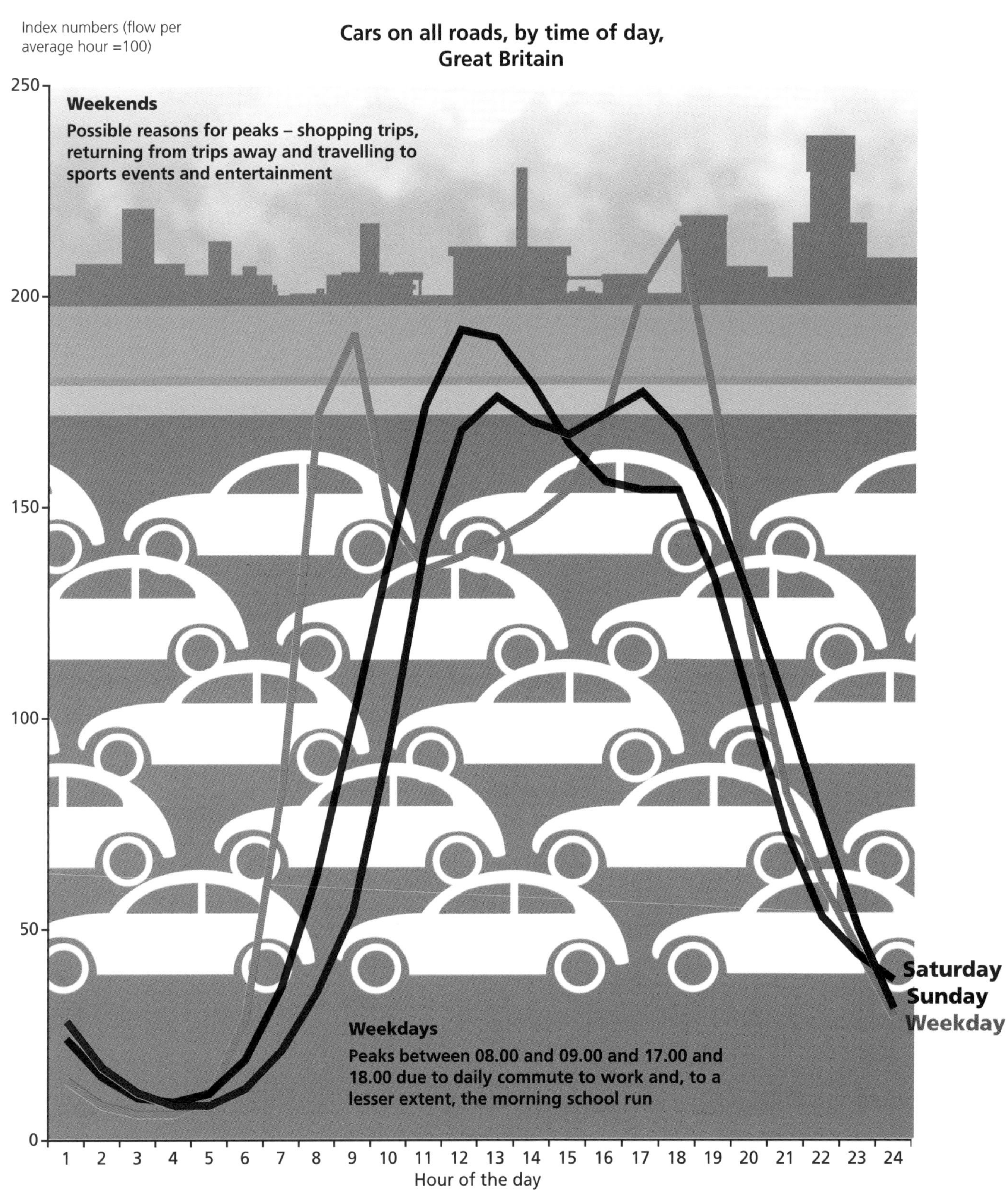
Index numbers (flow per average hour =100)
Cars on all roads, by time of day, Great Britain
250
200
150
100
50
0
Weekends
Possible reasons for peaks – shopping trips, returning from trips away and travelling to sports events and entertainment
Weekdays
Peaks between 08.00 and 09.00 and 17.00 and 18.00 due to daily commute to work and, to a lesser extent, the morning school run
Saturday
Sunday
Weekday
1 2 3 4 5 6 7 8 9 10 11 12 13 14 15 16 17 18 19 20 21 22 23 24
Hour of the day

Source: Department for Transport © Crown copyright 2008
http://www.dft.gov.uk

Rough ride

Motorcyclists are 43 times more likely to die in an accident than car users

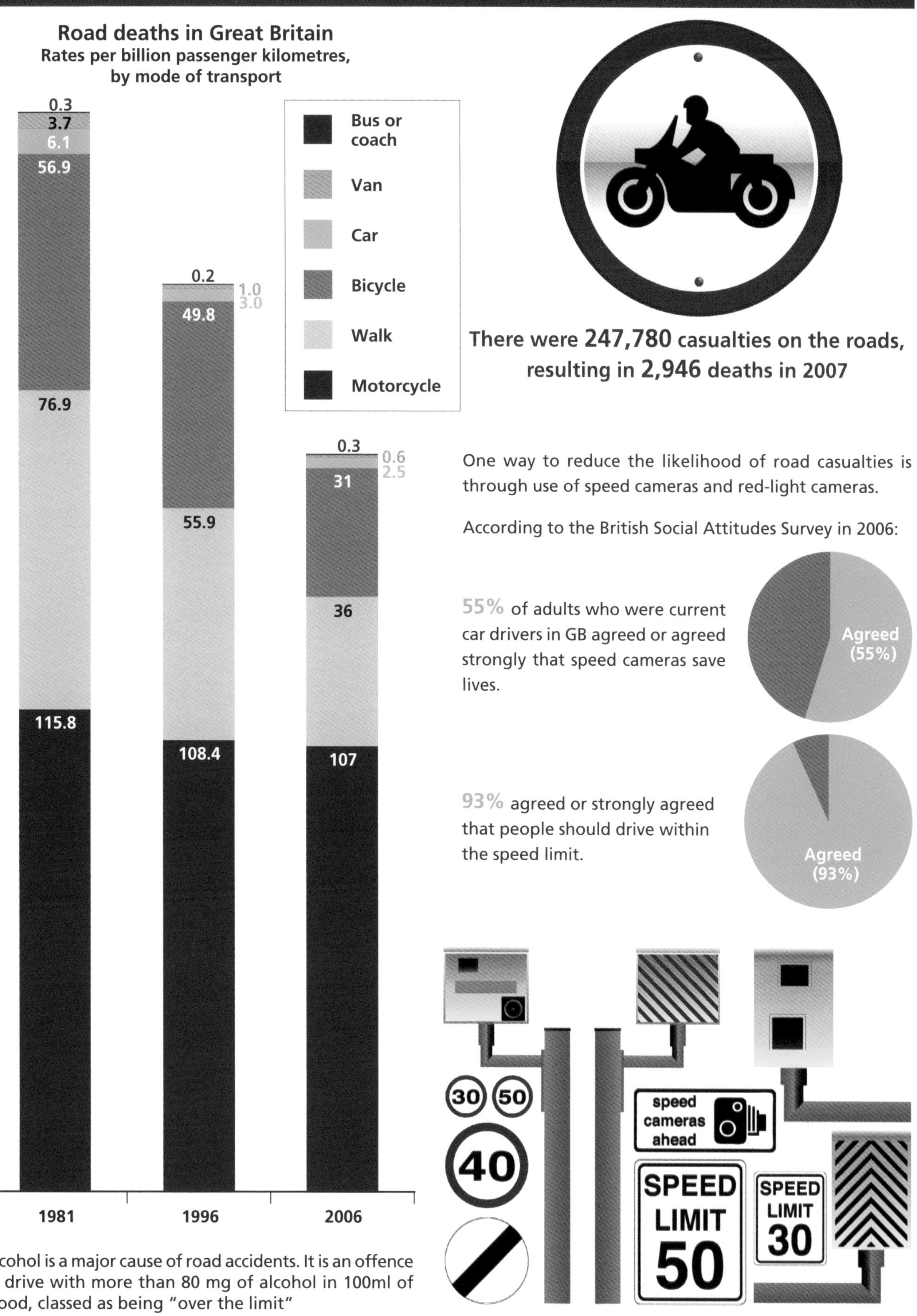

Road deaths in Great Britain
Rates per billion passenger kilometres, by mode of transport
Bus or coach
Van
Car
Bicycle
Walk
Motorcycle
1981
0.3
3.7
6.1
56.9
76.9
115.8
1996
0.2
1.0
3.0
49.8
55.9
108.4
2006
0.3
0.6
2.5
31
36
107
There were 247,780 casualties on the roads, resulting in 2,946 deaths in 2007
Agreed (55%)
Agreed (93%)
30
50
40
speed cameras ahead
SPEED LIMIT 50
SPEED LIMIT 30

One way to reduce the likelihood of road casualties is through use of speed cameras and red-light cameras.

According to the British Social Attitudes Survey in 2006:

55% of adults who were current car drivers in GB agreed or agreed strongly that speed cameras save lives.

93% agreed or strongly agreed that people should drive within the speed limit.

Alcohol is a major cause of road accidents. It is an offence to drive with more than 80 mg of alcohol in 100ml of blood, classed as being "over the limit"

Source: Social Trends © Crown copyright 2008
http://www.statistics.gov.uk

Flying high?

Although passenger numbers increased, the airline industry is not flourishing

Passengers at UK airports (millions)

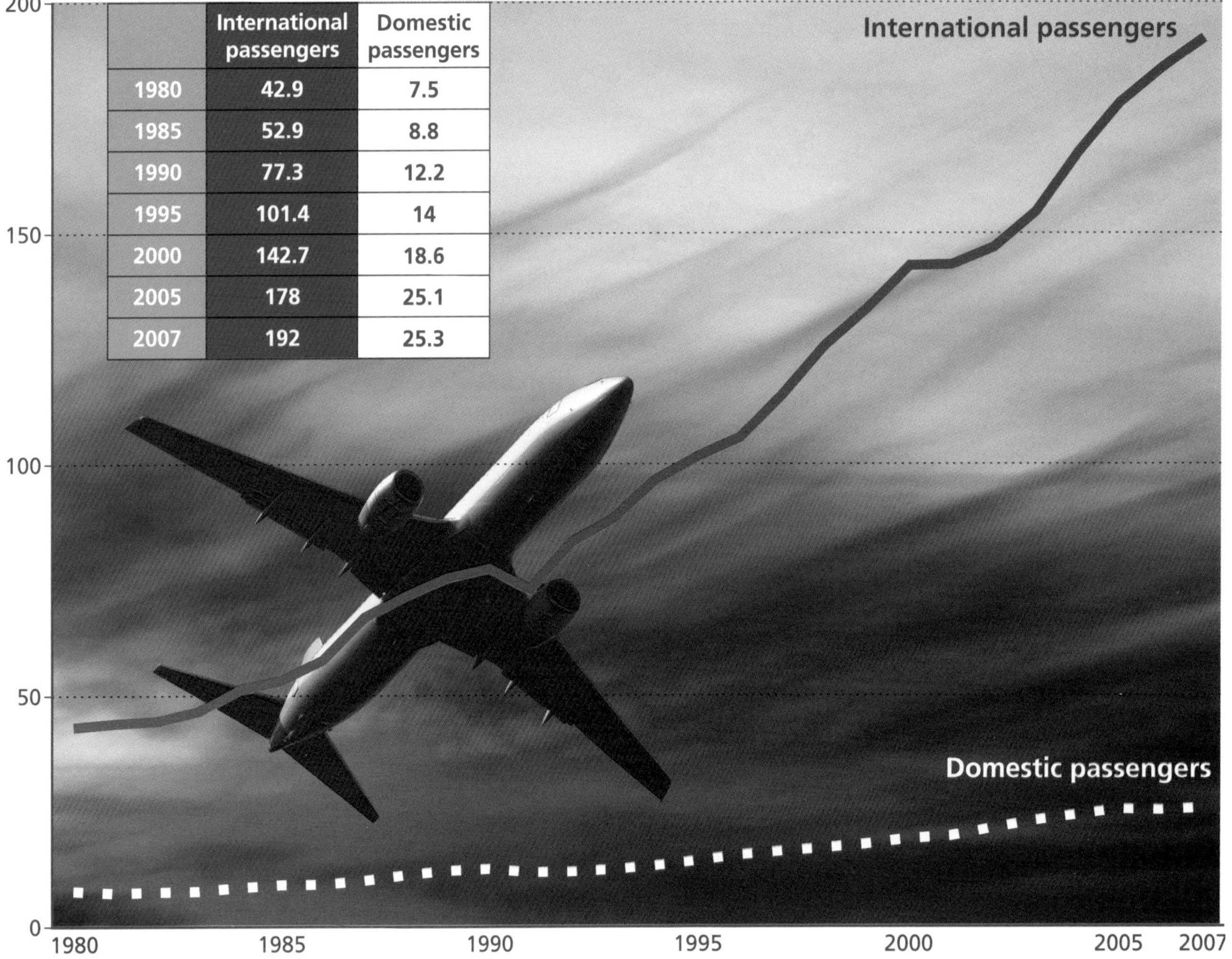

	International passengers	Domestic passengers
1980	42.9	7.5
1985	52.9	8.8
1990	77.3	12.2
1995	101.4	14
2000	142.7	18.6
2005	178	25.1
2007	192	25.3

International passengers
Domestic passengers
200
150
100
50
0
1980
1985
1990
1995
2000
2005
2007

- Growth in domestic air travel seems to have been mainly affected by competition from other means of transport, particularly due to improvements in long distance rail services and changes in airport security that have increased total journey times for air travel.
- Airlines and passengers have also experienced cost increases, particularly through rising jet fuel prices, but also through the doubling of Air Passenger Duty in 2007.
- The growth rate of no frills services from the UK eg easyJet etc has declined, but remains around 10%. By contrast, both full service and charter services are now showing negative annual growth rates.
- Regional airports have continued to grow at a faster rate than London airports and in 2006 handled 42% of passengers at UK airports.
- 8 regional airports now offer daily scheduled flights to 12 or more international destinations, whereas only Birmingham and Manchester did in 1990.

Source: Civil Aviation Authority
http://www.caa.co.uk

Plane problem

Passengers are more menacing as manners are declining

Incidents of air rage continue to rise!

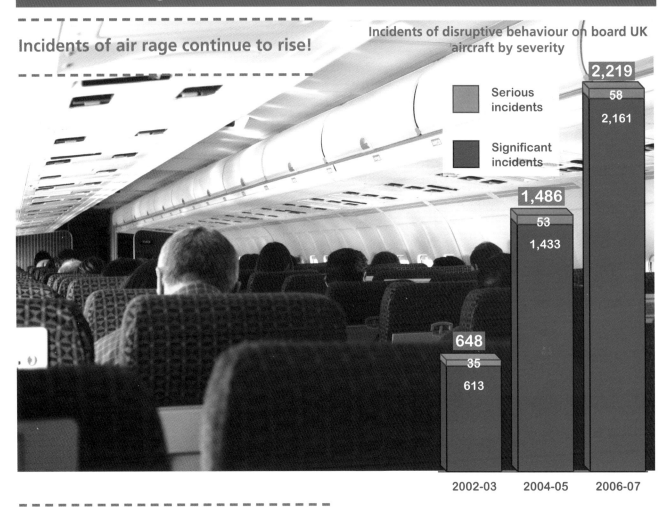

Incidents of disruptive behaviour on board UK aircraft by severity

	2002-03	2004-05	2006-07
Serious incidents	35	53	58
Significant incidents	613	1,433	2,161
Total	648	1,486	2,219

So why the decline in airline etiquette?

According to new research released by travel search engine Kayak.co.uk:

- **73%** of British travellers say that fellow passengers have become ruder in recent years
- **41%** blame long queues, disruptive security measures and cancelled or delayed flights as the primary causes of increased rudeness amongst fellow airline passengers
- **76%** agree fellow travellers should not spend more than five minutes in the toilet
- When it comes to straining passengers' nerves, the biggest gripes on long-haul flights are screaming babies (**29%**), sitting between two overweight passengers (**24%**), and being placed next to someone with bad body odour (**16%**).

Incidents of disruptive behaviour on board UK aircraft by type

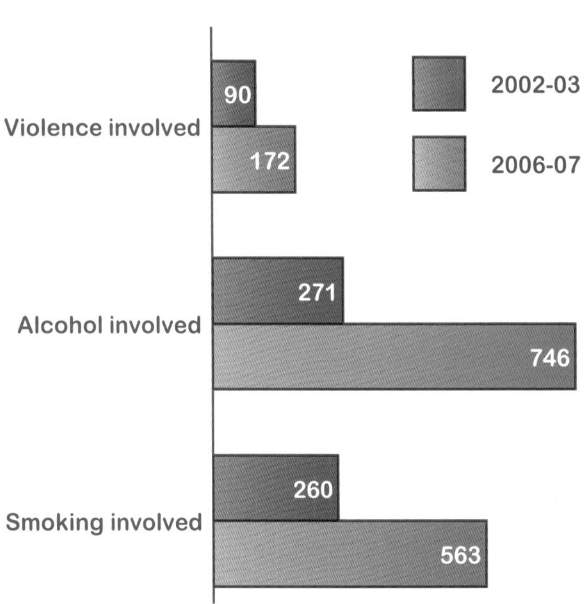
2002-03
2006-07
Violence involved
90
172
Alcohol involved
271
746
Smoking involved
260
563

Source: Disruptive behaviour on board UK aircraft, DFT
http://www.dft.gov.uk
http://www.kayak.co.uk

Holiday UK?

We like to holiday in the UK – but mainly for our short breaks

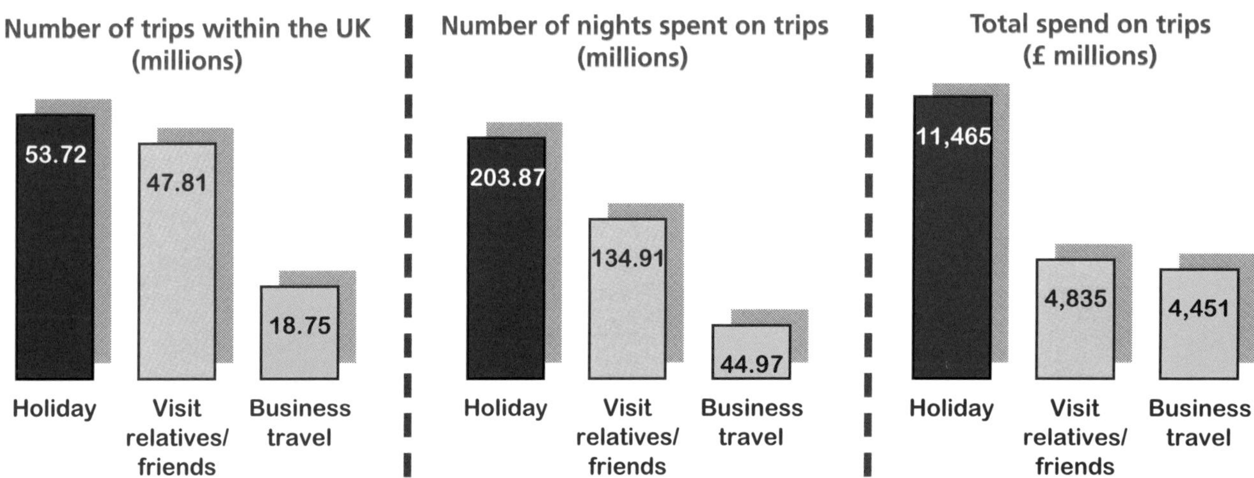
2007
Number of trips within the UK (millions)
53.72
47.81
18.75
Holiday
Visit relatives/ friends
Business travel
Number of nights spent on trips (millions)
203.87
134.91
44.97
Holiday
Visit relatives/ friends
Business travel
Total spend on trips (£ millions)
11,465
4,835
4,451
Holiday
Visit relatives/ friends
Business travel

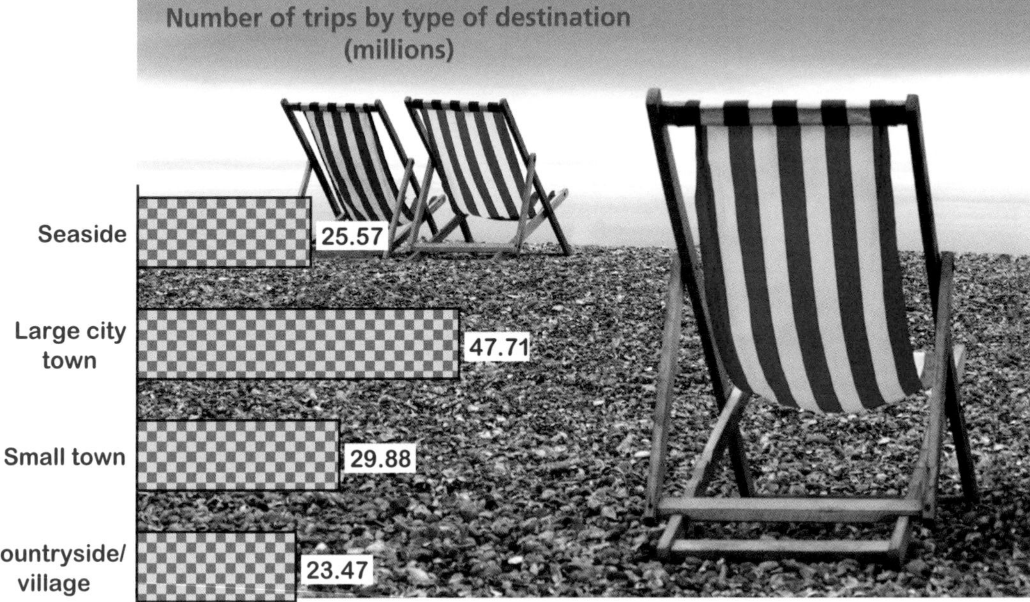
Number of trips by type of destination (millions)
Seaside
25.57
Large city town
47.71
Small town
29.88
Countryside/ village
23.47

While we spend more nights and money on holiday, large cities and towns are where we're mainly going, probably due to the large number of trips taken for business or to visit relatives or friends.

Party size	Number of trips 2007 (millions)
One	37.99
Two	40.94
Three	14.11
Four	17
Five	6.64
Six to ten	4.15
Ten or more	0.08

In 2007 as part of our trips within the UK we spent a total of **126.66 million** nights in large cities and towns, **106.82 million** by the seaside, **97.83** million in small towns and **87.14 million** nights in the countryside or a village.

Trips taken in the UK are mainly taken alone or in a couple. Only 32.44 million trips were taken with children under 15.

Source: United Kingdom Tourism Survey 2007
http://www.enjoyengland.com

Travel trends

UK residents made a record 69.5 million visits abroad

Top 10 countries visited

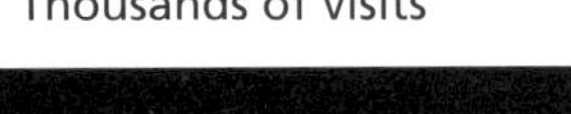

Thousands of visits

Country	Thousands of visits
Spain	14,428
France	10,854
Irish Republic	4,682
US	3,986
Italy	3,380
Germany	2,698
Greece	2,436
Netherlands	2,410
Portugal	1,937
Belgium	1,815

Top 10 countries for holidays

Thousands of visits

Country	Thousands of visits
Spain	12,587
France	7,112
Italy	2,440
US	2,363
Greece	2,241
Irish Republic	1,793
Portugal	1,654
Turkey	1,206
Netherlands	1,198
Cyprus	1,087

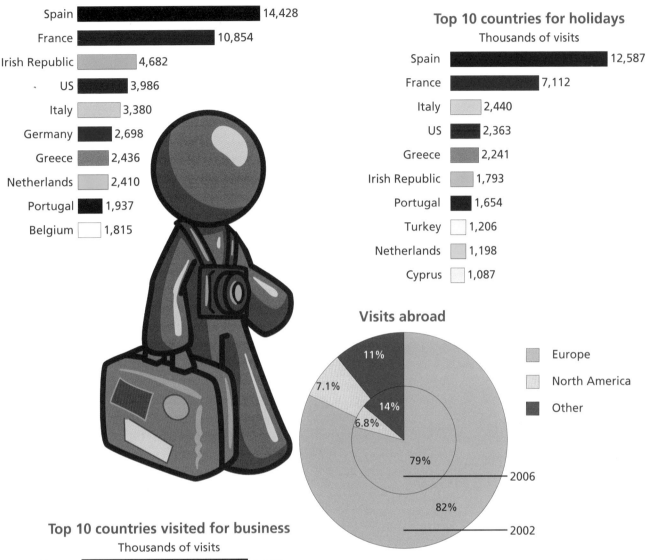

Visits abroad

	2006	2002
Europe	79%	82%
North America	6.8%	7.1%
Other	14%	11%

Top 10 countries visited for business

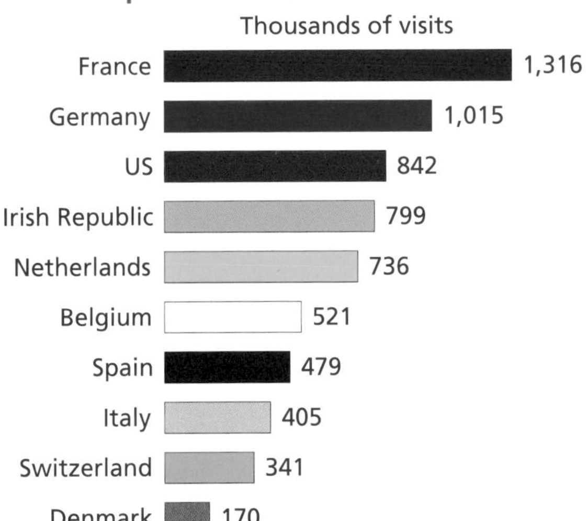

Thousands of visits
France 1,316
Germany 1,015
US 842
Irish Republic 799
Netherlands 736
Belgium 521
Spain 479
Italy 405
Switzerland 341
Denmark 170

Top 10 countries for visiting friends/relatives

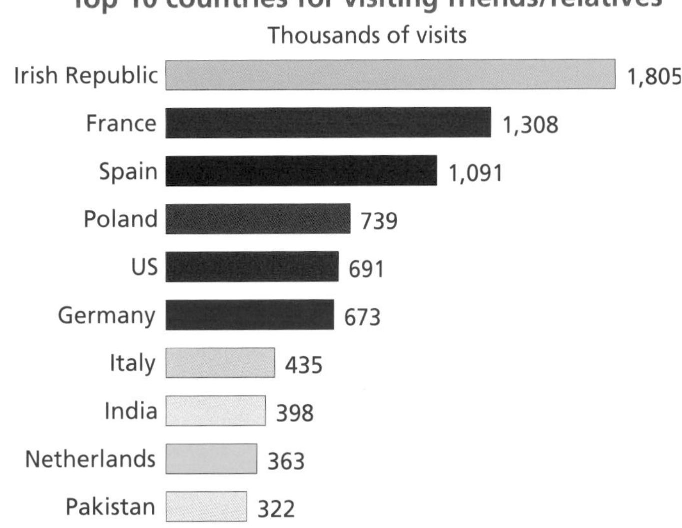

Thousands of visits
Irish Republic 1,805
France 1,308
Spain 1,091
Poland 739
US 691
Germany 673
Italy 435
India 398
Netherlands 363
Pakistan 322

Source: Travel Trends 2006 © Crown copyright 2008
http://www.statistics.gov.uk

Brits abroad

From accidents to abduction, help is available

Top 10 countries where British nationals required any consular assistance, 2007

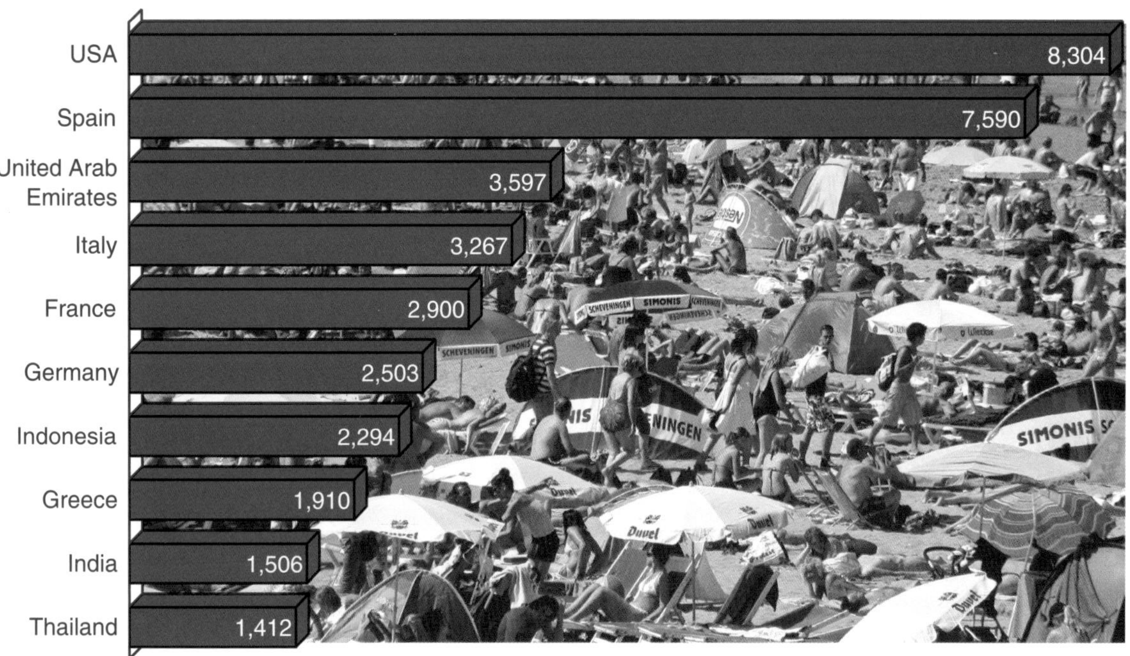

USA 8,304
Spain 7,590
United Arab Emirates 3,597
Italy 3,267
France 2,900
Germany 2,503
Indonesia 2,294
Greece 1,910
India 1,506
Thailand 1,412

Serious assistance cases can include arrests, hospitalisation and even child abduction and forced marriages.

- Taking into account the number of British visitors and residents, Indonesia showed a very high rate of serious assistance cases (10.05 for every 1,000 Brits) followed by Pakistan (1.95) and then India (1.37).
- Reasons for Indonesia's high rates of serious assistance cases include accidents, theft of money and passports and involvement in drugs.
- Although 2,032 Brits were arrested in Spain last year – 33% more than the year before and more than any other country – as a proportion of visitors and residents, Brits were more likely to be arrested in Cyprus, closely followed by the USA and United Arab Emirates.
- Spain had the highest number of hospitalisations but in fact Thailand had the highest proportion. The next highest was Greece. The five locations where injuries are most likely to occur are roads, beaches, hotels, remote locations and ski slopes.
- While more Brits visit European holiday spots, proportionally they are likely to need assistance in countries that are further away.

Country	Estimated number of British visits	Total number of serious assistance cases	Total arrests	Hospitalisation	Deaths	Reported rapes
USA	6,500,000	2,765	1,415	75	95	2
Spain	17,000,000	5,470	2,032	695	1,591	29
United Arab Emirates	1,100,000	606	230	20	51	2
Italy	3,500,000	619	38	171	156	2
France	14,800,000	1,572	153	246	385	6
Germany	2,372,320	1,739	162	29	294	1
Indonesia	140,673	1,525	18	25	2	0
Greece	3,000,000	1,405	230	602	131	28
India	600,000	866	46	45	126	1
Thailand	860,000	1,066	141	324	269	2

Source: British Behaviour Abroad Annual Report 2008, Foreign & Commonwealth Office
http://www.fco.gov.uk/en/

War & conflict

Pierre Holtz | UNICEF CAR | hdptcar.net

Military morale

Almost half of UK military personnel 'feel like quitting'...

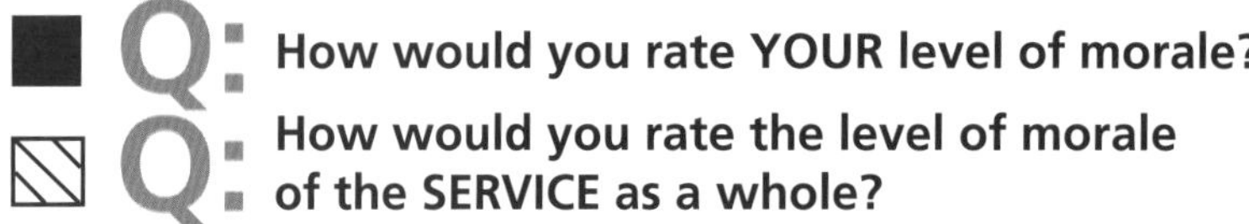

Q: How would you rate YOUR level of morale?
Q: How would you rate the level of morale of the SERVICE as a whole?

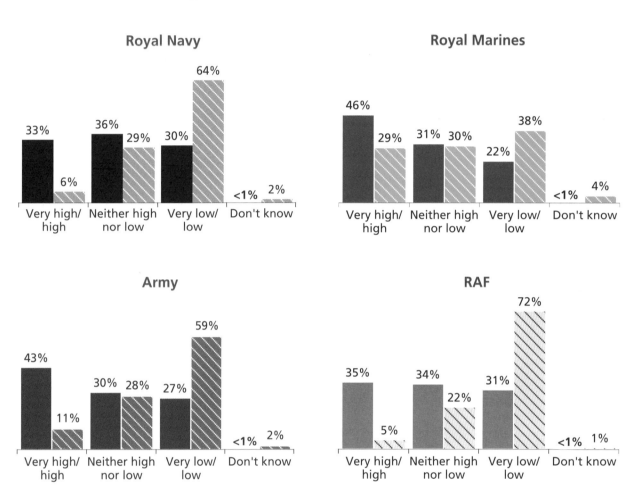

Royal Navy

	Very high/ high	Neither high nor low	Very low/ low	Don't know
YOUR level of morale	33%	36%	30%	<1%
SERVICE as a whole	6%	29%	64%	2%

Royal Marines

	Very high/ high	Neither high nor low	Very low/ low	Don't know
YOUR level of morale	46%	31%	22%	<1%
SERVICE as a whole	29%	30%	38%	4%

Army

	Very high/ high	Neither high nor low	Very low/ low	Don't know
YOUR level of morale	43%	30%	27%	<1%
SERVICE as a whole	11%	28%	59%	2%

RAF

	Very high/ high	Neither high nor low	Very low/ low	Don't know
YOUR level of morale	35%	34%	31%	<1%
SERVICE as a whole	5%	22%	72%	1%

I regularly feel like leaving the Service for good

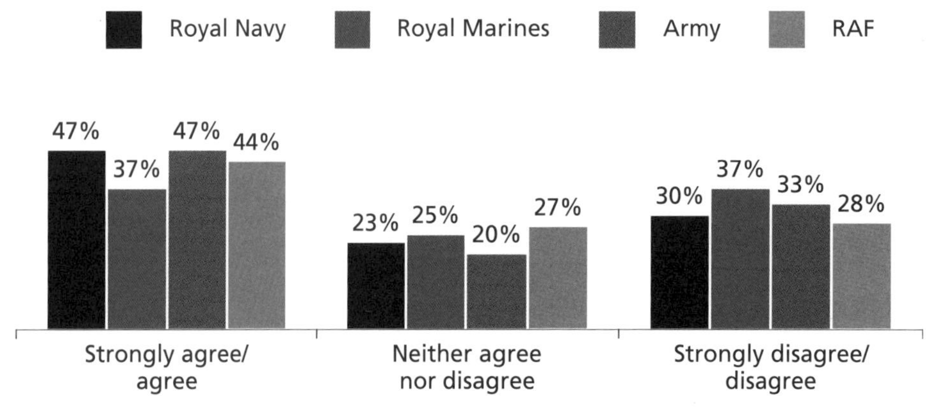

Royal Navy
Royal Marines
Army
RAF
47%
37%
47%
44%
23%
25%
20%
27%
30%
37%
33%
28%
Strongly agree/ agree
Neither agree nor disagree
Strongly disagree/ disagree

Figures may not add up to 100% due to rounding

Base: A sample of all members of the armed forces (24,760) were surveyed, 36% responded (8,857)

...but over half of the armed forces are satisfied with their job...

How satisfied are you with your job in general?

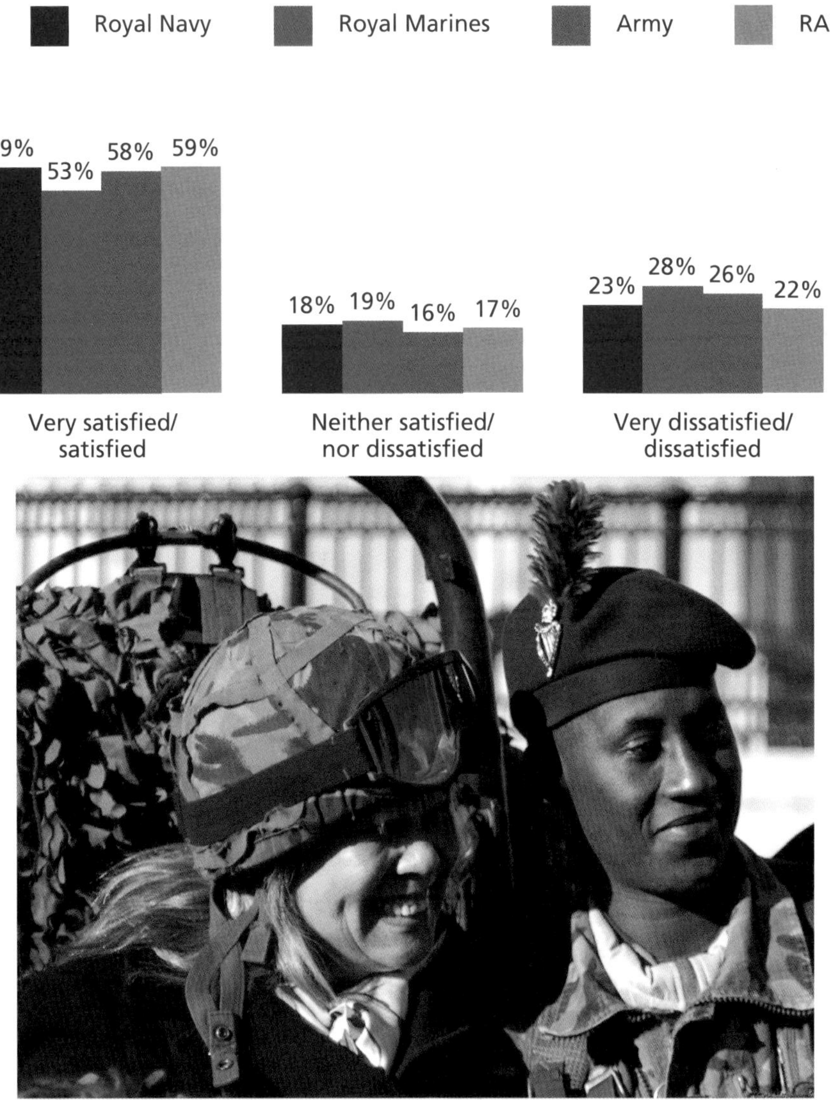

Royal Navy
Royal Marines
Army
RAF
59%
53%
58%
59%
18%
19%
16%
17%
23%
28%
26%
22%
Very satisfied/ satisfied
Neither satisfied/ nor dissatisfied
Very dissatisfied/ dissatisfied

...and they also feel proud to be in the service

I feel proud to be in the Service

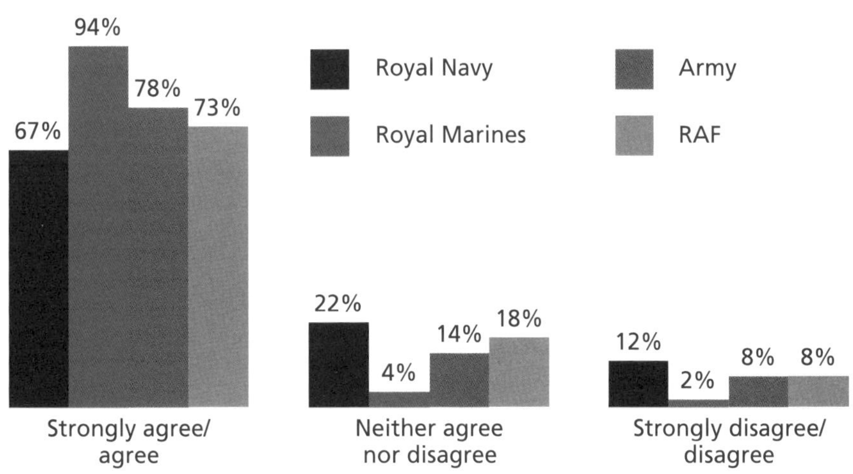

Royal Navy
Army
Royal Marines
RAF
67%
94%
78%
73%
22%
4%
14%
18%
12%
2%
8%
8%
Strongly agree/ agree
Neither agree nor disagree
Strongly disagree/ disagree

Source: Armed Forces Continuous Attitude Survey, Ministry of Defence © Crown copyright 2008

http://www.mod.uk

World of weapons

The USA accounts for nearly half of world military spending

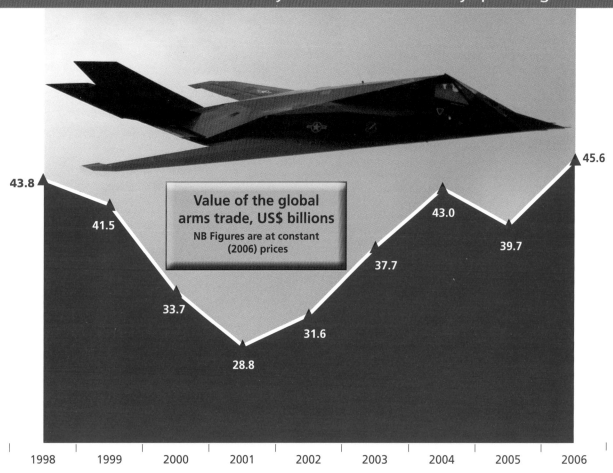

Value of the global arms trade, US$ billions
NB Figures are at constant (2006) prices

1998	1999	2000	2001	2002	2003	2004	2005	2006
43.8	41.5	33.7	28.8	31.6	37.7	43.0	39.7	45.6

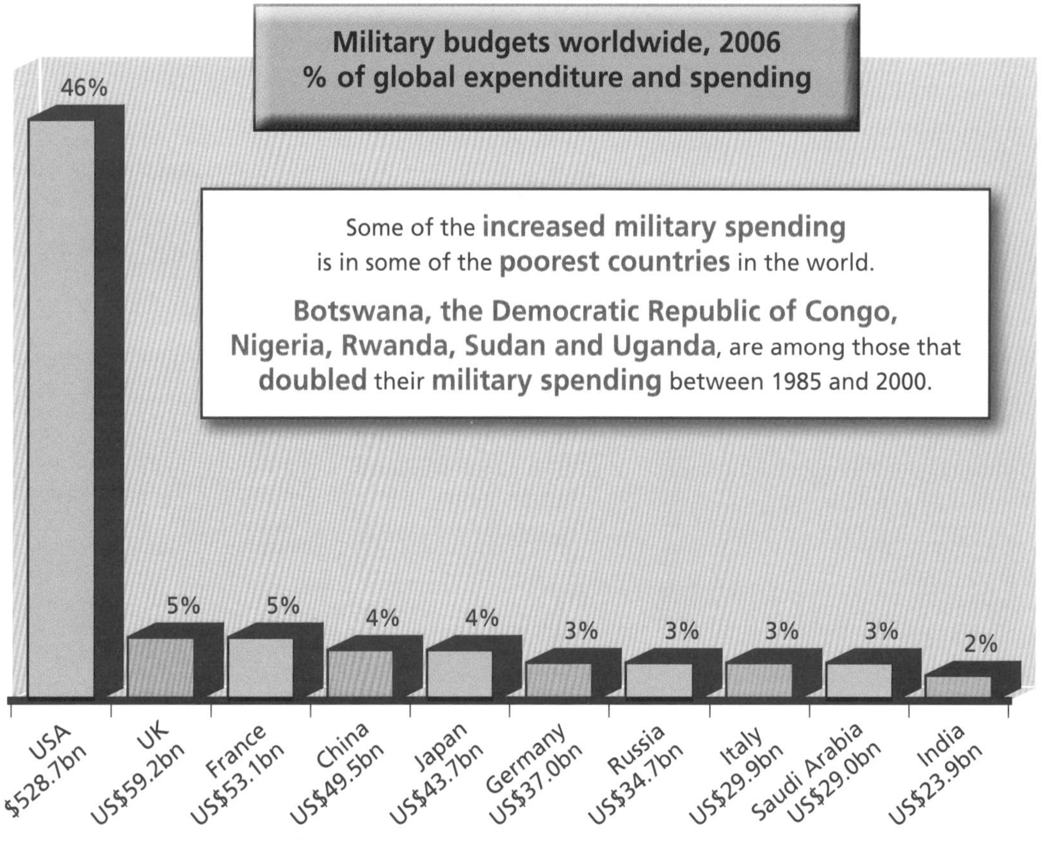
Military budgets worldwide, 2006
% of global expenditure and spending
Some of the increased military spending is in some of the poorest countries in the world.
Botswana, the Democratic Republic of Congo, Nigeria, Rwanda, Sudan and Uganda, are among those that doubled their military spending between 1985 and 2000.
46%
5%
5%
4%
4%
3%
3%
3%
3%
2%
USA $528.7bn
UK US$59.2bn
France US$53.1bn
China US$49.5bn
Japan US$43.7bn
Germany US$37.0bn
Russia US$34.7bn
Italy US$29.9bn
Saudi Arabia US$29.0bn
India US$23.9bn

Source: Campaign against arms trade

httpl/:www.caat.org.uk

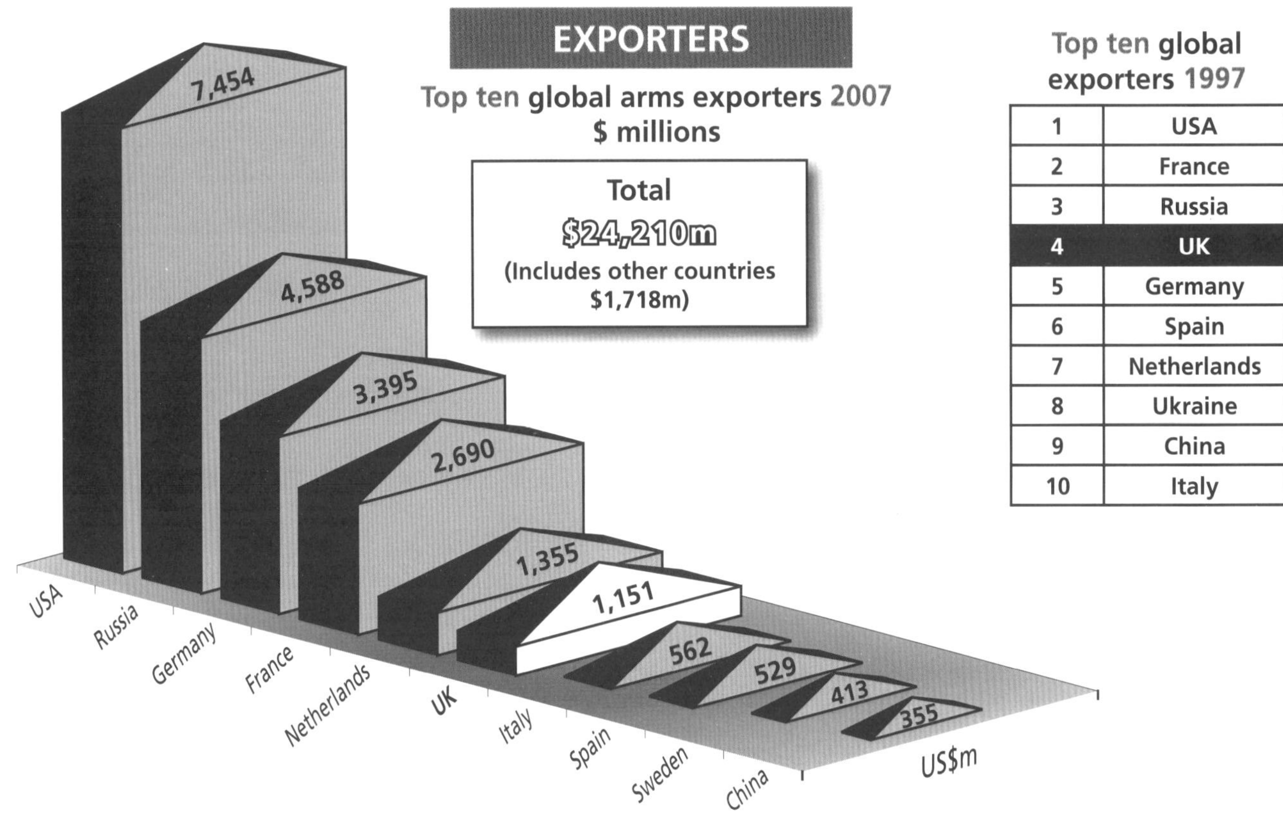
EXPORTERS
Top ten global arms exporters 2007
$ millions
Total
$24,210m
(Includes other countries
$1,718m)
7,454
4,588
3,395
2,690
1,355
1,151
562
529
413
355
USA
Russia
Germany
France
Netherlands
UK
Italy
Spain
Sweden
China
US$m

Top ten global exporters 1997

1	USA
2	France
3	Russia
4	UK
5	Germany
6	Spain
7	Netherlands
8	Ukraine
9	China
10	Italy

Emerging exporters

- While the industrialised countries remain the world's major arms exporters, a growing number of companies in the developing world, backed by their governments, are gaining a significant share of the global arms market
- The number of arms companies in the top 100 based in countries not previously considered as major exporters has more than doubled since 1990
- These emerging exporters include Israel, India, South Korea, Brazil, Singapore and South Africa

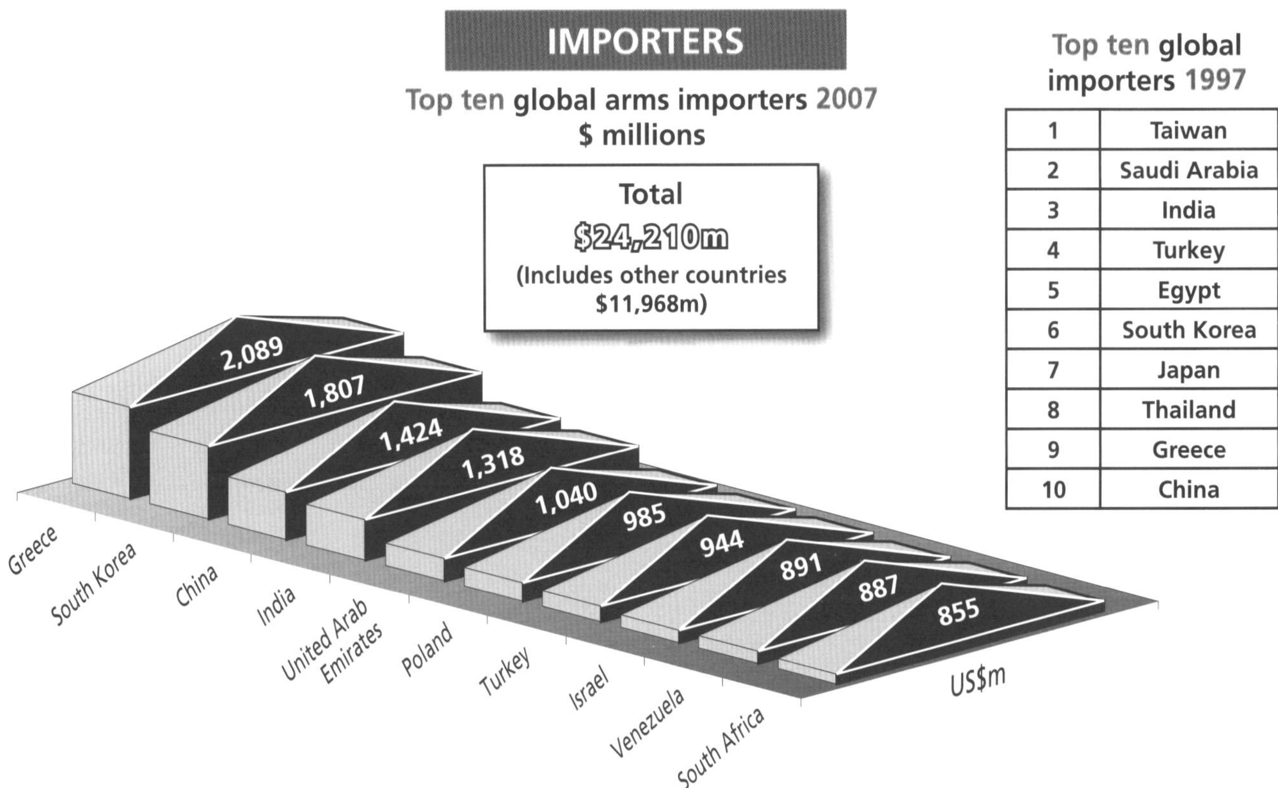
IMPORTERS
Top ten global arms importers 2007
$ millions
Total
$24,210m
(Includes other countries
$11,968m)
2,089
1,807
1,424
1,318
1,040
985
944
891
887
855
Greece
South Korea
China
India
United Arab Emirates
Poland
Turkey
Israel
Venezuela
South Africa
US$m

Top ten global importers 1997

1	Taiwan
2	Saudi Arabia
3	India
4	Turkey
5	Egypt
6	South Korea
7	Japan
8	Thailand
9	Greece
10	China

NB Figures are at constant (1990) prices.
Figures do not add up due to rounding

Source: Stockholm International Peace Research Institute
http://www.sipri.org

Deadly toys

Every thirty minutes someone is injured or killed by an encounter with the remnants of war

- In 2006 **casualties** from **landmines and explosive remnants of war** (ERW) were recorded in **68 states**
- **1,367** people were **killed, 4,296 injured** with **88 status unknown**
- **75%** of recorded casualties were **civilians**
- **89%** were **male**

ERW includes unexploded artillery shells, grenades, mortars, rockets, air-dropped bombs and cluster bombs.

Cluster bombs are launched from the ground or the air. The containers open and disperse 'bomblets' over a wide area.

Many of these bomblets fail to detonate and can harm civilians decades after a conflict has ended.

Landmine/ERW casualties worldwide, 2006

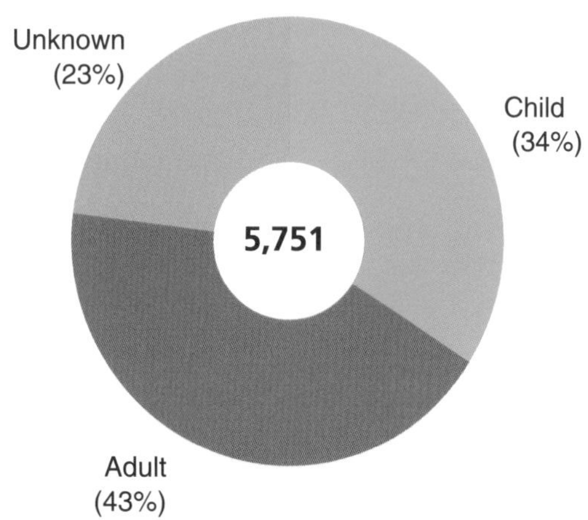
Unknown (23%)
Child (34%)
5,751
Adult (43%)

Countries with the most child casualties from landmines/ERWs, 2006

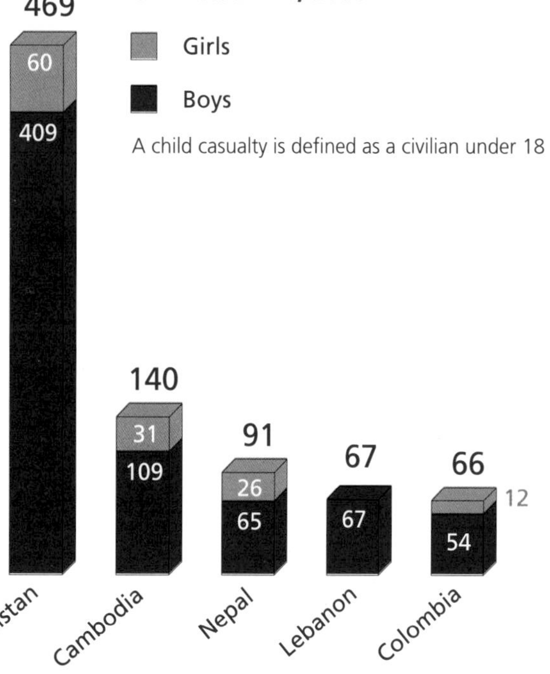
469
60
409
Girls
Boys
A child casualty is defined as a civilian under 18
140
31
109
91
26
65
67
67
66
12
54
Afghanistan
Cambodia
Nepal
Lebanon
Colombia

Whoever activates a mine, whether it is a child or a soldier – will be its next victim

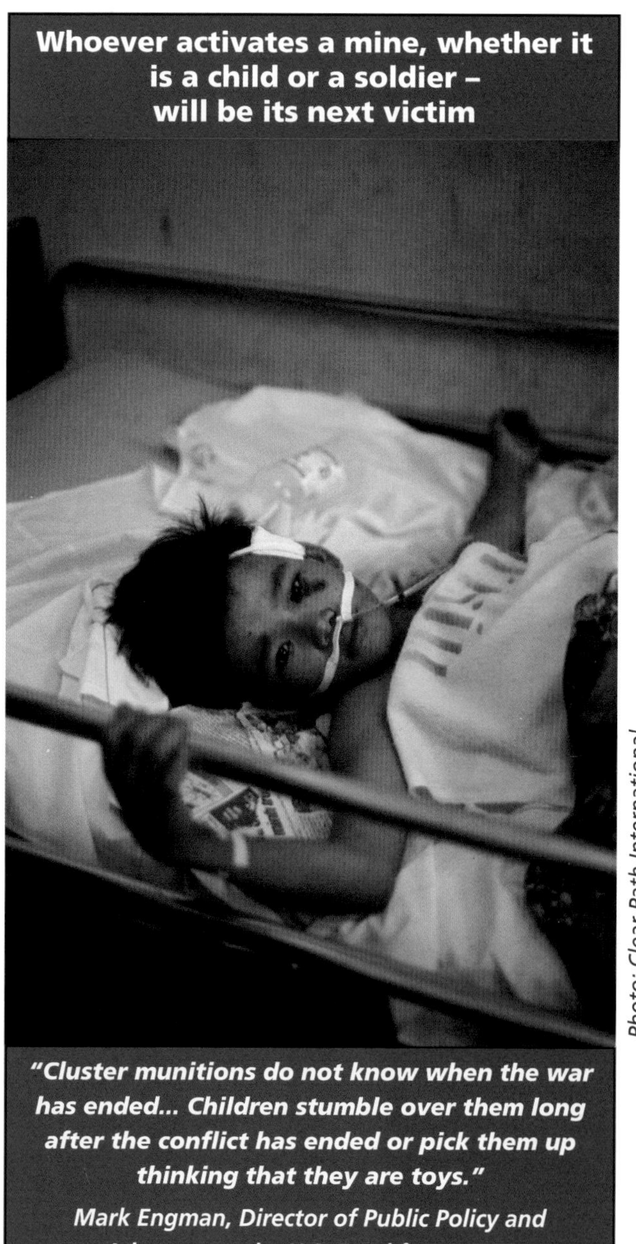

Photo: Clear Path International

"Cluster munitions do not know when the war has ended... Children stumble over them long after the conflict has ended or pick them up thinking that they are toys."

Mark Engman, Director of Public Policy and Advocacy at the U.S. Fund for UNICEF

Countries with the highest percentage of child casualties from landmines/ERWs

(The number of child casualties shown in brackets)

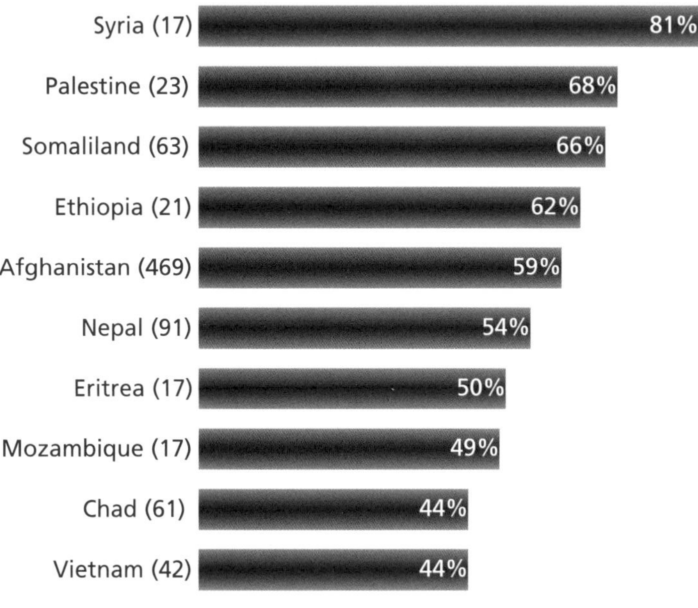
Syria (17) 81%
Palestine (23) 68%
Somaliland (63) 66%
Ethiopia (21) 62%
Afghanistan (469) 59%
Nepal (91) 54%
Eritrea (17) 50%
Mozambique (17) 49%
Chad (61) 44%
Vietnam (42) 44%

Only countries with 20 or more casualties are included

Total female casualties were **200 women**, **209 girls** and **55** whose **ages** were **unknown**.

Female child casualties are often among the most under-reported groups, as in some countries disability is seen as a stigma that needs to be hidden, especially when it occurs among girls.

In countries like Yemen, where girls traditionally herd sheep, they constitute a high-risk group. For example, five girls were injured by an antipersonnel mine in an area they thought had been cleared.

In Lao People's Democratic Republic, **children** were **49%** of all casualties and **girl** casualties were **30%** of child casualties, a percentage considerably higher than the international average.

In Nepal, **82%** of casualties resulting from intentional handling of ERW were children.

Photo: Clear Path International

Children are attracted to playing with unknown devices as they travel to school and while bored during other tasks, such as tending animals.

Recovering and selling metal from ERW provides children with pocket money or can be the child's contribution to the family's income.

The 1997 Mine Ban Treaty is an international agreement that bans landmines. As of March 2008, there are 156 member states and 39 states that remain outside the treaty these include: China, Russia and the United States.

On 30 May 2008 in Dublin, representatives of 110 nations completed negotiations on a new international treaty that commits their governments to stop using cluster bombs and to destroy their existing stockpiles within eight years.

The USA – historically, the world's largest producer, stockpiler, and user of these deadly weapons – did not participate and actively campaigned to weaken the treaty.

Source: Clear Path International, Landmine Monitor 2008
http://www.cpi.org
http://www.icbl.org/lm

Peaceful places

Which countries reject violence and conflict?

Ten most peaceful countries
1. Iceland
No army and lowest ratio of people in jail
2. Denmark
3. Norway
4. New Zealand
5. Japan
6. Ireland
7. Portugal
8. Finland
9. Luxembourg
10. Austria

The UN defined a culture of peace as involving values, attitudes and behaviours that reject violence; endeavour to prevent conflicts by addressing root causes and aim at solving problems through dialogue and negotiation

The Global Peace Index (GPI) is a measurement of peace.

140 countries were analysed in 2008 using **24 indicators** ranging from a nation's level of military expenditure to its relations with neighbouring countries and the level of respect for human rights.

The indicators were grouped into three themes:

- **Ongoing domestic and international conflict**
- **Safety and security in society**
- **Military build-up in the country**

Each of the indicators was given a value and the final calculation gave more weight to internal than external factors.

Small, stable and democratic countries are the most peaceful – **16 of the top 20 countries** are **western or central European** democracies. Most of them are members of the European Union. **Three Scandinavian countries** are in the **top ten**.

Three of the world's major military/diplomatic powers score relatively badly overall, with **China** at **67th**, the **US** at **97th** and **Russia** at **131st**.

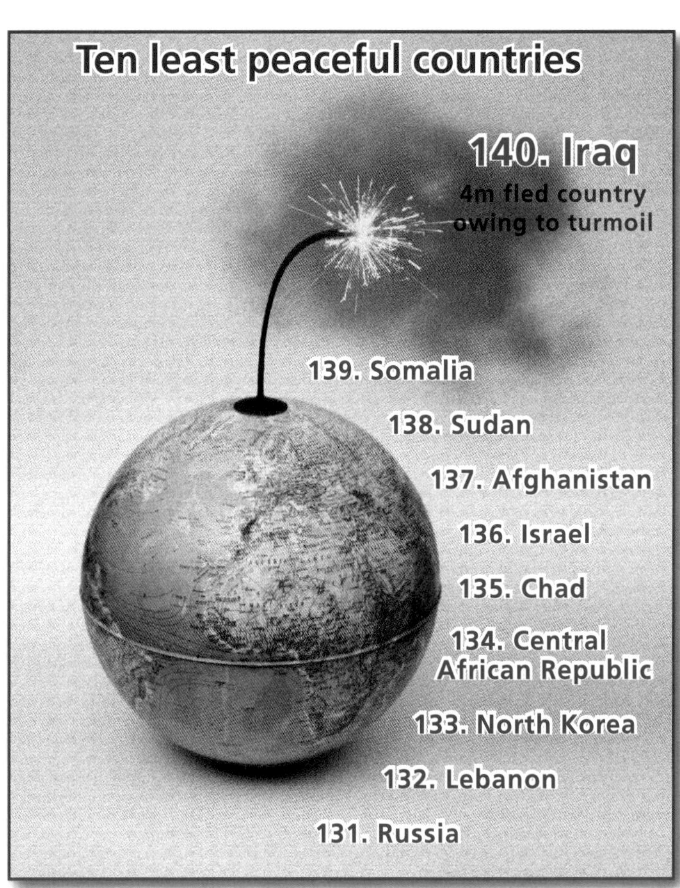
Ten least peaceful countries
140. Iraq
4m fled country owing to turmoil
139. Somalia
138. Sudan
137. Afghanistan
136. Israel
135. Chad
134. Central African Republic
133. North Korea
132. Lebanon
131. Russia

Western Europe

The majority of countries are in the **top 20**. However, **Spain (30th)**, **Cyprus (52nd)** and **Greece (54th)** ranked lower because of **internal conflicts**. The rankings for **UK** at **49th** and **France (36th)** are lowered by **high levels of militarisation**, sophisticated **weapons industries** and **arms exports** and the **UK's** battlefield **troop losses**.

State of peace

- Very high
- High
- Medium
- Low
- Very low
- Not included

Central and Eastern Europe

Recent members of the EU generally did well: **Slovenia (16th)**, **Czech Republic (17th)**.

Russia (131st) scored especially poorly on **internal peace** with high scores for **homicides, jailed population, distrust amongst citizens, violent crime** and **respect for human rights**.

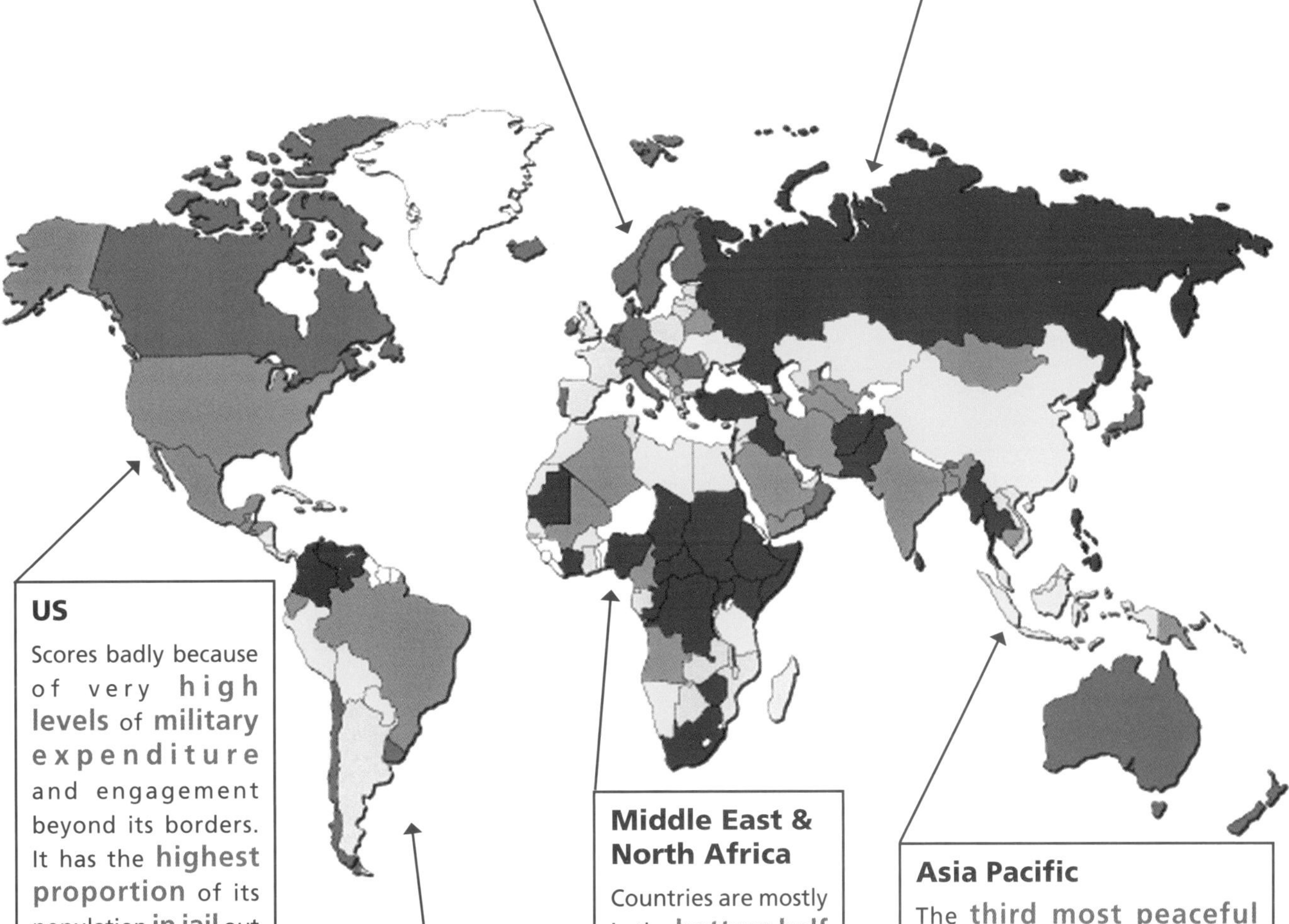

US

Scores badly because of very **high levels** of **military expenditure** and engagement beyond its borders. It has the **highest proportion** of its population **in jail** out of the 140 countries and comparatively **high levels of homicide**.

Latin America

A broad spread, led by **Chile (19th)** and **Uruguay (21st)**, but with **Venezuela** ranking **123rd** and **Colombia 130th**.

Middle East & North Africa

Countries are mostly in the **bottom half** of the GPI, with **Iraq** the country **least at peace**. However, **Oman, Qatar and United Arab Emirates** are all in the **top 30**.

Asia Pacific

The **third most peaceful region**, but with wide variation. **New Zealand (4th)** and **Japan (5th)** have very strong scores for **domestic peace** and **low levels of militarisation**. But **internal conflicts** and **high levels of militarisation** give **Afghanistan (137th), North Korea (133th), Pakistan (127th), Burma (126th)** and **India (107th)** low rankings.

Map Source: Economist Intelligence Unit

Source: Global Peace Index Rankings 2008
http://www.visionofhumanity.org

Displaced

4.7 million Iraqis have been uprooted as a result of the crisis in their country

As a result of initial optimism after the fall of the Saddam Hussein regime in 2003, over 300,000 Iraqi refugees returned home during the two years following the war – mainly from Iran.

However by mid 2007 2.2m Iraqis were still living outside Iraq and few are returning voluntarily.

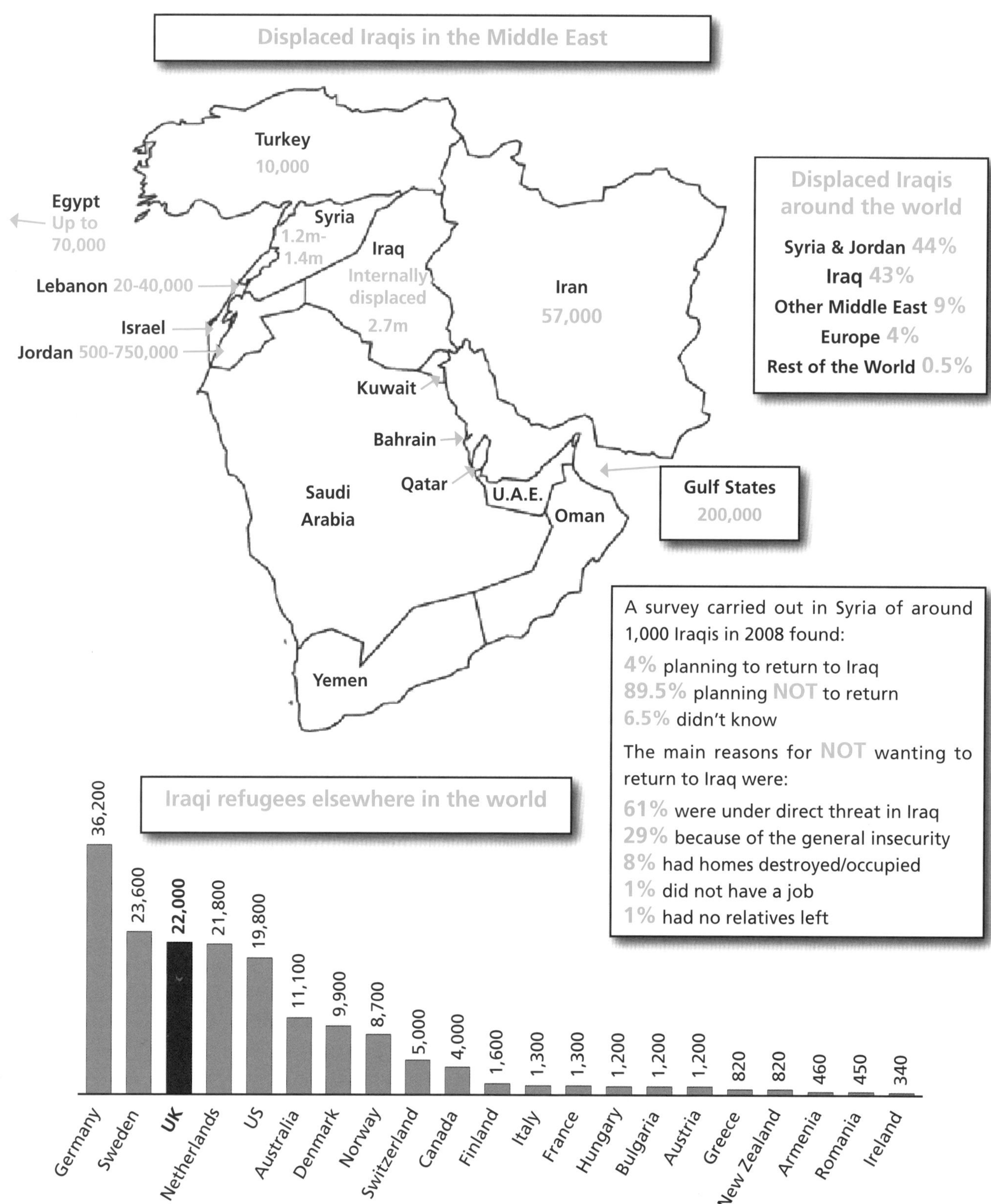

Displaced Iraqis in the Middle East
Turkey
10,000
Egypt
Up to
70,000
Syria
1.2m-
1.4m
Iraq
Internally
displaced
2.7m
Iran
57,000
Lebanon 20-40,000
Israel
Jordan 500-750,000
Kuwait
Bahrain
Qatar
U.A.E.
Saudi
Arabia
Oman
Yemen
Gulf States
200,000
Displaced Iraqis around the world
Syria & Jordan 44%
Iraq 43%
Other Middle East 9%
Europe 4%
Rest of the World 0.5%
A survey carried out in Syria of around 1,000 Iraqis in 2008 found:
4% planning to return to Iraq
89.5% planning NOT to return
6.5% didn't know
The main reasons for NOT wanting to return to Iraq were:
61% were under direct threat in Iraq
29% because of the general insecurity
8% had homes destroyed/occupied
1% did not have a job
1% had no relatives left
Iraqi refugees elsewhere in the world
36,200
23,600
22,000
21,800
19,800
11,100
9,900
8,700
5,000
4,000
1,600
1,300
1,300
1,200
1,200
1,200
820
820
460
450
340
Germany
Sweden
UK
Netherlands
US
Australia
Denmark
Norway
Switzerland
Canada
Finland
Italy
France
Hungary
Bulgaria
Austria
Greece
New Zealand
Armenia
Romania
Ireland

NB Estimates include recognised refugees, asylum seekers and other Iraqis who may be in need of international protection

Totals do not add up to 100% due to rounding

Source: UNHCR
http://www.unhcr.org

Wider world

State of democracy

36% of the world's population have no political freedom or civil liberties

Countries are classed as

Free
where there is a chance for different political parties to compete for votes, freedom to move around and associate with others and independent media.
Free countries include:
UK, South Africa and Indonesia

Partly Free
where there is limited respect for political rights and civil liberties. Partly Free states frequently suffer from an environment of corruption, weak rule of law and ethnic and religious strife.
Partly Free countries include:
Turkey, Nigeria and Lebanon

Not Free
where basic political rights are absent and basic civil liberties are widely and systematically denied.
Not Free countries include:
Russia, Saudi Arabia and China

Freedom in the world

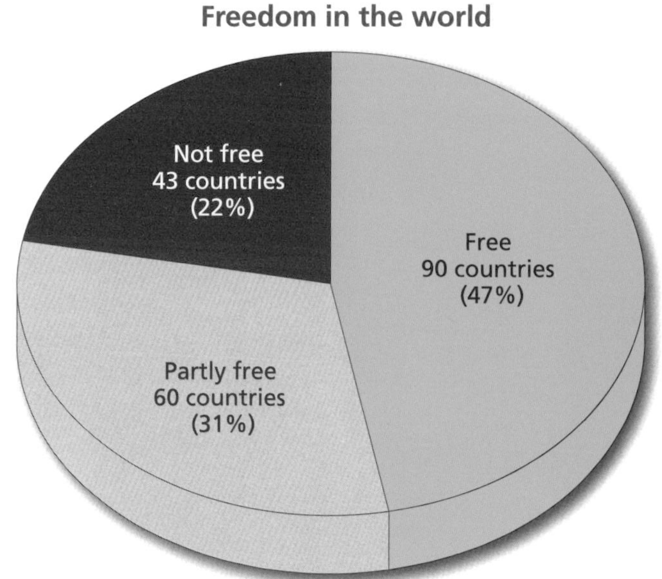

Not free
43 countries
(22%)
Free
90 countries
(47%)
Partly free
60 countries
(31%)

State of democracy

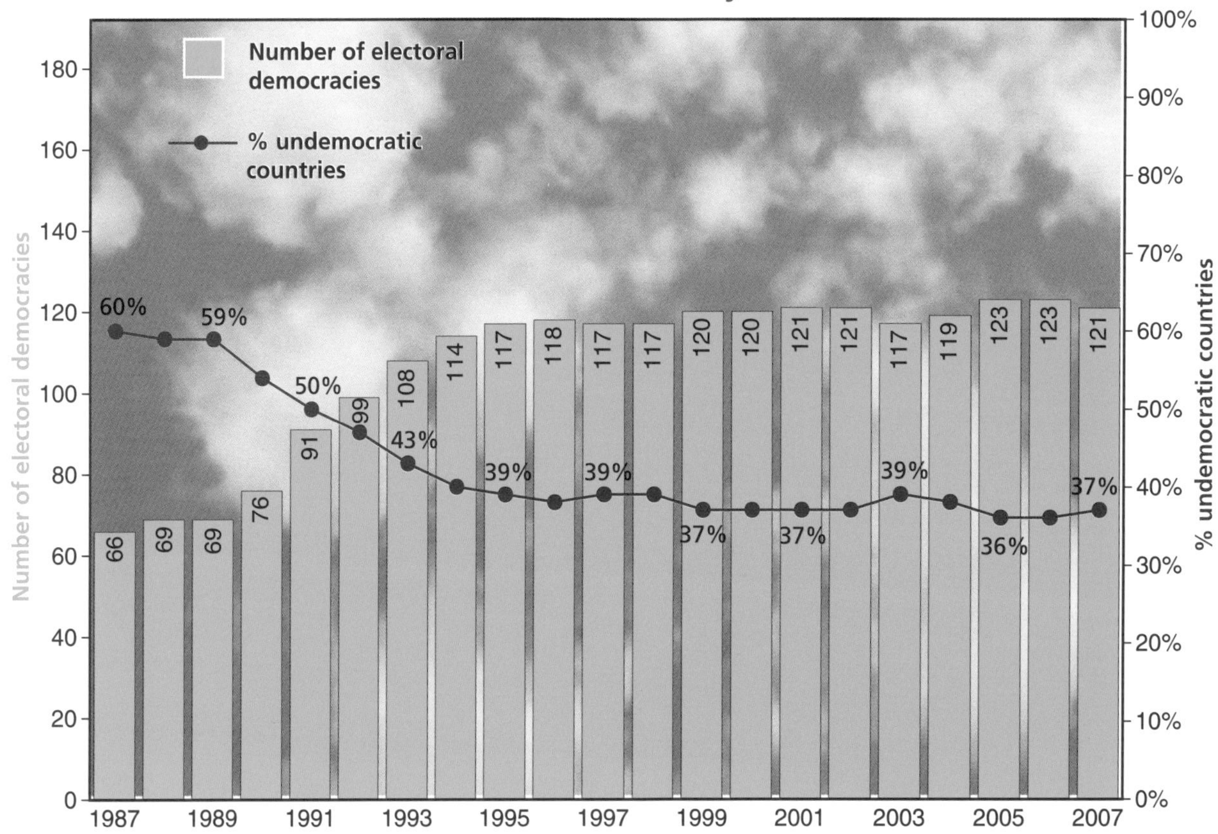

Number of electoral democracies
% undemocratic countries
Number of electoral democracies
% undemocratic countries
180
160
140
120
100
80
60
40
20
0
100%
90%
80%
70%
60%
50%
40%
30%
20%
10%
0%
1987
1989
1991
1993
1995
1997
1999
2001
2003
2005
2007
66
69
69
76
91
99
108
114
117
118
117
117
120
120
121
121
117
119
123
123
121
60%
59%
50%
43%
39%
39%
37%
37%
39%
36%
37%

In 2007, Mauritania qualified as an electoral democracy whilst Philippines, Bangladesh and Kenya were disqualified

Afghanistan, Bangladesh, Pakistan, and Sri Lanka all experienced downturns in freedom due to increased restrictions on civil society and, in three of the four cases, increased military activity. Declines were also noted in the Philippines, Burma, and Malaysia.

Freedom in Asia Pacific

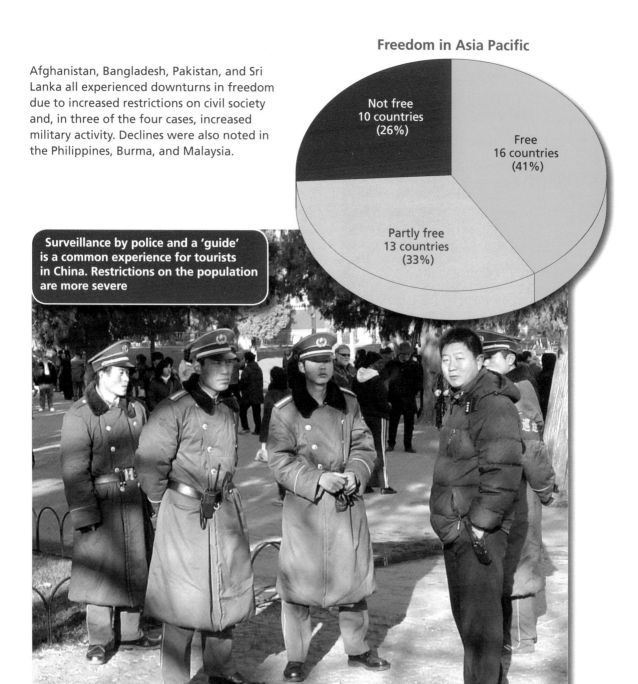

Not free
10 countries
(26%)

Free
16 countries
(41%)

Partly free
13 countries
(33%)

Surveillance by police and a 'guide' is a common experience for tourists in China. Restrictions on the population are more severe

Half of the world's population living in countries designated Not Free live in China

There was a notable setback for global freedom in 2007. The decline, which was reflected in a downward trend in one-fifth of the world's countries, was most pronounced in South Asia.

China imprisons more journalists than any other country in the world.

The Chinese government maintains one of the world's most sophisticated systems of blocking access to websites and monitoring its citizens' email communications.

The one-child policy leads to forced abortions, a shortage of females, and an increase in trafficking of people.

FREEDOM
HOUSE

65 crimes in China carry the death penalty.

The Chinese government has supported extremely repressive regimes such as those governing Burma, Sudan and Zimbabwe.

Tibetan Buddhists, Christians, Muslims and practitioners of other religions face frequent harassment.

Thousands of North Korean refugees who escape into China are sent back to North Korea to face arrest, torture, and sometimes death.

Public protests have been on the increase in recent years.

Source: Freedom House
http://www.freedomhouse.org/

A matter of faith

For the first time in history there are more Muslims worldwide than Catholics

Number of Muslims and Catholics worldwide and where they live

Muslims 1.322 billion

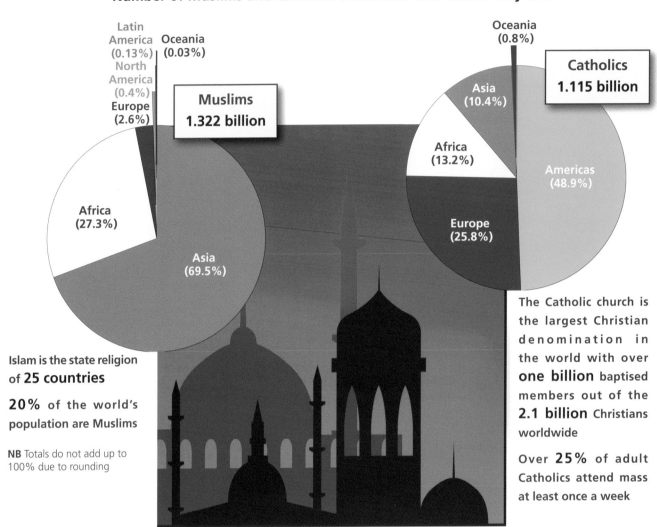

Asia (69.5%)
Africa (27.3%)
Europe (2.6%)
North America (0.4%)
Latin America (0.13%)
Oceania (0.03%)

Catholics 1.115 billion

Americas (48.9%)
Europe (25.8%)
Africa (13.2%)
Asia (10.4%)
Oceania (0.8%)

Islam is the state religion of **25 countries**

20% of the world's population are Muslims

NB Totals do not add up to 100% due to rounding

The Catholic church is the largest Christian denomination in the world with over **one billion** baptised members out of the **2.1 billion** Christians worldwide

Over **25%** of adult Catholics attend mass at least once a week

Cuba and North Korea are the only officially atheist states but many states are officially secular.

Allegiance to a single religion is professed by at least two-thirds of the population in more than **80%** of the world's states.

Top 10 countries with the most people who say they are atheists/agnostics/non-believers in God

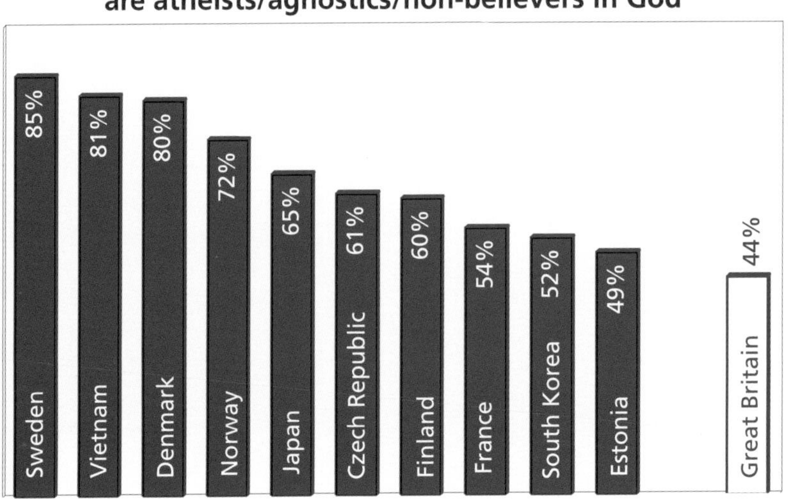

Sweden 85%
Vietnam 81%
Denmark 80%
Norway 72%
Japan 65%
Czech Republic 61%
Finland 60%
France 54%
South Korea 52%
Estonia 49%
Great Britain 44%

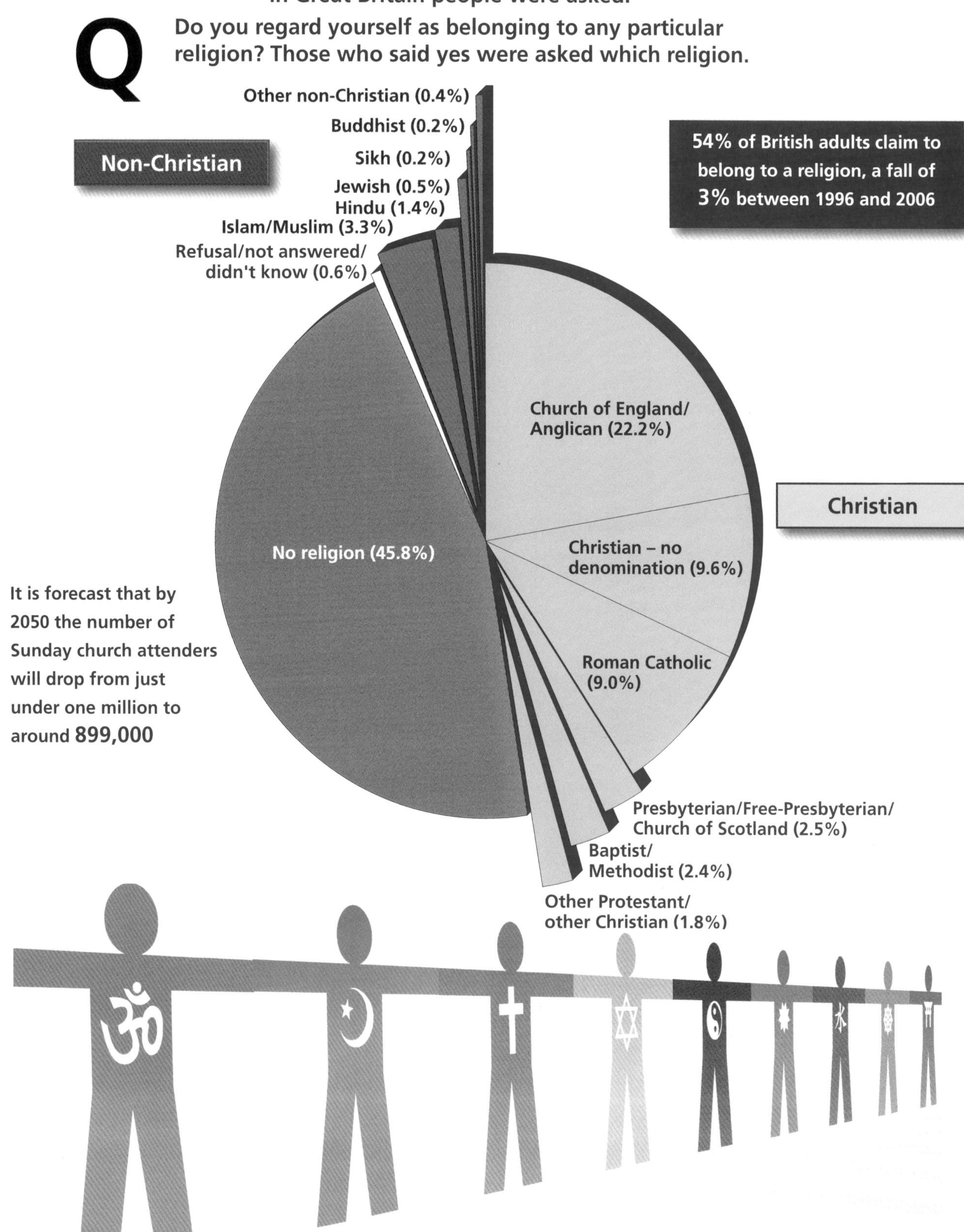
In Great Britain people were asked:
Q
Do you regard yourself as belonging to any particular religion? Those who said yes were asked which religion.
Other non-Christian (0.4%)
Buddhist (0.2%)
Non-Christian
Sikh (0.2%)
Jewish (0.5%)
Hindu (1.4%)
Islam/Muslim (3.3%)
Refusal/not answered/ didn't know (0.6%)
54% of British adults claim to belong to a religion, a fall of 3% between 1996 and 2006
Church of England/ Anglican (22.2%)
Christian
No religion (45.8%)
Christian – no denomination (9.6%)
It is forecast that by 2050 the number of Sunday church attenders will drop from just under one million to around 899,000
Roman Catholic (9.0%)
Presbyterian/Free-Presbyterian/ Church of Scotland (2.5%)
Baptist/ Methodist (2.4%)
Other Protestant/ other Christian (1.8%)

4,000 churches could face closure by 2020 if present rates of decline continue

In contrast the number of active Muslims is predicted to grow to **2,960,000** in 2050, three times the number of predicted Sunday churchgoers

Bucking the trend, principally due to immigration from EU countries and in particular Poland, Catholic congregations in Britain continue to increase in size

Source: The Atlas of Religion. Top 50 Countries with highest proportion of atheists/agnostics, Zuckerman, 2005
http://www.adherents.com

British Social Attitudes Survey, National Centre for Social Research, Religious Trends, Christian Research
http://www.natcen.ac.uk
http://www.christian-research.org.uk

Unequal chance

Economic growth does not necessarily mean improvements in child mortality

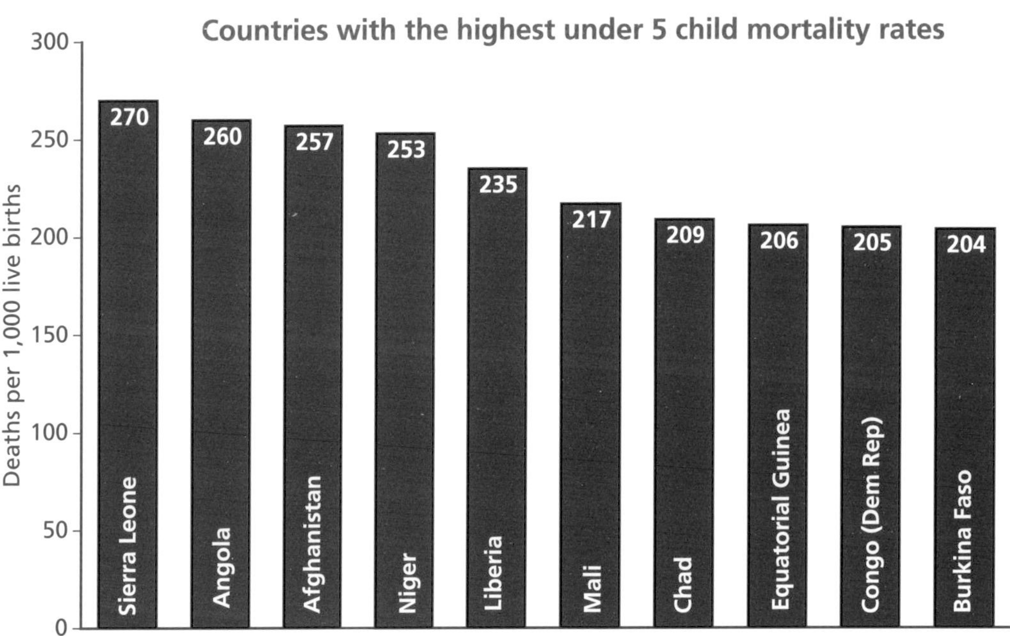
Countries with the highest under 5 child mortality rates
Deaths per 1,000 live births
300
250
200
150
100
50
0
Sierra Leone 270
Angola 260
Afghanistan 257
Niger 253
Liberia 235
Mali 217
Chad 209
Equatorial Guinea 206
Congo (Dem Rep) 205
Burkina Faso 204

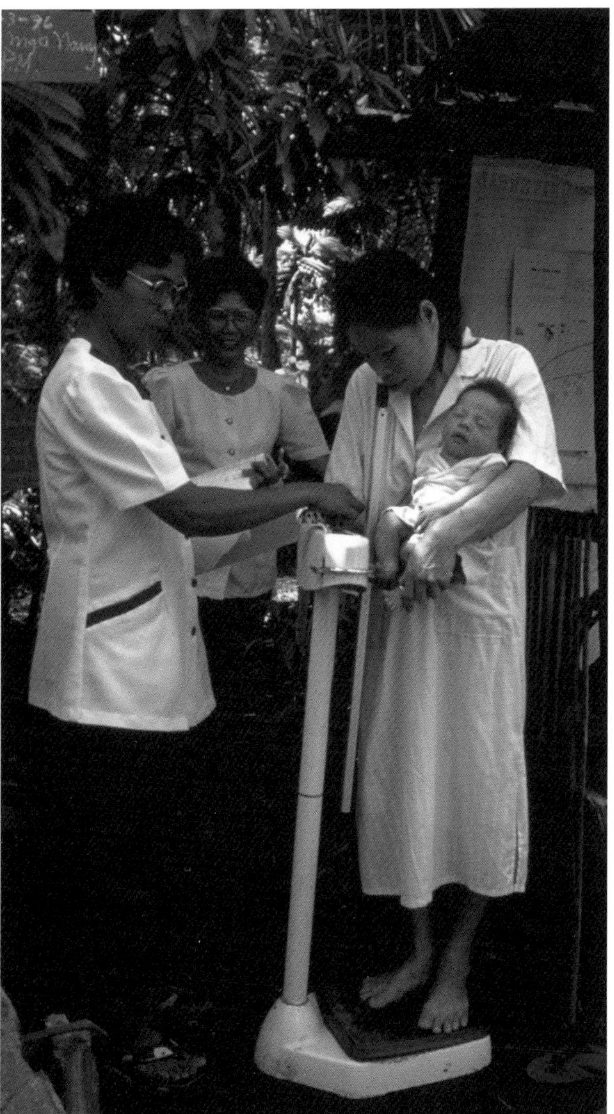

UNICEF/ HQ96-1005/Shehzad Noorani

- **99%** of all child deaths occur in developing countries
- Sub-Saharan Africa has only **11%** of the world's population yet accounts for nearly half (4.8 million) of total child deaths worldwide
- South Asia accounts for around **3.1 million** child deaths annually
- The child mortality rate is **160 per thousand** in sub-Saharan Africa and **83 per thousand** in South Asia which compares with **6 per thousand** in the UK
- 6 countries – India, Nigeria, Congo (Dem Rep), Ethiopia, Pakistan and China – account for **50%** of all deaths of children under 5
- The countries with the worst child mortality rates tend to be very poor and to have experienced war or violent conflict

Recent conflicts in the countries with the highest under 5 child mortality rates

Sierra Leone 1991-2000

Angola 1975-2002

Afghanistan 1978-ongoing

Niger 1992-1997

Liberia 1989-2003

Mali 1990-1994

Chad 1988-ongoing

Congo (Dem Rep) 1996-2001

The Wealth and Survival Index measures child mortality in relation to national income in the 41 countries that account for **90%** of child deaths

A nil score shows a country is performing as well as expected

A positive number means the country is experiencing higher child mortality than its Gross National Income (GNI) per person would suggest

A negative number indicates that it has lower child mortality than would be expected for its level of income per person

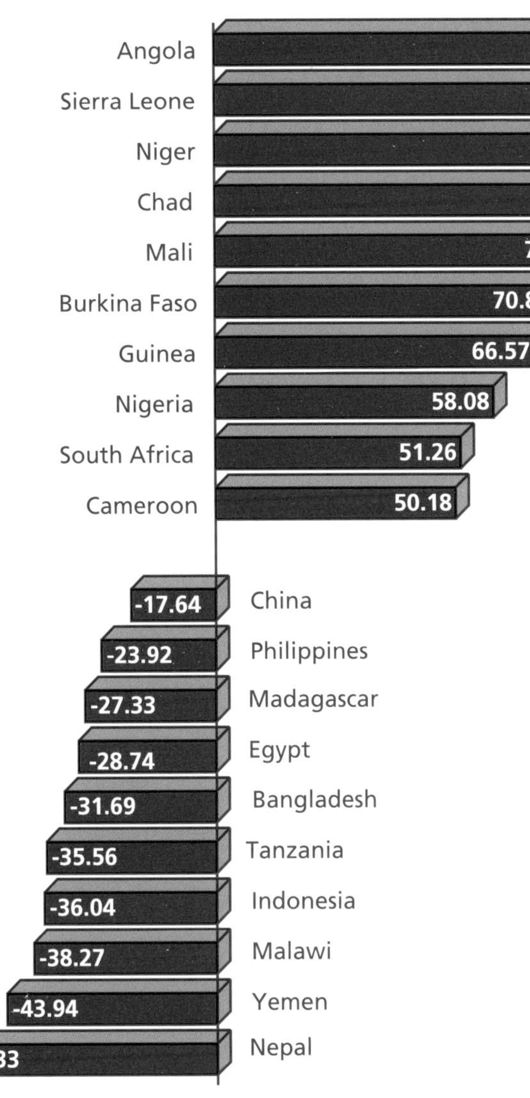
Countries in the Wealth and Survival Index – best and worst performers
Angola 162.00
Sierra Leone 117.58
Niger 100.94
Chad 84.35
Mali 77.52
Burkina Faso 70.89
Guinea 66.57
Nigeria 58.08
South Africa 51.26
Cameroon 50.18
China -17.64
Philippines -23.92
Madagascar -27.33
Egypt -28.74
Bangladesh -31.69
Tanzania -35.56
Indonesia -36.04
Malawi -38.27
Yemen -43.94
Nepal -56.33

Data not available for Afghanistan, Iraq, Myanmar (Burma) and Somalia

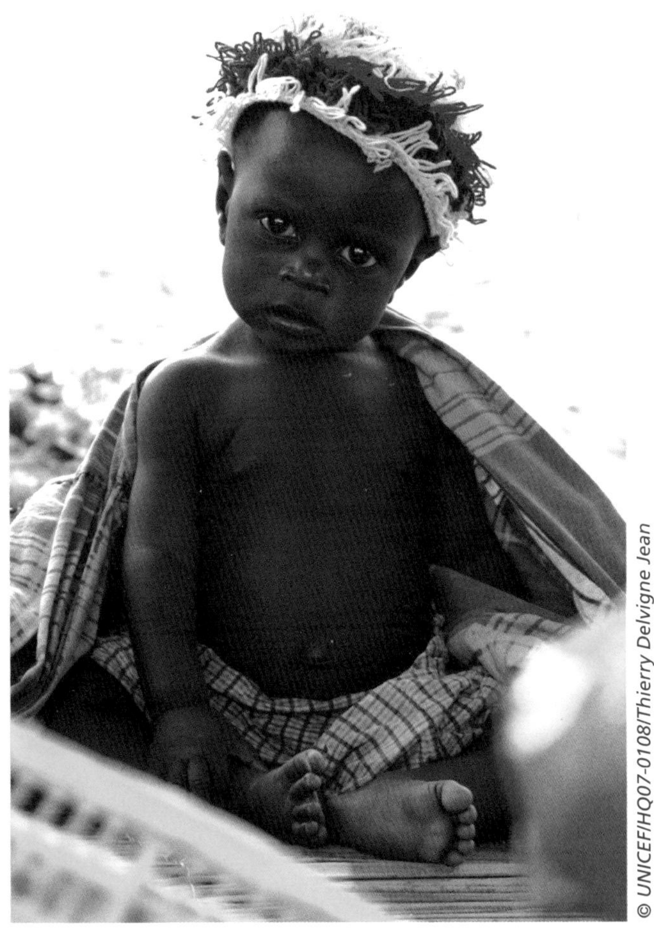

- It is estimated that more than half of the babies who die in Angola could be saved if its wealth were more fairly allocated
- Some of the poorest countries in the world – Nepal, Malawi, Tanzania and Bangladesh – are among the top ten performers in this index, showing success in cutting mortality
- Some countries are better at translating their economic growth into saving children's lives, eg between 2000 and 2006 Bangladesh's GNI per person grew **23%,** and its child mortality rate dropped by **25%**, whereas India's GNI per person increased by **82%** but its child mortality rate only declined by **19%**

Source: Saving Children's Lives © Save the Children Fund 2008
http://www.savethechildren.org.uk

Sanitation solution?

About 40% of the world's population lack what we take for granted: a toilet

In September 2000, 189 countries endorsed the Millennium Declaration, setting out goals to be reached by 2015.

Goal 7, Environmental Sustainability, contains the target to reduce by half the proportion of people without access to improved sanitation. This is central to meeting all the Millennium Development Goals, yet is one towards which very little progress has been made.

Goal 1: Eradicate Extreme Hunger and Poverty

Halve the proportion of people whose income is less than $1 a day

Halve the proportion of people who suffer from hunger

Goal 2: Achieve Universal Primary Education

Ensure that children everywhere, boys and girls alike, will be able to complete a full course of primary schooling

Goal 3: Promote Gender Equality and Empower Women

Eliminate gender disparity in education

Goal 4: Reduce Child Mortality

Reduce the under-five mortality rate by two-thirds

Goal 5: Improve Maternal Health

Reduce the maternal mortality ratio by three-quarters

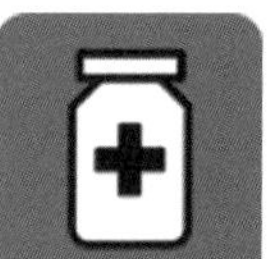

Goal 6: Combat HIV/AIDS, Malaria and other diseases

Halve and begin to reverse the spread of HIV/AIDS

Halve and begin to reverse the incidence of malaria and other major diseases

Goal 7: Ensure Environmental Sustainability

Integrate sustainable development into country policies and reverse the loss of environmental resources

Achieve a significant improvement in the lives of at least 100 million slum dwellers

Halve the proportion of people without sustainable access to safe drinking water and basic sanitation

Photo: UNEP/Bechtloff

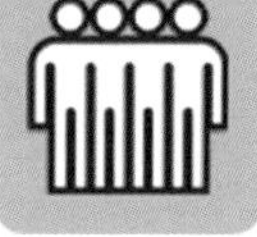

Goal 8: Develop a Global Partnership for Development

Develop an open, rule-based, predictable, non-discriminatory trading and financial system

Address the special needs of landlocked developing countries and small island developing states

Deal with the debt problems of developing countries

Develop and implement strategies for decent and productive work for youth

Provide access to affordable essential drugs in developing countries

Make available the benefits of new technologies, especially information and communications technologies

INTERNATIONAL YEAR OF
SANITATION
2008

Between 1990-2004, **1.2 billion** people gained access to improved sanitation

Due to population growth, **1.6 billion** people need to gain access to improved sanitation by 2015 to meet the MDG sanitation target – but even if this is achieved, **1.8 billion** people will still be without improved sanitation

2.6 billion people or nearly half of humanity lives without access to adequate sanitation. This:

- is an affront to human dignity
- causes widespread damage to human health and child survival prospects
- causes social misery especially for women, the elderly and sick
- depresses economic productivity and human development
- pollutes the living environment and water resources

Only **39%** of people living in rural areas have access to improved sanitation

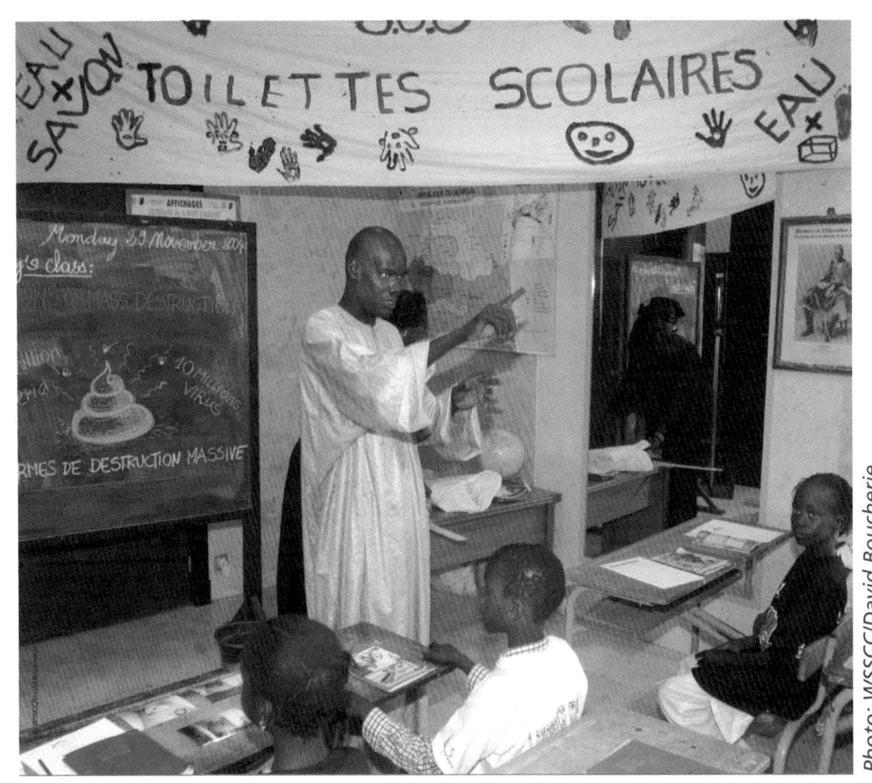
TOILETTES SCOLAIRES
SAVON
EAU
Monday 29 November 2004
RMES DE DESTRUCTION MASSIVE

Photo: WSSCC/David Boucherie

Diarrhoea is the 2nd highest single cause of child mortality (after pneumonia). More than 5,000 children under five die every day due to a lack of sanitation.

88% of diarrhoeal deaths are due to a lack of access to sanitation facilities

Regional progress towards basic sanitation target

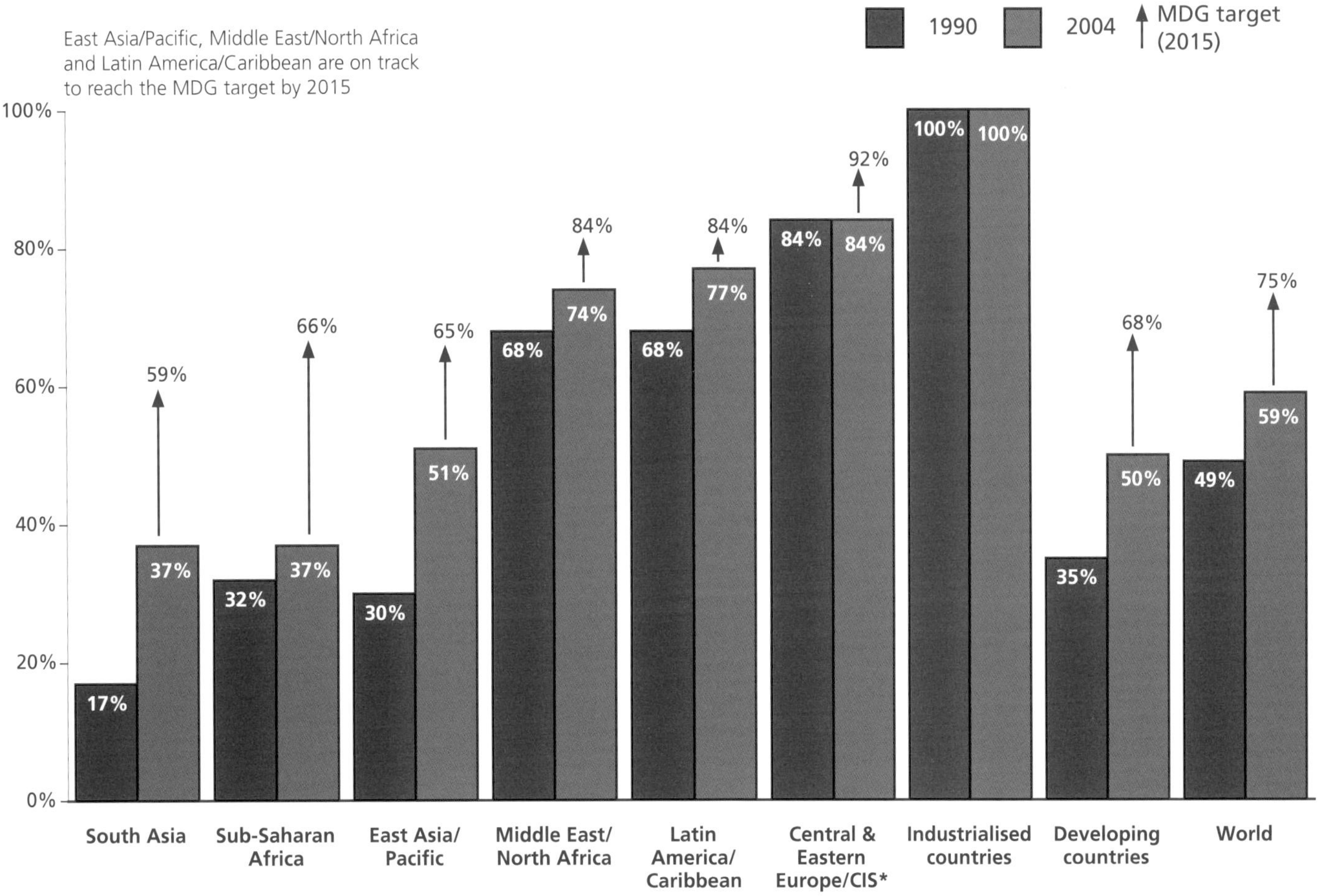

East Asia/Pacific, Middle East/North Africa and Latin America/Caribbean are on track to reach the MDG target by 2015

	1990	2004	MDG target (2015)
South Asia	17%	37%	59%
Sub-Saharan Africa	32%	37%	66%
East Asia/ Pacific	30%	51%	65%
Middle East/ North Africa	68%	74%	84%
Latin America/ Caribbean	68%	77%	84%
Central & Eastern Europe/CIS*	84%	84%	92%
Industrialised countries	100%	100%	
Developing countries	35%	50%	68%
World	49%	59%	75%

*Commonwealth of Independent States (former Soviet Union)

Source: Progress for Children, UNICEF

http://www.unicef.org
http://www.mdgmonitor.org

Living with HIV/AIDS

Around 30.8 million adults and 2.5 million children are affected

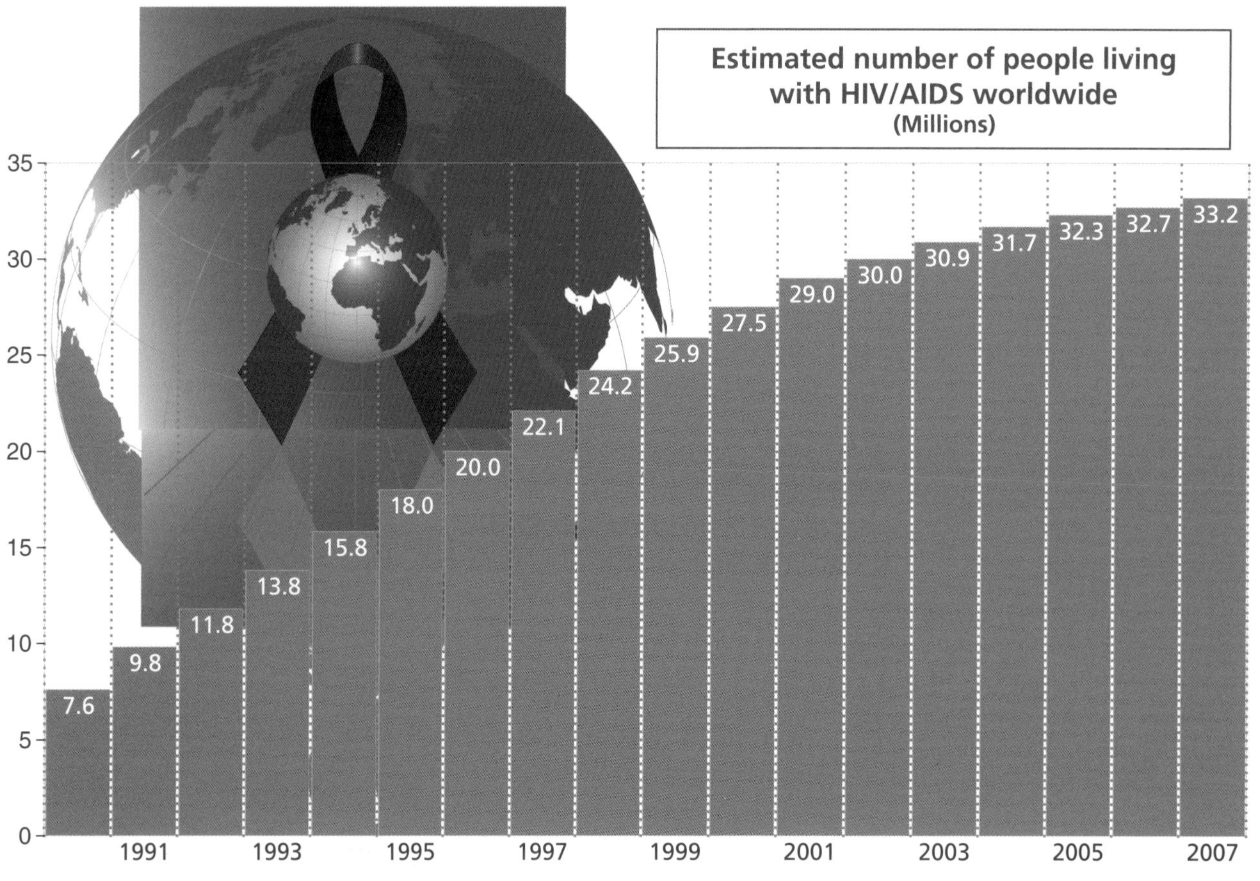

Estimated number of people living with HIV/AIDS worldwide
(Millions)
35
30
25
20
15
10
5
0
7.6
9.8
11.8
13.8
15.8
18.0
20.0
22.1
24.2
25.9
27.5
29.0
30.0
30.9
31.7
32.3
32.7
33.2
1991
1993
1995
1997
1999
2001
2003
2005
2007

Regional statistics for HIV and AIDS, end of 2007

Region	Adults & children living with HIV/AIDS	Adults & children newly infected	Adult prevalence (aged 15-49)	Deaths of adults & children
Sub-Saharan Africa	22.5 million	1.7 million	5.0%	1.6 million
North Africa & Middle East	380,000	35,000	0.3%	25,000
South & South-East Asia	4 million	340,000	0.3%	270,000
East Asia	800,000	92,000	0.1%	32,000
Oceania	75,000	14,000	0.4%	1,200
Latin America	1.6 million	100,000	0.5%	58,000
Caribbean	230,000	17,000	1.0%	11,000
Eastern Europe & Central Asia	1.6 million	150,000	0.9%	55,000
Western & Central Europe	760,000	31,000	0.3%	12,000
North America	1.3 million	46,000	0.6%	21,000
World total	33.2 million	2.5 million	0.8%	2.1 million

In 2007/08

- There were 12 million AIDS orphans in Africa
- Women accounted for 50% of all adults living with HIV worldwide, but 61% in sub-Saharan Africa
- Under 25-year-olds accounted for half of all new HIV infections
- In developing countries 9.7 million people were in immediate need of life-saving AIDS drugs, but, only 31% were receiving them

Source: Worldwide AIDS & HIV Statistics © AVERT
http://www.avert.org

Falling short

The world gave US$103.7 billion in aid but still did not reach the target

According to the United Nations the annual cost to stop all deaths caused by worldwide poverty is $195 billion per year.

In 2002 the 22 developed countries below pledged to work towards each giving 0.7% of their national income in international aid to raise this.

Aid from the world's major donors shown as a percentage of Gross National Income

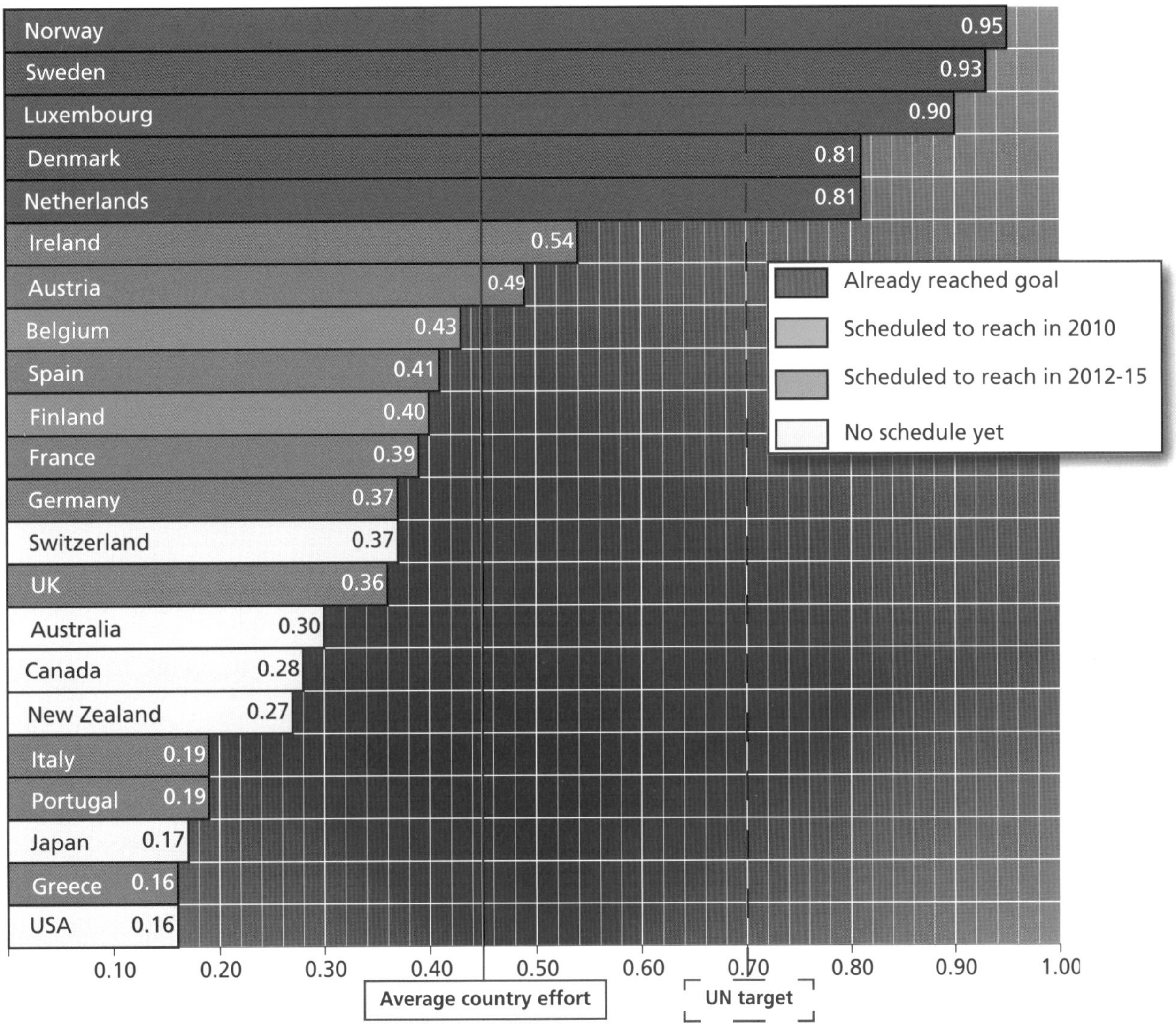

Norway	0.95
Sweden	0.93
Luxembourg	0.90
Denmark	0.81
Netherlands	0.81
Ireland	0.54
Austria	0.49
Belgium	0.43
Spain	0.41
Finland	0.40
France	0.39
Germany	0.37
Switzerland	0.37
UK	0.36
Australia	0.30
Canada	0.28
New Zealand	0.27
Italy	0.19
Portugal	0.19
Japan	0.17
Greece	0.16
USA	0.16

Already reached goal
Scheduled to reach in 2010
Scheduled to reach in 2012-15
No schedule yet

0.10 0.20 0.30 0.40 0.50 0.60 0.70 0.80 0.90 1.00

Average country effort

UN target

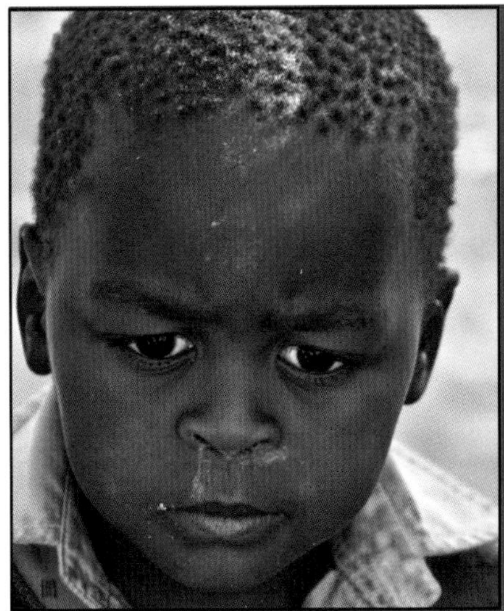

To look at the UN target another way – for every US$100 earned in the country, the country should give 70 cents in aid.

The pledges made at various summits, combined with other commitments, implied lifting aid from US$80 billion in 2004 to US$130 billion in 2010 (at constant 2004 prices).

Overall, most donors are not on track to meet their stated commitments to scale up aid; they will need to make unprecedented increases to meet their 2010 targets.

Source: OECD
http://www.oecd.org

Facts of death

By 2030 there will be more deaths due to road accidents than HIV/AIDS

Disease or injury 2004	Deaths (%)	Rank
Ischaemic heart disease	12.2	1
Cerebrovascular disease	9.7	2
Lower respiratory infections	7.0	3
Chronic obstructive pulmonary disease	5.1	4
Diarrhoeal diseases	3.6	5
HIV/AIDS	3.5	6
Tuberculosis	2.5	7
Trachea, bronchus, lung cancers	2.3	8
Road traffic accidents	2.2	9
Prematurity/low birth weight	2.0	10
Neonatal infections/other perinatal deaths	1.9	11
Diabetes mellitus	1.9	12
Malaria	1.7	13
Hypertensive heart disease	1.7	14
Birth asphyxia/ birth trauma	1.5	15
Self-inflicted injuries	1.4	16
Stomach cancer	1.4	17
Cirrhosis of the liver	1.3	18
Nephritis and nephrosis	1.3	19
Colon and rectum cancers	1.1	20
Liver cancer	1.1	21
Violence	1.0	22
Breast cancer	0.9	23
Oesophagus cancer	0.9	24
Alzheimer's and other dementias	0.8	25

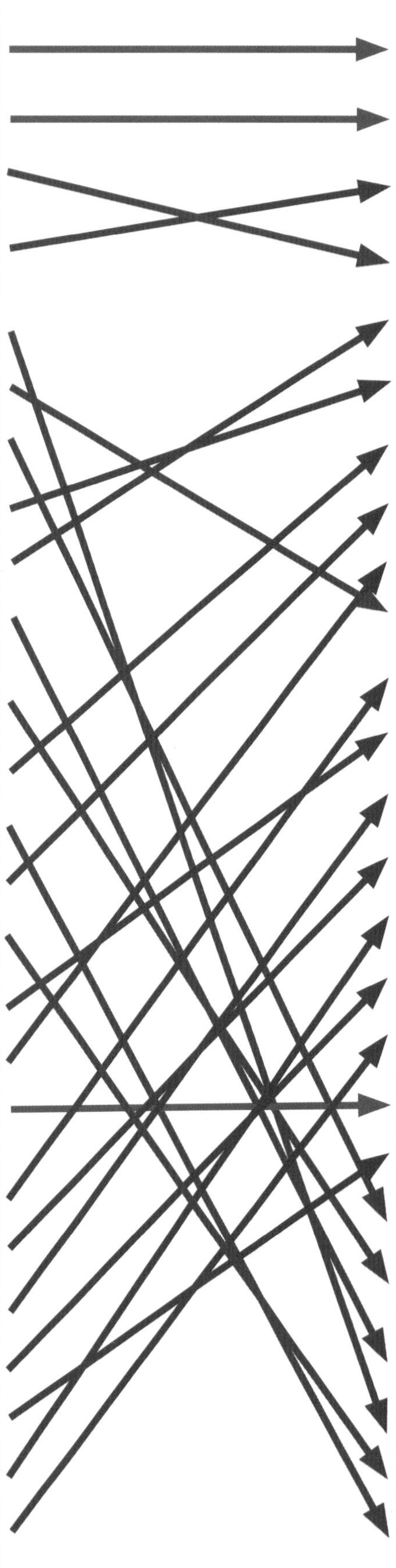

Rank	Deaths (%)	Disease or injury 2030
1	14.2	Ischaemic heart disease
2	12.1	Cerebrovascular disease
3	8.6	Chronic obstructive pulmonary disease
4	3.8	Lower respiratory infections
5	3.6	Road traffic accidents
6	3.4	Trachea, bronchus, lung cancers
7	3.3	Diabetes mellitus
8	2.1	Hypertensive heart disease
9	1.9	Stomach cancer
10	1.8	HIV/AIDS
11	1.6	Nephritis and nephrosis
12	1.5	Self-inflicted injuries
13	1.4	Liver cancer
14	1.4	Colon and rectum cancers
15	1.3	Oesophagus cancer
16	1.2	Violence
17	1.2	Alzheimer's and other dementias
18	1.2	Cirrhosis of the liver
19	1.1	Breast cancer
20	1.0	Tuberculosis
21	1.0	Neonatal infections/other perinatal deaths
22	0.9	Premature/low birth rate
23	0.9	Diarrhoeal diseases
29	0.7	Birth asphyxia/ birth trauma
41	0.4	Malaria

Causes of death

As global health care continues to improve and the population age continues to rise in middle- and low-income countries over the next 25 years, the proportion of deaths due to infectious diseases, poor nutrition and problems in childbirth and infancy will decline.

However, other causes of death will rise in prevalence. Some of these, such as chronic obstructive pulmonary disease, are associated with lifestyle choices, such as projected increase in tobacco use. Others, such as road traffic accidents, are associated with increased prosperity.

The 2030 projections are based on the assumption of a 'business as usual' scenario. This will take into account trends in economic and social development and cause-specific mortality, as well as economic growth in low- and middle-income countries.

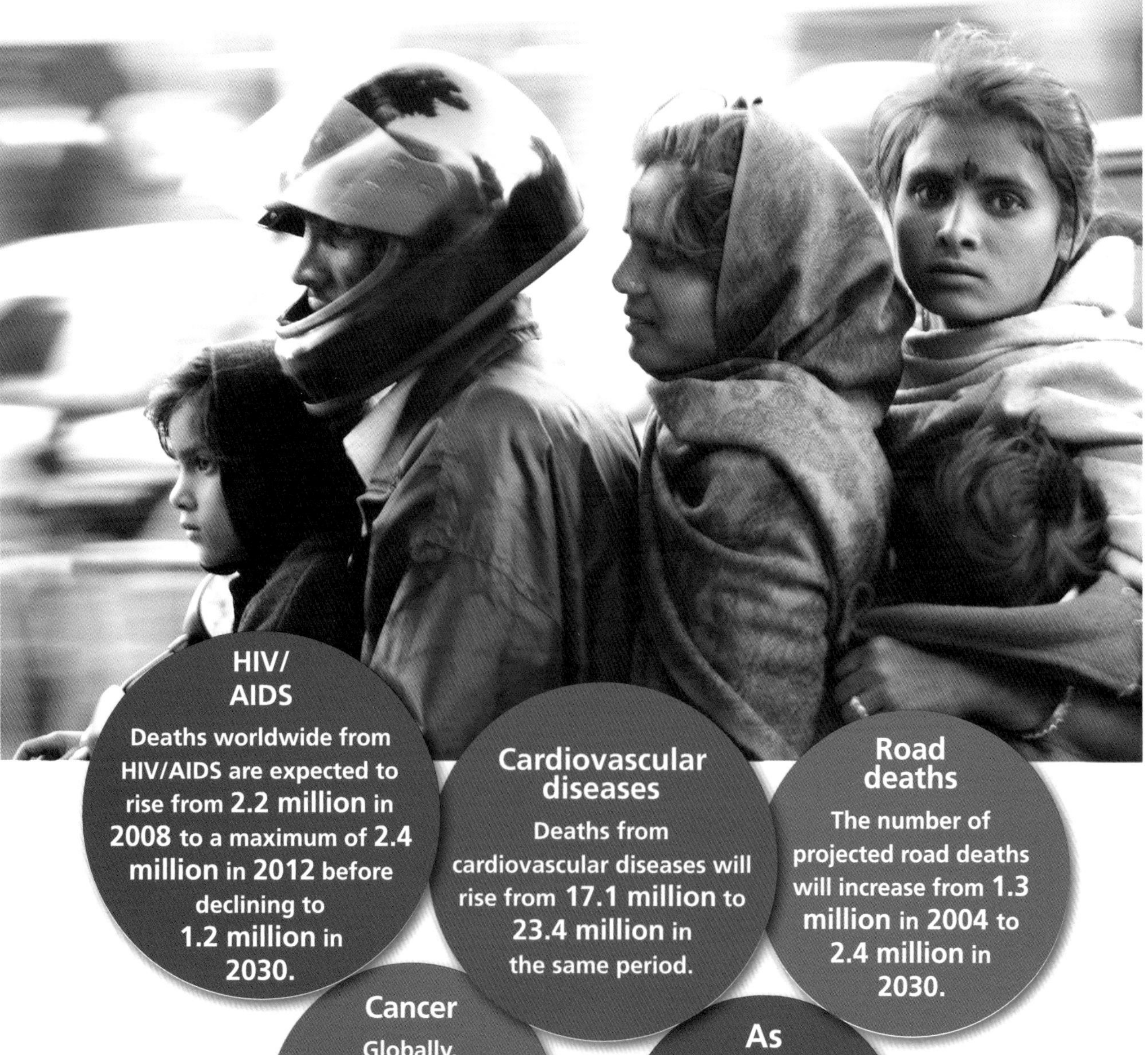

HIV/AIDS

Deaths worldwide from HIV/AIDS are expected to rise from **2.2 million** in **2008** to a maximum of **2.4 million** in **2012** before declining to **1.2 million** in **2030.**

Cardiovascular diseases

Deaths from cardiovascular diseases will rise from **17.1 million** to **23.4 million** in the same period.

Road deaths

The number of projected road deaths will increase from **1.3 million** in **2004** to **2.4 million** in **2030.**

Cancer

Globally, deaths from cancer will increase from **7.4 million** in **2004** to **11.8 million** in **2030.**

As the way we live changes, so too will the way we die!

Source: World Health Statistics 2008, World Health Organisation http://www.who.int

Stolen smiles

2.45 million people worldwide are in forced labour as a result of trafficking

What is sex trafficking?

The most common type of human trafficking is for sexual exploitation.

Although there is no universally accepted definition for this, the term includes:

• the organised movement of people, usually women, between countries and within countries

• forced prostitution or other forms of commercial sexual activities

• the use of physical coercion, deception and bondage through forced debt

Type of forced labour

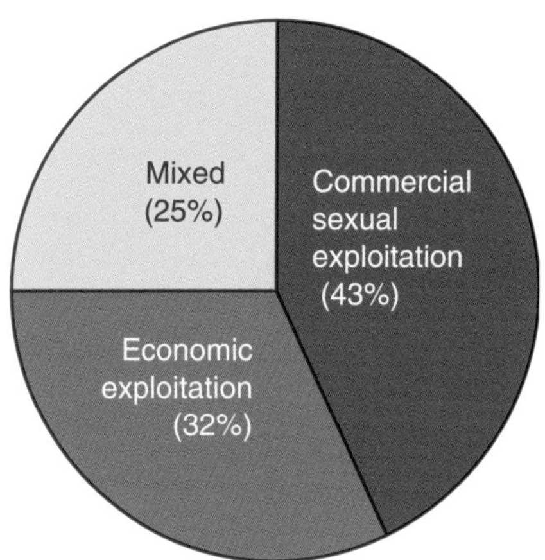
Mixed (25%)
Commercial sexual exploitation (43%)
Economic exploitation (32%)

Where are people trafficked from and to? (examples of some of the highest)

Country of Origin		Country of Destination
Very High Levels: Albania, Bulgaria, China, Nigeria, Romania, Russian Federation, Thailand, Ukraine		**Very High Levels:** Belgium, Germany, Greece, Israel, Italy, Japan, Netherlands, Thailand, Turkey, USA
High Levels: Bangladesh, Brazil, Czech Republic, Estonia, Ghana, Hungary, India, Mexico, Pakistan, Philippines, Poland	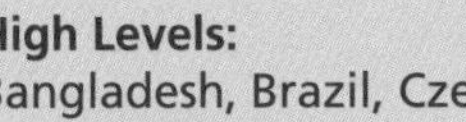 	**High Levels:** Australia, Austria, Canada, China, France, Spain, Switzerland, United Arab Emirates, United Kingdom

How does it happen?

Trafficked women and children often come from poverty-stricken countries. They are often promised work in the domestic or service industry of another country, but instead, when they get there, their passports and other identification papers are confiscated.

They may be beaten or locked up and promised their freedom only after earning – through prostitution – their purchase price, as well as their travel and visa costs. Some may never get their freedom at all.

Who does it?

Almost one in five women reported that a relative knew her trafficker. For some women, this was a case of betrayal by family. For others, relatives were acquainted with the trafficker, but unaware of his/her intentions. Numerous women were recruited by a friend or an acquaintance.

Who is affected?

98% of people trafficked are women and girls. A precise breakdown by age is not possible, as the exact age of victims is seldom reported. Many sources refer to the trafficking of young people without specifying their age. Nevertheless it is estimated that children represent between 40 and 50% of all victims.

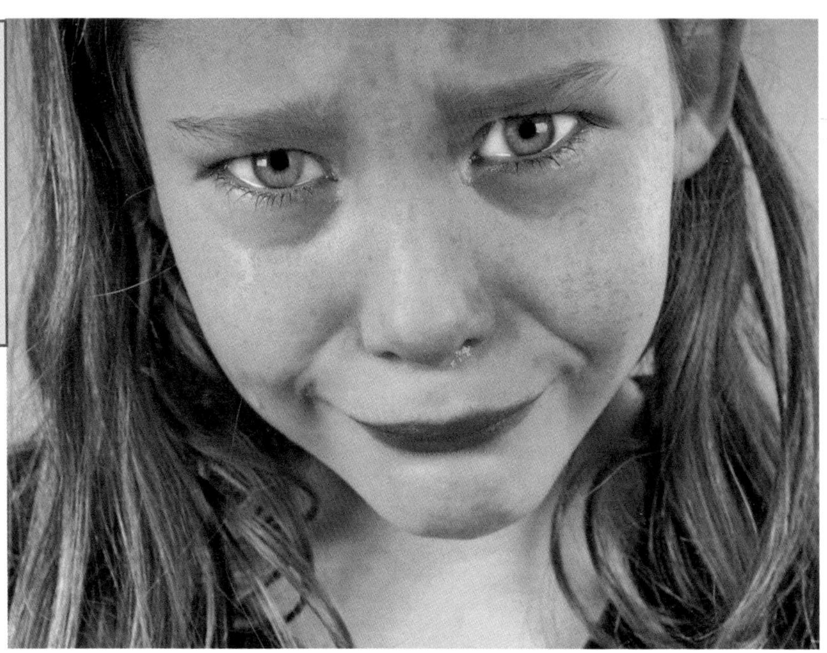

"I feel like they've taken my smile and I can never have it back."
Lithuanian woman trafficked to London

In the UK

The POPPY Project provides services for women trafficked into prostitution in the UK. Its unique position in conducting research alongside supporting those who have been trafficked results in detailed information. Its research confirms the presence of trafficked women in London's brothels.

In 2008, researchers found an absolute minimum of 1,933 women working in London brothels advertised through print media. The average age of the women in surveyed brothels was 21 years old, with an overall range between 18 and 55 years old. No brothel confirmed that they provided girls under 18 years old for sex. However, a number of premises offered 'very, very young girls' without divulging ages.

In total, 77 different nationalities and ethnicities of women were given by brothels surveyed, over half the women were European (55%), with nearly one-third stated to be from Asia (30%).

"I was locked in the basement with my friend. We were only free to work, and when the boss was drunk he would rape me."

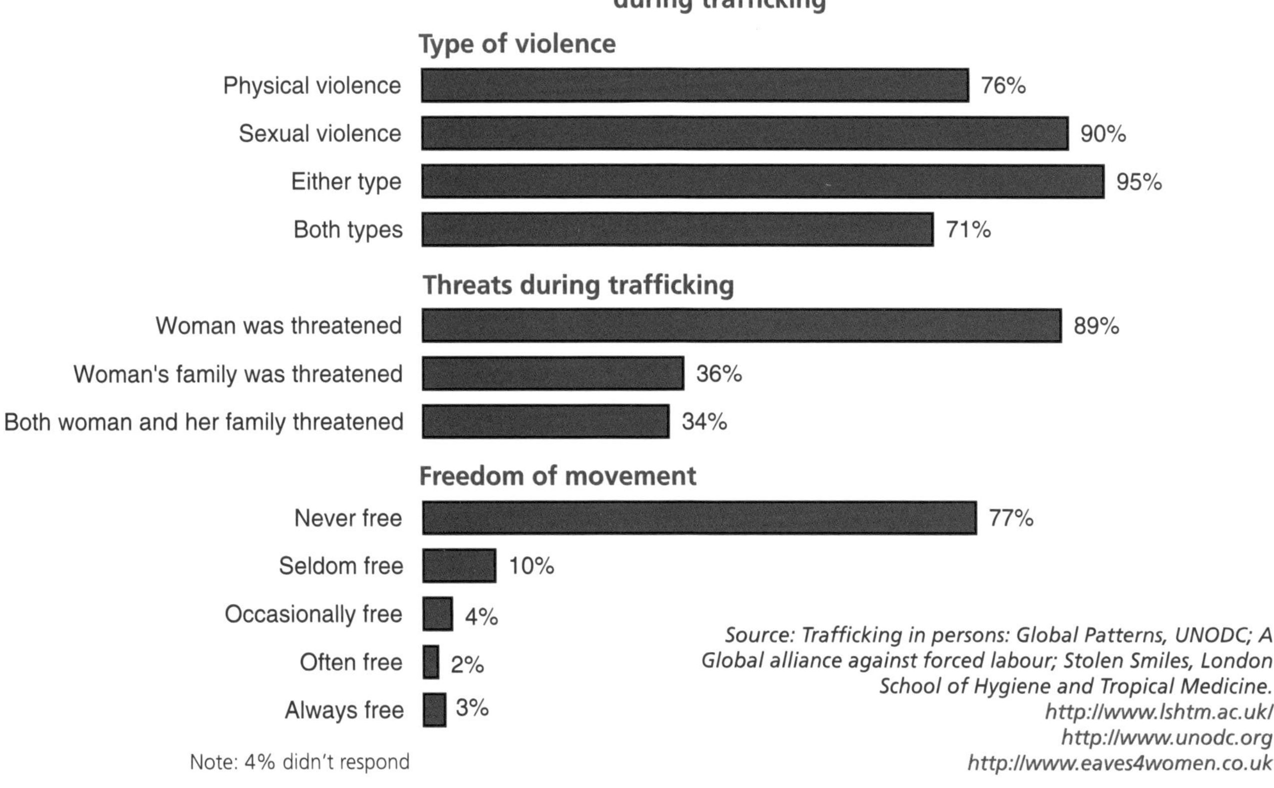
Experiences of violence and movement restriction during trafficking
Type of violence
Physical violence 76%
Sexual violence 90%
Either type 95%
Both types 71%
Threats during trafficking
Woman was threatened 89%
Woman's family was threatened 36%
Both woman and her family threatened 34%
Freedom of movement
Never free 77%
Seldom free 10%
Occasionally free 4%
Often free 2%
Always free 3%
Note: 4% didn't respond

Source: Trafficking in persons: Global Patterns, UNODC; A Global alliance against forced labour; Stolen Smiles, London School of Hygiene and Tropical Medicine.
http://www.lshtm.ac.uk/
http://www.unodc.org
http://www.eaves4women.co.uk

Chinadependence

As a nation we are increasingly dependent on goods from China

UK trade with China (£ millions)

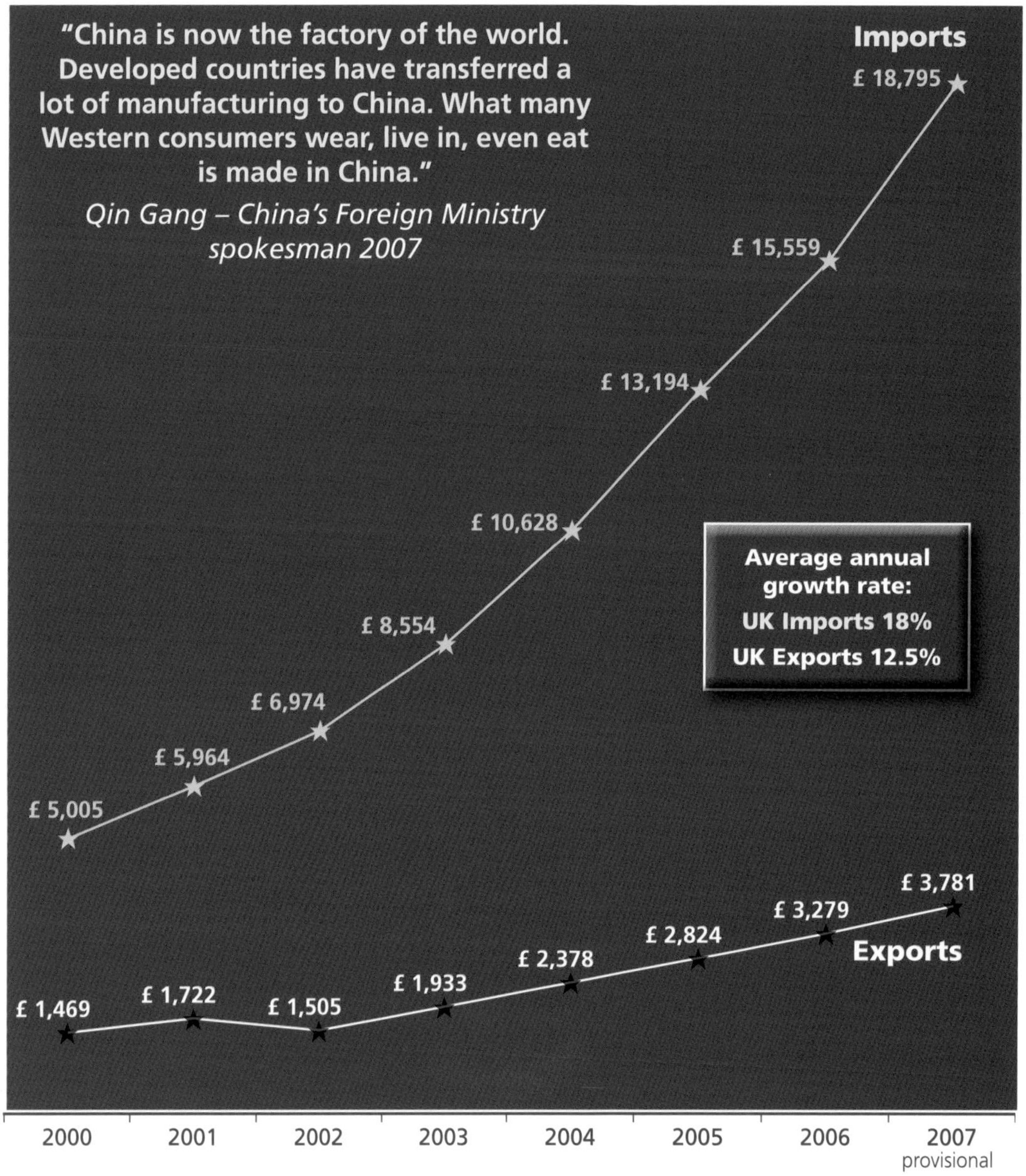

> "China is now the factory of the world. Developed countries have transferred a lot of manufacturing to China. What many Western consumers wear, live in, even eat is made in China."
>
> *Qin Gang – China's Foreign Ministry spokesman 2007*

	Imports	Exports
2000	£ 5,005	£ 1,469
2001	£ 5,964	£ 1,722
2002	£ 6,974	£ 1,505
2003	£ 8,554	£ 1,933
2004	£ 10,628	£ 2,378
2005	£ 13,194	£ 2,824
2006	£ 15,559	£ 3,279
2007 provisional	£ 18,795	£ 3,781

Average annual growth rate:
UK Imports 18%
UK Exports 12.5%

- As a nation we are increasingly turning to China to clothe ourselves, furnish our homes, supply our entertainment equipment and even provide our Christmas decorations.
- China is increasingly blamed for its levels of pollution in general, and its rising greenhouse gas emissions in particular. But it is demand from countries like the UK which leads to smoke from Chinese factories and power plants entering the atmosphere.
- The recent rapid growth in China over the past 20–25 years lifted over 400 million Chinese out of the most extreme category of poverty (living on less than $1 per day).

MADE IN CHINA

Top 10 imports to UK from China, 2006 (£ billion)

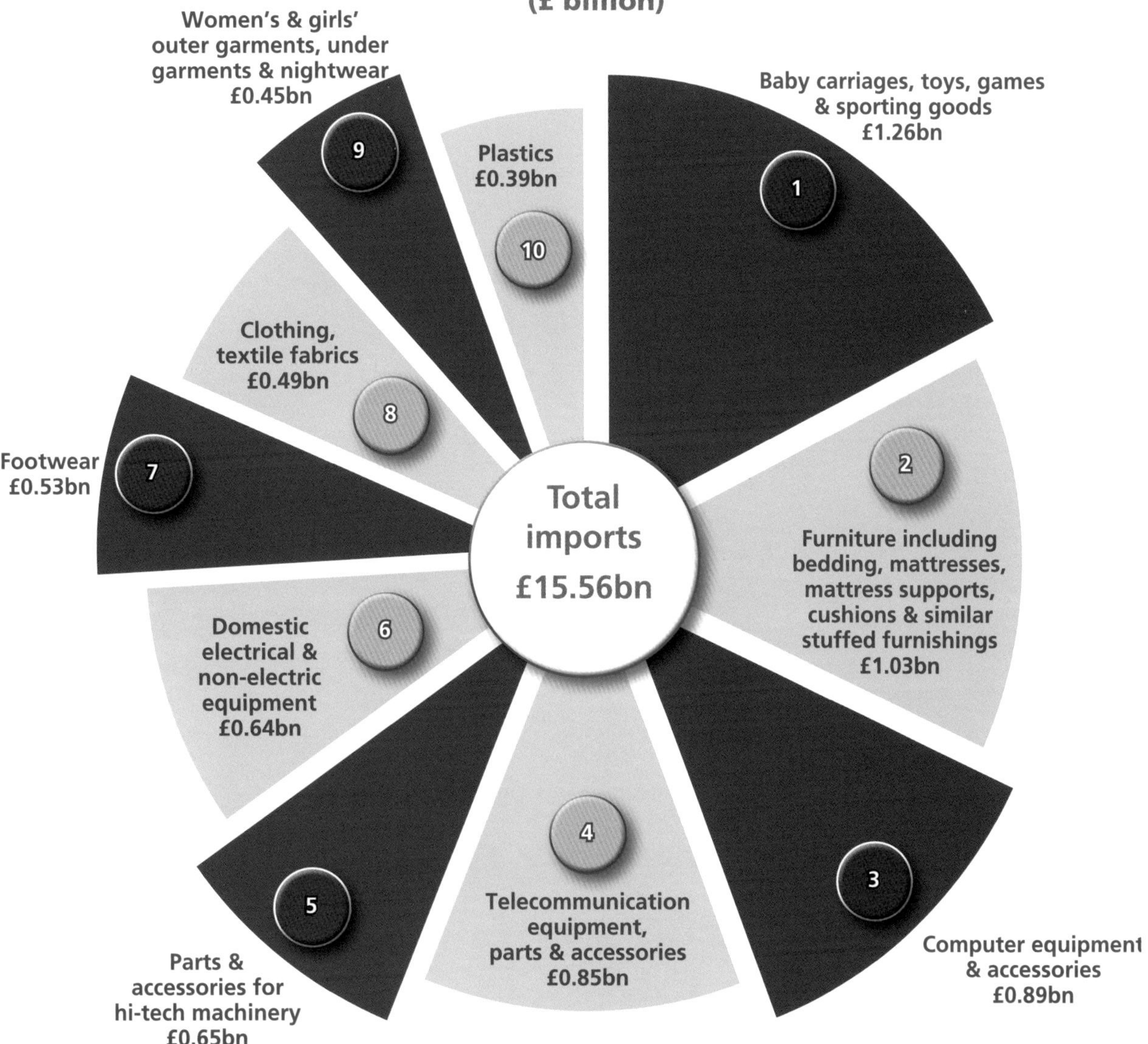
Women's & girls' outer garments, under garments & nightwear £0.45bn
9
Plastics £0.39bn
10
Baby carriages, toys, games & sporting goods £1.26bn
1
Clothing, textile fabrics £0.49bn
8
Footwear £0.53bn
7
2
Total imports £15.56bn
Furniture including bedding, mattresses, mattress supports, cushions & similar stuffed furnishings £1.03bn
Domestic electrical & non-electric equipment £0.64bn
6
4
3
5
Telecommunication equipment, parts & accessories £0.85bn
Computer equipment & accessories £0.89bn
Parts & accessories for hi-tech machinery £0.65bn

Weight of top 10 imports, 2006 (thousands of tonnes)

1	378.82
2	589.65
3	31.81
4	46.73
5	23.31
6	243.1
7	107.87
8	55.45
9	49.32
10	266.37
Total imports	**6,426.86**

These top ten represent 46% of the total imports, the remainder is split between 233 other commodities

Source: Chinadependence, HMRC Overseas trade statistics

http://www.neweconomics.org

How warm a welcome?

Sweden has the best policies in the EU to integrate migrants

The Migrant Integration Policy Index (MIPEX) measures policies to integrate non-EU migrants. It gives a percentage score in six policy areas which shape a migrant's journey to full citizenship.

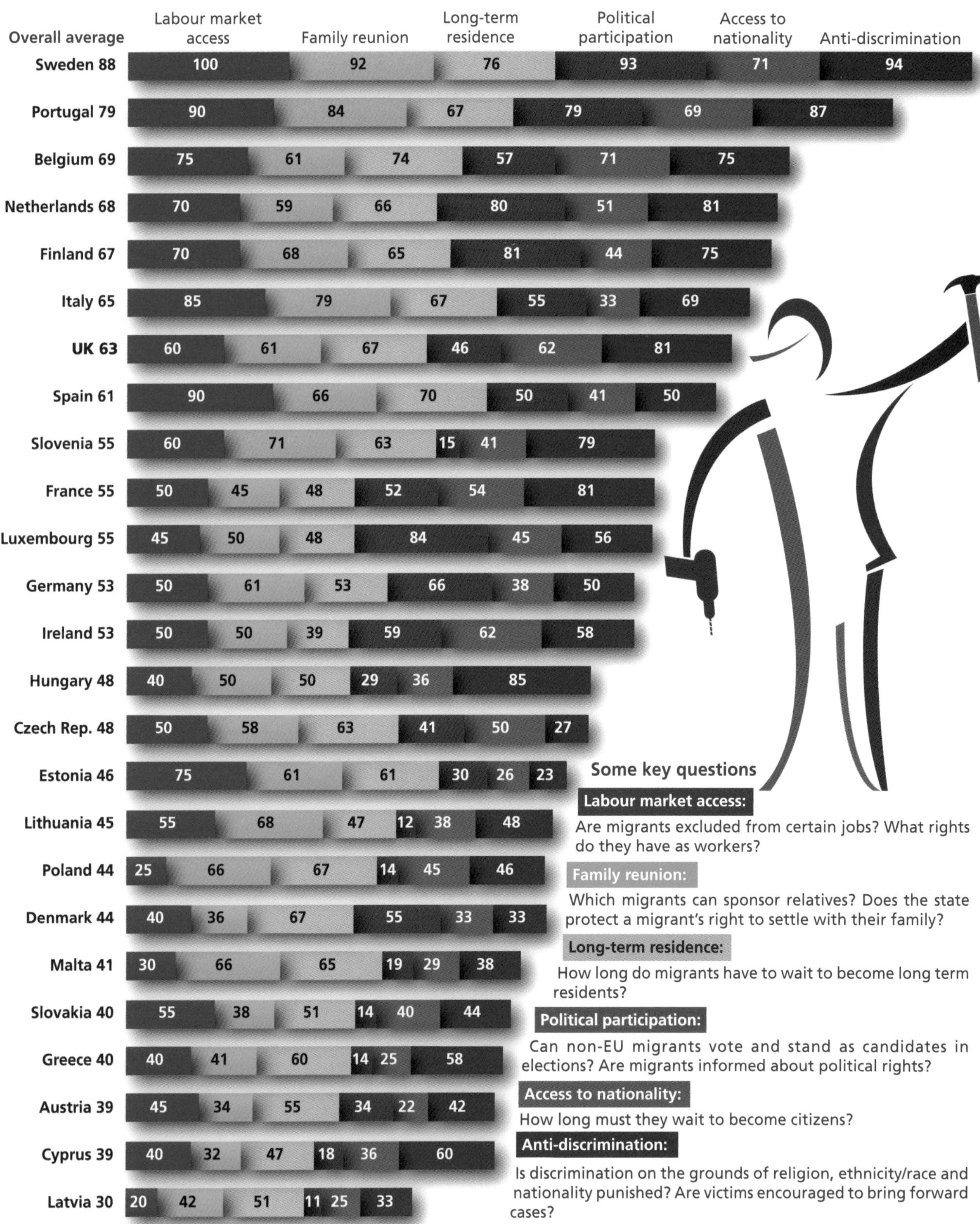

Overall average	Labour market access	Family reunion	Long-term residence	Political participation	Access to nationality	Anti-discrimination
Sweden 88	100	92	76	93	71	94
Portugal 79	90	84	67	79	69	87
Belgium 69	75	61	74	57	71	75
Netherlands 68	70	59	66	80	51	81
Finland 67	70	68	65	81	44	75
Italy 65	85	79	67	55	33	69
UK 63	60	61	67	46	62	81
Spain 61	90	66	70	50	41	50
Slovenia 55	60	71	63	15	41	79
France 55	50	45	48	52	54	81
Luxembourg 55	45	50	48	84	45	56
Germany 53	50	61	53	66	38	50
Ireland 53	50	50	39	59	62	58
Hungary 48	40	50	50	29	36	85
Czech Rep. 48	50	58	63	41	50	27
Estonia 46	75	61	61	30	26	23
Lithuania 45	55	68	47	12	38	48
Poland 44	25	66	67	14	45	46
Denmark 44	40	36	67	55	33	33
Malta 41	30	66	65	19	29	38
Slovakia 40	55	38	51	14	40	44
Greece 40	40	41	60	14	25	58
Austria 39	45	34	55	34	22	42
Cyprus 39	40	32	47	18	36	60
Latvia 30	20	42	51	11	25	33

Some key questions

Labour market access: Are migrants excluded from certain jobs? What rights do they have as workers?

Family reunion: Which migrants can sponsor relatives? Does the state protect a migrant's right to settle with their family?

Long-term residence: How long do migrants have to wait to become long term residents?

Political participation: Can non-EU migrants vote and stand as candidates in elections? Are migrants informed about political rights?

Access to nationality: How long must they wait to become citizens?

Anti-discrimination: Is discrimination on the grounds of religion, ethnicity/race and nationality punished? Are victims encouraged to bring forward cases?

NB Migrants does not refer to refugees or asylum seekers, or EU citizens exercising their free movement rights or EU citizens with immigrant origins.

Source: MIPEX Migrant Integration Policy Index
http://www.integrationindex.eu

Tight fit

Although the UK will have the largest EU population, it won't have the greatest density

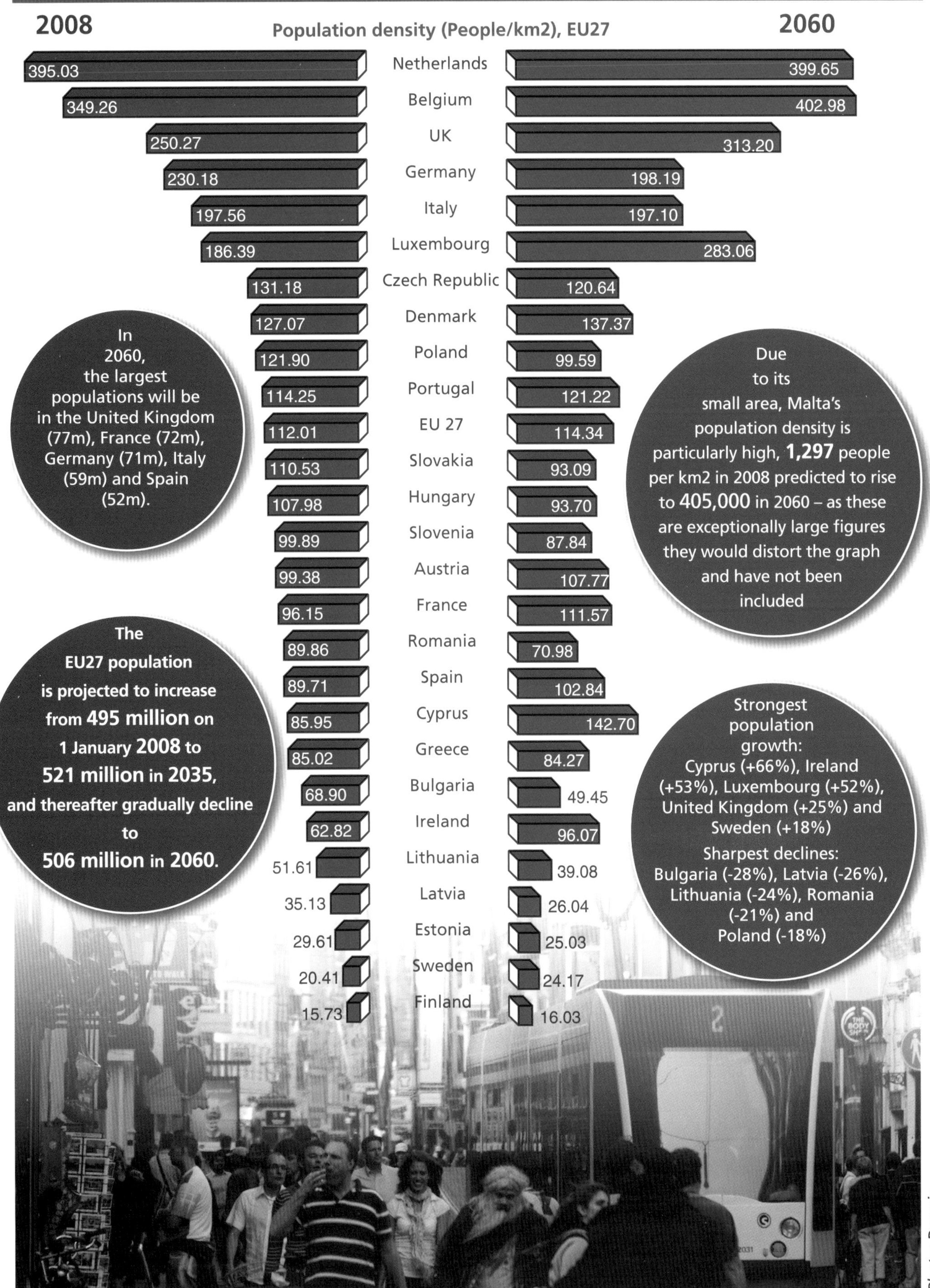
2008
Population density (People/km2), EU27
2060
395.03 Netherlands 399.65
349.26 Belgium 402.98
250.27 UK 313.20
230.18 Germany 198.19
197.56 Italy 197.10
186.39 Luxembourg 283.06
131.18 Czech Republic 120.64
127.07 Denmark 137.37
121.90 Poland 99.59
114.25 Portugal 121.22
112.01 EU 27 114.34
110.53 Slovakia 93.09
107.98 Hungary 93.70
99.89 Slovenia 87.84
99.38 Austria 107.77
96.15 France 111.57
89.86 Romania 70.98
89.71 Spain 102.84
85.95 Cyprus 142.70
85.02 Greece 84.27
68.90 Bulgaria 49.45
62.82 Ireland 96.07
51.61 Lithuania 39.08
35.13 Latvia 26.04
29.61 Estonia 25.03
20.41 Sweden 24.17
15.73 Finland 16.03
In 2060, the largest populations will be in the United Kingdom (77m), France (72m), Germany (71m), Italy (59m) and Spain (52m).
Due to its small area, Malta's population density is particularly high, 1,297 people per km2 in 2008 predicted to rise to 405,000 in 2060 – as these are exceptionally large figures they would distort the graph and have not been included
The EU27 population is projected to increase from 495 million on 1 January 2008 to 521 million in 2035, and thereafter gradually decline to 506 million in 2060.
Strongest population growth: Cyprus (+66%), Ireland (+53%), Luxembourg (+52%), United Kingdom (+25%) and Sweden (+18%)
Sharpest declines: Bulgaria (-28%), Latvia (-26%), Lithuania (-24%), Romania (-21%) and Poland (-18%)

Photo: Dsearis

Source: Eurostat http://epp.eurostat.ec.europa.eu

Gone to town

By 2030, 60% of the world's population will live in towns

How does the growth of towns affect the environment?

When people live in towns they change their environment through their consumption of food, energy, water and land. In turn, the polluted urban environment affects the health and quality of life of the population

The energy consumption of electricity, transport, cooking and heating is much higher in towns than in the country.

Percentage living in towns and cities, by region

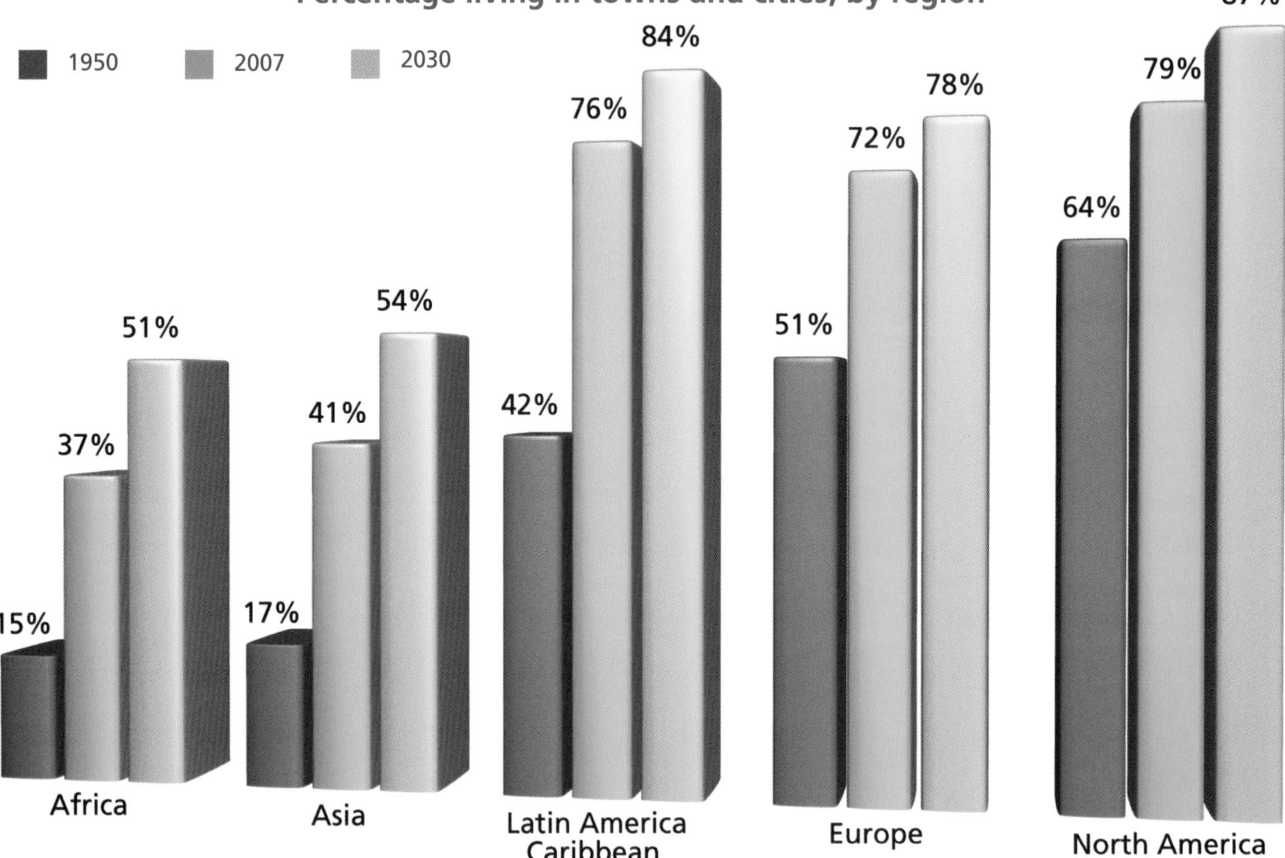

1950
2007
2030
15%
37%
51%
Africa
17%
41%
54%
Asia
42%
76%
84%
Latin America Caribbean
51%
72%
78%
Europe
64%
79%
87%
North America

29%
49%
60%
The World

The world

- The bulk of urban population growth is likely to occur in smaller cities and towns of less than 500,000
- Between 2000 and 2030, the urban population in Africa and Asia is set to double
- Asia's urban population will grow from **1.4 billion** to **2.6 billion**, Africa's from **294 million** to **742 million** and Latin America and the Caribbean from **394 million** to **609 million**
- Poor people will make up a large part of future urban growth
- Most urban growth is due to natural increase (more births than deaths) rather than migration

Source: 2007 World Population Data Sheet, Population Reference Bureau http://www.prb.org

Work

Good day at work?

Money can't buy happiness in the workplace

What is 'workplace happiness'?

'Happiness' is the culmination of a range of factors, which come together to create employees who look forward to going to work, feel challenged and supported and feel content about the place of their job and career in their broader lifestyle

The UK's **HAPPIEST** worker profile

- **Female**
- **Beauty therapist**
- **Over 60**
- **From the North East**

The UK's **UNHAPPIEST** worker profile

- **Man**
- **Builder**
- **40-49 year old**
- **From Northern Ireland**

Happiest professions 2008

(2,000 employees were surveyed across 20 professions)

Position	Profession
1	Beauty Therapists
2	Hairdressers
2	Armed Forces
4	Catering/Chefs
5	Retail Staff
6	Teachers
6	Marketing/PR
6	Accountants
9	Secretaries/Receptionists
9	Plumbers
9	Engineers
9	Architects
13	Journalists
13	Mechanics/Automotive
13	Human Resources
16	Call Centre
17	IT Specialists
17	Nurses
17	Banker/Finance
17	Builders/Construction

What secures workplace happiness?

Strong interest in what they do for a living

Good relationships with colleagues

Appreciates their work/life balance

Remain in the job as a direct result of salary

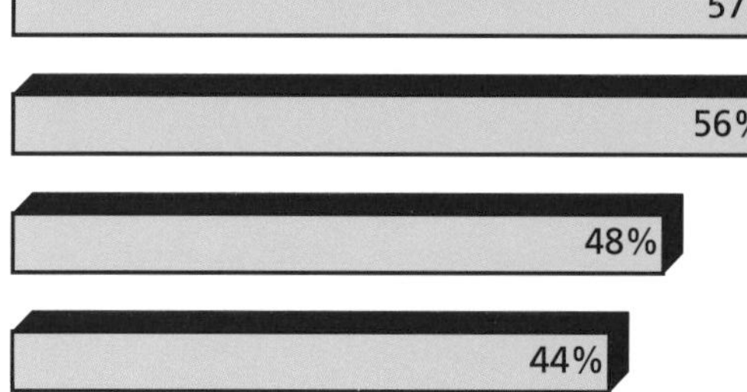
57%
56%
48%
44%

A keen interest in the job not only secures workplace happiness but is the main reason workers in the UK choose to stay with their employer

As UK workers face rising living costs and ever-longer working hours, they are sending a surprising message to their employers: the size of a payslip is NOT a guarantee of happiness and fulfilment at work

2,000 GB employed adults working in organisations with five or more employees, were asked:

How satisfied are you with the five aspects of your employment?

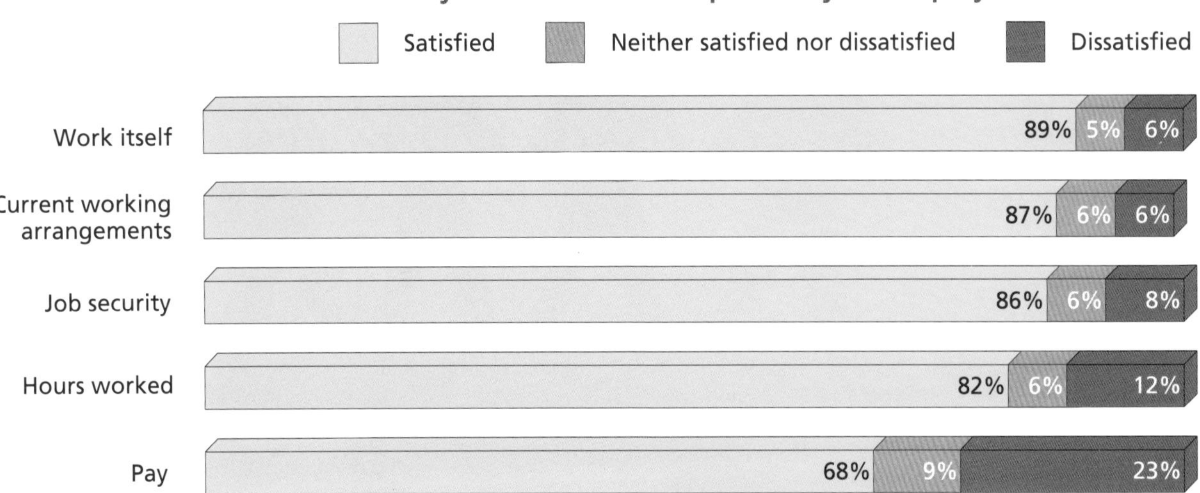

Satisfied
Neither satisfied nor dissatisfied
Dissatisfied
Work itself 89% 5% 6%
Current working arrangements 87% 6% 6%
Job security 86% 6% 8%
Hours worked 82% 6% 12%
Pay 68% 9% 23%

Source: The Third Work-Life Balance Employee Survey, Department for Trade and Industry © *Crown copyright 2008*
http://www.dti.gov.uk

Employees with flexible working patterns in the UK (2007)

	Men	Women	All
Full-time employees	%	%	%
Flexible working hours	10.1	14.9	12.0
Annualised working hours*	5.2	5.1	5.1
Four and a half day week	1.3	0.7	1.1
Term-time working	1.1	6.1	3.0
Nine day fortnight	0.4	0.3	0.3
Any flexible working pattern (inc. patterns not mentioned above)	18.3	27.4	21.8
Part-time employees			
Flexible working hours	7.4	9.2	8.9
Annualised working hours*	3.1	4.2	4.0
Term-time working	4.5	11.4	10.0
Job sharing	1.0	2.4	2.1
Any flexible working pattern (inc. patterns not mentioned above)	17.8	28.0	26.0

*The number of hours an employee has to work are calculated over a full year allowing for longer hours to be worked over certain periods of the year and shorter hours at others

Source: Labour Force Survey
http://www.statistics.gov.uk

The opportunity to work flexible hours can help people to balance home and work responsibilities

Source: City & Guilds happiness index
http://www.cityandguilds.com

Cut your losses

Union membership is falling, days lost to strikes are on the rise

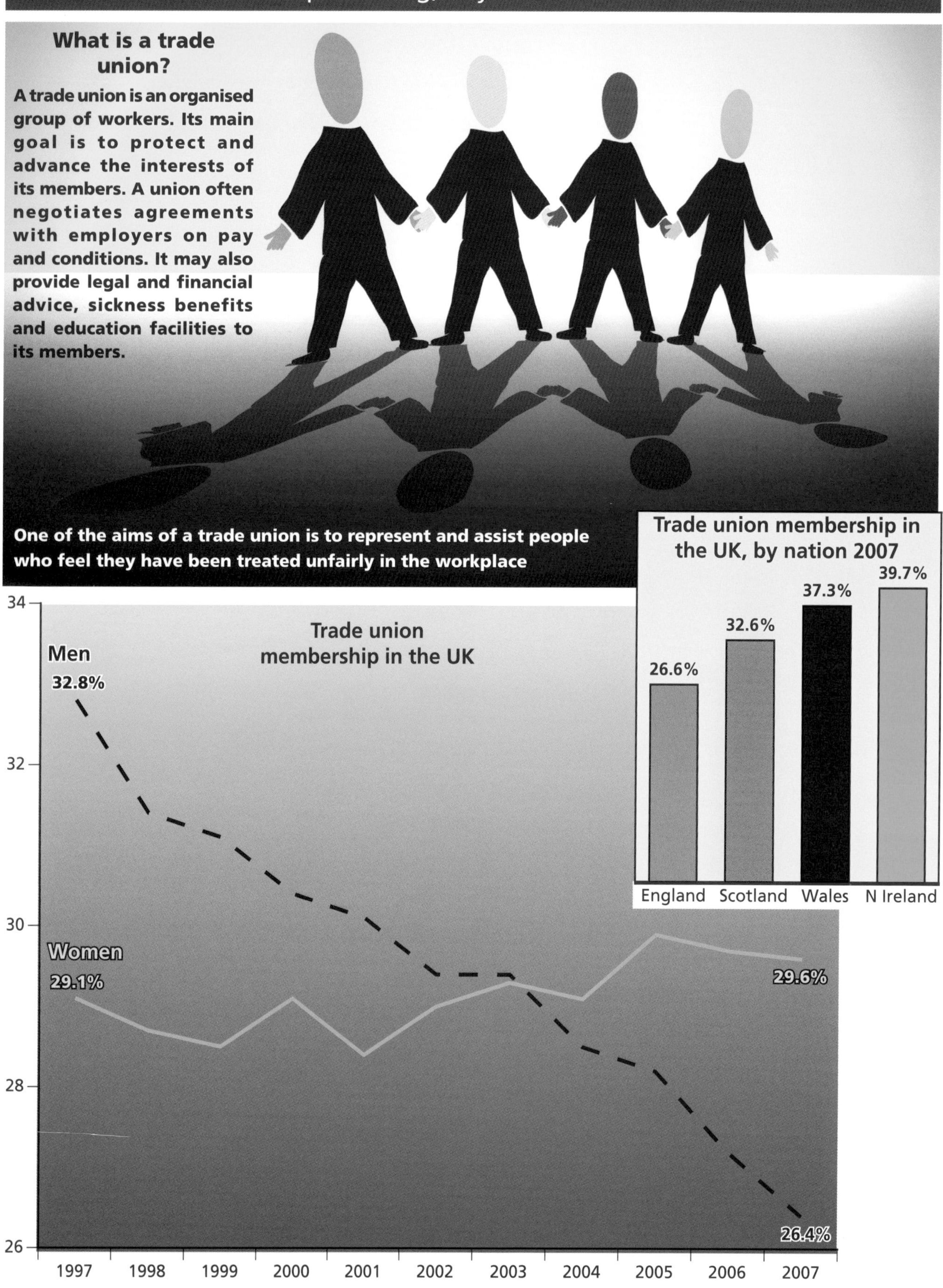

What is a trade union?
A trade union is an organised group of workers. Its main goal is to protect and advance the interests of its members. A union often negotiates agreements with employers on pay and conditions. It may also provide legal and financial advice, sickness benefits and education facilities to its members.
One of the aims of a trade union is to represent and assist people who feel they have been treated unfairly in the workplace
Trade union membership in the UK, by nation 2007
England 26.6%
Scotland 32.6%
Wales 37.3%
N Ireland 39.7%
Trade union membership in the UK
Men
32.8%
26.4%
Women
29.1%
29.6%
34
32
30
28
26
1997
1998
1999
2000
2001
2002
2003
2004
2005
2006
2007

Source: Trade Union membership 2007, The First Fair Treatment at Work Survey, BERR © Crown copyright 2008

http//www.berr.gov.uk

Forms of industrial action

Industrial action usually happens when a dispute in the workplace can't be resolved through negotiation

Industrial action is 'official' if it is formally backed by a trade union and members of that union are taking part in it

There are three main forms of industrial action:

- strike – when workers refuse to work for the employer
- action short of a strike – when workers take actions such as working to rule, go slows, overtime bans or call-out bans
- lock-out – a work stoppage when the employer stops workers from working

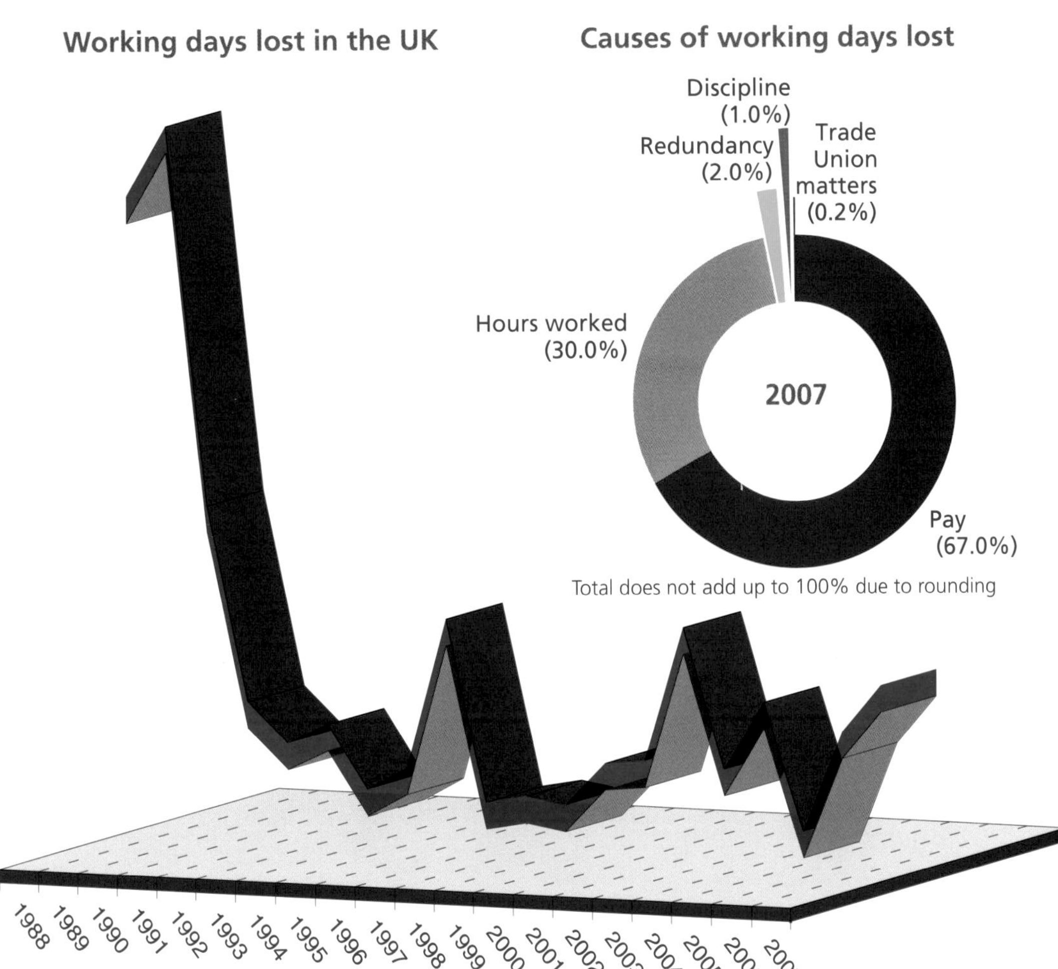

Working days lost in the UK
Causes of working days lost
Discipline (1.0%)
Redundancy (2.0%)
Trade Union matters (0.2%)
Hours worked (30.0%)
2007
Pay (67.0%)
Total does not add up to 100% due to rounding
1988 1989 1990 1991 1992 1993 1994 1995 1996 1997 1998 1999 2000 2001 2002 2003 2004 2005 2006 2007

(thousands)

Year	Days lost
1988	3,702
1989	4,128
1990	1,903
1991	761
1992	528
1993	649
1994	278
1995	415
1996	1,303
1997	235
1998	282
1999	242
2000	499
2001	525
2002	1,323
2003	499
2004	905
2005	157
2006	755
2007	1,041

In 2007

- The average number of working days lost per 1,000 employees was 38.
- The highest rate of working days lost was in the North West – 55 days per 1,000 employees. The lowest loss was in the East Midlands with 19.
- Just over a million working days were lost in the UK from 142 stoppages of work arising from labour disputes, with 96% of these being lost in the public sector.

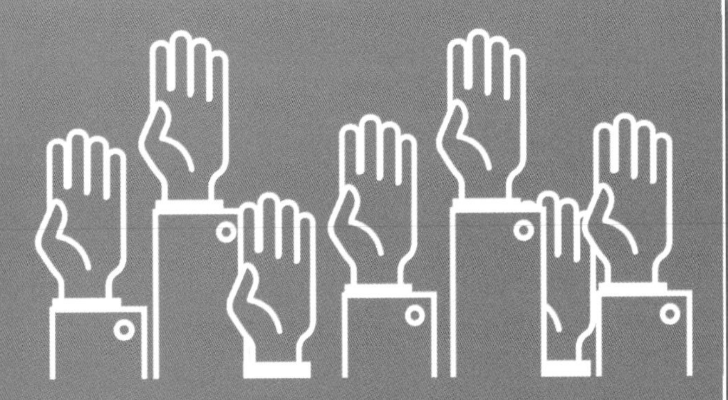

Source: Economic & Labour Market Review, June 2008

http://www.statistics.gov.uk

Unfair!

Almost one million employees are bullied at work

Q 'In the last 2 years with your employer, have you personally been treated unfairly because of the following?'

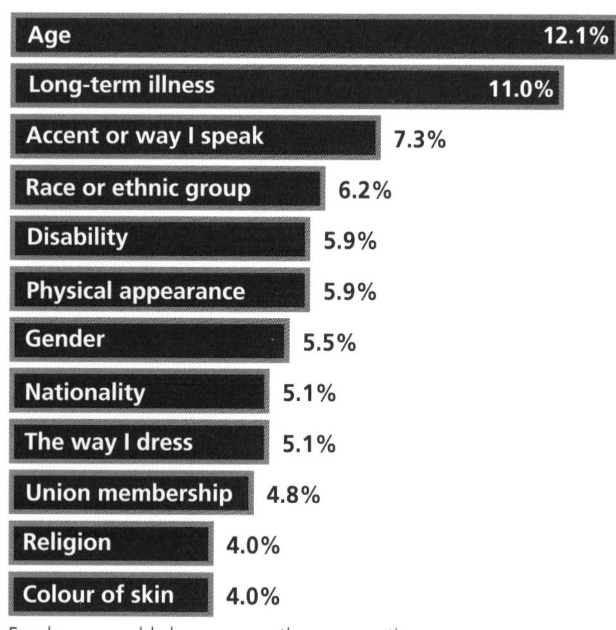

Age 12.1%
Long-term illness 11.0%
Accent or way I speak 7.3%
Race or ethnic group 6.2%
Disability 5.9%
Physical appearance 5.9%
Gender 5.5%
Nationality 5.1%
The way I dress 5.1%
Union membership 4.8%
Religion 4.0%
Colour of skin 4.0%

Employees could choose more than one option

- **4.9%** of women are bullied compared to **2.8%** men
- Foreign born employees were more at risk (**5%**) than UK born employees (**3.6%**)
- Among disabled women the rate was four times the national average
- The rate of bullying or harassment reported was twice as high in the public sector as the private
- Two thirds of cases involved the employee's supervisor or manager, the other third involve a work colleague
- **54%** said the bullying was still going on

Q 'In the last 2 years with your current employer have you experienced bullying or harassment at work?'

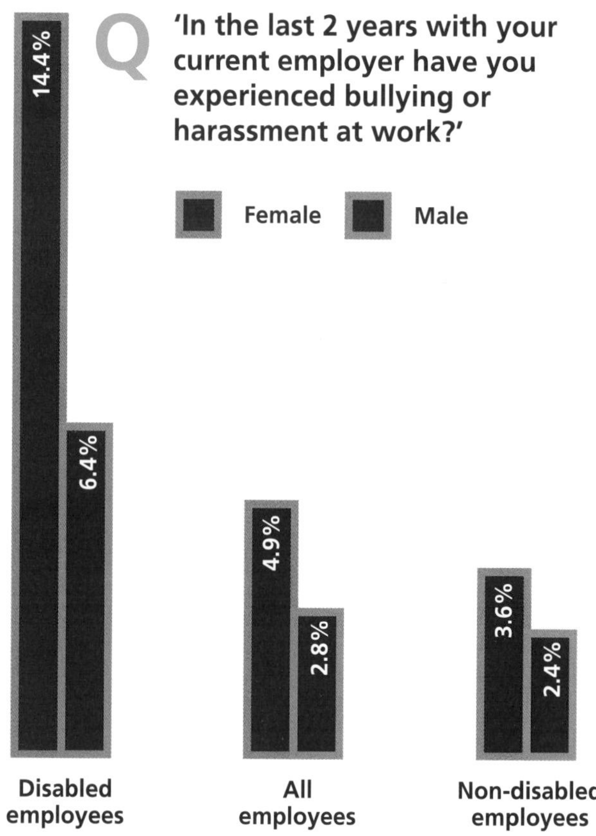

Female
Male
14.4%
6.4%
4.9%
2.8%
3.6%
2.4%
Disabled employees
All employees
Non-disabled employees

Base: Nearly 4,000 GB employees were interviewed face to face in the first official survey of unfair treatment at work

Source: The Fair Treatment at Work Survey, Department of Trade and Industry

http://www.berr.gov.uk

Under pressure

Stress can lead to physical and mental ill health

Work-related stress
is defined as
'the adverse reaction people have to excessive pressures or other demands placed on them'
Jobs with the highest levels of stress
Teaching/research professionals
Protective service occupations
Health/welfare associate professional
Customer services occupations
Managers/ senior officials tend to have the highest levels and skilled tradepersons the least
Top five industries for stress
Public admin
Health/social work
Education
Finance
Extraction/utilities

People reporting stress caused or made worse by work, Great Britain, 2006/07

(Estimates per 100,000 people ever employed)

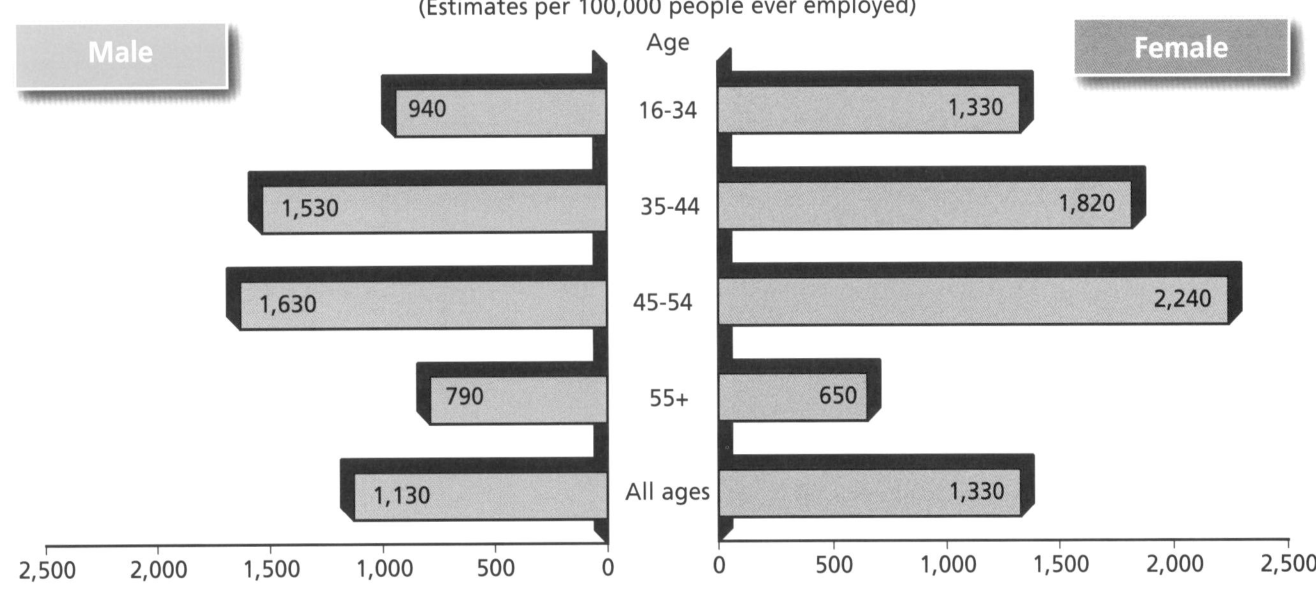
Male
Female
Age
16-34
35-44
45-54
55+
All ages
940
1,330
1,530
1,820
1,630
2,240
790
650
1,130
1,330
2,500
2,000
1,500
1,000
500
0
0
500
1,000
1,500
2,000
2,500

In 2006/07

530,000 people (approximately 237,000 males and 294,000 females) reported that they were suffering from stress, depression or anxiety that was caused or made worse by current or past work – that is 1,200 people for every 100,000, higher than the previous year.

13.8 million working days were lost to the condition.

On average, each person suffering took an estimated 30.2 days off in that 12 month period.

Source: Health and Safety Executive © Crown copyright 2008
http://www.hse.gov.uk

Snail's pace

Progress towards equality in top jobs is extremely slow

In 2008, **14.3 million** women are in the workforce alongside **16.9 million** men and we are moving to a position where women could eventually make up more than half the workforce. However women are under represented at the top.

Percentage of women in selected 'top jobs'

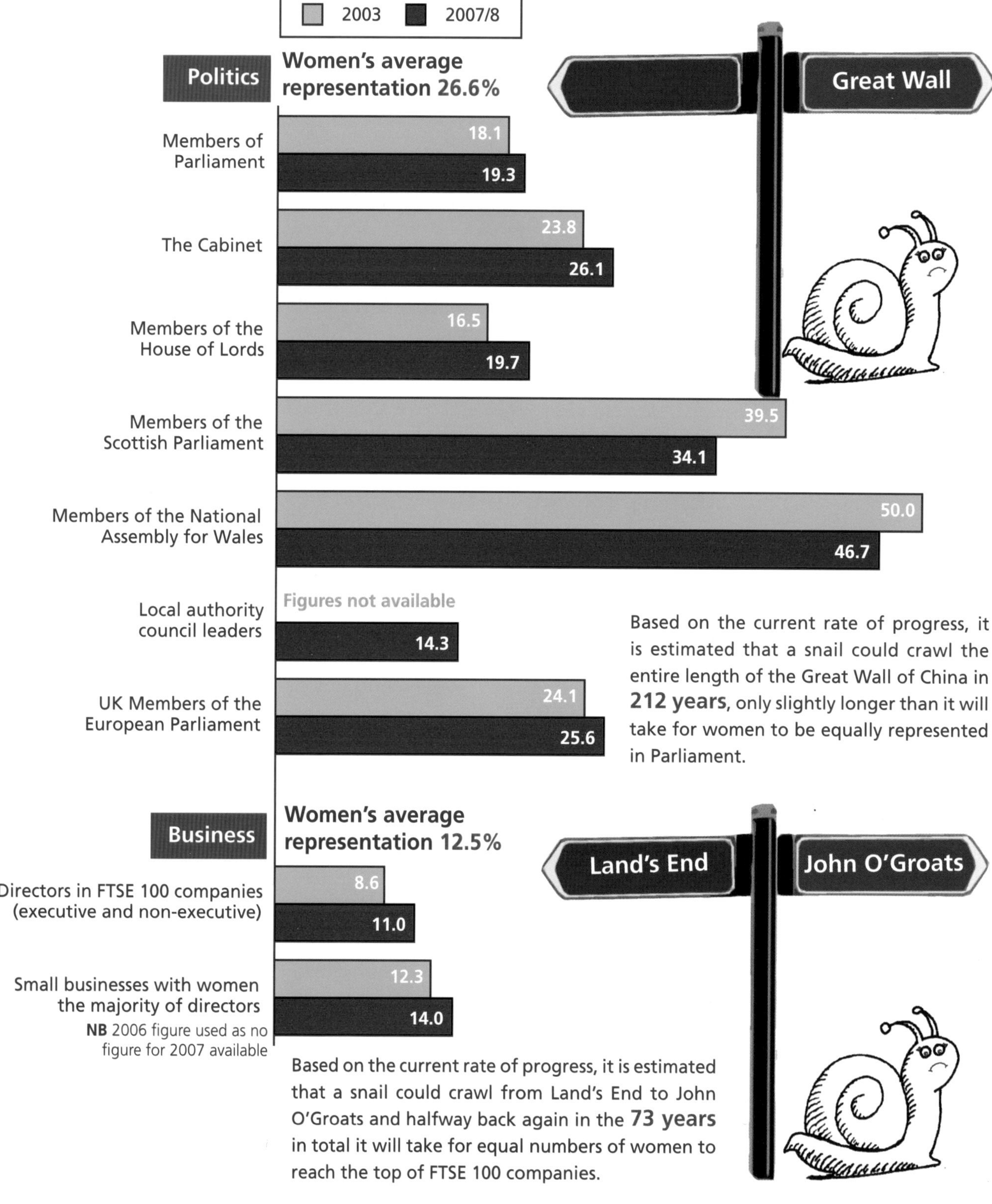
2003
2007/8
Politics
Women's average representation 26.6%
Great Wall
Members of Parliament 18.1 19.3
The Cabinet 23.8 26.1
Members of the House of Lords 16.5 19.7
Members of the Scottish Parliament 39.5 34.1
Members of the National Assembly for Wales 50.0 46.7
Local authority council leaders
Figures not available
14.3
UK Members of the European Parliament 24.1 25.6
Business
Women's average representation 12.5%
Land's End
John O'Groats
Directors in FTSE 100 companies (executive and non-executive) 8.6 11.0
Small businesses with women the majority of directors 12.3 14.0
NB 2006 figure used as no figure for 2007 available

Based on the current rate of progress, it is estimated that a snail could crawl the entire length of the Great Wall of China in **212 years**, only slightly longer than it will take for women to be equally represented in Parliament.

Based on the current rate of progress, it is estimated that a snail could crawl from Land's End to John O'Groats and halfway back again in the **73 years** in total it will take for equal numbers of women to reach the top of FTSE 100 companies.

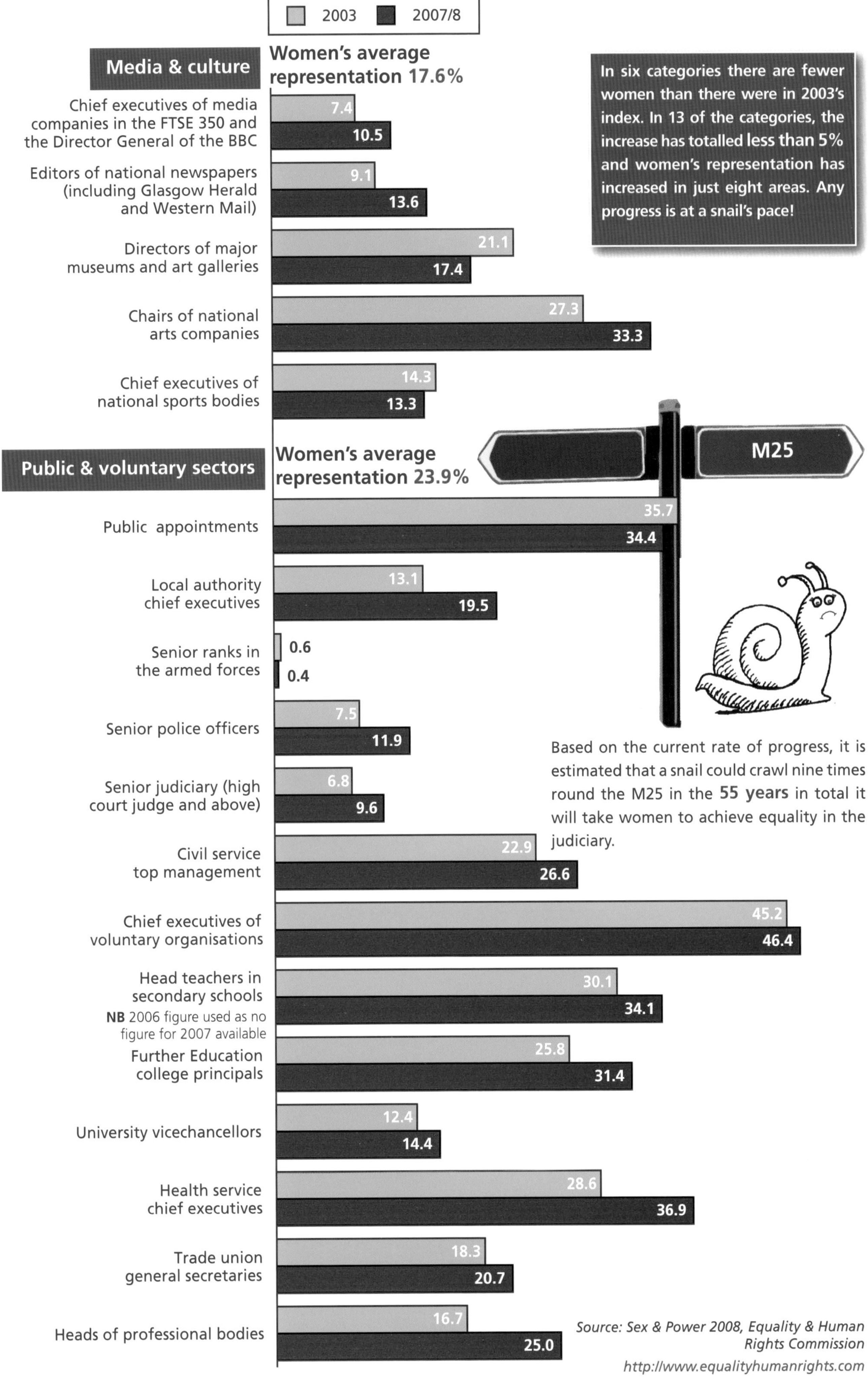
2003
2007/8
Media & culture
Women's average representation 17.6%
Chief executives of media companies in the FTSE 350 and the Director General of the BBC
7.4
10.5
Editors of national newspapers (including Glasgow Herald and Western Mail)
9.1
13.6
Directors of major museums and art galleries
21.1
17.4
Chairs of national arts companies
27.3
33.3
Chief executives of national sports bodies
14.3
13.3
In six categories there are fewer women than there were in 2003's index. In 13 of the categories, the increase has totalled less than 5% and women's representation has increased in just eight areas. Any progress is at a snail's pace!
M25
Public & voluntary sectors
Women's average representation 23.9%
Public appointments
35.7
34.4
Local authority chief executives
13.1
19.5
Senior ranks in the armed forces
0.6
0.4
Senior police officers
7.5
11.9
Senior judiciary (high court judge and above)
6.8
9.6
Based on the current rate of progress, it is estimated that a snail could crawl nine times round the M25 in the 55 years in total it will take women to achieve equality in the judiciary.
Civil service top management
22.9
26.6
Chief executives of voluntary organisations
45.2
46.4
Head teachers in secondary schools
NB 2006 figure used as no figure for 2007 available
30.1
34.1
Further Education college principals
25.8
31.4
University vicechancellors
12.4
14.4
Health service chief executives
28.6
36.9
Trade union general secretaries
18.3
20.7
Heads of professional bodies
16.7
25.0
Source: Sex & Power 2008, Equality & Human Rights Commission
http://www.equalityhumanrights.com

INDEX

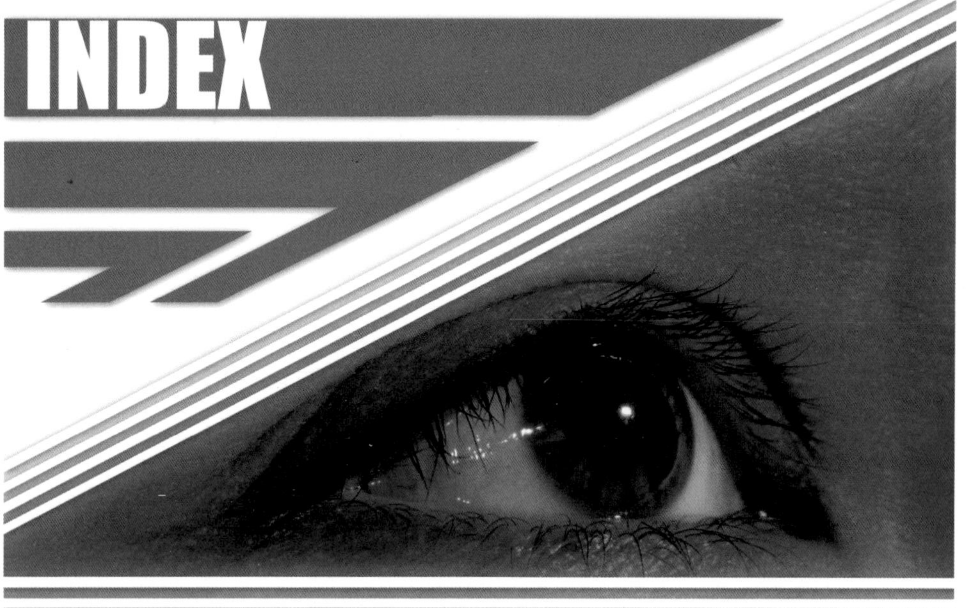

Entries in colour refer to main sections